Sally

Spreadsheets for Accountan Students

An Active-Learning Approach

for Lotus 1-2-3 release 2.0 and later; VP-Planner and VP-Planner Plus; As-Easy-As

Colston West

The author is a member of Bristol Business School, and has varied experience in industry and commerce, in addition to consultancy, business education and training

DP PUBLICATIONS LIMITED
Aldine Place
142/144 Uxbridge Road
London W12 8AW
1992

Acknowledgements

My thanks are due to the following:

Mr. Mike Bendrey and Professor Roger Hussey for permission to use examples from our book: ***Accounting and Finance for Business Students*** (DP Publications, 1st edn. 1989 and 2nd edn. 1992).

The staff of the Bristol Business School, particularly Dr. David Dugdale and Mr. Mike Behennah, for their help and encouragement with the second part of this book.

To my son, Mr. Nicholas West, of the staff of Peter L Mossman, Chartered Accountant, for his help in adding realism to many of the models in the second part of this book, and particularly for the design and detail of the model in sessions 33 and 34.

The many students in the Bristol Business School who used the experimental booklet which preceded this book, and to Kate, Molly and Nick who tried out various sessions of the first part of this book, for their time, patience, helpful comments and criticisms.

The many lecturers who responded to the questionnaire concerning ***Spreadsheets for Business Students*** for their kind interest and constructive comments.

A CIP record for this book is available from the British Library

ISBN 1 873981 86 4

Pageset by
Kai, 21 Sycamore Rise,
Cinderhill, Nottingham

Printed in Great Britain by
The Guernsey Press Co Ltd,
Guernsey, Channel Islands

Preface

1. Who should use this book?

This book has been designed for all students, but particularly accountancy students, on courses where acquaintance with the basics of spreadsheets is required.

In the first part of the book (sessions 1 – 13) students are taken from scratch and are given ***active learning*** experience in creating and printing worksheets, graphs, simple databases and macros. Basic skills are learnt through applying spreadsheet principles to solve various business problems. The examples have a business emphasis, and many have been taken from 'Accounting & Finance for Business Students' by Bendrey, Hussey and West (DP Publications, 1st edition 1989, 2nd expanded edition 1992), referred to as *AFBIS* in the text. However, this present book can be used quite independently, since all the examples are given in full. [This first part is, apart from minor amendments, the complete content of *Spreadsheets for Business Students*, first published in 1991.]

In the second half of the book (sessions 14 – 34) students are shown, again using the ***active learning*** approach, how to create models to solve problems in various areas of financial accounting, management accounting and financial management. Further spreadsheet skills continue to be learnt progressively through the sessions. The models cover such areas as regression analysis, pricing decisions, investment appraisal, variance analysis, accounting worksheets leading to financial accounts and the cashflow statement (FRS1), the analysed cashbook and bank reconciliation, product budgets and absorption costing, limiting factors and cost-volume-profit analysis.

2. The nature of the book

This is *not* a traditional manual or text-book.

The author has found that students learn little or nothing from lectures about spreadsheets, however well-presented. There are many manuals available for spreadsheets, particularly Lotus 1-2-3, and although these are mostly excellent and comprehensive, they are also mostly too expensive and perhaps too forbidding to be recommended to students starting to learn the basics of spreadsheets on their own.

The author experimented with a 24-page A4 'teach yourself'-type booklet which was issued free to students on HND, foundation and first-year degree courses. This has proved remarkably successful over the last few years.

This present book is an expansion of that booklet, and 'gets you cracking' straightaway. There are no boring introductory chapters explaining Function Keys and Menu Maps of Subcommands and what-have-you. These aspects are introduced gradually in the course of the sessions and are referred to or summarised in the appendices.

3. The scope of the book

A book of this size cannot be completely comprehensive. That is the function of the manuals and the £20 popular guides. Students can progress to these when they have overcome their apprehensions with the aid of this 'getting started' book.

The idea is to give students confidence in the basics of:

PART A:

- ❒ constructing spreadsheet models;
- ❒ saving and retrieving files;
- ❒ graphing;
- ❒ printing spreadsheets and graphs;
- ❒ using a spreadsheet as a database;
- ❒ creating and using macros.

PART B:

- ❒ solving a variety of accounting and costing problems;
- ❒ using short-cuts in entering labels, values and formulae;
- ❒ designing spreadsheets with separate input and output tables;
- ❒ using / commands and @ functions;

4. The layout of the book.

The first part of the book contains thirteen sessions. The first ten mostly contain work and instruction which should take the average student not more than an hour or two at the computer or computer terminal. If a student finds that a session is taking longer than the time available, instructions are given early in the course on how to save and retrieve the work already covered.

Each of these ten sessions has the following design:

- ❒ objectives of the session;
- ❒ instructions and explanation;
- ❒ summary of the session;
- ❒ activity for further practice;
- ❒ an objective test.

These ten sessions are followed by three practice sessions, in which students are invited to solve problems in simple management accounting topics by setting out the data on a worksheet and designing a format to solve the problem. Guidance is provided, and solutions are explained and illustrated.

The second part of the book contains twenty-one sessions. Each of these sessions usually contains the following headings:

- ❒ Objectives
- ❒ Introduction
- ❒ The problem
- ❒ Design of the model
- ❒ Notes on creating the model
- ❒ An explanation of the model
- ❒ Graphing the model (where appropriate)
- ❒ Activity

In each session the design of the model is illustrated with (usually) two Figures:

Figure XXa: which shows how the model will appear on the monitor;

Figure XXb: which repeats Figure XXa, but showing all the underlying formulae.

The idea is that, with the aid of these illustrations and the notes contained in the *Notes on creating the model* paragraph, students should be able to construct the model for themselves, learning as they do so.

Ideally a student might benefit most from working through all the sessions consecutively. However, in practice, time constraints may make this impracticable. Some sessions build on previous sessions and where this applies, this is clearly stated at the start of the session. Most sessions in the second part can be tackled independently; where a session demands skills covered in a previous session, reference is made to that session whenever it is considered helpful. As the book progresses, particularly in the second part, detailed instructions tend to diminish when procedures should be sufficiently familiar from practice with previous sessions, particularly those covered in the first part of the book.

5. Effective use of the book

- ❒ *By students on a taught course:*
  - ❒ Your lecturer will advise you which sessions to practise and when.
  - ❒ Work through the instructions and explanations *slowly* and *carefully.*
  - ❒ Remember that you are learning by doing.
  - ❒ Each time you do something, watch what happens on the screen, ask yourself why, and read the explanation.

- ❒ *By lecturers on a taught course*:
  - ❒ The first few sessions can be set early in the course, so that students can gain confidence.
  - ❒ Subsequent sessions can be set in accordance with the requirements of the course. For example, the sessions on cash flow forecasts could be set several weeks before an assignment which required the preparation of a cash flow forecast.
  - ❒ The objective tests could be used at tutorials, allowing, say, two minutes for the students to make their choice, and then asking a particular student to explain his/her choice.
  - ❒ Activities could be suggested or set, depending on the time available.
- ❒ *By students studying independently*:
  - ❒ Follow the suggestions above for students on a taught course.
  - ❒ Answers to the objective tests are given at the end of this book.
  - ❒ If you have difficulty with any of the activities suggested at the end of each session, repeat the session again, slowly and carefully.

6. Note on spreadsheets

This book uses Lotus 1-2-3 version 2.0 or 2.01. It was tempting to use later versions such as 2.2, 2.3, 3.0, 3.1, or Windows versions 1.0 or 1.1, but although these contain some improvements and enhancements, students might find it annoying if keystrokes or mice-clicking in the text did not work. In any case, later versions have retained the keystrokes of version 2, and this book is intended to teach the basic skills. Printing, for example, with ALLWAYS (provided with version 2.2) is more sophisticated than 'ordinary' printing, but I feel that 'ordinary' skills should precede the more sophisticated ones.

'Compatible' spreadsheets, such as VP-Planner (and VP-Planner Plus) and As-Easy-As are in common use. There are some minor differences between them and Lotus 1-2-3, and I have attempted to point out the differences throughout the book to help students who might otherwise get confused. Minor differences, for example the use of *General* for *Global*, are ignored, since the keystroke *G* is the same. Also the messages in the control panel are quoted for Lotus 1-2-3; the messages given by the other programs quite often have different wording, but the same intent, and to have quoted all the variants would be tedious for the reader. However, wherever the actual keystrokes are different (and this applies particularly to As-Easy-As) and also where a different procedure is required, the instructions are given in full for each particular program. The reader should note the references for the program being used are set out in *Conventions Used In This Book* which follows.

7. Conventions used in this book

term	**meaning**
{123}	Instructions specific to **Lotus 1-2-3**
{VP}	Instructions specific to **VP-Planner** and **VP-Planner Plus**
{VPP}	Instructions specific to **VP-Planner Plus**
{AEA}	Instructions specific to **As-Easy-As**, version 4.00Q. [Earlier versions may lack some features described in this book. These variations, where known, are noted in the text at points where they might cause confusion.]
Press <Esc>	Press the key marked 'Esc'
Press <Ctrl>+<Break>	Press and hold down the key marked 'Ctrl', and press the 'Break' key. Then release the 'Ctrl' key
Press /wey or /WEY	Press the keys as indicated, ignoring uppercase or lowercase. In Session 1, lowercase is shown for clarity, but uppercase from Session 2 onwards. See note in Session 2, paragraph 3
Type Total	Type the letters shown in bold type, in this case 'Total'
[range]	Specify a range by typing it in, or pointing, as described in Session 3
AFBIS	***Accounting and Finance for Business Students***: Reference to examples in ***Accounting and Finance for Business Students*** by **Bendrey, Hussey and West** (*DP Publications 1st edition 1989, 2nd edition 1992*) are to chapter and paragraph numbers. (See paragraph 1 of this Preface)

8. Free lecturers' supplement

The lecturers' supplement is a copyright-free PC-compatible disk, incorporating files for the models in the book. Files are in.WKS and .WK1 format suitable for all four programs (123,VP,VPP,AEA). This disk is available free from the publishers to bona fide lecturers who adopt this book as a course text.

Contents

\WGF TEXT

PRINTING p42
- condensed p46
- formula p50

ALIGNING LABELS p37
COMMAS IN FIG p37
\ Rpt's following character
/ RE erases cell
copying formulae p19

/WGC – widening columns

WGFT – formula then save

WGL ~~RPE~~ – aligning labels

WGF – commas

' left align " right align ^ centre

SESSION 1
Getting Started

1. Objectives

At the end of this session, you will be able to:

- ❑ load a blank worksheet (**Lotus 1-2-3, VP-Planner, VP-Planner Plus** or **As-Easy-As**);
- ❑ enter names into cells;
- ❑ correct your typing before entry into a cell;
- ❑ edit your typing after entry into a cell;
- ❑ move the cursor around the screen;
- ❑ understand <ESCAPE>, the panic button;
- ❑ end the session correctly.

2. Introduction

This book is intended for students who want to learn the basics of spreadsheets.

Many students look at a blank spreadsheet and wonder what on earth to do next. This book tells you what to do next.

You will be instructed what key to press and then told what should have happened on the screen, and why.

> **Advice**
> - ❍ Work initially at a very slow pace.
> - ❍ Follow the instructions carefully.
> - ❍ Inspect the screen after each single keystroke.
> - ❍ Ask yourself 'What has changed?'.
> - ❍ Ask yourself 'What did the keystroke achieve?'.

If you go too fast, you will learn little and get into a mess. But don't worry if you do get in a mess: you will be shown how to get out of it.

Throughout this book, **Lotus 1-2-3** is used. If you are using **VP-Planner** or **VP-Planner Plus** or **As-Easy-As**, you may occasionally have to use slightly different keystrokes. In the early stages at least you will be told what to do when differences between the design of spreadsheets arise. For example, instructions specific to **VP-Planner** will be indicated like this: {VP}. See *Conventions used in this book* preceding this Session.

Before we start, you need to have a blank spreadsheet on the screen before you.

If you have already got that far, skip to paragraph *6. The screen.*

If you have not, read one of the following sections, *3. If you have a hard disk*, *4. If you have no hard disk* or *5. If you are at a college or polytechnic.*

3. If you have a hard disk

❶ LOTUS 1-2-3

When you see the command prompt **C>** or **C:\>**,

type `cd\123` Press <Enter>

This should switch you to the directory in which Lotus 1-2-3 is installed. 'CD' stands for 'Change Directory'. Note particularly the backslash \ is *not* a forward slash /.

You should get a prompt **C>** or **C:\123>**.

If you get a message on the screen 'Invalid Directory', Lotus 1-2-3 may have been installed in another directory. For example the directory may be called 'Lotus', in which case, you would have to

type `cd\lotus` Press <Enter>

To find the name of the directory, you could, at the **C>** prompt,

type `dir/p` Press <Enter>

and look for a likely name against the <DIR> entries.

When you have succeeded,

type `lotus` Press <Enter>

☞ You will see on the screen the Lotus Access System Screen.

Read what it says.

Since we want a 1-2-3 empty spreadsheet, make sure that the menu pointer (the highlight bar at the top of the screen) is over 1-2-3. If it is not (eg if you have accidentally moved the pointer with the right or left arrow keys to highlight one of the other items on the top line), move the pointer back to 1-2-3, using the arrow keys.

> *Tip:* If the arrow keys do not work and you hear a 'beep', you are using a keyboard which combines the numeric keypad with the arrow keys. Press <Num Lock> to change the keys back to being arrow keys. <Num Lock> is a 'toggle' between the two modes. The Access Screen will show Press [NUM LOCK] at the bottom of the screen if <Num Lock> is on. Pressing <Num Lock> turns it off.

❷ VP-PLANNER

The program is probably installed in a directory called VP or VPP. See the instructions for 1-2-3 above to find the name of the directory.

Type `cd\vp` (or whatever the directory is called). Press <Enter>

The prompt will be C> or C:\VP> or similar.

Type `vp` Press <Enter>

☞ The VP-Planner Access System Screen will appear.

Make sure the menu pointer (the highlighted rectangle) is over

`1. Worksheet only`

and Press <Enter>

The blank worksheet should appear.

② VP-PLANNER PLUS

The program is probably installed in a directory called VPP.

Type `cd\vpp` Press <Enter>

[If this does not work, follow the instructions under 1-2-3 above for finding the name of the directory.]

At the prompt C> or C:\VPP> or similar

Type `vpp` Press <Enter>

☞ An introductory screen with a copyright message will appear, then a blank spreadsheet with the same message.

Press <Enter>

The worksheet loses the message and becomes blank.

❸ AS-EASY-AS

The program is probably installed in a directory called "Aseasy".

Type `cd\aseasy` Press <Enter>

[If this does not work, follow the instructions under 1-2-3 above for finding the name of the directory.]

At the prompt C> or C:\ASEASY>,

Type `aseasy` Press <Enter>

☞ The program will load and a screen full of information will appear. ...

Press any key.

A blank worksheet will appear, but possibly with a message.

To get rid of the message,

Type `/wey`

Don't worry about what happens on the screen while you are typing /wey. You will understand in time!

The message will disappear, and you will be left with a blank worksheet.

4. If you have no hard disk

1. Start you computer as usual with the DOS disk
2. Wait for the A> prompt
3. Remove the DOS disk
4. Insert your system disk
5. Type A: Press <Enter> to make sure drive A is the current drive
6. Type lotus or vp or vpp or aseasy
7. Press <Enter>
8. Follow the directions in paragraph 3 above, from the point marked ☞ in the section for your particular spreadsheet program.

5. If you are at a college or polytechnic

The terminal may be "networked".

The procedures vary, and instructions are probably on the machine.

A typical procedure might be:

1. Turn on the machine
2. Follow the instructions on the screen

Typical instructions might be:

a. Choose UTILITIES to FORMAT your floppy disk

b. Choose APPLICATIONS (move the menu bar to APPLICATIONS on the screen using the arrow keys on the keyboard and press <Enter>

c. Choose SPREADSHEETS

d. Choose the spreadsheet as available and required.

6. The screen

You should now have a blank worksheet on your screen.

There is a HORIZONTAL BORDER containing a one or two letter name for each COLUMN of the worksheet. Columns A to H are visible.

There is a VERTICAL BORDER containing a NUMBER for each ROW of the worksheet. Numbers 1-20 are visible.

There is also a CONTROL PANEL of 3 or 4 lines at the top or bottom of the screen (depending on the spreadsheet version).

Cell A1 should be highlighted sometimes with a blinking cursor.

In the control panel (on the left-hand side), A1 or A1: confirms that the cursor is on cell A1 of the worksheet.

Also in the control panel, there is a MENU INDICATOR which shows READY.

{123} shows READY in the top right-hand corner.

{VP} and {VPP} show READY in the bottom right-hand corner.

{AEA} shows READY at the top centre.

7. Entering names into cells

Type `Nebuchadnezzar` Press <Enter>

The name now appears in cell A1 on the worksheet.

I chose this name because it is difficult to spell!

If you made a mistake when typing it, leave the mistake for the moment. Your version, whether correct or incorrect, should be in the CONTROL PANEL, and if you look carefully, you will see that it is preceded by an apostrophe ('). I'll explain about this in due course.

You will notice that some of the letters spill over into cell B1. This is because, at present, each cell contains room for only 9 letters. Count the letters in cell A1 to check this. The fact that Nebuchadnezzar spills over into cell B1 does not matter, unless to want to type something into cell B1.

Suppose you typed Nebuchadnezzar incorrectly.

There are several ways to make a correction:

(a) Type `Nebuchadnezzar` again. Press <Enter>

The new entry replaces the old one in cell A1.

(b) EDIT the present contents of the cell.

Press `<F2>`

<F2> is the function key on the top or left-hand side of the keyboard.

8. Editing a cell entry

Note what happened when you pressed <F2>.

The MODE INDICATOR has chenged to EDIT, and 'Nebuchadnezzar' appears again in the second line of the control panel, ready for editing.

In EDIT mode, the following keys can be used:

Cursor Movement

Left arrow	Cursor moves one character to the left
Right arrow	Cursor moves one character to the right
<Shift>+<Tab>*	Cursor moves 5 {AEA:8} characters to left
<Tab>*	Cursor moves 5 {AEA:8} characters to right
<Home>	Cursor moves to the first character
<End>	Cursor moves to the last character

* The <Tab> key is sometimes marked with two arrows facing in opposite directions with a bar at the arrowhead.

Deleting Characters

<← del>*	Deletes the character to left of cursor
<Del>*	Deletes the character at cursor position

* The <← del> key is the key with a left facing arrow, usually above the <Enter> key. The <Del> key is usually marked 'Del', and can found near the bottom right-hand corner of the keyboard.

Inserting Characters

There are two ways to insert characters:

(a) Insert Mode

Place the cursor over the character AFTER the position where you wish to insert a character. For example, if you wish to insert a 't' into 'Lous' to make 'Lotus', place the cursor over the 'u' and type 't'.

(b) Replace or Overtype Mode

Press the <Ins> key once.

[Note: {123,AEA} OVR appears at foot of screen

{VP,VPP} blinking cursor size reduces to underline]

Place the cursor over the character you wish to replace. For example, if you wish to replace the 'b' in 'Lobus' to make 'Lotus', place the cursor over the 'b' and type 't'.

Note that the <Ins> key is a 'toggle-switch' (i.e. it changes to and fro) between Insert and Replace modes. Usually Insert mode is the more useful, and it is probably best to keep the toggle in Insert mode.

While you are in Edit mode, practise with some of the above keystrokes, altering Nebuchadnezzar as many times as you want.

When he is spelt correctly, press <Enter> to transfer him to cell A1, and return to READY mode.

9. Moving the cursor

Now for some more practice.

I assume the cursor is still on cell A1. If it is not,

Press `<Home>`

which returns the cursor to cell A1.

Press `<↓>` (down-arrow) once.

The cursor moves to cell A2.

Press `<↓>` `<↓>` `<→>` `<→>`

The cursor should now be in cell C4.

Press `<F5>` Type `a5` Press `<Enter>`

The cursor moves to cell A5. <F5> is the 'GoTo' key. Follow it with any cell reference, and the cursor will go there.

With the cursor on cell A5,

Type `Shadrach` Press `<↓>`

Note that you have pressed the down-arrow instead of <Enter>.

'Shadrach' appears in cell A5, and the cursor moves to cellA6, i.e. one cell in the direction of the down-arrow.

Type `Meshach` Press `<↓>`

'Meshach' appears in cell A6 and the cursor moves to cell A7.

Type `Abednego` Press `<→>`

'Abednego' appears in cell A7 and the cursor moves to cell B7.

If you have mis-spelt any of the names, try correcting them with the <F2> Edit key, as described above.

10. Altering an entry before pressing <Enter> or an arrow key

Move the cursor to cell A8.

Type `Belteshassar` BUT DO NOT PRESS <Enter>.

You should have typed 'Belteshazzar', i.e. zz instead of ss.

You can use the <← del> key or the <Del> keys to erase the last characters typed.

Press `<← del>` four times

This erases 'ssar'.

Type `zzar`

'Belteshazzar' is now ready for entry into cell A8.

Alternatively, you could have pressed <Esc> (before pressing <Enter>, but this would have wiped out the whole of 'Belteshassar', and then you would have had to type 'Belteshazzar' in full.

11. <ESCAPE> – The panic button

Sometimes you find that you have 'got in a mess', and things appear on the screen that you do not understand, due, perhaps, to pressing the wrong keys.

If this happens, pressing <Esc> will usually get you back to the READY mode. You may have to press <Esc> more than once.

Try this:

Press `/ w g f`

What to do next? You don't know yet?

Press `<Esc>` four times, and you are back where youstarted!

Now: {123, VP, VPP only}

Press `/ w g f` again.

Press `<Ctrl>+<Break>`

and again you are back where you started, in READY mode.

<Ctrl>+<Break> has the effect of pressing <Esc> innumerable times.

12. Before you end this session

You may be wondering about a number of things:

How do you 'blank out' a cell easily?

How do you alter the width of a column?

How do you clear the whole worksheet of the names you have been entering?

How do you move quickly to other parts of the worksheet?

How big is your total worksheet?

Why have I only let you enter names so far?

How do you save the data you have entered on the worksheet?

Where will it all end?

All these questions (apart from the last one) will be answered in the following sessions. Be patient!

Unless you have time or inclination to carry out the following activity, you can finish this session:

Press [/]

Note that this is the </> key, NOT the <\> key.

The main menu will appear in the control panel or as a drop-down menu.

Move the cursor to QUIT or EXIT and press <Enter>

Then:

{123} and {AEA}	Move the cursor to 'Yes' and press <Enter>
	If you returned to the Access screen,
	Choose 'Exit' with the cursor and press <Enter>
{VP} and {VPP}	Type 'Y' for Yes
{VP only}	Move cursor to 'Quit' and press <Enter>

You should now be back at the DOS prompt C> or C:\123 or whatever the directory is called. Park your hard disc if necessary.

If you are on a network system, you should be at the menu screen, in which case press <Esc> to go back through the menus and then follow the instructions on the screen.

Note that we are losing all the names we have been using for practice in this session, and we shall start the next session with a blank worksheet.

13. Summary

In this session you should have achieved the objectives set out at the start of this session.

In particular, you have become acquainted with:

</>		the MENU key
<F2>		the EDIT key
<F5>		the GOTO key
<Esc>		the PANIC button
<Ctrl>+<Break>		the multiple <Esc> keys
<Home>	in READY mode	the return to cell A1 key
<Home>	in EDIT mode	the return to first character key
<End>	in EDIT mode	the move to last character key
<Ins>		the Insert or Replace toggle.

14. Activity

Move the cursor to any blank cell and practise entering names (not numbers). Make deliberate mistakes in your typing, and correct them

(a) before pressing <Enter>, and

(b) after pressing <Enter>, i.e using the <F2> Edit key.

15. Objective test ☐ A ☐ B ☑ C ☐ D

1. When first loaded, a blank worksheet shows columns A-H. Each column has a (default) column-width of

   ☐ A 7 characters

   ☐ B 8 characters

   ☐ C 9 characters

   ☐ D 10 characters

2. In order to edit an entry in a cell, the edit key to press is

   ☐ A <Enter>

   ☐ B <F2>

   ☐ C <F3>

   ☐ D <F5>

3. In edit mode, the key to press to move the cursor to the first character is

   ☐ A <Tab>

   ☐ B <Shift>+<Tab>

   ☐ C <End>

   ☐ D <Home>

4. In edit mode, the key to toggle between Insert and Replace modes is

   ☐ A <Num Lock>

   ☐ B <Del>

   ☐ C <Ins>

   ☐ D <Esc>

5. If you are ready to make an entry into cell D4, and you want to press the key which will make the entry and move the cursor to cell E5, the key to press is

   ☐ A <→>

   ☐ B <↓>

   ☐ C <F5>

   ☐ D none of these

6. The <Goto> key is

   ☐ A <F2>

   ☐ B <F3>

   ☐ C <F4>

   ☐ D <F5>

7. If you have "got lost" after pressing **/ R F F**, and you don't know what to do, you can get back to the READY mode by pressing

   ☐ A <Esc> four times

   ☐ B <Ctrl>+<Ins>

   ☐ C <Enter> three times

   ☐ D none of these

8. The cursor is in cell B2, and you wish to move it to cell C5. The least number of key-presses to achieve this is

☐ A <→><→><→><↓>

☐ B <F5><c><5><Enter>

☐ C <→><↓><↓>

☐ D <↓><↓><→>

9. You want to enter 'Daniel' into a cell. You have typed 'Saniel', and realise you have made a mistake, but have not yet pressed <Enter>. The quickest way to correct this is to

☐ A press <Esc> and type 'Daniel'

☐ B press <Home>, then <Ins> to get into replace mode, and then type 'Daniel"

☐ C press <←del> 6 times, and type 'Daniel'

☐ D none of these

10. You need a cup of coffee, and you want to leave your worksheet and the spreadsheet program, without saving any of your entries. The first key to press is

☐ A </>

☐ B <\>

☐ C <Esc>

☐ D <Home>

SESSION 2
A Simple Worksheet

1. Objectives

At the end of this session, you will be able to:

- ❑ appreciate what a worksheet looks like
- ❑ enter more labels into a worksheet
- ❑ align labels to the left, right and centre of a cell
- ❑ use the GoTo (F5) key to move around the worksheet
- ❑ widen a column from the default width
- ❑ make dotted lines using the repeat key (\)
- ❑ copy cells, including pointing with the cursor
- ❑ clear a cell completely
- ❑ enter values into cells
- ❑ enter formulae into cells
- ❑ copy formulae into other cells
- ❑ save a new worksheet to disk
- ❑ save an updated worksheet to disk
- ❑ change data entries and observe the effect on related cells containing formulae.

2. Introduction

In this session you will create a worksheet containing some simple VAT calculations. You will learn some new skills as you do so.

The worksheet you will create looks something like the table on the following page.

L. Marshfield	**VAT Calculations**				
	Description of Items				
	Boxes	@ per box	Amount	VAT @ 15%	Total
	No.	£	£	£	£
Sale	50	12	600	90	690
Purchase	50	10	500	75	575

Summary:	£
Output tax =	90
Input tax =	75

[Note: This table is taken from AFBIS, chapter entitled *Deductions from Pay and Value Added Tax*.]

3. Entering the labels

LABELS include words such as Nebuchadnezzar. You may remember from Session 1 that when you entered his name into a cell, an apostrophe (') appeared before his name in the Control Panel.

This apostrophe is the DEFAULT LABEL PREFIX, and will appear in the Control Panel if your cell entry starts with a letter (as distinct from a number or one of the special numeric symbols which we shall describe later on).

DEFAULT means that the program inserts this for you unless you do something specific to the contrary.

LABEL PREFIX is a symbol placed before the label, telling the program how you want the label to appear in the cell.

In this case, the apostrophe tells the program that you wish the label to appear in the cell *left-aligned*, i.e. with the left-hand letter flush with the left-hand side of the cell.

Start this session with a blank worksheet, as you learnt in Session 1.

If you still have some entries in your worksheet, you can clear them by typing **/ W E Y** (/ Worksheet Erase Yes). I am assuming that you do not want to preserve these entries, because /WEY loses them unless you have already saved the worksheet. Later on in this session, you will learn how to save a worksheet.

[Note: From this point onwards, in the interest of consistency, commands such as /WEY are printed in uppercase (CAPITALS). However, you do not need to press <Shift>+w, for example, for the W of /WEY. Command letters can be pressed in either uppercase or lowercase, so simply press the key shown; it does not matter if <Caps Lock> has been activated. To continue to print /WEY as /wey might prove irritating, since W stands for Worksheet, E stands for Erase and Y for Yes, as shown in the control panel.]

Press `<Home>` if your cursor is not in cell A1.

Type `L. Marshfield` <Enter>

L. Marshfield will appear in cell A1, and A1: 'L. Marshfield will appear in the Control Panel.

Note the apostrophe before the label in the Control Panel, indicating that the label is left-aligned.

Now enter some more labels, as follows:

Press	<→> <→>	The cursor should now be in cell C1	
Type	VAT Calculations		
Press	<↓> <↓> <←>	The cursor should now be in cell B3	
Type	Description of Items		
Press	<↓> <↓>	The cursor should now be in cell B5	
Type	"Boxes	Press	<→>

Note that you typed ``Boxes. The inverted comma (``) is a label prefix which right-aligns the label in the cell.

The cursor should now be in cell C5.

Type	"per box	Press	<→>
Type	"Amount	Press	<→>
Type	VAT @ 15%	Press	<→>
Type	"Total	Press	<Enter>

The cursor should be positioned over the last entry in cell F5.

Note that *per box*, *Amount* and *Total* are right-aligned in the cells. The other label VAT @ 15% is exactly 9 characters, and therefore fills the default cell-width of 9 characters.

Press `<f5> a8` <Enter>

<F5> is the GoTo key, and the cursor should now be in cell A8.

Type	Sale	Press	<↓>	(Cell A9)
Type	Purchase	Press	<↓> <↓>	(Cell A11)

Type ^Summary: Press <↓><↓> (Cell A13)

Note: the caret (^) is a label-prefix which centres the label.

Type Output tax = Press <↓> (Cell A14)

Type Input tax = Press <Enter> (Cell A14)

4. Widening a column

You have probably noticed that there is a problem about entering figures in column B: the labels in column A overflow into column B. The default width of all columns is 9 characters, and it is possible to alter the column width of all columns. However, in this particular worksheet, only column A is too narrow.

Place the cursor over Output tax =, i.e. cell A13, which is the widest label in column A, apart from the label *L. Marshfield* which does not matter, since it overflows into cell B2, which is empty.

Press / W C S (/ Worksheet Column Set-width)

The Control Panel reads Enter column width (1..240): 9

({AEA} reads Enter Column Width (1..72) ? 9)

You could type the number 12, and press <Enter> which would widen the column to cover all of Output tax =. However, try this:

Press <→> <→> <→>

The cursor should now cover Output tax = (12 characters including spaces), and the 9 should have changed to 12 in the Control Panel.

Press <Enter>

and column A now has a width of 12.

[For {123}{AEA}, note the [W12] in the Control Panel. If you move the cursor to the other columns, this message does not appear for columns of the default width. Try it and see.]

5. Making dotted lines

Now you need some dotted lines. You could type them in as a row of hyphens, but here is a short-cut.

Move the cursor to cell A10

Type \- <Enter>

A row of twelve hyphens fills cell A10.

The backslash (\) is a label prefix which repeats the character which follows it, in this case a hyphen.

6. Copying cells

You need hyphens in cells B10 to F10 inclusive. You could repeat the technique in paragraph 5 for each of these cells. But there is an easier way.

Make sure the cursor is on cell A10.

Press `/ C` (/ Copy)

The Control Panel reads Enter range to copy FROM: A10..A10

A10..A10 means cell A10! (We shall look at larger ranges later.)

You want accept this cell as the cell to be copied, so

Press `<Enter>`

The Control Panel now reads Enter range to copy TO: A10.

A10 is given because that is where the cursor is.

The range you want to copy to is B10..F10.

Press `<→>` This moves the cursor to B10.

Press `.(a full stop!)`

This full stop ANCHORS the cursor which can now be extended to cell F10.

Press `<→> <→> <→> <→>`

The cursor should now cover cells B10, C10, D10, E10 and F10.

Press `<Enter>`

The hyphens should now extend from cells A10 to F10 inclusive. Move the cursor along this line. You will see from the Control Panel that each cell contains the repeating label \-.

Note: This method is known as Pointing with the cursor, i.e. moving the cursor over the range required after anchoring the cursor with a full stop. You could, instead, have typed in the range in after pressing /C<Enter>, i.e typed b10.f10 - a single full stop will suffice - and then pressed <Enter>. If you prefer this method in the future, by all means use it. However, POINTING with the cursor is probably safer: you can see the range on the screen, whereas it is easy to make a mistake in typing in the reference cells of the range.

You should now be able to put dotted lines (using \- and the / Copy command) into the following cells:

B4 to C4 inclusive

B6 to F6 inclusive

A12

7. More labels and copying

You need some headings on line 7.

Cell B7 needs No. right-aligned

Cells C7 to F7 inclusive need the £ sign, right-aligned.

You should now be able to enter these labels. Try it!

If you still find this difficult, here are the key-presses:

Move to cell B7

Press `"No.` `<→>` `"£` <Enter> `/C` <Enter>

`<→>` `. (a full stop)` `<→>` `<→>` <Enter>

8. Clearing a cell

It is unlikely that you have managed so far without making some mistakes in your key-presses. In session 1 you learnt how to correct mistakes, particularly by editing entries in cells.

Here is a way to clear a cell completely:

Move the cursor to cell A16.

Type `Rubbish` <Enter>

Press `/RE` <Enter>

Note that after pressing / Range Erase, the Control Panel reads *Enter range to erase: A16..A16*. By pressing <Enter>, you erase the range A16..A16, i.e. cell A16.

9. Entering values

Numbers are now needed in cells B8, B9, C8 and C9.

These numbers are values, as distinct from labels. When you perform the following keypresses, look at the mode indicator after you make each keystroke. A cell entry which starts with a letter is treated as a label, whereas a cell entry which starts with a number is treated as a value. If you wish to have a label which is in fact a number (e.g. the year 1991), you would have to use a label-prefix.

Move the cursor to cell B8.

Type `50` `<↓>` `50` `<→>` `10` `<↑>` `12` `<→>`

The cursor should now be on cell D8.

10. Entering formulae

The numbers in the remaining cells (refer to the worksheet in paragraph 2 of this session) can be calculated from the values which you entered in cells B8, B9, C8 and C9. You will therefore enter formulae into these cells, as follows:

With the cursor over cell D8,

Type `+b8*c8` <Enter>

You have now typed in a formula which multiplies any data figure entered in cell B8 by any data figure entered in cell C8. The + sign before the b of b8 tells the program that it is not a label. The asterisk (*) is the multiplication symbol. Note that the figure 600 appears in the cell, whereas the formula appears in the control panel.

Move the cursor to cell E8.

Type `+d8*15%` <Enter> [Not {AEA} early versions: see ** below.]

This formula multiplies the figure in cell D8 by 15%. You will note that the figure in cell E8 is 90, whereas the formula appears in the control panel as +D8*0.15. The program has converted 15% to 0.15, which is the same thing. You could, of course, have typed 0.15 instead of 15%, and this is necessary in early versions of {AEA}**.

Move the cursor to cell F8.

Type `+d8+e8` <Enter>

This formula adds the figure in cell D8 and the figure in cell e8. Again you will see the result of the addition in cell F8 (690) and the formula in the control panel.

11. Copying formulae

The formulae you require for line 9 (cells D9, E9 and F9) are similar to those in line 8. You could type in the formulae, substituting a 9 for an 8 in each case, but there is a quicker way:

Move the cursor to cell D8.

Type `/ C` <→> <→> <Enter> <↓> `.` <→> <→> <Enter>

Note the full stop to anchor the cursor when you get to Enter range to copy TO: D9 in the control panel.

What you have done is copy the formulae in cells D8, E8 and F8 into cells D9, E9 and F9, and the program has converted the formulae to make them relative to line 9 instead of line 8.

Check that the figures in cells D9, E9 and F9 are 500, 75 and 575 respectively.

Check the formulae in these cells and compare them with those in line 8 above by moving the cursor over them and looking at the formulae in the control panel.

12. Completing the worksheet

You need to enter cell references in cells B13 and B14 in the 'Summary' to complete the worksheet.

Move to cell B13.

Type `+e8` `<↓>` `+e9` `<Enter>`

Cells B13 and B14 now show the same figures as cells E8 and E9 respectively.

13. Saving your worksheet

The worksheet is now complete. In paragraph 15, you can experiment with altering the data and seeing how the worksheet responds, before you end this session.

However, you may want to save your masterpiece in its present state, so that you can experiment with it on some future occasion.

At present (unless there has been a power-cut or some similar disaster) the worksheet is still only in the memory of the computer. In order to be able to recall it when next you turn the computer on, the worksheet must be saved to a disk - either the hard disk (usually drive C: or perhaps D:) or your floppy disk (usually drive A: or B:).

Type `/ F S`

The control panel shows a message: *Enter save file name:* (or similar message) followed, perhaps, by something like:

C:\123.wk1* or *A:*.wks* or *B:*.wk1*

depending on the program you are using.

The C:\, A:\ or B:\ indicate the drive to which your worksheet will be saved. In the case of drives A: or B:, you should ensure that you have a suitable formatted disk in the appropriate drive.

The 123\ (usually only for the hard disk, drive C:) is the subdirectory to which your file will be saved.

The *.wk1 or *.wks is a 'blank' for the file name. The file name consists of the name (which will replace the *) and the extension (.wk1 or .wks). The extension is supplied automatically by the program. You must choose the file name.

If you are happy that this is the place where you want your worksheet to be saved, simply

Type `VATCALCS` <Enter>

and your worksheet will be saved to disk with the name VATCALCS.

If the program does NOT indicate where it will save your file,or if the indicated location is NOT where you want to save it, you should FIRST follow the following procedures, depending on the program you are using. Although the procedures are similar in principle, the details vary.

If the program does NOT indicate where it will save your file,or if the indicated location is NOT where you want to save it, you should FIRST follow the following procedures, depending on the program you are using. Although the procedures are similar in principle, the details vary.

If you are using {123} or {VPP}:

Either:

Press `<Esc>` until the mode indicator shows READY.

Type `/ F D`

The message *Enter current directory:* or *Enter Path:* appears.

Press <Enter> to accept the directory shown, or type in the directory you require. For example if the directory shown is *C:\123* and you want to save to your floppy disk in drive A:,

Type `A:` <Enter>

This means that whenever, during the current session, you save by pressing /FS, the directory shown will be what you want.

Press `/ F S`

Type `vatcalcs` <Enter>

The worksheet will saved as VATCALCS.WK1 or VATCALCS.WKS

Or:

After pressing /FS, (if the directory shown is not what you want), press <Esc> and then type in the full drive name, pathname i.e subdirectory name (if necessary) and then the name of the file,

e.g. `<Esc>` `c:\123\vatcalcs` `<Enter>`

or `<Esc>` `a:\vatcalcs` `<Enter>`

If you are using {VP} (Planner NOT Plus)

Pressing /FS produces the message *Enter File Name:* but this is not followed by any indication of the drive or path. However, a list appears in the second line of the control panel showing files (if any) which have previously been saved to the directory, and this may be sufficient clue for you.

To make sure which directory your present worksheet will be saved to,

Press `<Esc>` three times to get back to READY

Type `A:` <Enter>

This means that whenever, during the current session, you save by pressing /FS, the directory will be what you want.

Press `/ F S`

Type `vatcalcs` <Enter>

The worksheet will be saved as VATCALCS.WKS in the directory you specified.

If you are using {AEA}:

Pressing /FS produces the message *STORE:Name of file ?* followed by the flashing cursor inviting you to enter the filename. There is no indicaton of the drive or path. However, pressing <Esc> shows this information, together with a list of all files (if any) which have already been saved to the directory shown.

If this IS the directory to which you wish to save your worksheet,

Type `vatcalcs` <Enter>

If this is NOT the directory to which you wish to save your worksheet,

either:

type in the full drive name, pathname i.e subdirectory name (if necessary), and the the name of the file,

e.g. `c:\myfiles\vatcalcs` <Enter>

or `a:\vatcalcs` <Enter>

or:

press `<Esc>` `/ F D`

and then, when you see the message *Directory is >>*, type in the directory you require, e.g. c:\myfiles or a: and then <Enter>

Then press `S (for Store)` `vatcalcs` <Enter>

The worksheet will be saved (stored) as VATCALCS.WKS in the directory you specified.

Note concerning Filenames

The file name can be up to eight characters long, followed by a full-stop and the 'extension' such as wk1 or wks. depending on which program you are using.

The eight characters of the file name can be letters (A-Z) or numbers (0-9) . Some other characters are acceptable, depending on the program you are using, but it is safer to keep to letters and or numbers, at least for the time being.

You can type the letters of the filename in small letters: the program will convert them to capitals.

14. Saving your worksheet again

If, in a session, you have already saved your worksheet and given it a name, and you wish, as is prudent, to save it from time to time to update your additions to it, you can repeat the /fs command.

Try this:

Move the cursor on your VATCALCS worksheet to cell B12.

Type `"£` <Enter>

Type `/ F S`

The control panel should read: *Enter save file name:* followed by the name that you previously gave to your worksheet file, i.e. VATCALCS.

Press `<Enter>` `R (Replace)`

The revised VATCALCS worksheet is now saved with the addition of your recent entry into cell B12.

15. Changing your data

Before you end this session, you may like to experiment with changing the data entered into cells B8, B9, C8 and C9.

For example, alter the figure in cell B8 to 100.

Move the cursor to cell B8.

Type `100` <Enter>

The sale figures in cells D8, E8, F8 and B13 will have doubled.

Be careful not to type over the cells containing formulae. You will learn how to protect such cells from alteration in a later session.

When you have finished experimenting, you can end this session using the method described in session 1. Any changes to the data which you made in this paragraph will, of course, not be saved, unless you have used /FS again after the changes.

16. Summary

In this session you should have achieved the objectives set out at the start of this session.

In particular, you should have become acquainted with:

`'`	the left-align label prefix
`"`	the right-align label prefix
`^`	the centre label prefix
`\`	the repeat label prefix
`/WCS`	Worksheet Column Set-width
`/C`	the Copy command, including anchoring with a full-stop and pointing with the cursor
`/RE`	the Range Erase command
`+`	to precede a cell reference
`*`	the multiplication sign
`/FS`	the File Save command, and how to use it on first and subsequent occasions.

17. Activity

Create a worksheet from the following table:

Jean Landown	**VAT Calculations**				
			Net £	VAT(15%) £	Gross £
Sales:	20 bracelets @ £35 each		700	105	805
Purchases:	20 bracelets @ £20 each		400	60	460
Summary:	Output tax =	£105			
	Input tax =	£60			
Payable to HM Customs & Excise =		£45			

[Note: this table is taken from AFBIS, chapter entitled *Deductions from Pay and Value Added Tax*.]

You should try to convert this table to a format suitable for a worksheet, e.g. 'Bracelets' could be a heading for a column.

18. Objective test ☐ A ☐ B ☑ C ☐ D

1. **The label prefix `` results in the label entered in a cell being**

   ☐ A left aligned
   ☐ B right aligned
   ☐ C centred
   ☐ D repeated

2. **If you enter no label prefix before a label, then the default is for the label to appear**

   ☐ A left aligned
   ☐ B right aligned
   ☐ C centred
   ☐ D none of these

3. **In order to widen a single column to a width of 12, the key presses are**

   ☐ A /wcs12<Enter>
   ☐ B /rcs12<Enter>
   ☐ C \rcs12<Enter>
   ☐ D /wcs<Enter>12<Enter>

4. **In order to make a row of hyphens entered in a cell, the key presses are**

   ☐ A /-<Enter>
   ☐ B \-<Enter>
   ☐ C /\-<Enter>
   ☐ D ---------

5. **In order to copy a row of hyphens from cell A7 to cells B7, C7 and D7, the key presses are, starting with the cursor over cell A7,**

   ☐ A /C<→><→><→>.<Enter>
   ☐ B \C<→><→><→>.<Enter>
   ☐ C /C<Enter><→>.<→><→><Enter>

☐ D \C<Enter><→>.<→><→><Enter>

6. In order to clear cell A7 completely of its contents, the key presses, when the cursor is over cell A6, are

☐ A <→>\RE<Enter>

☐ B /RE<↓><Enter>

☐ C \REA7<Enter>

☐ D <↓>/RE<Enter>

7. If you wish to multiply the number 11 in cell A9 by the number 9 in cell B9, and obtain the result in cell C9, the formula to enter in cell C9 is

☐ A +a9xb9

☐ B +a9*b9

☐ C 11x9=

☐ D none of these

8. With the number 11 in cell A10 and the number 7 in cell B10, in order to obtain the product in cell C10, the way to copy the correct formula from cell C9 in question 7 above to cell C10 requires the following key presses, assuming the cursor is over cell C9:

☐ A /C<↓><Enter>

☐ B /C<Enter><↓><Enter>

☐ C <↓>/C<Enter><↑><Enter>

☐ D both B and C

9. For {123} and {VPP} users only:

You are saving a worksheet for the first time with the name BEDTIME. If when you press /FS, the control panel shows:

Enter save file name: C:\123\works*.wk1

in order to save your worksheet to a floppy disk in drive A:, you type:

☐ A bedtime<Esc>

☐ B <Esc><Esc>a\bedtime<Enter>

☐ C <Esc>a:bedtime<Enter>

☐ D <Esc><Esc>a:\bedtime<Enter>

9. For {VP} and {AEA} users only:

You are saving a worksheet for the first time with the name BEDTIME. If when you press /FS, the control panel shows:

Enter File Name: or STORE:Name of file ?,

in order to save your worksheet to a floppy disk in drive A:, you type:

- ☐ A bedtime<Esc>
- ☐ B <Esc><Esc>a\bedtime<Enter>
- ☐ C <Esc>a:/bedtime<Esc>
- ☐ D a:bedtime<Enter>

10. Assuming you have saved your worksheet BEDTIME correctly, and have made some additions which you now wish to save with it, under the same name, you should make the following key presses:

- ☐ A /FS<Enter>R
- ☐ B /FS<Enter><Enter>
- ☐ C /FSTeatime<Enter>
- ☐ D /FS<Enter>

SESSION 3
Bristol: Cash Flow Forecast

1. Objectives

At the end of this session, you will be able to:

- ❑ know the layout of a Cash Flow Forecast
- ❑ save a keystroke in copying to a range of cells
- ❑ widen a range of cells
- ❑ use the @SUM formula to total a range of cells
- ❑ practise saving the worksheet
- ❑ use pointing in entering a formula
- ❑ align a range of labels
- ❑ put commas into figures using /WGF
- ❑ translate a Cash Flow Forecast into a worksheet format

2. Introduction

In this session, you will create a worksheet containing a CASH FLOW FORECAST, and you will learn some more skills as you do so.

A Cash Flow Forecast is a financial statement of the cash expected to flow into and out of a business for a specified future period. The statement is usually presented as an analysis which shows detailed cash inflows at the top of the statement and detailed cash outflows below, with analysis columns for suitable periods of time, frequently months. At the foot of each column appears the balance of cash in hand expected at the end of the period to which the column relates. The purpose of the forecast is to aid cash planning and decision making. Control can be achieved by regular comparison of the planned cash flow with the actual flow. It is therefore a document which needs to be updated frequently, and its preparation in spreadsheet format enables this to be done more easily than with pencil and rubber or perhaps by re-typing.

'Cash' is usually taken to mean both cash-in-hand and cash-at-bank, i.e. money which is easily accessible.

3. Bristol: Cash Flow Forecast

The Cash Flow Forecast which you will be shown how to create on a worksheet is shown below. It is a personal cash flow forecast for a Mr. B. Bristol who expects to have savings in hand of £250 on 1st January, but knows that he must have £500 available by the end of June to be able to afford a holiday. The forecast shows his 'take-home' pay for the next six months, as well as his anticipated outgoings for the same period. The foot of each column shows his anticipated balance of cash at the end of each month.

[This example is taken from AFBIS, chapter entitled *Cash Planning and Personal Cash Flow*.]

	A	B	C	D	E	F	G	H
1	B. BRISTOL: CASH FLOW FORECAST							
2	for the six month period January - June							
3								
4	------------------	------	------	------	------	------	------	------
5		JAN	FEB	MAR	APL	MAY	JUN	TOTAL
6		£	£	£	£	£	£	£
7	CASH INFLOWS							
8	Salary	700	700	700	700	700	700	4,200
9		------	------	------	------	------	------	------
10	Total Inflows A	700	700	700	700	700	700	4,200
11	CASH OUTFLOWS:	======	======	======	======	======	======	======
12	Rates				160			160
13	Rent	200	200	200	200	200	200	1,200
14	Electricity			180			180	360
15	Travel	50	50	50	50	50	50	300
16	Insurances	10	40	10	130	10	10	210
17	Sundries	120	120	120	120	120	120	720
18	Food	150	150	150	150	150	150	900
19	Holiday						500	500
20		------	------	------	------	------	------	------
21	Total Outflows B	530	560	710	810	530	1,210	4,350
22		======	======	======	======	======	======	======
23	NET CASH FLOW: A - B	170	140	(10)	(110)	170	(510)	(150)
24	Balances:							
25	Start of month	250	420	560	550	440	610	250
26	End of month	420	560	550	440	610	100	100
27	==================	======	======	======	======	======	======	======

Note: cells B25 and H25 = savings at 1st January

4. Approach

You could, of course, compose the worksheet in the same way as you entered VATCALCS in session 2, i.e. first labels, then values, and finally formulae.

However, in this session you will work down the worksheet more or less from top to bottom. i.e. a mixture of labels, values and formulae as you go. The idea is that once you get the hang of a principle, you may feel confident enough to make entries which are similar to previous entries on your own, without pressing or typing as instructed in detail. On the other hand, you may feel that you will learn more easily by carrying out the detailed instructions, and watching the screen carefully after each keystroke as suggested in session 1. The choice is yours! If you think you have made the wrong choice, you can always erase as much as you want and try the other method.

5. Entering the headings

Start this session with a blank worksheet, as you learnt in session 1.

Move the cursor to cell A1 (press Home if it is not already there).

Type `B. BRISTOL: CASH FLOW FORECAST` Press `<Enter>`

You will note that what you have typed now appears in cell A1, and that it spreads over into cells B1, C1 and D1. This does not matter, since you do not want to enter anything into those cells.

If you have made a typing error, you can either retype correctly, or use the <F2> edit key as you learnt in session 1, paragraph 8.

Press `<↓>` (Cell A2)

If you used <Caps Lock> for cell A1, turn it off now!

Type `for the six month period January - June`

Press `<↓> <↓>` (Cell A4)

Press `\-` Press <Enter>

This fills cell A4 with a line of hyphens.

Press `/C` <Enter>

This is the /Copy command.

Press `<→>` to move the cursor to cell B4

Type `.(a full stop)` to anchor the cursor

Move the cursor to cell H4 using the <→> key

Press `<Enter>`

This /Copy command should have copied the hyphens from cell A4 to cells B4 - H4 inclusive and the cursor should still be at cell A4.

Press <↓><→> (Cell B5)

Type JAN <→> FEB <→> MAR <→> APL <→>

MAY <→> JUN <→> TOTAL <Enter>

Press <F5> b6 <Enter> (Cell B6)

Type '£ <Enter>

Note that a label prefix is necessary before the £ sign (except for {AEA}).

Type /C <Enter>

The control panel reads *Enter range to copy TO: B6*. You want to copy the £ sign to cells C6 - H6 inclusive. You have learnt that the next keystrokes are .(full stop), move cursor to H6, and <Enter>. You may find the following to be easier:

Press .(full stop) <→> six times <Enter>

You omitted to move the cursor to C6 before anchoring the cursor with the full stop. This means that you copied cell B6 on to itself, as well as to the cells to the right. Why not, if it's easier?

6. Entering the inflows

Press <↓> <←> (Cell A7)

Type CASH INFLOWS: <Enter>

You will notice that this label overflows into cell B7, but unlike your entries into cells A1 and B1, this does now matter, since you wish to enter figures into column B.

You must now widen column A to accomodate the maximum number of letters and spaces you wish to enter into it. If you refer to the table in paragraph 3 above, you will see that the longest label from the first column is:

NET CASH FLOW: A - B

There are a total of 20 letters and spaces. So you need to widen column A to 20, as follows:

Press /WCS20 <Enter>

You could have used the <→> key (as you did in session 2, 4) but in this case typing *20* is quicker.

You will notice that the worksheet is now larger than can be seen at once on the screen. Columns G and H are off-screen to the right. This does not matter, but since columns B - H inclusive are wider than you need, you can, for convenience narrow columns B - H from 9 to 7 characters:

Press [/WGC7<Enter>] (Worksheet, Global, Column-Width)

This / Worksheet, Global ({AEA} General), Column-width command sets the default column-width for every column on the worksheet which has not already been individually set beforehand by /WCS. Since you altered column A by /WCS to a width of 20, column A remains unaffected by this global setting.

[Note: {VP} has a /RCS (Range, Column-width, Set) command, which you could use as an alternative in this instance, as follows:

Move cursor to cell B7

Press [/RCS] Move cursor to H7 Press <Enter>

Type [7] <Enter>

This gives columns B - H only a width of 7. In {VP} /WGC sets the default column-width for all columns of the worksheet which have not been individually set beforehand by either /WCS or /RCS.]

Now you can enter the detailed inflows:

Move the cursor to cell A8

Type [Salary] [<→>] [700] [<Enter>]

Next, copy the 700 in cell B8 to cells C8 - G8 inclusive, as you did for the £ sign in row 6:

Press [/C<Enter>.] [<→>] 5 times [<Enter>] (Cell B8)

Now move the cursor to cell H8 (press <F5>h8<Enter>), where you require the total of the figures in cells B8 - G8 inclusive:

Press [@sum(b8.g8)] <Enter>

The figure of 4200 should appear in cell H8, with the formula in the status line of the control panel. [If the figure 0 appears in cell H8, make sure you have not entered the values of 700 as labels!]

Note that entering the formula requires only a single fullstop, though the control panel shows two full stops.

The formula @SUM totals all figures in the range entered between the brackets. This is simpler than entering: +b8+c8+d8+e8+f8+g8 as the formula.

Press [<f5>b9] [<Enter>] (Cell B9)

Press [\-] [<Enter>] [/C] [<Enter>] [.] [<→>] six times [<Enter>]

A line a hyphens should extend from cell B9 to cell H9.

Press [<F5>a10<Enter>] (Cell A10)

* + cell number enter /C

Type [Total Inflows A] [<→>] (Cell B10)

Press [+b8] [<Enter>] [/C] [<Enter>] [.] [<→>] six times [<Enter>]

This enters the formula +B8 into cell B10 (thereby copying the number 700 from cell B8 into cell B10), and then copies this formula to cells C10 to H10 inclusive.

Move the cursor over cells B10 to H10, and notice the formulae displayed on the status line of the control panel as you do so.

Press [<F5>b11<Enter>] (Cell B11)

Press [\=] [<Enter>] [/C] [<Enter>] [.] [<→>] six times [<Enter>]

This enters a row of = signs from cells B11 to H11.

7. Saving your worksheet

Before you enter the Cash Outflows, why not save the worksheet so far?

Check that you will be saving the worksheet to the correct drive and directory. If you have forgoten how to do this, refer to session 2, paragraph 13.

Press [/FS]

Type [bristol] <Enter>

and the worksheet so far is saved to a file BRISTOL.WKS or BRISTOL.WK1 (depending on the program you are using) in the drive and directory you have specified.

You should get into the habit of saving your worksheet frequently with /FS. The next time you decide to do so, say in 10 minutes time, type **/FS<Enter>R**. The 'R' is for *replace*, i.e. to replace or update the worksheet as previousy saved with the name *BRISTOL*.

[You could, if you wish, save the file separately each time you save it, e.g. with the names *BRISTOL*, *BRISTOL1*, *BRISTOL2*, and so on. The advantage of this is that if you decide that the changes you have made since you saved the worksheet for the first time as *BRISTOL* are not to your liking, you could retrieve *BRISTOL* and make new changes. You will learn how to retrieve a file in the next session.]

8. Entering the outflows

Move the cursor to cell A11

Type [CASH OUTFLOWS:] [<↓>] (Cell A12)

Type [Rates] <Enter>

Move the cursor to cell E12, and

Type [160] <Enter>

In cell H12, you want the total of cells B12..G12. To do so, you will copy the formula from cell H8, as follows:

Move the cursor to cell H8

Type [/C] <Enter>

Move the cursor to cell H12

Type [<Enter>]

Move the cursor from H8 to H12, and inspect the formula on the status line of the control panel. You will see that it reads:

@SUM(B12..G12)

Next, type in the labels for cells A13 to A19 inclusive:

Cell	Label
A13	Rent
A14	Electricity
A15	Travel
A16	Insurances
A17	Sundries
A18	Food
A19	Holiday

Next, type in the figures from the Bristol: Cash Flow Forecast sheet in paragraph 3 above, into cells B13..G19. (This is how to define a rectangular range of cells, by defining the top left and bottom right corners.) Leave the blank cells empty.

Do NOT enter the total column figures into column H, because these will be represented by formulae.

Did you take advantage of the arrow keys (when entering figures) and also the /Copy command for copying identical figures?

Now for the total formulae in cells H13..H19.

Move the cursor to cell H12

Type [/C<Enter>.] (Don't forget the full stop!)

Move the cursor to cell H19, and press <Enter>

The correct totals should now appear in cell H13..H19, and the status line of the control panel should show the appropriate formula for each cell.

Move the cursor to cell B20

Type [\-] <Enter> [/C] <Enter> [.]

Move the cursor to cell H20, and press <Enter>

This produces a line of hyphens from cell B20 to H20. (Did you remember the full stop?)

Move the cursor to cell A21

Type [Total Outflows B] [<→>] (Cell B21)

Type [@sum( ] and no more yet!

You are now going to enter the rest of the formula by pointing.

Move the cursor up to cell B12

Type [.] (a full stop)

Move the cursor down to cell B19

The status line should now read: **@SUM(B12..B19 but with no end bracket. You have to** supply this:

Type [ )] and then press <Enter>

Cell B21 should show 530 and the status line the formula.

Next, copy the formula from B21 to cells C21..H21:

Type [/C] <Enter> [.]

Move the cursor to cell H21, and press <Enter>

Now, draw a line of = signs from B22 to H22:

Move the cursor to cell B22

Type [\=] <Enter> [/C] <Enter> [.]

Move the cursor to H22, and press <Enter>

[Why not save the worksheet to date?]

Type [/FS<Enter>R]

9. Entering the balances

Move the cursor to cell A23

Type [NET CASH FLOW A - B] <→> (Cell B23)

Type [+b10-b21] <Enter>

Type [/C] <Enter> [.]

Move the cursor to H23, and press <Enter>

Note how positive and negative values are displayed

Now enter the following labels:

Cell	Label
A24	Balances:
A25	Start of month
A26	End of month
A27	\=

Move to cell B25, and type `250` <Enter>

Move to cell H25, and type `+b25` <Enter>

Note: the contents of cell H25 must always be the same as the figure entered in cell B25. This is because it is not the total of line 25, but the start of the month figure at the beginning of the six month period.

Move to cell B26

Type `+b23+b25` <Enter>

Move the cursor to cell C25

Type `+b26` <Enter>

Next, copy cell C25 to D25..G25, as follows:

Type `/C` <Enter> `.`

Move the cursor to G25, and press <Enter>

[Do not worry about the '0's (or blanks) in the cells; the formulae will have something to work on when you have completed line 26.]

Now, copy cell B26 to C26..H26, as follows:

Move to cell B26

Type `/C<Enter>` `.`

Move the cursor to H26, and press <Enter>

Finally, copy the = signs in cell A27 across the page:

Move to cell A27

Type `/C<Enter>` `.`

Move the cursor to cell H27, and press <Enter>

At last! The worksheet is complete. But before you end this session, you will do a few things to improve its appearance.

10. Aligning a range of labels

The month headings in row 5 and the £ signs in row 6 are at present all left-aligned. This is because you entered them using the default label-prefix (').

Perhaps they would look better centre-aligned, as follows:

Move the cursor to cell B5

{123}{VP} Press `/RLC` (Range, Label, Center)

{AEA} Press `/RPC` (Range, Prefix, Centre)

Now you will move the cursor to cell H5, but using a new technique:

Press `<End><→>` (Cell H5)

Note: The <End> key, when pressed before any of the arrow keys, moves the cursor in the direction of the arrow key to the cell on the boundary of any empty and filled space.

[If you are outside the area of your worksheet, you can see how large the whole spreadsheet is. Try it sometime, NOT NOW! Move the cursor outside the worksheet, press <End><↓><End><→>. Lotus 123 version 2 goes to column IV and line 8192. Press <Home> to get back to cell A1.]

Press `<↓>` (Cell H6)

This illuminates the range B5..H6 (the top-left and bottom-right corners of the range rectangle).

Press `<Enter>`

Do you like the revised appearance? Perhaps the labels would look even better if right-aligned:

Move the cursor to cell B5, if not there.

{123}{VP} Press `/RLR<End><→><↓><Enter>`

{AEA} Press `/RPR<End><→><↓><Enter>`

11. Putting commas in figures

Finally, you will put some commas into your figures,so that, for example, 4350 appears as 4,350.

Press `/WGF, (a comma!) 0 (number 0)` <Enter>

and there you are.

As an experiment,

Press /WGF, (a comma!) <Enter>

Note that this time you did not alter the default decimal position from 2, and therefore all figures appear with pence added, e.g. 700 reappears as 700.00.

In addition, some of the cells are filled with asterisks (*******).

The reason is that 4,200.00 plus a blank following is 9 characters, and you have set the column widths for B..H to 7. Therefore figures which cannot fit in appear as *******.

You could alter the column widths back to 9 using /WGC9<Enter>, but in this case, to keep all the figures horizontally visible on the screen, and also because pence are unnecessary:

Press /WGF,0<Enter> again.

Enough for this session.

Do not forget to SAVE your BRISTOL worksheet. You will be recovering it in the next session, and printing it out.

12. Summary

In this session you should have achieved the objectives set out at the start of this session.

In particular, you should have become acquainted with:

/WGC	Worksheet Global Column-width
/RCS	(VP) Range Column Set
@SUM	the formula to total a range of cells
/RLC	Range Label Center
/RLR	Range Label Right
/WGF,	Worksheet Global Format ,(comma) to enter commas into figures, and set the decimal place

13. Activity

13.1 BRISTOL REVISED

Three months have passed, and Mr. Bristol is revising his budget to reflect the actual figures for January, February and March.

These are as shown in the table on the following page:

CASH INFLOWS: As per budget

CASH OUTFLOWS: Actual:

	JAN	FEB	MAR
Rates	–	–	–
Rent	200	200	200
Electricity	–	–	220
Travel	50	60	60
Insurances	10	60	10
Sundries	120	150	130
Food	150	150	150
Holiday	–	–	–
Total Outflows	530	620	770

Type *Actual* in each of the cells B3, C3 and D3.

Alter the figures for January to March from budget to actual. Inspect the changes to the 'Balances: End of month' figures. What is the revised budgeted balance at the end of June? Assume his budgeted figures for the next three months are unchanged, but alter his budget for food (Mr. Bristol is somewhat overweight) for the months of April, May and June, so that he will still have a £100 balance at the end of June, even after paying for his holiday.

13.2 Personal Budget

Draw up a personal cash flow forecast for yourself for the next year, and translate it into a worksheet, using the techniques you have acquired in the current session.

Save it, and update it throughout the year with the actual figures and revised budget figures.

14. Objective test ☐ A ☐ B ☑ C ☐ D

1. If you type: **Cash Flow** and **cASH fLOW** appears on the screen, you should delete and retype after pressing

   ☐ A <Num Lock>

   ☐ B <Caps Lock>

   ☐ C <Ins>

   ☐ D <Scroll Lock>

2. To change the widths of all columns on a worksheet which have not already been changed using /WCS (or /RCS for {VP}), the keys to press are

   ☐ A /WGC

   ☐ B /WCS

   ☐ C /RGS

   ☐ D /GCS

3. To total cells D6..D12 in cell D13, the formula to enter in cell D13 is

   ☐ A '@SUM(D6..D12)

   ☐ B @SUM[D6..D12]

   ☐ C /SUM(D6..D12)

   ☐ D @SUM(D6..D12)

4. If all the labels in cells B2..H2 are left-aligned, and column H is the extreme right-hand column with any entries, in order to change all the labels in cells B2..H2 to right-aligned, the key presses required after moving the cursor to cell B2 are [{AEA} read P for L]

   ☐ A /RLC <End><→><Enter>

   ☐ B /RLC<Enter><End><→><Enter>

   ☐ C /RLR <End><→><Enter>

   ☐ D /RLR<Enter><End><→><Enter>

5. If all the currency figures entered into your worksheet have no commas, e.g. 4,000 appears as 4000, and you want to show all the figures with commas, and with pence as well, e.g. 4,000.00, the key presses required are

   ☐ A /WGFC<Enter>

   ☐ B /WGF,<Enter>

   ☐ C /WGC,<Enter>

   ☐ D /WGCC2<Enter>

6. If after the correct key presses for question 5 above, some of the cells are full of asterisks, the reason is

   ☐ A you have made a dreadful mistake

   ☐ B the computer has gone wrong

   ☐ C it's time you went to bed

   ☐ D the columns are too narrow

7. Only one of the following formulae is incomplete. It is:

   - [ ] A +D2+E2
   - [ ] B D2*E2
   - [ ] C +D2*E2
   - [ ] D @SUM(D2..E2)

8. If you entered SUM(D2.E2) in to a cell, the cell would show:

   - [ ] A SUM(D2.E2)
   - [ ] B the total of figures in cells D2 and E2
   - [ ] C ERROR in the mode indicator box
   - [ ] D none of these

9. There are the following figures in the following cells:

Cell	Figure
C4	23
D4	34
C5	12
D5	45

To get a total of 114 in cell B5, the formula to be entered into cell B5 is

   - [ ] A +C4+D4+C5+D5
   - [ ] B @SUM(D4..C5)
   - [ ] C @SUM(C4..D5)
   - [ ] D any of these

10. If you have saved your file with /fs several times, and then make some subsequent alterations, without saving it, if you then quit and turn off the computer,

   - [ ] A only the alterations are lost
   - [ ] B the whole file is lost
   - [ ] C only the first 'save' is saved
   - [ ] D none of these

SESSION 4
Printing Your Worksheet

1. Objectives

At the end of this session you will be able to:

- ❑ retrieve a worksheet
- ❑ prepare your printer
- ❑ obtain a print-out of your worksheet
- ❑ adjust the page-length for your type of paper
- ❑ print your worksheet in condensed print
- ❑ adjust the margins of your print-out
- ❑ look at all the formulae in your worksheet

2. Introduction

In this session, you will learn how to retrieve and print out the 'BRISTOL' worksheet which you created and saved in session 3.

You will also learn how to look at all the formulae of your spreadsheet rather than one at a time in the control panel.

3. Retrieving your worksheet

In session 2, you learnt how to save a worksheet in the directory of your choice. It is probably a good idea at the beginning of a session to make that directory the current directory. This could save time when you come to save and retrieve worksheets.

If you have forgotten how to use the /FD command, refer back to session 2, paragraph 13.

[Note: {123} {VP} If you regularly use one directory only,

Press `/WGDD` (Worksheet, Global, Default, Directory)

and edit the 'Directory at startup:' to your requirements.

Press `<Enter>UQ` (<Enter>, Update, Quit)

This will ensure that you have the correct directory each time you start a session after previously quitting the program.]

Make sure that the mode indicator shows READY.

Press `/FR` (File, Retrieve)

A list of files in the current directory appears in the control panel or on a drop-down menu. If BRISTOL.WKS or BRISTOL.WK1 is not shown, use the cursor (using the arrow keys) to find it. You can move the cursor off the screen or menu to see more files. Usually the cursor movement is circular, i.e. when you go beyond the end of the menu, the cursor moves back to the beginning.

{123} In addition you can press <F3>, (the List Names key) if you want to view more files at the same time.

When the cursor is over your BRISTOL file name,

Press `<Enter>` to retrieve it on to the screen.

4. Preparing your printer

Your printer should be properly connected to your computer. Make sure that it is switched on and 'On Line'. Printers vary in the facilities provided, but usually there is a light to show when it is 'On Line'. Some printers have 'Form Feed' and 'Line Feed' buttons which operate when the printer is 'Off Line', and move perforated tractor feed paper to the next perforation (Form Feed) or one line at a time (Line Feed).

Before you print your worksheet, assuming you are using continuous (perforated tractor feed paper), make sure the print head is just below the page perforation. You can do this by Form Feed or Line Feed (if the printer can do so) or by manually turning the platen knob. Some printers can be damaged if you manually turn the platen knob while the printer is turned on. Be on the safe side, and read your printer manual!

It is also good practice to tell your program that the print head is in fact at the top of a page.

Press `/PPAQ` (Print, Printer, Align, Quit)

[Note: {AEA} The keypress A is named Adjust, not Align]

The 'Quit' returns you to READY mode. Using the *Align* command should be part of your printing routine as you will see shortly.

5. Basic printing of the 'Bristol' worksheet

The following instructions assume that your printer 'default' is to print in some orthodox manner, e.g. draft at 10 cpi (characters per inch). You will learn how to change this later on. The odds are that the following instructions will produce a basic printout of your 'BRISTOL' worksheet.

(1) Make sure you have the 'BRISTOL' worksheet on the screen.

(2) Check that the mode operator is at READY, and that the cursor is in cell A1 (Press <Home> if it is not).

(3) Press `/PPR` (Print, Printer, Range)

The control panel displays *Enter Print range: A1*

(4) Press `. (full-stop)`

(5) Move the cursor to cell H27. This can be done as follows:

Press `<End><Home>`

(This moves the cursor to the bottom right hand corner of the worksheet you have created, and highlights the range A1..H27.)

(6) Press `<Enter>`

(7) Press `AGP` (Align, Go, Page)

Align has been explained above in paragraph 4. *Go* instructs the printer to print the worksheet. *Page* instructs the printer to advance the paper to the top of the next sheet.

(8) Press `Q` (Quit)

This leaves the *Print* menu, and returns you to READY mode.

Your printout should be a replica of the worksheet on the screen, excluding the borders (column letters and row numbers) and information from the control panel.

Your printout should look something like Figure 4a, with column letters and row numbers added for you to refer to.

[If the £ signs did not print, try replacing them with # signs on the worksheet (Cells B6..H6) and press /AGP again]

Before you continue, save your settings in the present worksheet:

Press `/FS<Enter>R`

6. Adjusting the page-length

Check that the *Page* command worked. If you are using continuous stationery, the perforation should be just below the printhead, as it was before you printed the worksheet. If it is not, adjust the paper from the printer, as instructed above in paragraph 4.

Press `/PPOP` (Print, Printer, Options, Page-length)

The message in the control panel will read:

Enter *Lines per Page (1..100):* followed by a number, which may be the default number 66.

If you are using 8.5″ by 11″ paper, assuming your printer prints 6 lines per inch, then the number should be 66 lines per page, i.e. 11″ times 6 lines per inch = 66 lines. If the default 66 is showing in the control panel, accept it and return to READY mode by pressing <Enter>QQ.

Figure 4a

	A	B	C	D	E	F	G	H
1	B. BRISTOL: CASH FLOW FORECAST							
2	for the six month period January - June							
3								
4	------------------	----------	----------	----------	----------	----------	----------	----------
5		JAN	FEB	MAR	APL	MAY	JUN	TOTAL
6		£	£	£	£	£	£	£
7	CASH INFLOWS							
8	Salary	700	700	700	700	700	700	4,200
9		----------	----------	----------	----------	----------	----------	----------
10	Total Inflows A	700	700	700	700	700	700	4,200
11	CASH OUTFLOWS:	==========	==========	==========	==========	==========	==========	==========
12	Rates				160			160
13	Rent	200	200	200	200	200	200	1,200
14	Electricity			180			180	360
15	Travel	50	50	50	50	50	50	300
16	Insurances	10	40	10	130	10	10	210
17	Sundries	120	120	120	120	120	120	720
18	Food	150	150	150	150	150	150	900
19	Holiday						500	500
20		----------	----------	----------	----------	----------	----------	----------
21	Total Outflows B	530	560	710	810	530	1,210	4,350
22		==========	==========	==========	==========	==========	==========	==========
23	NET CASH FLOW: A - B	170	140	(10)	(110)	170	(510)	(150)
24	Balances:							
25	Start of month	250	420	560	550	440	610	250
26	End of month	420	560	550	440	610	100	100
27	==================	==========	==========	==========	==========	==========	==========	==========

If, however you are using A4 continuous paper, which is 8.25" by 11.67", then the number should be changed (typed over) to 70, which is 11.67" times 6 lines per inch = 70 lines, before pressing <Enter>QQ.

If you have any other size paper, measure it and use the above principles to calculate the correct number of lines.

This corrects the page length for the current worksheet.

[Note: {123} {VP} If you want to adjust the page-length for all future sessions (i.e. alter the global default setting):

Press `/WGDPP` (Worksheet, Global, Default, Printer, Page-Length)

Type in the page-length you require, then:

Press `<Enter>QUQ` (Quit, Update, Quit) to return to READY.]

7. Printing in condensed print

In paragraph 5, you printed the BRISTOL worksheet at your printer's default, probably at 10 cpi (characters per inch).

You can calculate how many characters wide the worksheet is, as follows:

Column A	20
Columns B – H, 7 columns x 7 characters =	49
Total	69

Normal screens are able to display 72 or 76 characters (depending on the program). Many printers are able to print 80 characters on 8.5" wide or A4 paper. A normal default for a spreadsheet program is 72 characters, and later you will learn how to change this.

However, assuming that 72 is a normal limit, this means that the BRISTOL worksheet, at 69 characters, just managed to print out without some right-hand columns being printed below the other columns.

There are several solutions to printing out wide worksheets which will not fit normal 8.5" or A4 paper at 10 cpi. One is to alter the cpi from 10 cpi to, say, 17 cpi.

This is called compressed (or small) print. If your printer is a dot-matrix printer (and not a daisy-wheel) printer you should be able to change to this.

With the BRISTOL worksheet retrieved, and in READY mode,

Press `/PPOS` (Print, Printer, Options, Set-up)

You should see the prompt in the control panel:

Enter Setup String:

This where you enter some codes to tell your printer to print in compressed print. The codes vary from printer to printer.

If your printer is an Epson (or Epson-compatible) the code to try is \027\015 or \015. [For {AEA} press \<F1>, move the cursor to CND-ON and press <Enter>. This enters the code \015 for you!]

If this code does not work, consult your printer manual for the decimal code for compressed print. Note that it must be the decimal code. If the code is given in another format, e.g. ESC+SI or 1B,0F (Hex. code) for 027,015 (decimal), you will have to look up a conversion table to convert it to decimal format. Note also that the decimal three-digit codes must be preceded by a back-slash.

Some printers can also be set to print in condensed print from the printer's operator panel. (The printer manual should explain how to do this.) If this is possible, then it is not necessary to enter a printer set-up string from the spreadsheet program.

{123} {VP} If you wish to clear a set-up string which you already entered to the global default (usually blank), **press /PPCFQ** (Print, Printer, Clear, Format, Quit).

{AEA} To clear a set-up string, press **/PPOS<Esc>**

When you have entered the set-up string,

Press | <Enter>QQ | to return to READY mode.

If you now want to print out in compressed print, follow the procedure in paragraph 5 above. If you saved the range settings, then the keystrokes are:

Press | /PPAGP | (Print, Printer, Align, Go, Page)

With any luck, you should obtain a print-out in compressed print, and the paper (if continuous) should be at the top of the next sheet. * Adjust margin too.

8. Adjusting the margins

Your print-out in compressed print will be at the top left-hand corner of your paper.

It is possible to move your print-out to a more central position by altering the margin settings.

{123} {VP} If you wish to see the current default settings,

Press | /WGDS | (Worksheet, Global, Default, Status)

You will see such items as your current defaults for page-length and printer set-up strings.

> {AEA} You will see the defaults later, when you press /PPOM.

Margins are what we are interested in at present.

The defaults are probably (unless somebody has changed them):

> Left: 4 Right: 76 Top: 2 Bottom: 2

> {AEA} The defaults are Left: 0 Right: 80

The top and bottom margins are the distance in lines of print from the top and bottom edges of the paper default, e.g. 66 lines from top to bottom. If you changed the default in paragraph 6 above to 70 (for A4 paper) the default shows as 70 lines.

How many lines of your worksheet can be printed out on one page can be calculated as follows:

Assume that the page-length is set for 66 lines, and top and bottom margins at 2 lines each. You might expect that 66 less 2 less 2 = 62 lines of worksheet can be printed. However, the programs (unless you change the settings) allow in addition for headers and footers, i.e. items which can be typed in at the top and bottom of each page.

> {123}{VP} One line of header or footer can be typed in, and the programs allow 2 extra lines of space between these single lines and the text. Thus 6 extra lines (3 for headers and 3 for footers) have to be deducted, i.e. 62 less 6 = 56 lines.

{AEA} One line of header or footer can be typed in, and the program allows 1 extra line of space between these single lines and the text. One line at the top and bottom of the page is reserved for a perf-skip feature. Thus 6 extra lines have to be deducted, i.e. 62 less 6 = 56 lines.

The following table should make this clear:

Program	{123}{VP}		{AEA}	
Paper type	11"	A4	11"	A4
Perf-skip			1	1
Top margin	2	2	2	2
Header space	3	3	2	2
Body of text	56	60	56	60
Footer space	3	3	2	2
Bottom margin	2	2	2	2
Perf-skip			1	1
	66	70	66	70

[Note: headers and footers will be covered in a later session]

The left and right margin figures are the distance in *characters* from the *left-hand side of the paper*. This is a frequent cause of misunderstanding. [Some students assume that the right margin figure is measured from the right-hand side of the paper, and set the margin figure accordingly, say at 6 characters. This would result in a very narrow print-out of 2 (6 minus 4) characters!]

Now for some calculations. Your *BRISTOL* worksheet is 69 characters wide. With compressed print at 17 cpi, you should be able to get, say, 8 inches times 17 cpi = 136 characters on your A4 or 8.5" x 11" paper. In order to centre the printout, you could have a margin each side of 136 minus 69 = 67 divided by two = (say) 33 characters. So you could set the left margin at 33, and the right margin at 33 plus 69 = 102 (not forgetting that the measurement is from the left-hand edge of the paper.

The *BRISTOL* worksheet is 27 rows deep. Assume you have 56 lines available for printing on your paper (see above for {123}{VP} 11" paper). This means you have 56 - 27 = 29 lines spare. In order to centre the worksheet approximately you could increase the top margin of 2 lines by half the 29 spare lines, say 14, and alter the top margin to 16 lines.

Now to try it out, remembering that you are adjusting the margins for the current worksheet only:

Press **/PPOM** (Print, Printer, Options, Margins)

The control panel reads: *Left* *Right* *Top* *Bottom*

Press **L33<Enter>**

[You are returned to the Margins menu each time.]

Press **MR102<Enter>**

Press `MT16<Enter>`

Press `MB2<Enter>` or `MB<Enter>` if 2 is displayed.

Assuming you have not changed your printer set-up string, your range or page-length, to print out:

Press `Q` (Quit returns you to the Printer sub-menu)

Press `AGPQ` (Align, Go, Page, Quit)

Your printout should look something like Figure 4b, with column letters and row numbers added for you to refer to.

Figure 4b

	A	B	C	D	E	F	G	H
1	B. BRISTOL: CASH FLOW FORECAST							
2	for the six month period January - June							
3								
4	----------	----------	----------	----------	----------	----------	----------	----------
5		JAN	FEB	MAR	APL	MAY	JUN	TOTAL
6		£	£	£	£	£	£	£
7	CASH INFLOWS							
8	Salary	700	700	700	700	700	700	4,200
9		----------	----------	----------	----------	----------	----------	----------
10	Total Inflows A	700	700	700	700	700	700	4,200
11	CASH OUTFLOWS:	==========	==========	==========	==========	==========	==========	==========
12	Rates				160			160
13	Rent	200	200	200	200	200	200	1,200
14	Electricity			180			180	360
15	Travel	50	50	50	50	50	50	300
16	Insurances	10	40	10	130	10	10	210
17	Sundries	120	120	120	120	120	120	720
18	Food	150	150	150	150	150	150	900
19	Holiday						500	500
20		----------	----------	----------	----------	----------	----------	----------
21	Total Outflows B	530	560	710	810	530	1,210	4,350
22		==========	==========	==========	==========	==========	==========	==========
23	NET CASH FLOW: A	170	140	(10)	(110)	170	(510)	(150)
24	Balances:							
25	Start of month	250	420	560	550	440	610	250
26	End of month	420	560	550	440	610	100	100
27	==========	==========	==========	==========	==========	==========	==========	==========

9. Looking at the formulae

You can, of course, inspect the formula for a particular cell by positioning the cursor on it, and reading the formula from the status line of the control panel.

Sometimes, however, it is useful to be able to look at all the formulae.

Before you do so, save your BRISTOL worksheet and the margin changes you have made with /FS<Enter>R.

Press `/WGFT` (Worksheet, Global, Format, Text)

Now you can see the formulae, but some of them are too wide to fit in the columns.

You must widen columns B..H. How wide? The longest formula is, for example, in cell B21: @SUM(B12..B19), i.e 15 characters (including a space after the final bracket).

Press `/WGC` (Worksheet, Global, Column-Width)

Press `15<Enter>` (or move <→> until width is 15 <Enter>)

You should now be able to see all the formulae, though the whole worksheet is no longer visible on the screen. You will have to move the cursor to see columns which are off-screen.

Now save this file under the name BRISTOLF (the F is for formulae).

Press `/FS` Type `BRISTOLF` Press `<Enter>`

Figure 4c is a printout of this file.

Figure 4c

B. BRISTOL: CASH FLOW FORECAST
for the six month period January - June

	JAN £	FEB £	MAR £	APL £	MAY £	JUN £	TOTAL £
CASH INFLOWS							
Salary	700	700	700	700	700	700	@SUM(B8..G8)
Total Inflows A	+B8	+C8	+D8	+E8	+F8	+G8	+H8
CASH OUTFLOWS:							
Rates				160			@SUM(B12..G12)
Rent	200	200	200	200	200	200	@SUM(B13..G13)
Electricity				180			@SUM(B14..G14)
Travel	50	50	50	50	50	50	@SUM(B15..G15)
Insurances	10	40	10	130	10	10	@SUM(B16..G16)
Sundries	120	120	120	120	120	120	@SUM(B17..G17)
Food	150	150	150	150	150	150	@SUM(B18..G18)
Holiday						500	@SUM(B19..G19)
Total Outflows B	@SUM(B12..B19)	@SUM(C12..C19)	@SUM(D12..D19)	@SUM(E12..E19)	@SUM(F12..F19)	@SUM(G12..G19)	@SUM(H12..H19)
NET CASH FLOW:	+B10-B21	+C10-C21	+D10-D21	+E10-E21	+F10-F21	+G10-G21	+H10-H21
Balances:							
Start of month	250	+B26	+C26	+D26	+E26	+F26	+B25
End of month	+B23+B25	+C23+C25	+D23+D25	+E23+E25	+F23+F25	+G23+G25	+H23+H25

In order to see the worksheet as it was, without the formulae in the cells,

Press `/WGFG` (Worksheet, Global, Format, General)

The worksheet has now been saved as BRISTOL (with revised margin settings) and BRISTOLF (with formulae showing and wider columns) and there is no need to save it again. In fact, if you saved it now, it would have column-widths saved which are wider than necessary.

You can end this session in the normal way. If you have forgotten how, refer back to session 1, paragraph 12.

10. Summary

In this session you should have achieved the objectives set out at the start of this session.

In particular, you should have become acquainted with:

/WGDD	Worksheet, Global, Default, Directory *
/FR	File, Retrieve
/PPAQ	Print, Printer, Align, Quit
/PPR	Print, Printer, Range
/PPAGP	Print, Printer, Align, Go, Page
/PPOP	Print, Printer, Options, Page-length
/WGDPP	Worksheet, Global, Default, Printer, Page-length
/PPOS	Print, Printer, Options, Set-up
/WGDS	Worksheet, Global, Default, Status *
/PPOM	Print, Printer, Options, Margins
/WGFT	Worksheet, Global, Format, Text
/WGFG	Worksheet, Global, Format, General

Note * = not (AEA)

11. Activity

Print out the BRISTOLF worksheet, showing all the formulae.

Hints: You will have to alter the margins. The principles for the calculations were demonstrated in paragraph 8 above. Check that the correct range is specified and that the printer set-up string is correct for condensed print.

12. Objective test ☐ A ☐ B ☑ C ☐ D

1. In order to retrieve a worksheet file which you have already saved, the keystrokes required to retrieve it from the READY mode are

   ☐ A /WR

   ☐ B \WR

   ☐ C /FR

   ☐ D \FR

2. In order to tell your program that your printer is at the top of a new page, and to return to READY mode, the keypresses, from READY mode, are

   ☐ A /PPA

   ☐ B /PPAQ

   ☐ C /PAQ

   ☐ D /SPQR

3. You wish to define the range A1..H27 for printing where H27 is the bottom right-hand corner of your worksheet. From READY mode the keypresses are

   ☐ A /PPR.<End><Home><Enter>

   ☐ B /PRP.<Home><End><Enter>

   ☐ C /PPR<Enter>.<Home><End><Enter>

   ☐ D /PRP<Enter>.<Home><End><Enter>

4. In order to adjust the page length from the present default of 66 lines to 70 lines (for A4 paper), the keypresses from READY mode are

   ☐ A /PPP70<Enter>

   ☐ B /PPOP<Enter>70<Enter>

   ☐ C /POPPY70<Enter>

   ☐ D /PPOP70<Enter>

5. In order to enter a set-up string to instruct your printer to use condensed print, the keypresses from READY mode are

   ☐ A /PPS

   ☐ B /POPS

   ☐ C /PPOS

   ☐ D /PPROS

6. The set-up string for an Epson (or compatible) printer for condensed print is

☐ A /027/015

☐ B \027\015

☐ C \015\027

☐ D /015/027

7. You have defined the range settings, adjusted the page-length and entered any required set-up string ready for printing. In order to print your file, the keypresses from READY mode are

☐ A /PPAGP

☐ B /AGP

☐ C /PPGAP

☐ D /PPAP

8. You have pressed /PPOML6<Enter> to give you a margin of 6 characters from the left-hand side of the page. You now wish to set the right-hand margin to 6 characters from the right-hand side of the page which you calculate is 82 characters from the left-hand side of the page. The keypresses are

☐ A MR76<Enter>

☐ B R76<Enter>

☐ C MR6<Enter>

☐ D R6<Enter>

9. In order to see all the formulae, rather than the values resulting from the formulae, of your worksheet, the keypresses from READY mode are

☐ A /WFGT

☐ B /WGFT

☐ C /WGFG

☐ D /WFTG

10. Following the correct keypresses in question 9 above, to return to normal values, rather than formulae, visible in the cells, the keypresses from READY mode are

☐ A /WFGT

☐ B /WGGF

☐ C /WGFG

☐ D /WFTG

SESSION 5
Pontefract Financial Budgets

1. Objectives

At the end of this session you will be able to:

- ❑ create a worksheet into which you can enter data and from which a cash flow forecast, trading and profit & loss account, and balance sheet are automatically produced and updated
- ❑ understand what is meant by a data-block
- ❑ learn more about formulae, particularly + - * /
- ❑ save and print various versions of the same worksheet
- ❑ understand the logical function @IF
- ❑ protect labels and formulae from inadvertant alteration

2. Introduction

In this session, you will create a worksheet which is the solution to a budgeting problem.

The problem is adapted from an example in AFBIS (chapter entitled *The Relationship between Financial Statements*) and is set out in full in paragraph 3 below.

The solution to this problem is set out in figures 5a and 5b, which are a printout of the worksheet which you will create.

In order to create this worksheet, you will not be given individual keypresses as you were in the previous sessions. Instead, you are referred to figures 5c and 5d, which show the whole worksheet with column letters, row numbers, labels, values and formulae.

Most of the format of this worksheet will be familiar to you from what you have learnt in the previous sessions. There are some new aspects, however, and these are explained in paragraphs 4 and following.

You are advised to make your worksheet an exact replica of figures 5c and 5d, so that when you print it out, it should look like figures 5a and 5b.

This is not so formidable a task as you might think. You will be given advice about column-widths and margin settings etc., though should feel free to experiment for yourself.

If you find this session too much for one sitting, don't forget to save your work before leaving the program! It is good practice to save your work every 10 minutes or so in any case.

It is suggested that you save the worksheet with the filename PONTEF01. Then you can save subsequent versions as PONTEFxx, where xx represents various version references.

The problem and comments on its solution follow in paragraphs 3 and 4. It is not essential that you understand these in order to create the worksheet, though it is obviously better if you do!

3. Pontefract: The problem

Peter Pontefract has inherited £30,000, and plans to commence a confectionery business trading as PONTEFRACT on 1st April, 19x1.

His plans include the following:

(1) Equipment costing £16,000 will be bought and paid for on 1st April. Further equipment will be bought and paid for on 1st July, costing £8,000. Peter estimates that this equipment will last 10 years with no scrap value, and he will charge depreciation in his accounts from the date of purchase on a straight-line basis.

(2) Wages will be £2,000 per month for the first 3 months, and £3,000 per month thereafter.

(3) Selling and administration costs are expected to be £1,200 per month for the first 3 months, rising to £1,400 per month thereafter, payable in the month when the costs are incurred.

(4) Premises will be rented at £7,200 per annum, payable quarterly in advance starting on 1st April, 19x1.

(5) Selling price of goods is calculated at purchase price plus 50%.

(6) Terms of trade are for customers to pay in the month following receipt of goods, and Peter has arranged with his suppliers for payment to be made two months after the month of purchase.

Peter's planned sales and purchases are:

	Sales (£000s)	Purchases (£000s)
April	12	30
May	16	24
June	20	20
July	24	20
August	24	20
September	24	20
Totals	120	134

Required:

Prepare for PONTEFRACT the following BUDGETED documents:

(a) Cash Flow Forecast for the first 6 months of trading, showing the expected bank balances at the end of each month.

(b) Trading and Profit & Loss Account for the 6 months to 30.9.19x1.

(c) Balance Sheet as at 30.9.19x1.

4. Pontefract: The solution

The solution to this problem is set out in figures 5a and 5b.

The workings are as follows:

(1)

	Sales (£000s)		Purchases (£000s)	
	Invoiced	Cash	Invoiced	Paid
April	12		30	
May	16	12	24	
June	20	16	20	30
July	24	20	20	24
August	24	24	20	20
September	24	24	20	20
Totals	120	96	134	94
	Debtors	24	Creditors	40
		120		134

(2) Depreciation of equipment:

£16,000 x 10% p.a. =	£1,600 p.a.: 6 months =	£800
£8,000 x 10% p.a. =	£800 p.a.: 3 months =	£200
		£1,000

(3) Stock: See Trading Account (Figure 5b, Table C):

Sales are £120,000 (data) which is 50% added on to cost of sales - see note (5) of problem (para. 3 above).

Cost of sales is therefore two-thirds of sales value, i.e. £80,000.

Stock is therefore the difference between purchases of £134,000 (data) and cost of sales of £80,000.

5. Notes on the design of the worksheet

Please refer to figures 5a, 5b, 5c and 5d.

↔ 20   9 × 8 → H. = 72

Figure 5a

	A	B	C	D	E	F	G	H
1	PONTEFRACT							
2	==========	======	======	======	======	======	======	======
3	TABLE A: DATA							
4	Month:	April	May	June	July	August	Sept	Total
5		£	£	£	£	£	£	£
6	Capital	30,000						
7	Equipment	16,000			8,000			24,000
8	Nages	2,000	2,000	2,000	3,000	3,000	3,000	15,000
9	Selling & Admin	1,200	1,200	1,200	1,400	1,400	1,400	7,800
10	Rent of Premises	1,800			1,800			3,600
11	Sales	12,000	16,000	20,000	24,000	24,000	24,000	120,000
12	Purchases	30,000	24,000	20,000	20,000	20,000	20,000	134,000
13	Cash at start	0						
14	==========	======	======	======	======	======	======	======
15	TABLE B: CASH FLOW FORECAST for the first six months of trading							
16								
17	Month:	April	May	June	July	August	Sept	Total
18		£	£	£	£	£	£	£
19	RECEIPTS:							
20	Capital	30,000						30,000
21	Sales		12,000	16,000	20,000	24,000	24,000	96,000
22		------	------	------	------	------	------	------
23	Total A	30,000	12,000	16,000	20,000	24,000	24,000	126,000
24		======	======	======	======	======	======	======
25	PAYMENTS							
26	Purchases			30,000	24,000	20,000	20,000	94,000
27	Wages	2,000	2,000	2,000	3,000	3,000	3,000	15,000
28	Selling & Admin	1,200	1,200	1,200	1,400	1,400	1,400	7,800
29	Rent	1,800	0	0	1,800	0	0	3,600
30	Equipment	16,000	0	0	8,000	0	0	24,000
31		------	------	------	------	------	------	------
32	Total B	21,000	3,2CO	33,200	38,200	24,400	24,400	144,400
33		======	======	======	======	======	======	======
34	NET CASH FLOW A-B	9,000	8,800	(17,200)	(18,200)	(400)	(400)	(18,400)
35		------	------	------	------	------	------	------
36	Balances:							
37	Start of month	0	9,000	17,800	600	(17,600)	(18,000)	0
38	End of month	9,000	17,800	600	(17,600)	(18,000)	(18,400)	(18,400)
39	==========	======	======	======	======	======	======	======

Figure 5b

	A	B	C	D	E	F	G	H
40	TABLE C: BUDGETED TRADING AND PROFIT & LOSS ACCOUNT for the period							
41	of six months ending 30th September, 19x1							
42								
43					£	£		£
44	Sales							120,000
45	less Cost of Sales:							
46	Purchases					134,000		
47	less Closing Stock					54,000		
48						-------		
49								80,000
50								-------
51	Gross Profit							40,000
52	less Expenses:							
53	Wages					15,000		
54	Selling & Admin					7,800		
55	Rent					3,600		
56	Depreciation:							
57	Original Equipment				800			
58	Later Equipment				200			
59					-------	1,000		
60						-------		27,400
61								-------
62	Net Profit							12,600
63								=======
64								
65	TABLE D: BUDGETED BALANCE SHEET as at 30th September, 19x1							
66				£		£		£
67	FIXED ASSETS			Cost		Acc.Dep'n		NBV
68	Equipment			24,000		1,000		23,000
69				=======		=======		
70	CURRENT ASSETS							
71	Stock			54,000				
72	Debtors			24,000				
73				-------		78,000		
74	CURRENT LIABILITIES							
75	Creditors			40,000				
76	Overdraft			18,400				
77				-------		58,400		
78	Net Current Assets					-------		19,600
79								-------
80	Capital Employed							42,600
81								=======
82	Represented by:							
83	Capital					30,000		
84	Profit for 6 months					12,600		
85						-------		42,600
86								=======
87	==							

Figure 5c

	A	B	C	D	E	F	G	H
1	PONTEFRACT							
2	====================	====================	====================	====================	====================	====================	====================	====================
3	TABLE A: DATA							
4	Month:	April	May	June	July	August	Sept	Total
5		£	£	£	£	£	£	£
6	Capital	30,000						
7	Equipment	16,000		8,000				@SUM(B7..G7)
8	Nages	2,000	2,000	2,000	3,000	3,000	3,000	@SUM(B8..G8)
9	Selling & Adm:	1,200	1,200	1,200	1,400	1,400	1,400	@SUM(B9..G9)
10	Rent of Premi:	1,800			1,800			@SUM(B10..G10)
11	Sales	12,000	16,000	20,000	24,000	24,000	24,000	@SUM(B11..G11)
12	Purchases	30,000	24,000	20,000	20,000	20,000	20,000	@SUM(B12..G12)
13	Cash at start	0						@SUM(B13..G13)
14	====================	====================	====================	====================	====================	====================	====================	====================
15	TABLE B: CASH FLOW FORECAST for the first six months of trading							
16								
17	Month:	April	May	June	July	August	Sept	Total
18		£	£	£	£	£	£	£
19	RECEIPTS:							
20	Capital	+B6						@SUM(B20..G20)
21	Sales		+B11	+C11	+D11	+E11	+F11	@SUM(B21..G21)
22		--------------------	--------------------	--------------------	--------------------	--------------------	--------------------	--------------------
23	Total A	+B20	+C21	+D21	+E21	+F21	+G21	@SUM(B23..G23)
24		====================	====================	====================	====================	====================	====================	====================
25	PAYMENTS							
26	Purchases			+B12	+C12	+D12	+E12	@SUM(B26..G26)
27	Wages	+B8	+C8	+D8	+E8	+F8	+G8	@SUM(B27..G27)
28	Selling & Adm:	+B9	+C9	+D9	+E9	+F9	+G9	@SUM(B28..G28)
29	Rent	+B10	+C10	+D10	+E10	+F10	+G10	@SUM(B29..G29)
30	Equipment	+B7	+C7	+D7	+E7	+F7	+G7	@SUM(B30..G30)
31		--------------------	--------------------	--------------------	--------------------	--------------------	--------------------	--------------------
32	Total B	@SUM(B26..I	@SUM(C26..C30)	@SUM(D26..D30)	@SUM(E26..E30)	@SUM(F26..F30)	@SUM(G26..G30)	@SUM(B32..G32
33		====================	====================	====================	====================	====================	====================	====================
34	NET CASH FLOW	+B23-B32	+C23-C32	+D23-D32	+E23-E32	+F23-F32	+G23-G32	+H23-H32
35		--------------------	--------------------	--------------------	--------------------	--------------------	--------------------	--------------------
36	Balances:							
37	Start of month	+B13	+B38	+C38	+D38	+E38	+F38	+B37
38	End of month	+B34+B37	+C34+C37	+D34+D37	+E34+E37	+F34+F37	+G34+G37	+H34+H37
39	====================	====================	====================	====================	====================	====================	====================	====================

Figure 5d

	A	B	C	D	E	F	G	H
40	TABLE C: BUDGETED TRADING AND PROFIT & LOSS ACCOUNT for the period							
41	of six months ending 30th September, 19x1							
42								
43					£	£		£
44	Sales							+H11
45	less Cost of Sales:							
46	Purchases					+H12		
47	less Closing Stock					+F46-H49		
48						-------------		
49								+H11*2/3
50								-------------
51	Gross Profit							+H44-H49
52	less Expenses:							
53	Wages					+H8		
54	Selling & Admin					+H9		
55	Rent					+H10		
56	Depreciation:							
57	Original Equipment				+B7/10*6/12			
58	Later Equipment				+E7/10*3/12			
59					-------------	+E57+E58		
60						-------------		@SUM(F53..F59)
61								-------------
62	Net Profit							+H51-H60
63								=============
64	=============	=============	=============	=============	=============	=============	=============	=============
65	TABLE D: BUDGETED BALANCE SHEET as at 30th September, 19x1							
66				£		£		£
67	FIXED ASSETS			Cost		Acc.Dep'n		NBV
68	Equipment			+H7		+F59		+D68-F68
69				=============		=============		
70	CURRENT ASSETS							
71	Stock			+F47				
72	Debtors			+H11-H21				
73				-------------		+D71+D72		
74	CURRENT LIABILITIES							
75	Creditors			+H12-H26				
76	Overdraft			-H38				
77				-------------		+D75+D76		
78	Net Current Assets					-------------		+F73-F77
79								-------------
80	Capital Employed							+H68+H78
81								=============
82	Represented by:							
83	Capital					+B6		
84	Profit for 6 months					+H62		
85						-------------		+F83+F84
86								=============
87	=============	=============	=============	=============	=============	=============	=============	=============

TABLE A: DATA

This is a data-block into which the data of the problem can be entered. You will see from figure 5c that it consists mainly of labels and values. The only column which contains formulae is column H, which adds columns B..G.

[At the end of this session, you will protect (so that it cannot be inadvertently altered) all of this table except for the range B6..G13 in which the values of the data are entered.]

TABLES B, C and D

You will see from figures 5c and 5d that these tables contain only labels, and formulae which refer to cells in table A as well as cells within tables B, C and D.

[At the end of this session, you will protect all of these three tables. In other words, only the values in in the range of cells B6..G13 in table A can be altered.]

This means that, when you have created the whole worksheet, if you alter any of the data values in cells B6..G13 in table A, then the figures in the cash flow forecast, budgeted trading and profit & loss account and budgeted balance sheet will alter automatically.

6. Notes on creating the worksheet

Column A can be set at 17 characters wide.

Columns B..H can be set at 8 characters wide.

Cell H49: +H11*2/3

This formula takes cell H11 (total sales) and multiplies it by two-thirds. This gives the cost of sales figure. See paragraph 4 (3) for an explanation.

Cell F47: +F46-H49

This formula takes the contents of cell F46 (total purchases from cell H12) and deducts the contents of cell H49 (the cost of sales). This gives the closing stock figure. See paragraph 4 (3) for an explanation.

Cells E57 and E58:

These cells calculate depreciation on the equipment purchased during the six months.

For example, in cell E57 is the formula +B7/10*6/12.

This means:

+B7	£16,000 from cell B7
/10	divided by 10, because depreciation is for 10 years, straight-line method, and
*6/12	multiplied by 6 and divided by 12, i.e. 6 months of a full year's depreciation.

Similarly, the formula in cell E58, +E7/10*3/12 calculates the depreciation on the equipment to be bought in July for £8,000 for the 3 months of July to September.

Cell D76 -H38

This is the overdraft figure at the end of the six months from cell H38 in the cash flow forecast.

Since you need a positive figure under Current liabilities in the Balance Sheet, and the overdraft figure in cell H38 is negative (overdrawn), you use the minus and not the plus sign.

7. Saving and printing the worksheet

It is to be hoped that you have been saving your worksheet frequently as you created it, perhaps with the file-name PONTEF01, as suggested in paragraph 2 above.

You could now try printing it out in condensed print, using the skills acquired in session 4.

You should print out two ranges separately:

A1..H39 and A40..H87

Plan your margins carefully.

You may like to experiment as follows:

When you have successfully printed out the first range A1..H39, and are satisfied with the results, save the file as PONTEF5A. Then if ever you want to print it out again with the same settings, you can do so with no more effort.

Now retrieve PONTEF01, and print out the second range A40..H87. Again, if you are happy with the settings, save the worksheet as PONTEF5B.

If you are feeling particularly energetic, you could use /WGFT to see all the formulae. Then you could try printing out the two ranges separately, after adjusting the columns appropriately. Plan your margins very carefully! Again, these settings could be saved as PONTEF5C and PONTEF5D respectively.

8. The logical function @IF

If you want to create a balance sheet to cope with a positive (credit) balance figure at the bank, you will have to create a cell under Current Assets, e.g. at cell D73 with the reference +H38. Cell A73 could have the label ' Cash at Bank, cell F73 could have the formula +D71+D72+D73 or @SUM(D71..D73), and cell D74 could have a row of hyphens.

The problem then is that we would have the same figure from cell H38 entered twice on the balance sheet, i.e. under Current Assets in cell D73, and under Current Liabilities in cell D76.

The problem can be solved by using the logical function @IF, as follows:

Cash at Bank:	Cell D73:	@IF(H38>0,H38,0)
Overdraft:	Cell D76	@IF(H38<0,-H38,0)

The first formula instructs the program:

If the contents of cell H38 are greater than 0 (zero), then enter the contents of cell H38 into this current cell (D73); otherwise enter 0 (zero). For the present data, since cell H38 contains (£18,400) or -£18,400, i.e. a sum less than zero, then cell D73 will read 0.

The second formula instructs the program:

If the contents of cell H38 are less than 0 (zero), then enter the (negative) contents of cell H38 into this current cell (D76) as a positive amount. For the present data, since cell H38 contains (£18,400) or -£18,400, i.e. a sum less than zero, then cell D76 will read £18,400.

Enter these formulae into cells D73 and D76.

Enter 'Cash at bank' in cell A73.

Enter a line of hyphens in cell D74 (Press \-Enter>)

Alter (using edit <F2>) cell F73 from the formula +D71+D72 to the formula +D71+D72+D73

Alter (using edit <F2>) cell F83 from the formula +B6 to the formula +B6+B13

If you have altered PONTEF01 to incorporate these changes, why not save this revised version as PONTEF02?

Now you can try changing the data in table A, and see the effect on tables B, C and D. For example, enter cash at start (cell B13) as £20,000. You will note that cell H38 changes to £1,600 (positive), D73 to £1,600 and D76 to 0 (zero).

The balance sheet still balances, because the formula for capital in cell F83 is now +B6+B13, i.e the initial capital of £30,000 (cell B6) plus any extra cash which you inject into the business by entering it into cell B13.

[Note that in this model, if you alter sales, then the closing stock will be adjusted, not purchases. Cell H49 maintains a constant relationship between sales and cost of sales.]

9. Protecting the cells

The only cells which you wish to change are in the range B6..G13. The remaining cells can be protected from inadvertant alteration by the following:

Retrieve worksheet PONTEF01.

{123}{VP} Press /WGPE (Worksheet, Global, Protection, Enable)

This protects all the cells of the worksheet.

Move the cursor to cell B6

Press `/RU` (Range, Unprotect)

Move the cursor to cell G13, and press <Enter>

{AEA} Move the cursor to cell B6

Press `/RLN` (Range, Lock, No)

Move the cursor to cell G13, and press <Enter>

Press `/WGPE` (Worksheet, General, Protect, Enable)

This results in cells B6..G13 being unprotected, and it is now possible to change the values in those cells, but no others.

If you do want to alter a label or formula in the protected cells, you can press /WGPD (Worksheet, Global, Protect, Disable), and then, when you have made any changes, you can re-protect with /WGPE.

You can, if you wish, get some additional practice by protecting the labels and formulae on the other versions of the Pontefract worksheet which you have saved.

10. Summary

In this session you should have achieved the objectives set out at the start of this session.

In particular,you should have become acquainted with:

`@IF`	IF(Condition,True value,False Value) the logical function which results in one of two values: true value if condition is true, false value if condition is false
`/WGPE`	Worksheet, Global, Protection, Enable
`/WGPD`	Worksheet, Global, Protection, Disable
`/RU`	Range, Unprotect {123}{VP}
`/RLN`	Range, Lock, No {AEA}

17. Activity

Prepare some budgeted data for an enterprise of your choice, similar to that for Pontefract as set out in paragraph 3 above.

Try to make the values realistic in the sense that you want the business to have a satisfactory cash flow, profit and loss account, and balance sheet at the end of the six month period.

Retrieve your worksheet which you filed with the name PONTEF02, i.e the one with the facility to record either a bank balance or overdraft in the balance sheet. (See paragraph 8 above.)

Make sure that all the labels and formulae are protected. (See paragraph 9 above.)

Erase the range B6..G13, as follows:

Move the cursor to cell B6

Press `/RE`

Move the cursor to cell G13

Press `<Enter>`

Enter your own data, and then examine and comment on the results shown in tables B, C and D.

[Note: do not enter figures in cells C13..G13, since these will result in an incorrect capital figure in cell F83. It would, of course, be possible to adjust the design of the worksheet to accommodate this, but this is beyond the scope of this session.]

12. Objective test ☐ A ☐ B ☑ C ☐ D

1. The formula to add the values in cells D14..D17 is

   ☐ A @SUM(D14..D17)

   ☐ B @SUM(D17..D14)

   ☐ C +D14+D15+D16+D17

   ☐ D any of these

2. The value of an asset has been entered into cell D68 as £20,000. You require its depreciation to be calculated by a formula in cell F68. Depreciation is for the first 9 months of its life which is estimated at 5 years with no scrap value at the end. Assuming straight-line depreciaton, the formula to be entered into cell F68 is

   ☐ A £20,000/5x9/12

   ☐ B +D68/60x9

   ☐ C +D68/5*9/12

   ☐ D +D68+5x9+12

3. You have retrieved a file named WEARY. You have improved it, and want to save it in its new form while, at the same time preserving the file in its original form. To do so you press

   ☐ A /FS<Enter>WEARY01<Enter>R

   ☐ B /FSWEARY01<Enter>

   ☐ C /FSR<Enter>R<Enter>

   ☐ D none of these

4. You wish to protect all the cells of your current worksheet. The keypresses are

   ☐ A /RGPE

   ☐ B /RPE<Enter>

   ☐ C /WGPE<Enter>

   ☐ D /WGPE

5. You have correctly protected all the cells of your current worksheet. You wish to unprotect a range within the worksheet. The initial keypresses, before pointing the required range, are

   ☐ A /RU or /RLN {AEA}

   ☐ B /UR or /LNR {AEA}

   ☐ C /RRU or /RRLN {AEA}

   ☐ D /URU or /RNLI {AEA}

6. The @IF is a

   ☐ A statistical function

   ☐ B logical function

   ☐ C financial function

   ☐ D none of these

7. The following describes the @IF function:

   ☐ A (True value,False value,Condition)

   ☐ B (Condition,False value,True value)

   ☐ C (Condition,True value,False value)

   ☐ D none of these

8. The following is a correct entry for an @IF function:

   ☐ A @IF<H38>0,H38,0>

   ☐ B @IF[H38>0,H38,0]

   ☐ C @IF(H38>0;H38;0)

   ☐ D @IF(H38>0,H38,0)

9. Which of the following is the correct entry in a cell to convey this message to the program: "If the contents of cell H38 are less than zero, then enter the contents of cell H38 into the current cell; otherwise enter zero":

   ☐ A @IF(H38>0,H38,0)

   ☐ B @IF[H38>0,H38,0]

   ☐ C @IF<H38>0,H38,0)

   ☐ D none of these

10. You have protected your worksheet with the correct global command, and now you want to alter one of the formulae. Before you re-protect the worksheet, you can disable the protection by the keypresses:

    ☐ A /WGPD

    ☐ B /RGPD

    ☐ C /WGPD<Enter>

    ☐ D /RSVP

SESSION 6
Skegness: Accounting Ratios

1. Objectives

At the end of this session you will be able to:

- ❑ create a worksheet into which you can enter data and from which seven accounting ratios are automatically calculated
- ❑ appreciate how a simple model can be designed
- ❑ offset left-aligned labels
- ❑ format a range of figures to show only two decimal places
- ❑ print your worksheet with a heading
- ❑ centre the printed heading
- ❑ extend the worksheet by copying ranges of cells
- ❑ freeze the borders on the screen
- ❑ print borders and a separated range of cells

2. Introduction

In this session, you will create a worksheet which can calculate accounting ratios from data entered into a skeleton Profit & Loss Account and Balance Sheet.

The model is adapted from an example in AFBIS (chapter entitled *Accounting Ratios*).

As in session 5, you will not be given the individual keypresses as you were in the previous sessions. Instead, you are referred to figure 6a which shows the worksheet as it appears on the screen, and figure 6b which shows the same worksheet, but with the formulae required to produce the figures shown in figure 6a. Figure 6b shows column letters, row numbers, labels, values and formulae, from which you should be able to create the worksheet.

Paragraph 3 below describes the model.

Paragraph 4 contains notes on the design of the model.

Paragraph 5 gives notes on creating the worksheet.

Paragraph 6 advises on printing and saving the worksheet.

For the time being you could save your worksheet as you create it with the filename SKEGNESS.

You are advised to read through these paragraphs before starting to create the worksheet from figure 6b.

	A	B	C	D	E
1	SKEGNESS				
2	TABLE A: DATA (£000s)	Year ending	31.12.19x3	Year ending	31.12.19x4
3	PROFIT & LOSS ACCOUNT:	Data:- £	£	Data:- £	£
4	Sales (Turnover)	350		560	
5	Cost of Sales	280		462	
6	Gross Profit	----------	70	----------	98
7	Total Costs	49		56	
8	Net Profit	----------	21	----------	42
9	BALANCE SHEET:				
10	Buildings	35		105	
11	Equipment	70		161	
12	FIXED ASSETS	----------	105	----------	266
13	Stock	56		98	
14	Debtors	35		84	
15	Bank	84		63	
16	CURRENT ASSETS	----------	175	----------	245
17	Creditors	35		28	
18	Dividends	14		35	
19	Overdraft	0		0	
20	CURRENT LIABILITIES	----------	49	----------	63
21	NET CURRENT ASSETS		126		182
22	TOTAL NET ASSETS		231		448
23	Share Capital	140		350	
24	Retained Profit	91		98	
25	CAPITAL EMPLOYED	----------	231	----------	448
26	========================	==========	==========	==========	==========
27	TABLE B: RATIOS	Calcs.	Year ending		Year ending
28	(1) PERFORMANCE RATIOS		31.12.19x3		31.12.19x4
29	[A] Prime Ratio	PBIT x 100			
30	(percentage)	----------	9.09		9.38
31		CE			
32					
33	[B] Profit Margin	PBIT x 100			
34	(percentage)	----------	6.00		7.50
35		Sales			
36					
37	[C] Capital Turnover	Sales			
38	(times)	----------	1.52		1.25
39		CE			
40					
41	[D] Gross Profit	G.P't x 100			
42	(percentage)	----------	20.00		17.50
43		Sales			
44					
45	(2) LIQUIDITY RATIOS				
46	[E] Current Test	CA			
47	(ratio:1)	----------	3.57		3.89
48		CL			
49					
50	[F] Acid Test	CA-Stocks			
51	(ratio:1)	----------	2.43		2.33
52		CL			
53					
54	[G] Debt Collection	Drs. x 365			
55	Period (days)	----------	36.50		54.75
56		Sales			

Figure 6a

	A	B	C	D	E
1	SKEGNESS				
2	TABLE A: DATA (£000s)	Year ending 31.12.19x3		Year ending 31.12.19x4	
3	PROFIT & LOSS ACCOUNT:	Data:- £	£	Data:- £	£
4	Sales (Turnover)	350		560	
5	Cost of Sales	280		462	
6	Gross Profit	------------	+B4-B5	------------	+D4-D5
7	Total Costs	49		56	
8	Net Profit	------------	+C6-B7	------------	+E6-D7
9	BALANCE SHEET:				
10	Buildings	35		105	
11	Equipment	70		161	
12	FIXED ASSETS	------------	+B10+B11	------------	+D10+D11
13	Stock	56		98	
14	Debtors	35		84	
15	Bank	84		63	
16	CURRENT ASSETS	------------	@SUM(B13..B15)	------------	@SUM(D13..D15)
17	Creditors	35		28	
18	Dividends	14		35	
19	Overdraft	0		0	
20	CURRENT LIABILITIES	------------	@SUM(B17..B19)	------------	@SUM(D17..D19)
21	NET CURRENT ASSETS		+C16-C20		+E16-E20
22	TOTAL NET ASSETS		+C12+C21		+E12+E21
23	Share Capital	140		350	
24	Retained Profit	91		98	
25	CAPITAL EMPLOYED	------------	+B23+B24	------------	+D23+D24
26	====================	============	============	============	============
27	TABLE B: RATIOS	Calcs.	Year ending		Year ending
28	(1) PERFORMANCE RATIOS		31.12.19x3		31.12.19x4
29	[A] Prime Ratio	PBIT x 100			
30	(percentage)	------------	+C8*100/C25		+E8*100/E25
31		CE			
32					
33	[B] Profit Margin	PBIT x 100			
34	(percentage)	------------	+C8*100/B4		+E8*100/D4
35		Sales			
36					
37	[C] Capital Turnover	Sales			
38	(times)	------------	+B4/C25		+D4/E25
39		CE			
40					
41	[D] Gross Profit	G.P't x 100			
42	(percentage)	------------	+C6*100/B4		+E6*100/D4
43		Sales			
44					
45	(2) LIQUIDITY RATIOS				
46	[E] Current Test	CA			
47	(ratio:1)	------------	+C16/C20		+E16/E20
48		CL			
49					
50	[F] Acid Test	CA-Stocks			
51	(ratio:1)	------------	(C16-B13)/C20		(E16-D13)/E20
52		CL			
53					
54	[G] Debt Collection	Drs. x 365			
55	Period (days)	------------	+B14*365/B4		+D14*365/D4
56		Sales			

Figure 6b

3. Description of the model

Skegness is a wholesale trading company. Abbreviated results for two years, 19x3 and 19x4, are set out in Table A of figure 6a, and in Table B seven ratios are calculated from those figures.

The 'Calcs.' column of Table B shows how the ratios are calculated.

PBIT stands for *Profit Before Interest* and *Tax* which is taken here to be *Net Profit* from Table A (line 8)

CE stands for *Capital Employed* (line 25)

G.P't stands for *Gross Profit* (line 6)

CA stands for *Current Assets* (line 16)

CL stands for *Current Liabilities* (line 20)

Drs. stands for *Debtors* (line 14)

Sales stands for *Sales (Turnover)* (line 4)

4. Notes on the design of the model

If you study figure 6b, you will see that this is a print-out containing the formulae used for figure 6a. Both figures 6a and 6b show the cell references: column letters and line numbers. So you should be able to trace the cells to which the formulae refer.

For example, cell C30 contains the formula C8*100/C25. Cell C8 contains the net profit for the first year. This is divided by cell C25, which is the capital employed. The result is multiplied by 100 to give the percentage return (net profit) on capital employed, and this is known as the *Prime Ratio*.

In Table A, columns B and D are the columns into which data are entered. These columns in Table A should stay unprotected. The rest of the worksheet – labels and formulae should be protected. You will be reminded of how to do this in paragraph 5.

The model as it is presented in figures 6a and 6b is a modest one, designed to print out on A4 paper. It may be adequate for you as part of the learning process. However, it could be extended to more years for the same company, or for calculating and comparing the accounting ratios of, say, different companies in the same type of business. Tips on how to do this are given below in paragraph 7.

5. Notes on creating the worksheet

COLUMN-WIDTHS

The column-widths used for figure 6a are as follows:

Column A:	22
Column B:	10
Column C:	14
Column D:	10
Column E:	14

Have you forgotten how to do this? (Session 2, paragraph 4) Position the cursor in the appropriate column, and

Press `/WCS`

and type in the column-width, or use the right/left arrow keys, followed by <Enter>

OFFSET TEXT

You will see in column A that some text is offset, e.g in cell A4, the label *Sales (Turnover)* is offset one space to the right of the left-hand side of the cell. To achieve this, simply place the cursor over cell A4, and press the space-bar once, before typing **Sales (Turnover)**. There is no need to type an inverted comma to indicate a left-aligned label before pressing the space-bar. This is done automatically by the program.

Cell A6 contains *Gross Profit* preceded by two spaces, and so on.

TWO DECIMAL PLACES

The ratios shown in table B, columns C and E, are shown in figure 6a with 2 decimal places. In order to achieve this,

Move the cursor to cell C29

Press `/RFF` (Range, Format, Fixed)

The message appears: *Enter number of decimal places (0..15): 2*

Press `<Enter>` to accept 2 decimal places

Move the cursor to cell C56 using the down-arrow key

Press `<Enter>` and the mode returns to *READY*.

Do the same for the range E29..E56.

PROTECTING LABELS AND FORMULAE

The only cells which you wish to change are in the data-block (Table A), in the ranges B4..B24 and D4..D24.

In case you have forgotten what you learnt in session 5, paragraph 9, here is the procedure:

Make sure you are in *READY* mode

Move the cursor to cell B4

{123}{VP} Press `/RU` (Range, Unprotect)

{AEA} Press `/RLN` (Range, Lock, No)

Move the cursor to cell B24, and press <Enter>

Follow the same procedure for cells D4..D24.

Press `/WGPE` (Worksheet, Global, Protection, Enable)

6. Printing and saving with a heading

If you followed the suggestion in paragraph 2 above, you have been saving the worksheet with the filename *SKEGNESS*. Retrieve this worksheet if necessary.

If you wish to print out at 10 cpi (characters per inch), assuming that your printer prints at 10 cpi as a default, then here are suggestions for settings. It is a bit of a tight fit to print on 8.25" or 8.5" wide paper, but it is worth trying, if only for experience!

Press `/PPO` (Print, Printer, Options)

What appears on the screen depends on your program.

Press `H` (Header)

You are about to enter the heading *ACCOUNTING RATIOS*

Press `¦ ACCOUNTING RATIOS` (Header)

The ¦ is the bar which is usually <Shift>+<\>, and is sometimes printed on the key as a broken bar (like --) turned through ninety degrees. This means that the header will be centred. [In order to left-align the header, do not precede the header with a bar. In order to right-align the header, precede it with two bars.]

Press `<Enter>`

You are returned to the Options menu.

Now set your margins. Refer to session 4, paragraph 8 if you have forgotten the procedure.

Set the Margins as follows:

Left: 4 Right: 82 Top: 2 Bottom: 2

SETUP can be left blank, since you are using the printer default, though you may care to enter the decimal code for whatever type-style your printer is capable of at 10 cpi

(Refer to session 4, paragraph 7).

Check Page-length, and alter as necessary for your paper type (Refer to session 4, paragraph 6).

Press `Q` (Quit) to return to the Print, Printer menu)

Press `R (Range)` and specify the range A1..E56.

(Refer to session 4, paragraph 5 if necessary.)

{VP} If you like, you can check your settings fron the Print, Printer menu by pressing S (Status) or /PPS from *READY* mode.

When you are happy with your settings, and while still in the Print, Printer menu,

Press `AGP` (Align, Go, Page)

With any luck, you should obtain a good print-out. It is very easy to forget something before pressing Go, and the easiest one to forget is to specify the range. Setup strings are also easy to get wrong. If the printer prints most of the worksheet on the first page, and then proceeds to print something on the next sheet, it is probably due to the setting of the margins.

If you feel that your print-out is rather large for the page, you could try printing it out at 17 cpi. You should refer back to session 4, paragraph 7 if you have forgotten how to do this.

When you find a combination of settings which proves satisfactory, you can save your worksheet with these settings with a new file-name, e.g. if you obtain a good print-out at 17 cpi, and are likely to want to repeat the printout, you could save this version of the worksheet with the filename SKEG17.

7. Extending the worksheet

This paragraph describes how you can extend the worksheet to provide extra columns for analysis, so that it can calculate the ratios for additional years for the same company, or compare the accounting ratios of, say,different companies in the same type of business.

Retrieve your original file *SKEGNESS*

Move the cursor to cell D2

Press `/C` (Copy)

Highlight the range D2..E56

Press `<Enter>`

Move the cursor to cell F2, and press <Enter>

Note: there is no need to specify more than the top left-hand corner of the destination range.

The range F2..G56 is now a replica of the range D2..E56.

To blank the data cells F4..F5, F7, F10..F11, F13..F15, F17..F19, F23..F24, use /Range, Erase. For example, to erase the data in cells F4..F5:

Move the cursor to cell F4

Press | /RE<↓> | <Enter>

You could also edit the heading in cell F2 to read *Year ending*:

8. Freezing borders on the screen

If you move the cursor to look at columns F and G, you can no longer see the labels in column A. This is inconvenient, and the problem can be solved by specifying column A so that it will not scroll with the rest of the screen.

Move the cursor to column B

When you carry out the following keystrokes, the column to the left of column B will be treated as a title {123}{VP} or border {AEA}

{123}{VP} Press | /WTV | (Worksheet, Titles, Vertical)

{AEA} Press | /WBV | (Worksheet, Borders, Vertical)

Now move the cursor to column F. You will see that column A stays frozen on the screen.

Save this version of the worksheet with the filename *SKEGVBOR* which is meant to be a mnemonic for SKEGNESS saved with a Vertical BORder.

[Note: If you want to freeze rows above the cursor, use /WTH (Worksheet, Titles, Horizontal) ({AEA} /WBH)

If you want to freeze, for example, row 1 and column A, position the cursor in cell B2, and use /WTB (Worksheet, Titles, Both) ({AEA} use /WBB or /WBH and /WBV separately.)

To unfreeze the borders, you will use /WTC (Worksheet, Titles, Clear) ({AEA} /WBC) in the next paragraph.]

9. Printing borders

If you want to print out, say, columns A, and D..G, here is the procedure:

Press | /WTC | {AEA} | /WBC |

This clears the border column A which you froze in paragraph 8 above.

Move the cursor to column A

{123}{VP} Press | /PPOBC | (Print, Printer, Options, Border, Column)

{AEA} Press | /PPBC | (Print, Printer, Border, Column)

Press `<Enter>`

IMPORTANT: When specifying the range to be printed, DO NOT include column A, i.e. the border. Choose only the range D1..G56. Otherwise column A will be printed twice.

Now follow the usual procedures for printing.

10. Summary

In this session you should have achieved the objectives set out at the start of this session.

In particular, you should have become acquainted with:

/RFF	Range, Format, Fixed
/PPOH	Print, Printer, Options, Header
/WTV	Worksheet, Titles, Vertical {123}{VP}
/WBV	Worksheet, Borders, Vertical {AEA}
/WTH	Worksheet, Titles, Horizontal {123}{VP}
/WBH	Worksheet, Borders, Horizontal {AEA}
/WTB	Worksheet, Titles, Both {123}{VP}
/WBB	Worksheet, Borders, Both {AEA}
/WTC	Worksheet, Titles, Clear {123}{VP}
/WBC	Worksheet, Borders, Clear {AEA}
/PPOBC	Print,Printer,Options,Border,Column {123}{VP}
/PPBC	Print, Printer, Border, Column {AEA}

11. Activity

Retrieve the worksheet which you saved as *SKEGVBOR* in paragraph 8 above. This version of the worksheet should have column A frozen, and three sets of columns for data and ratio analysis, i.e. B and C, D and E, F and G.

Obtain the report and accounts for a company of your choice for two successive years. The first year should have comparative figures for the previous year, making three years' figures available to you.

Alter the headings in cells B2..G2 appropriately.

[To alter the heading in cell A1 from *SKEGNESS* to the name of your chosen company, you can **either** unfreeze column A, make the alteration and then refreeze it, **or** (not {AEA}) press

<F5>, the GoTo key, type A1 and press <Enter>, alter cell A1 in the duplicate copy of column A which appears, and then move the cell pointer to the right until the duplicate column A disappears.]

Enter the appropriate figures from the accounts into the data block (Table A) of the worksheet, and examine the resulting ratios in Table B.

You may have to exercise some ingenuity in entering figures in the Profit and Loss Account, since some published accounts are not very informative. A non-trading company, for example, may have nil 'Cost of Sales'. Also figures from the Balance Sheet may have to be grouped and entered under the limited number of headings in the model. If necessary, alter the headings in column A to broaden their cover.

The Skegness model is a simplified one, and you may feel inspired to redesign it to make it more comprehensive.

12. Objective test ☐ A ☐ B ☑ C ☐ D

This test covers skills acquired in this and previous sessions.

1. In order to widen a single column to 20 characters, the keypresses, after moving the cursor to the required column, are

   ☐ A /WGC20<Enter>

   ☐ B /RC20<Enter>

   ☐ C /WCS20<Enter>

   ☐ D none of these

2. To set a range of cells to show the figures with 3 decimal places, the keypresses required (where [range] means specify the range by typing it in or pointing) are

   ☐ A /RF3F<Enter>[range]<Enter>

   ☐ B /RFF[range]<Enter>3<Enter>

   ☐ C /RFF3<Enter>[range]<Enter>

   ☐ D any of these

3. You wish to print a worksheet with the right-aligned header which reads Table A. Starting from READY mode, the keypresses are

   ☐ A /PPOH|Table A<Enter>

   ☐ B /PPOHTable A<Enter>

   ☐ C /PPOH||Table A<Enter>

   ☐ D /PPOH\Table A<Enter>

4. If you press /WTV (or {AEA} /WBV) while the cursor is on cell C3, the effect on the worksheet will be that

☐ A column C and row 3 are frozen

☐ B rows 1 and 2 are frozen

☐ C columns A and B are frozen

☐ D none of these

5. If you press /WTH (or {AEA} /WBH) while the cursor is on cell C2, the effect on the worksheet will be that

☐ A row 1 is frozen

☐ B column A is frozen

☐ C rows 1 and 2 are frozen

☐ D columns A and B are frozen

6. If you have frozen some columns and/or rows, and you now want to unfreeze them, the keypresses are (for {AEA} read B for T)

☐ A /WGCT

☐ B /WGT

☐ C /WGTC

☐ D /WTC

7. You have just wasted a lot of continuous paper due to setting your right-margin at 12 instead of 82. To correct this before pressing Go again, the keystrokes from READY mode are

☐ A /PPOMR82<Enter>Q

☐ B /PPOMR<Enter>82<Enter>Q

☐ C /PPMR82<Enter>Q

☐ D /PPOMR82<Enter>

8. The labels in cells C2..H2 have been entered at the default (left-aligned). You wish the centre them. The keypresses required, where [range] means specify the range by typing it in or pointing), are (for {AEA} read P for L)

☐ A /WGLC[Range]<Enter>

☐ B /RCL[Range]<Enter>

☐ C /RLC[range]<Enter>

☐ D /LGOC[range]<Enter>

9. You have entered a rude word in cell X99. You wish to erase it before anyone sees it. The best way to do so, with the cursor on cell X99, is to press

   - ☐ A /RE<Enter>
   - ☐ B /RD<Enter>
   - ☐ C /Q<Enter>
   - ☐ D /WE<Enter>

10. You are half-way through working on a worksheet, and you want a cup of coffee. You have saved your worksheet with a suitable name several times so far. Before going for your coffee, you should press

    - ☐ A /FSR<Enter>
    - ☐ B /FS<Enter>R
    - ☐ C /FS<Enter>
    - ☐ D /TTFN<Enter>

SESSION 7
Creating Graphs

1. Objectives

At the end of this session, you will be able to:

- ❑ create a worksheet in a format suitable for creating graphs
- ❑ create some formulae which conform to the requirements of the data
- ❑ define the necessary set-up for a graph
- ❑ enhance a graph with titles and legends
- ❑ name a graph
- ❑ save a graph ready for printing
- ❑ create bar, line, stacked-bar and pie graphs

2. Introduction

In this session, you will create a worksheet which sets out the budgeted sales data for a bicycle manufacturing company in a table of suitable format, and then produce graphs from that table which improve the presentation and facilitate interpretation of the data.

As in sessions 5 and 6, you will not be given all the individual keypresses. Instead, you are referred to figure 7a which shows the worksheet as it appears on the screen, and figure 7b which shows the same worksheet, but with the formulae required to produce the figures shown in figure 7a. Figure 7b shows column letters, row numbers, labels, values and formulae, from which you should be able to create the worksheet.

Paragraph 3 below sets the problem and describes the model.

Paragraph 4 contains notes on the design of the model.

Paragraph 5 gives notes on creating the worksheet.

Paragraphs 6, 7, 8 and 9 show you how to define, enhance, name and save a bar graph based on the worksheet.

Paragraphs 10, 11 and 12 show you how to do the same for line, stacked-bar and pie graphs.

Figure 7a

	A	B	C	D	E	F
1			The Zed Bicycle Company			
2			Budgeted Sales for Next Year			
3						
4	Qtr:-	Spring	Summer	Autumn	Winter	Totals
5	------------	------------	------------	------------	------------	------------
6	Model:-	£	£	£	£	£
7	Alpha	80,000	96,000	115,200	138,240	429,440
8	Beta	90,000	99,000	108,900	119,790	417,690
9	Gamma	80,000	80,000	90,000	90,000	340,000
10	Delta	60,000	54,000	58,600	52,740	225,340
11	------------	------------	------------	------------	------------	------------
12	Totals	310,000	329,000	372,700	400,770	1,412,470
13	============	============	============	============	============	============

Figure 7b

	A	B	C	D	E	F
1				The Zed Bicycle Company		
2				Budgeted Sales for Next Year		
3						
4	Qtr:-	Spring	Summer	Autumn	Winter	Totals
5	------------	------------	------------	------------	------------	------------
6	Model:-	£	£	£	£	£
7	Alpha	80000	+B7*1.2	+C7*1.2	+D7*1.2	@SUM(B7..E7)
8	Beta	90000	+B8*1.1	+C8*1.1	+D8*1.1	@SUM(B8..E8)
9	Gamma	80000	+B9	+C9+10000	+D9	@SUM(B9..E9)
10	Delta	60000	+B10*.9	(C10*.9)+10000	+D10*.9	@SUM(B10..E10)
11	------------	------------	------------	------------	------------	------------
12	Totals	@SUM(B7..B10)	@SUM(C7..C10)	@SUM(D7..D10)	@SUM(E7..E10)	@SUM(F7..F10)
13	============	============	============	============	============	============

That should be enough for this session, and in session 8 you will print out the graphs created and saved in this session.

3. Description of the model

The ZED BICYCLE COMPANY manufactures four models of bicycle: the Alpha, Beta, Gamma and Delta. The sales manager has just completed his budgeted sales figures for next year, which, for budget purposes, is sub-analysed into spring, summer, autumn and winter quarters.

For the spring quarter, he anticipates sales as follows:

	£
Alpha	80,000
Beta	90,000
Gamma	80,000
Delta	60,000

He also anticipates growth of sales in each quarter over the previous quarter, as follows:

Alpha	20%
Beta	10%
Gamma	nil
Delta	-10%

In view of the nil growth rate for the Gamma, and the negative growth rate for the Delta, he plans to spend some money on advertising for these two models. As a result of that advertising, he expects that sales of each model will increase by £10,000 in the autumn quarter, on top of the originally budgeted sales figures. In the winter quarter, he expects sales to change by the usual growth rates (nil and -10%) over the autumn quarter's sales which include the additional sales in the autumn quarter resulting from the advertising.

These expectations have been translated into a table, which is shown in figure 7a. In figure 7b, you will see the budgeted values for the spring quarter, and the formulae required to calculate the budgeted sales for the last three quarters of next year.

4. Notes on the design of the model

If you study figure 7b, you will see that this is a print-out containing the formulae used for figure 7a. Both figures 7a and 7b show the cell references: column letters and row numbers. So you should be able to trace the cells to which the formulae refer.

Cells B7..B10 contain the values for the budgeted sales for the spring quarter. The range C7..E10 contains formulae directly or indirectly derived from the range B7..B10. Cells C7..C10 calculate the sales for the summer quarter, using the values in cells B7..B10 multipled by the growth factors supplied by the sales manager. Note that cell C9 has a nil growth factor, and therefore simply has the entry +B9. Cells D7..D10 use the resulting values in cells C7..C10, again multiplied by the same growth factors. However cells D9 and D10 each have £10,000 added, for the extra budgeted sales arising from additional advertising. Cells E7..E10 use the resulting values in cells D7..D10 (including the extra £10,000s), multiplied by the growth factors.

All these formulae are designed to conform with the information supplied by the sales manager.

Cells F7..F10 and B12..F12 contain formulae which total the respective rows and columns.

5. Notes on creating the worksheet

The following notes refer to figure 7a.

COLUMN-WIDTH

Before entering the labels, values and formulae, it is suggested that you set the global column-width at 11:

Press `/WGC11<Enter>`

Comments on suitable column-widths and printer option settings are given below (at the end of this paragraph).

ENTERING THE LABELS

The labels in rows 1 and 2 are in cells C1 and C2. The label in C1 is preceded by three spaces. Starting a label with a space does not require a ' to be typed.

Cells A4..F4 and B6..F6 (Fig 7a) are right-aligned.

Cells A6..A10 and A12 and also B6.. F6 (Fig 7b) are left-aligned.

[If you find that the £ signs in cells B6..F6 do not print out, try substituting a # sign. This depends on the your program and printer. This was mentioned in session 4, paragraph 5, and you may have solved the problem then.]

ENTERING THE VALUES

Cells B7..B10 contain the values. Do not forget to enter these values **without** commas or £ sign preceding them.

To obtain the commas,

Press `/WGF,0<Enter>`

[Note: to obtain £ signs in front of every figure (values as well as figures resulting from formulae), you would press: **/WGFC0<Enter>**. To cancel both commas and £ signs, you would press **/WGFG**.]

ENTERING THE FORMULAE

Cell C7: this contains the formula +B7*1.2. To enter this, you could type it in as shown, or you could try:

Press `+b7*120%<Enter>`

Note: some keyboards have a very convenient set of keys at the top right-hand side, which duplicate the keys for:

/ * – +

These are convenient for entering formulae, since the <Shift> key is not required, and they are easy to locate.

When you have entered cells C7..C10, copy this range to the range D7..E10. You will see that the formulae are all relative to the cell to the left, which is what we require in this instance.

Cells D9 and D10 only: Edit (using the <F2> key) the formulae and add +10000 after the existing formulae in each cell.

Cell D9: The brackets are not strictly necessary; * is calculated before +.

Cell B12: Don't forget that you can **point** to cells B7..B10 when entering the formula *@SUM(B7..B10)*. If you have forgotten how to do this, refer back to session 3, paragraph 8). You can use the same technique for cell F7.

Cell F7 can be copied to cells F8..F10, and cell B12 can be copied to cells C12..F12.

COLUMN-WIDTHS AND PRINTER SETTINGS

The global column-width chosen for figure 7a is the global column-width of 11. This could be less, but 11 was chosen because there is adequate room for printing out at 10 cpi on A4 paper at this width, and the wider columns give a less cramped appearance.

If you want to print out this worksheet later, the following settings are suggested for 10 cpi: ML 4, MR 80, MT 10, MB2.

You could set them now, before you forget, using /PPOM.

[Don't forget to define the Range, and to enter any Setup string required to print at 10 cpi.]

When you have defined satisfactory print options, save the worksheet as *ZED7A*.

Figure 7b used /WGFT (Worksheet, Global, Format, Text) to display all the formulae. The global column-width chosen is 17. This, again, could be less, but the print-out at 17 cpi is less cramped with the slightly wider columns.

Suggested settings for margins, to print at 17 cpi on A4 paper, are: ML 10, MR 132, MT10, MB 2

You may feel that the labels in the range B4..F4 would look better left-aligned:

Use `/RLLB4.F4<Enter>` (AEA) `/RPLB4.F4<Enter>`

This version of the worksheet could be saved as *ZED7B*.

6. Defining the bar graph

Retrieve the worksheet which you saved as ZED7A.

From *READY* mode, press `/GTB` (Graph, Type, Bar)

[You are advised, as usual, to proceed slowly, observing the changes to the menus in the control panel, or drop-down menus.]

You have now selected a bar type of graph, and you are returned to the main graph menu.

Press `A`

Move the cursor to cell B7

Press `.` (a full stop)

Move the cursor to cell E7, and press <Enter>

You have now defined graph range A for the Alpha bicycle. There are 6 graph ranges available, A – F inclusive. You are going to use the first four of these, A – D inclusive, covering the four models of bicycle.

From now on, when you see [range] in these instructions, define the range following [range]. For example, the instructions for defining the A range above will be shown as:

Press `A [range]B7..E7 <Enter>`

You can, of course, type the range in (type b7.e7), if you prefer doing so to pointing.

Press `B [range]B8..E8 <Enter>`

Press `C [range]B9..E9 <Enter>`

Press `D [range]B10..E10 <Enter>`

You should now be back at the graph menu, and you should see View in the control panel or drop-down menu.

{AEA} Do not view yet, until you have defined the X range.

Go to the start of the next paragraph.

{123}{VP} Press `V` (View)

A bar graph should appear on your monitor (assuming you have a graphics card and a monitor which supports graphics).

[This graph should be similar to figure 8a or 8b (in session 8), but without most of the words.]

Press `<Esc>` to return to the graph menu.

7. Enhancing the bar graph

Press `X [range]B4.E4` <Enter>

This defines the X range (Spring..Winter)

Press `V` to view the addition of the labels added to the X axis data points.

Press `<Esc>` to return to the graph menu.

Press `O` (Options)

You will use the *Legend* and *Titles* options in this Option sub-menu.

Press `LA` (Legend, A range)

{123}{VP} Press `\A7` <Enter>

{AEA} Type `Alpha` <Enter>

{123}{VP} Cell A7 contains the legend *Alpha* and typing in \A7 against the prompt saved you having to type in Alpha.

Note: More characters can be displayed by this cell-reference method than by typing in a legend. The numbers vary between programs.

{123}{VP} Press `LB\A8` <Enter>

{AEA} Type `LBBeta` <Enter>

{123}{VP} Press `LC\A9` <Enter>

{AEA} Type `LCGamma` <Enter>

{123}{VP} Press `LD\A10` <Enter>

{AEA} Type `LDDelta` <Enter>

Press `QV` (Quit, View) to view the graph with legends added.

Press `<Esc>` to return to the main graph menu.

Press `OT` (Options, Titles)

You are now going to specify titles.

{123}{VP} Press `F\C1` <Enter>

{AEA} Type `FThe ZED Bicycle Company` <Enter>

This enters *The ZED Bicycle Company* at the top of the graph.

{123}{VP} Press `TS\C2` <Enter>

{AEA} Type `SBudgeted Sales for Next Year` <Enter>

This enters *Budgeted Sales for Next Year* on the second line.

Press **{123}{VP}** `TX` **{AEA}** `X`

Type `Budgeted Sales per Quarter`

Press `<Enter>`

Press {123}{VP} `TY` {AEA} `Y`

Type `Pounds`

Press `<Enter>`

Press {123}{VP} `QV` (Quit, View) {AEA} `QQV`

You should now see the graph with legends and titles on your monitor. You can check for mistakes, and repeat any sequence of keystrokes necessary to correct them.

8. Naming the bar graph

Your program can maintain only one set of graph definitions at any time, unless you have given a name to each set of definitions.

Return to the main graph menu.

Press `NC` (Name, Create)

Type `ZEDBAR`

Press `<Enter>`

The worksheet has already been saved with the file name *ZED7A* (and *ZED7B*, if you saved the /WGFT version at the end of paragraph 5). Now save it again with the name *ZEDGRAPH* :-

Press `Q/FS`

Type `ZEDGRAPH`

9. Saving the bar graph

{AEA} has a different method of printing, which is shown as Plot in the Graphics menu. Some of this paragraph (9) is therefore inapplicable. Details of how to use the Plot sub-menu will be given in the next session. However, you should work through paragraphs 9, 10, 11 and 12 of this session (session 7), but you should ignore the Save commands, where they are marked: {not AEA}.

To save the graphic image for printing, it should be saved with a separate file-name. In the next three paragraphs, you will be creating a line graph, stacked-bar graph and pie graph, and each one should be named and saved separately if you want to print them later.

So far you have defined and named a bar graph for the Zed Bicycle Company sales budget. Now you will save it in what is known as a *PIC* file, i.e. one with a *.PIC* extension, in this case *ZEDBAR.PIC*.

You should now be back at the main menu (READY mode).

Type `/GNU` (Graph, Name, Use)

The name *ZEDBAR* should appear, and since it is the only named graph so far, it should be high-lighted.

Press `<Enter>` to accept it

You have now made *ZEDBAR* the current graph, and the graph should appear on the monitor as a check that you have the correct graph current.

Press `<Esc>` to get back to the graph menu.

{notAEA} Press `S` (Save)

{notAEA} Type `ZEDBAR`

{notAEA} Press `<Enter>`

{notAEA} You have now created a file called *ZEDBAR.PIC* and saved it to disk.

In the next session (Session 8) you will print out your *ZEDBAR* graph. Before doing so, (unless you cannot wait) you can create, name and save some more graphs, based on the same data.

10. Line graph

You may feel competent now to create, name and save a line graph (and other graphs) without any further help. If so, carry on! If not, carry out the abbreviated instructions in this paragraph (and the next two paragraphs for stacked-bar and pie graphs).

You should still be in the main graph menu.

Press `TLV` (Type, Line, View)

Press `<Esc>NC` (Name, Create)

Type `ZEDLINE` <Enter>

Press `NU` (Name, Use)

Highlight `ZEDLINE` <Enter> <Esc>

{notAEA} Press `S` (Save)

{notAEA} Type `ZEDLINE` <Enter>

11. Stacked-bar graph

Press **TSV** (Type, Stacked-bar, View)

Press **<Esc> NC** (Name, Create)

Press **ZEDSTACK** <Enter>

Press **NU** (Name, Use)

Highlight **ZEDSTACK** <Enter> <Esc>

{notAEA} Press **S** (Save)

{notAEA} Type **ZEDSTACK** <Enter>

12. Pie Graph

Press **TP** (Type, Pie)

You will now have to alter the definitions slightly, since the A range is set for cells B7..E7, which is for the Alpha bicycle, and you need total sales for each quarter.

Press **A**

The range B7..E7 is highlighted.

Press **<Esc>**

Move the cursor to cell B12, type a full-stop, move the cursor to cell E12 and press <Enter>

The range already set for X is B4..E4, which is what you require.

Press **V** (View), and check that this is the graph you require.

Press **<Esc>** to return to the graph menu

Press **NC** (Name, Create)

Type **ZEDPIE** <Enter>

Press **NU** (Name, Use)

Highlight **ZEDPIE** <Enter> <Esc>

{notAEA} Press **S** (Save)

{notAEA} Type `ZEDPIE` <Enter>

Do not forget to save the current ZEDGRAPH worksheet before you end this session:

Press `Q/FS<Enter>R`

13. Summary

In this session you should have achieved the objectives set out at the start of this session.

In particular, you should have become acquainted with:

`/WGF,0`	Worksheet, Global, Format, Comma, Zero
`/WGFC0`	Worksheet, Global, Format, Currency, Zero
`/WGFG`	Worksheet, Global, Format, General
`/ * - +`	Duplicate keys for entering formulae
`/GTB`	Graph, Type, Bar
`/GTL`	Graph, Type, Line
`/GTS`	Graph, Type, Stacked-bar
`/GTP`	Graph, Type, Pie
`/GX`	Graph, X-range
`/GA`	Graph, A-range
`/GOL`	Graph, Options, Legend
`/GOT`	Graph, Options, Titles
`/GNC`	Graph, Name, Create
`/GNU`	Graph, Name, Use
`/GS`	Graph, Save (not{AEA})

14. Activity

Invent some budgeted data for an organisation for three or four activities or products, for a period of six separate months.

Create (and save!) a worksheet which conforms with your data.

Define, enhance, name and save bar, line, stacked-bar and pie graphs created from the data in your worksheet.

15. Objective test ☐ A ☐ B ☑ C ☐ D

1. To enter £7,000 into a cell, you should type, before pressing <Enter>

   ☐ A 7000

   ☐ B 7,000

   ☐ C £7,000

   ☐ D any of these

2. With a value of 7000 entered into a cell, the keypresses required to show 7,000 in the cell, before pressing <Enter> are

   ☐ A /WFG,

   ☐ B /WFG,0

   ☐ C /WF,0

   ☐ D /WGF,0

3. To enter a formula into cell A3 which increases the value in cell A1 by 20%, the formula to be entered is

   ☐ A +a1x120%

   ☐ B +A1+20%

   ☐ C +A1*1.2

   ☐ D +A1*20%

4. To define a bar graph, the initial keystrokes from READY mode are

   ☐ A /GTB

   ☐ B /WGTB

   ☐ C /WGB

   ☐ D /GB

5. From READY mode, legends can be added to a graph for the A range after the keypresses:

   ☐ A /WGLA

   ☐ B /GTLA

   ☐ C /GOLA

   ☐ D /GTOLA

6. From READY mode, titles can be added to a graph for the X-Axis after the keypresses:

☐ A /GTX

☐ B /GOTX

☐ C /GTOX

☐ D /WGTOX

7. Once you have defined and enhanced a graph, you should name it before defining and enhancing another graph from the same data. You can do this by the following keypresses from READY mode:

☐ A /GNC

☐ B /GONC

☐ C /GTNC

☐ D /ONC

8. You have named a graph with the name CHOCBAR. To make this the current graph, you should press, before you highlight CHOCBAR and press <Enter>, starting from the Graph menu:

☐ A ONU

☐ B NU<Enter>

☐ C NU

☐ D NC<Enter>

9. You have finished defining, enhancing and naming a bar graph. You now want to view a line graph from the same data. From the graph menu, the keypresses are:

☐ A TLV

☐ B OTLV

☐ C OTVL

☐ D none of these

10. A graph is on the screen, and you want to get rid of it. So you press:

☐ A <Space-bar>

☐ B <Enter>

☐ C either A or B

☐ D neither A nor B

SESSION 8
Printing Graphs

1. Objectives

At the end of this session (assuming you have a graphics printer) you will be able to:

- ❑ print out any of the graphs which you created in session 7
- ❑ appreciate the capabilities of the printing facilities available for your particular spreadsheet program

2. Introduction

In session 7, you created and named four types of graph.

Also {123}{VP} you saved them with the file-names:

ZEDBAR.PIC
ZEDLINE.PIC
ZEDSTACK.PIC
ZEDPIE.PIC

In this session you will learn how to print them out on paper.

It is important to note that you must have a graphics printer to print graphs.

The programs used in this book have different graph-printing support. Refer to the paragraphs below which are relevant to your program.

Program	Paragraphs
{123}	3, 4, 5
{VP}	6
(AEA}	7

3. {123} Acessing Printgraph

In session 1 , you were shown how to get a blank worksheet by going through the Lotus Access System Screen. This screen shows when you type *Lotus* at the C:> or C:\123> prompt (once you have changed to the *1-2-3* sub-directory). So far you have chosen only *1-2-3* from the menu to obtain a blank worksheet. The choice to the right of 1-2-3 is *PrintGraph,* and this is a separate program which you will use to print your graphs.

[If you want to go straight to a blank worksheet, without going through the Access screen, you can type **123 <Enter>** at the prompt. However, if you then want to use the PrintGraph program, you have to Quit the 1-2-3 program, and (assuming you are still in your 1-2-3 sub-directory) type **Printgraph** at the C:> prompt.]

Start this session by accessing a blank worksheet by typing Lotus at the prompt, and then press <Enter> with the high-light over *1-2-3*.

Refresh your memory of the four graphs you created in session 7 by looking at them on your monitor.

Press `/FR`

Press `<F3>` to list the files you have created

Move the cursor to *ZEDGRAPH* and press <Enter>

Press `/GNU` (Graph, Name, Use)

Select the graph you want to see on screen with the cursor, and press <Enter>

To view another graph,

Press `<Esc> NU` (Name, Use)

Select the next graph with the cursor.

Press `<Enter>`

> **Tip:** After viewing one graph and pressing **<Esc>**, the cursor will already be on *Name*. Press <Enter> and the cursor will be on Use. Press **<Enter>** again, and you can now select the graph you want. Also, pressing other keys besides **<Esc>** works to take you from the graph on the screen back to the main graph menu. So, when you have finished viewing one graph, and want to view another, you could simply press **<Enter>** three times, to achieve the same result as pressing **<Esc>NU**. Try it and see. As you use spreadsheets, look out for short-cuts!

Practise viewing the graphs until the process becomes easy.

4. {123} Preparing Printgraph

Before you print your graphs, it is necessary to check and, if necessary, change the printgraph settings, so that your graphs print out correctly.

After viewing your last graph, press <Enter> to return you to the main graph menu.

Press `Q` (Quit)

This takes you back to READY mode

Press `/QY` (Quit, Yes)

You should now be back at the 1-2-3 Access System Screen. If not, see paragraph 2 above.

Move the cursor to *PrintGraph* and press <Enter>

You will see a menu, with a status screen below.

Move the cursor to *Settings* and press <Enter>

Move the cursor to *Hardware* and press <Enter>

You will see a menu with selections corresponding to the headings under *HARDWARE SETUP* in the status screen.

Check each item to see if it is correct.

Graphs Directory should show the drive and directory where your graphs were saved, i.e. the same directory as *ZEDGRAPH*. If the directory shown is incorrect, choose *Graphs-Directory* in the menu and press **<Enter>**; then type in the correct drive and directory, such as *A:* or *B:* or *C:\123*.

Fonts Directory should show the drive and directory where your font (.FNT) files are. For example, if your font files are in the subdirectory 123 of drive C:, the entry should be C:\123. If the entry is incorrect, choose *Fonts-Directory*, press **<Enter>** and type in the correct drive and directory.

Interface refers to the way your printer is connected to your computer. Do not make any changes unless you understand fully your type of printer. The most common setting is Parallel 1, which is the first option when you choose *Interface* from the menu. Your printer manual should tell you what interface you need. Other options can be read from the control panel by moving the right- or left- arrow keys. Do NOT press <Enter> unless you need to make a change. Press <Esc> to keep the setting on the status screen as it is.

Printer Type: Check that your printer is shown in the status screen. If not, choose *Printer* from the menu. Follow the instructions on the screen. [If no options are displayed, or if your printer is not listed, you will have to return to the Install program.]

Paper Size: Alter width and length if necessary. Follow the instructions on the screen.

Press	Q	(Quit)
Press	S	(Save) if you want to save your current settings for future sessions
Press	Q	(Quit) to return to the main menu

5. {123} Printing your graphs

At last! It may seem tedious to have to check the settings as described in the previous paragraph, but, once the settings have been saved, you will not have to do it again unless you make a change, e.g. to your printer or paper size.

Press `I` (Image-Select)

You should see a list of your four graph (.PIC) files, with the date and time you saved them, and also the file sizes.

Move the cursor (if necessary) to *ZEDBAR*

Press `<Spacebar>`

This marks *ZEDBAR* with a hash sign

Press `<Enter>` to select it

You are returned to the main menu, and you will see *ZEDBAR* listed under *GRAPH IMAGES SELECTED*

Press `AGP` (Align, Go, Page)

This is the same procedure as you learnt when printing your worksheet in session 4.

The *ZEDBAR* graph should print out and the paper (if continuous) should advance to the top of the next page.

Your graph should look similar to Figure 8a.

[If you want to view your graphs as a check before you print them (or to look at them in any case) you can do this when you select *Image-Select* by high-lighting the file you want to view and pressing <F10>. Press <Esc> to return to the *Image-Select* screen.]

Next, to print out *ZEDLINE* :

Press `I` (Image-Select)

Move the cursor to *ZEDBAR* and press **<Spacebar>**

This turns the mark (#) off

Move the cursor to *ZEDLINE* and press **<Spacebar>**

This turns the mark (#) on

Press `<Enter>` to select the marked graph and returnyou to the main menu.

You will see *ZEDLINE* listed under *GRAPH IMAGES SELECTED*

Press `AGP` (Align, Go, Page)

The *ZEDLINE* graph should print out and the paper (if continuous) should advance to the top of the next page.

Finally you will print out *ZEDPIE* and *ZEDSTACK* in one operation.

Press `I` (Image-Select)

Figure 8a

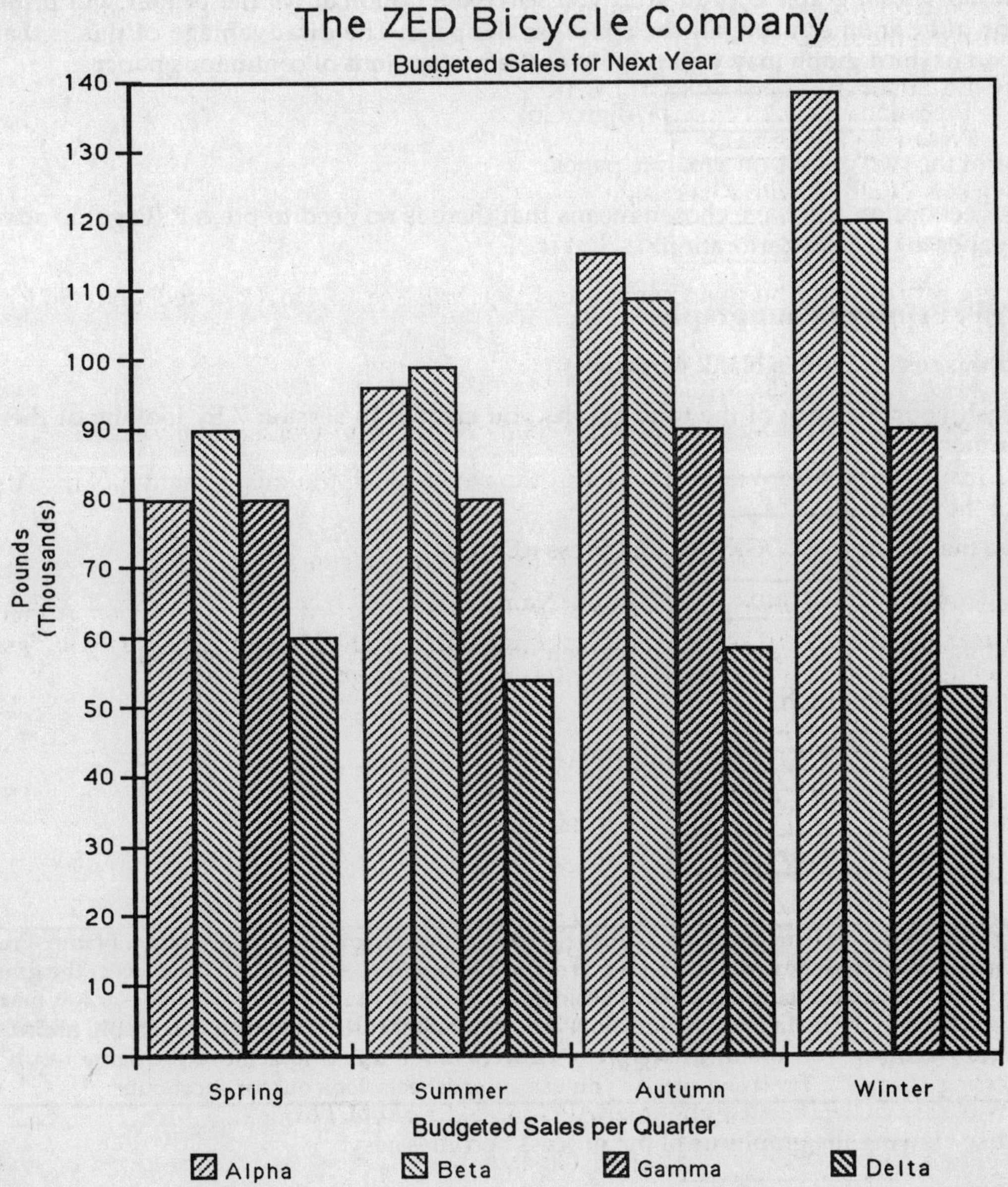

Cancel the mark against *ZEDLINE*, and mark *ZEDPIE* and *ZEDSTACK* using the **<Spacebar>**.

Press `<Enter>`

Press `SAEYQQ` (Settings, Action, Eject, Yes, Quit, Quit)

By setting *ACTION OPTIONS Eject* to *Yes* the printer will advance to the next page when each individual graph is printed. If you leave the option at *No* the printer will print one graph after another using all the space on the page. The disadvantage of this is that the second or third graph may well print over the perforations of continuous paper.

Press `AG` (Align, Go)

to print the two graphs on separate pages.

The Eject option you have chosen means that there is no need to press P (Page) to advance the paper to the next perforation.

6. {VP} Printing your graphs

Start this session with a blank worksheet.

Refresh your memory of the four graphs you created in session 7 by looking at them on your monitor.

Press `/FR`

Move the cursor to *ZEDGRAPH* and press **<Enter>**

Press `/GNU` (Graph, Name, Use)

Select the graph you want to see on screen with the cursor, and press **<Enter>**

To view another graph,

Press `<Esc> NU` (Name, Use)

Select the next graph with the cursor.

Press `<Enter>`

> *Tip:* After viewing one graph and pressing **<Esc>**, the cursor will already be on Name. Press **<Enter>** and the cursor will be on Use. Press **<Enter>** again, and you can now select the graph you want. Also, pressing other keys besides <Esc> works to take you from the graph on the screen back to the main graph menu. So, when you have finished viewing one graph, and want to view another, you could simply press **<Enter>** three times, to achieve the same result as pressing **<Esc>**NU. Try it and see. As you use spreadsheets, look out for short-cuts!

Practise viewing the graphs until the process becomes easy.

After viewing your last graph, press **<Enter>** to return you to the main graph menu.

Selecting V (View) from the main graph menu enables you to view the current (named with Name, Use) graph only.

You can also view your graphs which you saved in *.PIC* files. Select *Look* from the main graph menu, and your *.PIC* are listed for you to select for viewing.

[A current graph (after Name, Use) can also be viewed from *READY* mode by pressing <F10>.]

Printing with {VP} is simple:

From the Graph menu:

Press `NU` (Name, Use)

Highlight the graph name you wish to make current

Press `<Enter>`

The graph appears on the screen.

Press `<Esc>` to return you to the main graph menu.

Press `P` (Print)

The graph appears on the screen and the printer prints the current graph sideways.

[You may possibly be able to print a graph while it is displayed on your monitor after pressing (from *READY* mode) /GV (Graph, View) or /GL (Graph, Look) or <F10>, by pressing **<Shift>+<PrintScreen>**. You may waste paper trying!]

Once you have saved your graphs in a *.PIC* file, it can by readby other graphics programs for more elaborate print-outs.

If you have time, you could experiment by printing out your other graphs.

7. {AEA} Printing your graphs

Start this session with a blank worksheet.

Refresh your memory of the four graphs you created in session 7 by looking at them on your monitor.

Press `/FR`

Move the cursor to *ZEDGRAPH* and press **<Enter>**

Press `/GNU` (Graphics, Name, Use)

Select the graph you want to see on screen with the cursor, and press **<Enter>**

To view another graph,

Press `<Esc> NU` (Name, Use)

Select the next graph with the cursor.

Press `<Enter>`

> ***Tip:*** After viewing one graph and pressing **<Esc>**, the cursor will already be on *Name.* Press **<Enter>** and the cursor will be on Use. Press **<Enter>** again, and you can now select the graph you want. Also, pressing other keys besides **<Esc>** works to take you from the graph on the screen back to the main graph menu. So, when you have finished viewing one graph, and want to view another, you could simply press **<Enter>** three times, to achieve the same result as pressing **<Esc>NU**. Try it and see. As you use spreadsheets, look out for short-cuts!

Practise viewing the graphs until the process becomes easy.

After viewing your last graph, press **<Enter>** to return you to the main graphics menu.

Selecting **V** (View) from the main graph menu enables you to view the current (named with Name, Use) graph only.

[A current graph (after Name, Use) can also be viewed from *READY* mode by pressing <F10>.]

Printing with {AEA} is simple:

From the Graphics menu:

Press `NU` (Name, Use)

Highlight the graph name *ZEDBAR* to make it current

Press `<Enter>`

The graph appears on the screen.

Press `<Esc>` to return you to the main graph menu.

Press `P` (Plot)

This enters the *Graphics Plot* menu, from which a printed copy of the current graph can be produced.

The menu choices are:

Image	Density	Hardware	Paper	Orient	Eject	GO	Quit
High	Low	PIC	Height	Portrait			
Wide	High	LASER	Width	Landscape			
Top		FX/MX	Quit				
Bottom		24-PIN					
Left							
Quit							

Your menus may differ slightly from the above, depending on your version of the program. Many of these options are not available in version 3.

Full details of these menu items are given in the manual under *GRAPHICS COMMAND SUMMARY.*

You will now print out your *ZEDBAR* graph, using some of the choices available.

Press `IH` (Image, High)

The height of the graph is to be set in hundredths of an inch. So to make the graph 4 inches high, accept the default value of 400 by pressing **<Enter>**, or alter it to 400 if the default has changed.

Press `W` (Wide)

Accept the default value of 600 by pressing **<Enter>**, or alter it to 600 if the default has changed.

Press `T` (Top)

Type `50` (to set at half an inch)

Press `B` (Bottom)

Type `100` (to set at one inch, because the legends and titles need this space)

Press `L` (Left)

Type `100` (to set left margin at one inch)

Press `Q` (Quit, to return to the Graphics menu)

Press `D` (Density)

Choose *Low* or *High*. High gives a better print-out but takes longer to print. Choose L for a faster first-time printout, in case you want to alter the settings before producing a final high-quality print-out.

Press `H` (Hardware)

PIC sends the output to a *.PIC* file (which is a file which can be read by some other graphics and word-processing programs). If you remember, in session 7, you could not do this at that stage.

Your choice of one of the other three menu items depends on what printer you are using. *FX/MX* is for a 9-pin Epson or compatible dot-matrix printer.

Move the cursor to your type of printer

Press `<Enter>`

Press `P` (Paper)

The defaults are probably for 1100 x 800 (11″ x 8″) paper, but you should change this for A4 paper to 1166 x 825.

Press `H` and type in height required. Press `<Enter>`

Press `W` and type in width required. Press `<Enter>`

Press `Q` (Quit)

Press `O` (Orient)

Press `P` (Portrait) Press `<Enter>`

If you are happy that you have set-up your print-out correctly,

Press `G` (Go)

The mode indicator at the top of the screen will flash *WAIT*. The screen will read *Plotting...Press ESC to Stop* , and the progress of the printing is shown below as a percentage.

The speed of printing will vary with your choice of high or low density.

When the printing has stopped, move the paper to the top of the next sheet. You printer controls (line feed) may be better than pressing *Eject* which sometimes moves to the top of the next but one sheet of continuous paper.

Your graph should look similar to Figure 8b.

Press `QQ` (Quit, Quit) to return to READY! mode.

If you have time, you could experiment by printing out your other graphs.

8. Summary

In this session you should have achieved the objectives set out at the start of this session.

The basic principles of printing graphs with the various programs are:

- define, enhance, name and {notAEA} save individual graphs

{123}
- access the PrintGraph program
- check the PrintGraph settings
- choose Image-Select and your graph PIC file
- Align, Go, Page

{VP}
- /GNU (Graph, Name, Use)
- Select your graph
- P for Print

{AEA}
- /GNU (Graphics, Name, Use)
- Select your graph
- P for Plot
- check and alter Plot menu settings
- G for Go

Figure 8b

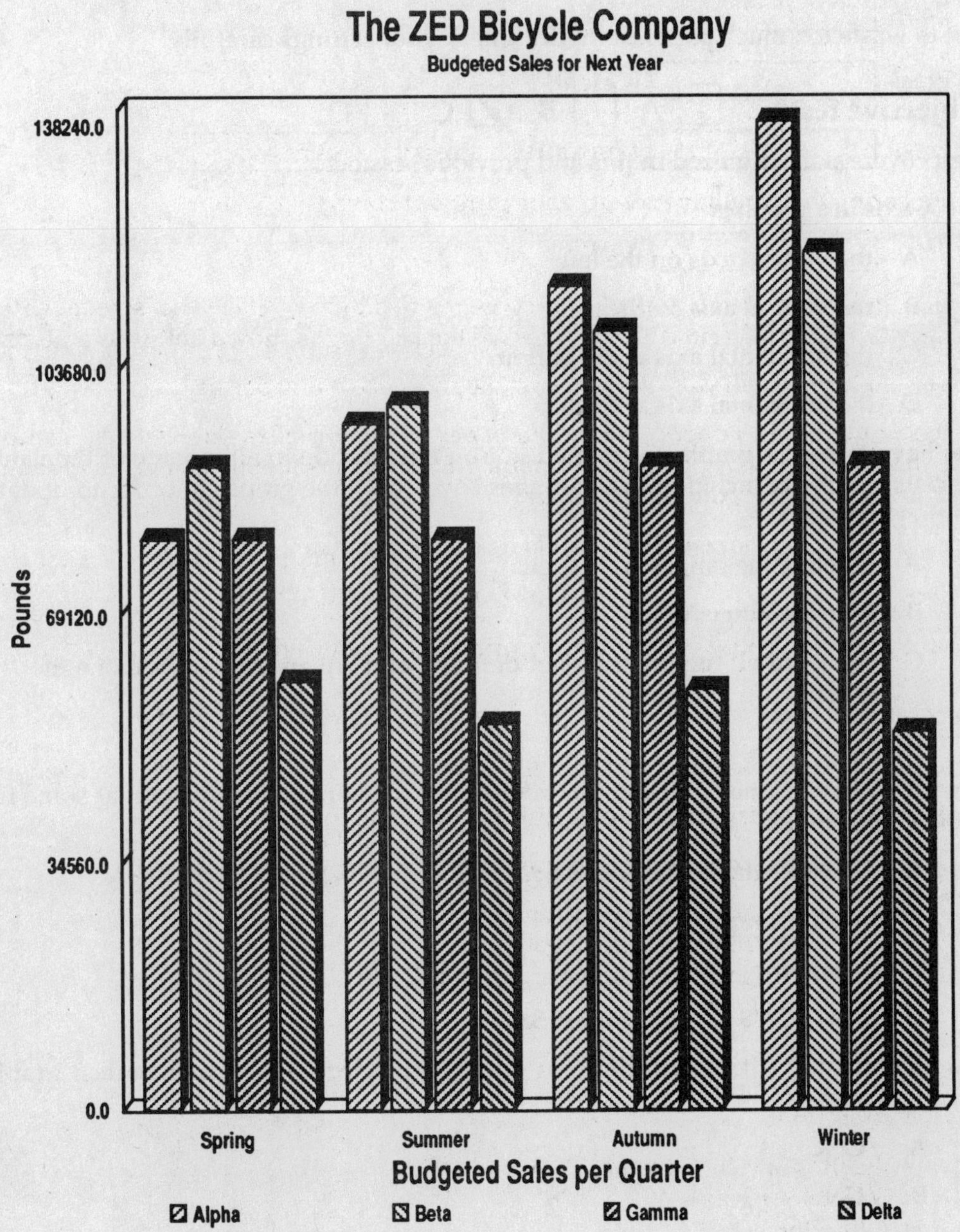
The ZED Bicycle Company
Budgeted Sales for Next Year
138240.0
103680.0
69120.0
34560.0
0.0
Pounds
Spring
Summer
Autumn
Winter
Budgeted Sales per Quarter
Alpha
Beta
Gamma
Delta

9. Activity

Print out the graphs which you created during the activity of the last session (Session 7, paragraph 14).

Try not to waste too much paper doing so! Check your settings carefully.

10. Objective test ☐ A ☐ B ☑ C ☐ D

This test covers skills acquired in this and previous sessions.

1. The X-axis in a graph is

   ☐ A the vertical axis on the left

   ☐ B the vertical axis on the right

   ☐ C the horizontal axis at the bottom

   ☐ D the horizontal axis at the top

2. You have created a graph and named it. You now decide to alter some of the values in the cells which are included in the ranges covered by the graph. In order to update the graph, you must

   ☐ A redefine the ranges A, B, C etc.

   ☐ B redefine range X only

   ☐ C carry out all the processes of defining and enhancing and rename the graph

   ☐ D do nothing

3. When you have named a graph, in order to use the named graph again at some future session, you should

   ☐ A save the whole worksheet with /FS

   ☐ B save the graph to a PIC file

   ☐ C do nothing

   ☐ D press /GNS (Graph, Name, Save)

4. You have named a series of different graphs. To select a particular named graph for viewing, you press

   ☐ A /GNC

   ☐ B /GNU

   ☐ C /GNV

   ☐ D none of these

5. The number of data ranges which you can plot on a particular graph is

☐ A 4 (A-D)

☐ B 6 (A-F)

☐ C 8 (A-H)

☐ D 12 (A-L)

6. You are viewing a graph on your monitor. You want to select a different graph which you have created and named. To select it and view it, the keypresses, before you highlight it and press <Enter> are

☐ A <Enter><Enter><Enter>

☐ B <Enter><Name><Use>

☐ C <Esc><Enter><Use>

☐ D any of these

7. One of the following formulae is incomplete. It is

☐ A (A14*1.2)+1000

☐ B A14*1.2+1000

☐ C +A14*1.2+1000

☐ D +A14*1.2+(1000)

8. You wish to protect all the cells of your current worksheet. The keypresses are

☐ A /WGPE

☐ B /WGPE<Enter>

☐ C /RGPE

☐ D /RPE<Enter>

9. The formula to add the values in cells F7..F9 is

☐ A @SUM(F7..F9)

☐ B @SUM(F9..F7)

☐ C +F7+F8+F9

☐ D any of these

10. You have protected your worksheet with the correct global command, and now you want to alter one of the formulae. Before you re-protect the worksheet,you can disable the protection by the keypresses:

- [ ] A /RGPD
- [ ] B /WGPD<Enter>
- [ ] C /WGDP
- [ ] D /WGPD

SESSION 9

A Simple Database

1. Objectives

At the end of this session, you will be able to:

- ❑ appreciate what a database is
- ❑ understand the meaning of records and fields
- ❑ create a simple database input range
- ❑ use the *data, fill* command to list numbers
- ❑ enter labels, dates and currency
- ❑ sort the database in various ways
- ❑ use the primary and secondary sort commands
- ❑ search the database for particular groups of records
- ❑ extract records from the database
- ❑ use some statistical functions
- ❑ alter the database with *move, insert, delete.*

2. Introduction

In the first eight sessions, you have been concerned with worksheets which have primarily calculated various numeric results.

In this session, you will learn how a spreadsheet can manipulate data.

A *database* is a collection of information about sets of things. These sets can be, for example, collections of books, compact disks, stamp collections. In business, examples are lists of customers, stocks of raw materials and stocks of finished goods.

In this session, you will create a small database of the personnel employed by the CDPublications Company. You will learn how to sort the database, search it for particular groups of employees and extract information from it. You will also learn how to calculate such things as the average salary.

3. Description of the model

CDPublications Company (referred to hereafter as CDP) have 20 staff on the payroll. These staff are listed in Figure 9a.

Each ROW is known as a RECORD, and contains details concerning a single member of staff.

Each COLUMN is known as a FIELD, and contains one particular piece of information concerning each record. The field NAMES are in row 3 (A3..G3).

For example, the record for Uriah Heep is in row 10 (A10..G10), and cell D10 is in the DEPARTMENT field (column D) and shows that he works in the ACCOUNTS department.

4. Notes on the design of the model

At present the employees are listed in numerical order of staff number (column A). However, you will soon learn to list them in any order you want, e.g. alphabetically by surname (column B).

Twenty staff are listed (rows 4..23), but obviously the list could be added to. Details of how to do this are given in paragraph 10 below.

There are seven fields (columns A..G), and again these could be added to. For example other fields could contain home addresses, home telephone numbers, National Insurance numbers, date started with the company etc.

5. Notes on creating the worksheet

The following notes refer to figure 9a.

COLUMN-WIDTHS

Column-widths are best set individually. Position the cursor over each column separately before using /WCS

Column A:	8
Column B:	14
Column C:	12
Column D:	12
Column E:	10
Column F:	3
Column G:	9

Column A

STAFFNO Label: left-aligned

The numbers in cells A4..A23 can be entered as follows:

Position the cursor over cell A4

Press `/DF.` (Data, Fill, <.>)

Move cursor to cell A23 (Try <PgDn> <↑>)

Press `<Enter>`

Figure 9a

	A	B	C	D	E	F	G
1	CDPublications Company: Staff Database						
2							
3	STAFFNO	SURNAME	FIRSTNAME	DEPARTMENT	DOB	SEX	SALARY
4	1	PICKWICK	SAMUEL	ADMIN	31-Dec-29	M	50000
5	2	SNODGRASS	AUGUSTUS	MARKETING	15-Jul-31	M	18000
6	3	TUPMAN	TRACY	MARKETING	16-Nov-32	M	18000
7	4	WINKLE	NATHANIEL	MARKETING	05-Apr-35	M	18000
8	5	BARDELL	MARTHA	ACCOUNTS	22-Aug-38	F	17000
9	6	COPPERFIELD	DAVID	SALES	24-Dec-69	M	12000
10	7	HEEP	URIAH	ACCOUNTS	04-Sep-52	M	16000
11	8	MICAWBER	WILKINS	SALES	29-Jul-40	M	9000
12	9	TROTWOOD	BETSEY	PERSONNEL	28-Feb-28	F	11000
13	10	TWIST	OLIVER	ADMIN	02-Sep-72	M	4000
14	11	DEDLOCK	LEICESTER	ADMIN	19-May-30	M	35000
15	12	CRATCHIT	ROBERT	ACCOUNTS	14-Mar-51	M	5000
16	13	SCROOGE	EBENEZER	ACCOUNTS	30-Jan-34	M	22000
17	14	CRATCHIT	BELINDA	PERSONNEL	02-Apr-69	F	12000
18	15	DEDLOCK	VOLUMNIA	PERSONNEL	02-Dec-71	F	20000
19	16	DEDLOCK	HONORIA	MARKETING	23-Jun-37	F	25000
20	17	SQUEERS	WACKFORD	SECURITY	01-Jul-50	M	7500
21	18	BUZFUZ	SERGEANT	SECURITY	30-May-52	M	7500
22	19	SQUEERS	FANNY	PERSONNEL	07-Oct-53	F	8000
23	20	JINGLE	ALFRED	SALES	20-Nov-48	M	19000

Type `1 <Enter>` against *Start* prompt

Type `<Enter>` against *Step: 1* prompt

Type **{notAEA}** `<Enter>` against *Stop: 8191* prompt

[The programs vary slightly in the prompt words and numbers]

The cells A4..A23 should be filled with numbers 1..20

Columns B, C, D and F

All cells are labels, left-aligned

Column E

Cell E3: Label, centred. Press ^DOB<Enter>

Cells E4..E23: Do NOT enter the dates as shown. Use the following method to enter with the @DATE formula.

Move the cursor to cell E4

Type @DATE(29,12,31)<Enter>

You will see the formula in the control panel and the number 10958 in the cell.

After @DATE, the figures entered in the brackets are (year,month,day), i e.:

(1) the last two digits of the year: 29 of 1929

[The programs start counting from the beginning of the 20th century. {123}{VP} 21st century: the year 2099 will be entered as 199. {VP} starts with 1801 as -99.]

(2) the month: Jan..Dec = 1..12

(3) the day of the month: 1..31 or 1..30 or 1..28 or 1..29, depending on the month

The number appearing in the cell, e.g. 10958 is the number of days since the 1st January, 1900. This is useful for the program to use in sort calculations. However, to see the date in the cell in a more usual format,

Move the cursor to cell E4

Press /RFD (Range, Format, Date)

Choose a suitable format from the menu, e.g.

{123} DD-MMM-YY {AEA} D-M-Y or {VP} D-MMM-Y and press <Enter>

Move the cursor to E23 to define the range and press <Enter>

The cells E4..E23 should now show the dates in the format shown in figure 9a, the formulae (in the control panel) should be as entered, and the program will remember the number of days since 1st January, 1900.

Now move to cell E5

Press @DATE(31,7,15)<Enter>

and so on for cells E6..E23.

Column G

Cell G3: Label, right-aligned. Press "SALARY <Enter>

Use /RFC0<Enter>[range]<Enter>

(Range, Format, Currency, 0) for the range G4..G23

Enter the salary figures from figure 9a into cells G4..G23, remembering that £50,000 must be entered as 50000

6. Sorting the database

Move the cursor to cell A4

Press `/DS` (Data, Sort)

These are the entry keys to data-sorting.

Press `D` (Data-Range)

Highlight the range A4..G23 and press <Enter>

Note that you did not include row 3, since the field names are not included in the sort.

Press `P` (Primary-Key)

You are going to sort the staff into alphabetical order, by Surname

Move the cursor to the SURNAME column. Any cell in the range B4..B23 will do.

Press `<Enter>A` (Ascending)

Pressing A for Ascending means that the names will be sorted in the order A..Z. Pressing D for Descending would sort the names in the order Z..A

Press `<Enter>`

You are returned to the *Sort* menu.

Press `G` (Go)

and the surnames are sorted A..Z, with Martha Bardell heading the list.

You will notice that the Dedlocks are together, but not necessarily in the order of their Firstnames. To correct this, you must also specify a Secondary-Key sort.

Press `/DSS` (Data, Sort, Secondary-Key)

Move the cursor to the *Firstname* field (range C4..C23)

Press `<Enter>A<Enter>G` (Ascending, Go)

and the Dedlocks should be in the order Honoria, Leicester, Volumnia.

Now try sorting the staff by date of birth, youngest first.

Press `/DSP`

Move the cursor to column E (press <Esc> if necessary first) and press <Enter>

Press `D<Enter>G`

Note that D for Descending was required, since the highest date-numbers are listed first.

Note that the Data-Range has already been set, and need only be changed if required before a fresh data-sort.

Next, try sorting the staff into departments, with the departments in alphabetical order, and, within the departments, the staff sorted in salary order, highest salaries first.

Press /DSP[rangeD4..D23]A<Enter>S[rangeG4..G23]D<Enter>G

Ebenezer Scrooge should head the list with the highest salary in the accounts department.

Incidentally, you could freeze the first three rows so that you can keep the headings visible when you scroll to row 23.

Move the cursor to row three, and press **/WTH {AEA} /WBH**

Now move the cursor to row 23 to see the security staff.

Feel free to carry out further primary and secondary sorts, until you are familiar with the procedure.

Finish up with re-sorting the database into the original order of staff numbers.

Press /DSP[rangeA4..A23]A<Enter>G<Home>

7. Searching the database

Move the cursor to cell A4 if it is not already there.

{123}{VP} Press /C<↑><Esc><↑>. (do not forget the full stop!)

{AEA} Press /WBC move cursor to A3 and press /C.

The cursor should now be on cell A3

Move the cursor to cell G3, and press **<Enter>**

Move the cursor to cell A30, and press **<Enter>**

Unless you have made a mistake, you should have copied the field names to cells A30..G30.

Cells A30..G30 are the first row of your criteria range.

Enter F in cell F31, i.e in the cell below *SEX*

{AEA} Enter * in cell A31

The F is the criteria for your search, and the criteria range is now A30..G31.

Press /DQC (Data, Query, Criterion)

Highlight the criterion range A30..G31 and press **<Enter>**

You are taken back to the Query menu

Press `I` (Input)

Highlight the Input range A3..G23 and press **<Enter>**

Note particularly that, unlike as in sorting, you have now *included* the field names in the input range.

{AEA} At this stage, you should define the OutRange (as well as the Criteria and InpRange, which you have just done). AEA works differently from 1-2-3, though the principles are the same. When you come to Extracting Records in the next paragraph, you will not need to define OutRange again. Copy A30..G30 to A40..G40. Press **/DQO** (Data, Question, OutRange). Highlight A40..G40 and press **<Enter>**.

Press `F` (Find)

{123}{VP} Row 8 should be highlighted for you, since Martha Bardell is the first female on the staff list. Press <↓> and Betsey Trotwood is highlighted. Keep pressing <↓> until the last female staff member is highlighted. [You will hear a beep when the last item of the Find is reached.]

{AEA} Menu-like cards appear, one for each record which contains an F under SEX. Martha Bardell appears first. Keep pressing <PgDn> to view all the female staff. [You will hear a beep when the last item of Find is reached.]

Press {123} <Esc>Q {VP} <Esc> {AEA} Q to get back to READY mode.

Move the cursor to cell F31

Delete the *F* with **/RE<Enter>**

Now to find all staff whose salaries are in the range £10,000 and £20,000.

Enter the following formula in cell G31:

+G4>=10000#and#+G4<=20000

What this formula says is this:

Is the salary of Samuel Pickwick (his salary is in cell G4) greater than or equal to £10,000, AND ALSO is his salary less than or equal to £20,000? If so indicate this with a figure 1 (true), but if it is not true, indicate this with a figure 0 (false). Since S. Pickwick's salary is over £10,000 but is NOT also less than or equal to £20,000, then the answer is no, and you will see a figure 0 (false) in cell G31.

Note that the *logical operator* #AND# has a # at the beginning and end of AND.

Press `/DQF` (Data, Query, Find) and the down arrow ({AEA} <PgDn>) to find all the staff within the specified salary range.

Return to *READY* mode.

Do NOT delete the formula in cell G31.

Now enter the following formula in cell E31:

+E4>=@DATE(40,1,1)

Press `/DQF` to find all staff born on or after 1st January, 1940 whose salaries are £10,000 or more, but £20,000 or less. There are only five of them.

Return to *READY* mode.

Delete cells E31 and G31 with /RE

Enter SALES in cell D31 and ACCOUNTS in cell D32.

{AEA} Enter * in cell A32 as well.

Press `/DQC` (Data, Query, Criterion)

Press `<↓>` to highlight the range A30..G32.

[The criterion range must contain all the criteria cells, but must not contain any blank rows; this principle applies to the Input range as well.]

Press `<Enter> /DQF` to find all staff in the Sales and Accounts departments.

You should now be able to experiment with other searches of your own choice. For example, you could search for all staff whose surnames begin with the letter D. To do this, enter D* in cell B31. ({AEA} Do not forget the * in cell A31.) The * is known as a *wildcard* which means *all characters to the end of the label*. You must also reduce the criterion range to include only rows 30 and 31, since a blank row in the criteria range results in all records being selected. Use /RE to erase previous criteria no longer needed.

[There are many other facilities available for searching; for further details refer to the manual for your particular program.]

8. Extracting records

You may need to extract selected records from the database, show them elsewhere on the spreadsheet so that they can be viewed separately and, if required, printed out.

Suppose the Chairman is disturbed by discontent among the lower-paid staff. He wants a list of all staff whose salaries are £10,000 or less.

Delete any entries in your criteria range (rows 31 and below)

Enter the following formula in cell G31

+G4<=10000

{AEA} Also enter * in cell A31

{123}{VP} Copy the range A3..G3 to row A40..G40

{AEA} You have already done this. Check!

Press `/DQC` (Data, Query, Criterion)

Specify the range A30..G31

Press `O` (Output)

The control panel shows: *Enter Output Range*

Specify the range A40..G49

[This range gives 9 rows for the extracted output, which should be adequate. If you do not specify an adequate range, you would have to enlarge the range when you get an error message. If you specify the range A40..G40, i.e. a single line only, the program will use as many rows as necessary, but may erase data below them. You are going to use rows 50..55 in the next paragraph.]

Press `E` (Extract)

Return to *READY* mode

View the extracted output in the range A40..G46

Micawber, Twist, Cratchit, W. Squeers, Buzfuz and F. Squeers should be listed.

You will note that they are listed in Staff Number order.

If the Chairman had wanted them listed in alphabetical order or in order of their salaries, you could have sorted the database appropriately before extracting the records.

Note that the Output range need not contain all the fields, and also the order of the output range need not be the field order of the database. To test this out, delete cells A41..G46, delete cell F40, alter cell B40 to read *FIRSTNAME* and cell C40 to read *SURNAME*. Press /DQE to view the revised extracted output. [You may have to reformat dates, widen columns, move headings together, depending on your program. Experiment!]

When you have finished experimenting, change A40..G40 back to its original form, i.e a copy of A30..G30, and reset column-widths, and delete output in rows 41 and below.

9. Database statistical functions

IF YOU ARE USING 1-2-3 OR VP

({AEA} see special section at the end of this paragraph.)

The database can be used to calculate, for example, the average salaries of the staff in the marketing and sales departments. To do so, you will use some of the database statistical functions.

In doing so, you will also learn about named ranges.

Move the cursor to cell A3

Press `/RNC` (Range, Name, Create)

Type `INPUT` (you can type in lowercase)

Press `<Enter>`

Specify the range A3..G23 and press <Enter>

Move the cursor to cell G31 and delete the formula there with **/RE<Enter>** or any other criteria you may have entered during your experiments.

Enter **MARKETING** in cell D31, and **SALES** in cell D32

Move the cursor to cell A30

Press `/RNC` (Range, Name, Create)

Type `CRITERIA` Press `<Enter>`

Specify the range A30..G32 and press <Enter>

You have now created two named ranges, and you will use these names in the formulae which follow below.

Enter the following labels in the appropriate cells:

A50:	**Marketing and Sales Staff:-**
B51:	**Average salary of staff**
B52:	**Highest paid staff member**
B53:	**Lowest paid staff member**
B54:	**Total staff salaries**
B55:	**Total number of staff**

Now enter the following formula in cell E51:

@DAVG($INPUT,6,$CRITERIA)

You should see the figure 17000 in cell E51. This is the average salary of all staff in marketing and sales.

Explanation:

The *@DAVG* is the formula for calculating the average salary of the salaries in column 6 (counting from the left, with column A being numbered 0), within the overall input range, and according to the criteria in the criteria range (marketing and sales). The formula is usually described as:

@DAVG(input,offset,criterion)

The dollar ($) signs are useful in this instance, because you are going to copy the formula to cells E52..E55. Without the dollar signs, the copied formulae would be relative, and would alter the input and criteria ranges. By copying the formula as it stands in cell E51, you can then edit the bits you want to change, thereby saving typing time.

Move the cursor to cell E51

Press /C<Enter><↓>.<↓><↓><↓><Enter>

This copies the formula in cell E51 to cells E52..E55

Now edit <F2> the copied formulae to read:

(The letters to replace AVG with are printed in BOLD, and note that you can enter the letters in lowercase.)

E52: @**DMAX**($INPUT,6,$CRITERIA)
E53: @**DMIN**($INPUT,6,$CRITERIA)
E54: @**DSUM**($INPUT,6,$CRITERIA)
E55: @**DCOUNT**($INPUT,6,$CRITERIA)

The results of the calculations should appear in the respective cells, i.e.:

E52: 25000; E53: 9000; E54: 119000; E55: 7

You could add £s and commas to E51..E54 with:

Move to cell E51

Press /RFC0<Enter><↓><↓><↓><Enter>

IF YOU ARE USING AEA [also of interest to users of {123} {VP}]

The database can be used to calculate, for example, the average salaries of the staff in the marketing and sales departments. To do so, you will use some of the statistical functions.

Move the cursor to cell G31 and delete the formula there with /RE<Enter> (and any other criteria you may have entered while experimenting).

Enter **MARKETING** in cell D31, and **SALES** in cell D32

Enter an * in each of cells A31 and A32.

Press /DQE to list Marketing and Sales staff in the output range A41..G47.

Enter the following labels in the appropriate cells:

A50: **Marketing and Sales Staff:-**
B51: **Average salary of staff**
B52: **Highest paid staff member**
B53: **Lowest paid staff member**
B54: **Total staff salaries**
B55: **Total number of staff**

Now enter the following formula in cell E51:

@AVG(G$41..G$47)

You should see the figure 17000 in cell E51. This is the average salary of all staff in marketing and sales.

Explanation:

The @AVG is the formula for calculating the average salary of the salaries in the range specified.

The dollar ($) signs are useful in this instance, because you are going to copy the formula to cells E52..E55. Without the dollar signs, the copied formulae would be relative. By copying the formula as it stands in cell E51, you can then edit the bits you want to change, thereby saving typing time.

Move the cursor to cell E51

Press `/C<Enter><↓>.<↓><↓><↓><Enter>`

This copies the formula in cell E51 to cells E52..E55

Now edit <F2> the copied formulae to read:

(The letters to replace AVG with are printed in BOLD below. Note that you can enter the letters in lowercase.)

E52: **@MAX**(G$41..G$47)

E53: **@MIN**(G$41..G$47)

E54: **@SUM**(G$41..G$47)

E55: **@COUNT**(G$41..G$47)

The results of the calculations should appear in the respective cells, i.e.:

E52: 25000; E53: 9000; E54: 119000; E55: 7

Note: instead of entering the range as G$41..G$47 you could first name the range using /RNC (Range, Name, Create), give it the name MARSAL (for example) and then use the name in the formula: @AVG(MARSAL). Use <F2> to edit cell E51 to try it.

You could now add £s and commas to E51..E54 with:

Move to cell E51

Press `/RFC0<Enter><↓><↓><↓><Enter>`

10. Altering the database

Before you end this session, you may like to learn how to move ranges and insert rows and columns.

First, sort the database (A4..G23) into alphabetical order:

Type `/DSP` (Data, Sort, Primary-Key)

Move the cursor to column B, press <Enter>A<Enter>G

Nicholas Nickleby has joined the admin. staff as staff no. 21, and you wish to enter him into the database.

Move the cursor to cell A15

Type `/WIR<Enter>` (Worksheet, Insert, Row)

Mr. Pickwick moves down to make room for Nicholas, and you can now enter Nicholas's details. You can decide details such as his salary.

You will have to format the date (/RFD) and salary(/RFC0).

[If you want to delete a row, use /WDR (Worksheet, Delete, Row).]

Suppose you want to move the range A51..E56 to somewhere else on the worksheet, to leave more room for the output range above it. [Note that inserting Nicholas Nickleby has moved all the rows below him down a row.]

Move the cursor to cell A51

Type `/M` (Move)

Highlight the range A51..E56 and press **<Enter>**

Move the cursor to cell I51 and press **<Enter>**

Suppose now you wish to move column M to the right, to improve the layout if you want to print the statistics out.

Move the cursor to column M (say cell M52)

Type `/WIC<Enter>`

To move it back again, make sure the cursor is in column M

Type `/WDC<Enter>`

If you wish to practise moving, inserting and deleting, arrange the worksheet as you want it, save it with /FS<Enter>R, and then experiment as much as you wish before you quit this session (without saving any mess you have made!).

11. Summary

In this session you should have achieved the objectives set out at the start of this session.

In particular, you should have become acquainted with:

`/DF`	Data, Fill
`@DATE`	@Date(Year,Month,Day)
`/RFD`	Range, Format, Date
`/RFC`	Range, Format, Currency

/DSD	Data, Sort, Data-Range
/DSP	Data, Sort, Primary-key
/DSS	Data, Sort, Secondary-key
/DSG	Data, Sort, Go
/DQI	Data, Query, Input
/DQC	Data, Query, Criterion
/DQO	Data, Query, Output
/DQF	Data, Query, Find
/DQE	Data, Query, Extract
/RNC	Range, Name, Create
@AVG	Average(List) calculates average of values in the list
@MAX	Maximum(List) determines maximum value in the list
@MIN	Minimum(List) determines minimum value in the list
@SUM	Sum(Range) sums a range of cells
@COUNT	Count(List) counts the number of cells in the list

{123} {VP}:-

@DAVG	@DAVG(Input,Offset,Criterion) calculates the average of values in the offset column of the input range which meet the criteria of the criterion range.
@DMAX	@DMAX(Input,Offset,Criterion) indicates the maximum value in the offset column of the input range which meets the criteria of the criterion range.
@DMIN	@DMIN(Input,Offset,Criterion) indicates the minimum value in the offset column of the input range which meets the criteria of the criterion range.

`@DSUM`

@DSUM(Input,Offset,Criterion) adds the values in the offset column of the input range which meet the criteria of the criterion range.

`@DCOUNT`

@DCOUNT(Input,Offset,Criterion) counts the (non-blank) cells in the offset column of the input range which meet the criteria of the criterion range.

12. Activity

Look up the Share Prices page of a suitable newspaper, and choose a block of about 20 shares. Create a database using a choice of the column-headings (e.g. High, Low, Stock, Price, Yield, Index Code) as fields. Sort, find and extract records. Use statistical formulae to calculate any interesting statistics. Print out the database (total input range) and also any statistics you have identified, and any output you have extracted, with suitable title and headings.

13. Objective test

☐ A ☐ B ☑ C ☐ D

1. In a database, the vertical cells contain
   - ☐ A records
   - ☐ B fields
   - ☐ C criteria
   - ☐ D outputs
2. To fill a column with the figures 1,2,3,4,5,6,7,8,9,10, the quickest way is to use the command
   - ☐ A /DF
   - ☐ B /WDF
   - ☐ C /RDF
   - ☐ D /RFD
3. To enter the date 25th December 1991 in a database cell, the following entry shoud be made
   - ☐ A '@DATE(91,12,25)
   - ☐ B @DATE(25,12,91)
   - ☐ C @DATE(91,12,25)
   - ☐ D 25-Dec-91

4. To sort a list of surnames in column B into alphabetical order, where <→B> means "move the cursor to column B", and assuming the Data-range has already been defined, the keypresses are

   - ☐ A /DS<→B>P<Enter>A<Enter>G
   - ☐ B /DSP<→B><Enter>D<Enter>G
   - ☐ C /DS<→B>P<Enter>D<Enter>G
   - ☐ D /DSP<→B><Enter>A<Enter>G

5. When finding or extracting records, the criteria range can be defined by starting with the following keypresses:

   - ☐ A /DC
   - ☐ B /DQI
   - ☐ C /DQC
   - ☐ D /DI

6. The formula to find staff in the salary range £5,000 to £15,000 inclusive could be

   - ☐ A +G4>=5000#AND#+G4<=15000
   - ☐ B +G4<=5000#AND#+G4>=15000
   - ☐ C +G4>=15000#AND#+G4<=5000
   - ☐ D +G4>=£5,000#AND#+G4<=£15,000

7. Before extracting records, it is necessary to have defined one of the following:

   - ☐ A the input range
   - ☐ B the output range
   - ☐ C the criterion range
   - ☐ D all of these

8. To name a range with the name FRED, the keypresses before defining the range are

   - ☐ A /WNCFRED
   - ☐ B /RNCFRED
   - ☐ C /RNC<Enter>FRED
   - ☐ D /UNCLEFRED

9. The keypresses to insert a row in a worksheet, after positioning the cursor over the place where you want the row inserted, are

   - ☐ A /RIR
   - ☐ B /RIC
   - ☐ C /WIR
   - ☐ D /WRC

10. One of the following statements is true; the others are false. The true statement is

   - ☐ A database fields can contain labels and values
   - ☐ B data sorts require the field names in the data-range
   - ☐ C query finds require the field names in the input range
   - ☐ D +E4>=@DATE(40.1.1) is a legitimate formula

SESSION 10
Simple Macros

1. Objectives

At the end of this session, you will be able to:

- ❑ appreciate what a macro is
- ❑ create simple keyboard macros to
    - ❑ add £s and commas to values
    - ❑ return currency format to general format
    - ❑ set a column-width to 20
    - ❑ insert rows
- ❑ create a pro-forma table for interest factors
- ❑ create a macro to form a table of present values (DCF)

and, if you complete the Activity:

- ❑ create macros to form tables for:
    - ❑ present values (annuities)
    - ❑ future values (compound interest)
    - ❑ future values (annuities)

2. Introduction

In this session, you will be introduced to macros. These are, in their simplest form, a means of automating a succession of keystrokes. In their most advanced form they provide a language of immense programming capabilities. We are not concerned in this session with the latter. However, by the end of this session you will be able to create simple macros which will automate your most frequently used keystroke sequences. In addition, to finish this session, you will construct a table from which, with simple macros, you can read future or present values.

Follow the instructions carefully, step by step. In doing so, you will start to learn how to construct macros, and perhaps begin to realise their potential.

3. A simple macro

You will need some material on which to practise your macros.

Retrieve your *ZEDGRAPH* worksheet which you saved in session 7 (paragraphs 8 and 12). This should appear on your monitor as range A1..F13 of figure 10a.

Figure 10a

	A	B	C	D	E	F
1			The Zed Bicycle Company			
2			Budgeted Sales for Next Year			
3						
4	Qtr:-	Spring	Summer	Autumn	Winter	Totals
5	----------	----------	----------	----------	----------	----------
6	Model:-	£	£	£	£	£
7	Alpha	80,000	96,000	115,200	138,240	429,440
8	Beta	90,000	99,000	108,900	119,790	417,690
9	Gamma	80,000	80,000	90,000	90,000	340,000
10	Delta	60,000	54,000	58,600	52,740	225,340
11	----------	----------	----------	----------	----------	----------
12	Totals	310,000	329,000	372,700	400,770	1,412,470
13	==========	==========	==========	==========	==========	==========
14						
15	\c	/wg	invokes the Worksheet Global command			
16		f	invokes the Format command			
17		c	invokes Currency, to add £s and commas to values			
18		0	chooses 0 (zero) to give no decimal places			
19		~	imitates the <Enter> key			
20						
21	\x	/wg	invokes the Worksheet Global command			
22		f	invokes the Format command			
23		g	General, returns Format to original condition			
24						
25	\t	/wcs	invokes Worksheet Column Set-Width			
26		20~	sets column-width at 20			
27						
28	\i	/wi	invokes Worksheet Insert			
29		r	invokes Row			
30		{down}{down}	moves cursor down to insert THREE rows			
31		~	imitates the <Enter> key			

You will see on figure 10a some strange entries below this range. These are macros, and you are about to create the first one.

Move the cursor to cell A15

Type `'\c` Press `<Enter>`

This entry is purely for reference purposes, as will be explained later. Note that it is important to enter it as a label, i.e. with a label prefix ('); otherwise the cell will fill with the letter c. This principle applies to other entries which follow.

Move to cell B15

Type `'/wg` Press `<Enter>`

This is the first line of the macro, and contains the instruction "press the / key, followed by the w key and then the g key".

The objective of this macro is to change all values in the worksheet from plain format (e.g. 80000) to currency format (e.g. £80,000). The full set of keystrokes is /WGFC0<Enter> (Worksheet, Global, Format, Currency, 0 (zero), <Enter>). When you have completed the macro, all you will have to do is press <Alt>+<c> and your macro will perform the keystrokes /WGFC0<Enter> for you.

You could enter the whole macro in cell B15. The disadvantage of this is that with longer and more complex macros, it would be difficult to understand it and detect any errors; also you might forget what it was meant to achieve. It is therefore customary to split the macro down into shorter pieces, with an explanation of each stage to the right of the commands.

Move the cursor to cell C15

Type `invokes the Worksheet Global command`

This is the explanation of the entries in cell B15, and is not part of the macro itself. The macro is listed in column B, starting in cell B15, and continuing down column B as far as is necessary. The macro stops when it encounters a blank line, in this case cell B20, if you refer to figure 10a.

Now enter the rest of the macro itself:

Cell B16: Type **f**

Cell B17: Type **c**

Cell B18: Type '0 (a zero, as a label)

Cell B19: Type ~ (a tilde, which is the squiggly line sign, like an inverted S on its side, on some keyboards placed over the # sign, i.e. <Shift>+<#>). This tilde sign has the same effect as pressing <Enter>.

Now enter the explanations into cells C16..C19:

C16: Type **invokes the Format command**

C17: Type **invokes Currency, to add £s and commas to values**

C18: Type **chooses 0 (zero) to give no decimal places**

C19: Type **imitates the <Enter> key**

The final stage before trying it out is to NAME the macro.

Move the cursor to the first line of the macro itself, i.e. cell B15, and

Press `/RNC` (Range, Name, Create)

Against the prompt *Enter name*

Type `\c` Press `<Enter>`

Press `<Enter>` again to accept the range B15..B15

The macro is now named \C which is the equivalent of <Alt>+<c>

[You can use any letter of the alphabet: total 26.]

Now the try out your macro.

Press `<Alt>+<C>`

and all the values in the worksheet should change to the currency format, unless you have made a mistake somewhere.

4. Three more macros

If you refer to figure 10a, you will see three more macros, in the same format as the one you have just created.

Using the same principles for entry as for the \c macro, enter these into your worksheet.

Here are some notes to help you:

Do not forget to enter all cells as labels; this is very easy to forget, so go slowly!

Do not forget to NAME (/RNC) the macro in the top cell in column B with the name which is entered in column A to help you remember.

You must leave a blank row between each macro; otherwise each macro will execute in turn once you activate the top one.

Warning: Save your worksheet frequently to disk, particularly before trying out a new macro. If the macro misbehaves, you could lose a lot of your work, but if you have saved to disk, you can always retrieve the most recently saved version of your worksheet. You have been warned.

\x This macro changes all the values in the worksheet back to the original plain format, e.g. £80,000 back to 80000.

\t This macro sets the column-width at 20 for the column on which the cursor is placed when the macro is invoked. This macro is useful for widening column A to enter labels, e.g. for a Profit & Loss Account.

\i Note the entry {down}{down} in cell B30. The keyword {down} is a special key representing the cursor key movement of <↓> or down-arrow. [Other examples are {up} {right} {left} {home} {end} {pgup} {pgdn}. Note the curly-brackets which are essential.]

{AEA} uses {dn} for {down} {rt} for {right} {lt} for {left}

See manual for full details.

Before trying out this macro, move the cell pointer to row 11 (over the dotted lines). Press <Alt>+<i>, and three blank rows appear for rows 11, 12 and 13; useful if you want to enter three more models of bicycle (? the Epsilon, Zeta and Eta).

These are four simple macros to introduce you to the idea. If you want to create some more for successive keystrokes which you use often, you can construct them using the principles which you have learned so far. You will need to refer to the manual for your particular program to advance further.

5. Moving the macros

So far you have placed the macros below the worksheet. This was done so that you could see the macros and worksheet easily. However, this was not a very good idea, because if you make changes to the worksheet itself, these changes (e.g. inserting columns and rows) could upset the macros. So it is customary to place the macros well away from the likely total working area. Try this:

Move the macros to cell GG999:

Move the cursor to cell A15

Press `/M` (Move)

Highlight the range A15..C31. Press <Enter>

Type `GG999` Press `<Enter>`

To find the macros, press **<End> <Home>**

To return to the worksheet table, press **<Home>**

The macros should still work. Try them!

6. Using the macros again

If you think you may want to use the four macros you have just created in a new worksheet, try this:

`/FS<Enter>R` (File, Save, Replace)

This saves *ZEDGRAPH* in its current form.

Press `<Home>`

Press `/RE` (Range, Erase)

Highlight the range A1..F13 Press <Enter>

Press `<F5>GG999` (Goto cell GG999)

Press `/FS`

Type `MACROS` Press `<Enter>`

This creates a new file called *MACROS*.

The next time you want to create a new worksheet containing your macros, retrieve *MACROS* and you will start at cell GG999, which reminds you that your macros are there. [You can at this stage erase any that you will not want to use.] Then press <Home> to get to the blank cells at the top left-hand corner of the spreadsheet. When you save your new worksheet (which should be soon!), save it with a new filename. You can then use your *MACROS* file as often as you need it.

In fact, you are now in the worksheet called *MACROS*.

To get back to your *ZEDGRAPH* worksheet,

Press `/FR` (File, Retrieve)

Highlight *ZEDGRAPH* and press **<Enter>**

7. A table of present value factors: Introduction

Now for a rather more ambitious project. You are going to create a *Present Value* or *Discounted Cash Flow (DCF)* table. If you want to see what one looks like, you can sometimes find one at the end of finance or management accounting text-books which cover the subject of Project Appraisal or Capital Budgeting. For example, AFBIS has one in the Appendix, where it is called *TABLE 1 - PRESENT VALUE FACTORS*. You do not need to understand the subject to construct this table; simply follow the instructions. However, if you want to have some idea of how the table can be used in business, you can find an explanation in AFBIS, section on *Project Appraisal*, or in any other appropriate text-book or manual.

The table you will construct will calculate present values automatically, by pressing <Alt>+<A>. If you want to expand the table in size, to make it more comprehensive, and to make it do other clever things, such as calculate future values and annuities, then you are referred to ACTIVITY paragraph 11 towards the end of this session. Guidance is given there on how to do this.

8. Creating the PV table

Start with a blank spreadsheet; do NOT start with the *MACROS* spreadsheet which you created in paragraph 6 because the macro names could conflict with those you will make here.

Make the following entries:- [You can check them against Figure 10b]

Cell A1:	**TABLE OF INTEREST FACTORS**
Cell A2:	\- and copy A2 to B2..H2
Cell A3:	**Press <Alt>+A for Present Values (DCF)**
Cell A7:	\- and copy A7 to B7..H7
Cell A9	\- and copy A9 to B9..H9

Cell A10: **PERIODS:**

Cell A11: **0** (a zero)

Cell A12: **+A11+1**

[Note: Rows 4, 5 and 6 are left blank, so that additional macro instructions can be entered here if you carry out the activity in paragraph 11 below. Row 8 is left blank so that each macro, when activated, can enter a description here.]

Move the cursor to cell A12

Press `/C<Enter><↓>. (a full stop)`

Move the cursor to cell A21, and press **<Enter>**

This copies the formula in cell A12 to cells A13..A21, and produces period numbers 0..10 in cells A11..A21.

Next you need interest rates in row 10.

You could, of course, enter all the rates from 1% to say 50% in stages of 1%, but this would create a very large worksheet which, at this stage in your learning process, would be rather inappropriate. Also large spreadsheets take longer to recalculate, unless you have a fast computer or maths co-processor chip. So for now, you will start at 5% and progress in 5% stages to 35%.

Enter in cell B10: **.05**

Enter in cell C10: **+B10+.05**

Copy cell C10 to cells D10..H10

[You should know how to do this by now!]

Move to cell B10

Press `/RFP0<Enter>` (Range, Format, Percent, zero)

Highlight the range B10..H10, and press **<Enter>**

This changes 0.05 to 5% in cell B10, and so on.

Next, to enter the macro itself. Make the following entries, being very careful to get them exactly right.

Cell A25: **'\a**

This is for reference purposes only, and gives the name of the macro. Don't forget the ' to make it a label.

Cell B25: **{goto}a8~Present Values of £1 at the end of n periods~**

This tells the cursor to go to cell A8, and enter the label which then appears in cell A8 to tell you what the table shows.

Cell B26: **{goto}b11~1/((1+b$10)^$a11)~**

This tells the cursor to go to cell B11, and enter the present value formula, which is the reciprocal of the compound interest formula, i.e 1 divided by (=reciprocal): 1 plus the interest rate (which is the 5% in cell B10), to the power of the number of years (which is the 0 in cell A11). The caret sign (^) is usually <Shift>+<6> on the keyboard, and stands for "to the power of". The $ signs are purely to keep the following numbers absolute rather than relative when copying the formula into other cells, which the next line of the macro performs. Don't forget the tildes (~) after b11 and at the end of the formula. Another easy thing to forget is that all brackets must be complete pairs e.g. (( )); there are two pairs in the formula.

[An explanation of the formula is given in AFBIS, chapter entitled *Principles of Discounted Cash Flow.*]

Cell B27: **'/cb11~b12.b21~**

Don't forget the ' to start with; otherwise your commands will be obeyed! And don't forget the tildes.

This tells the program to copy cell B11 to cells B12..B21

Cell B28: **'/cb11.b21~c11.h21~**

This tells the program to copy cells B11..B21 to cells C11..H21.

Finally, NAME the macro.

With the cursor on cell B25,

Press `/RNC\a<Enter><Enter>`

9. Testing the PV table

Now for the moment of truth.

Press `<Alt>+A`

How long the macro takes to work depends on the speed of your computer. Be patient. Row 8 should show the title, and cells B11..H21 should fill with figures. If this does not happen, or the figures look wrong, check that your entries in B25..B28 are correct. [When the author tried it, he had forgotten to enter one of the tildes.]

The figures in the table look rather untidy; they are shown to six decimal places (if the global column-width is set at 9). To make the figures show to three decimal places:

Press `/WGFF3<Enter>` (Worksheet, Global, Format, Fixed, 3)

Column A (Periods) now looks untidy, showing the periods (years) to three decimal places; so

Move the cursor to cell A11

Press `/RFF0<Enter>` (Range, Format, Fixed, 0)

Move the cursor to cell A21, and press <Enter>

Note that the percentage figures in row 10 were not affected by the Global Format command, since Range commands take precedence over global commands.

Your worksheet should look like Figure 10b.

Figure 10b

	A	B	C	D	E	F	G	H
1	TABLE OF INTEREST FACTORS							
2	--							
3	Press <Alt>+A for Present Values (DCF)							
4								
5								
6								
7	--							
8	Present Values of £1 at the end of n periods							
9	--							
10	PERIODS:	5%	10%	15%	20%	25%	30%	35%
11	0	1.000	1.000	1.000	1.000	1.000	1.000	1.000
12	1	.952	.909	.870	.833	.800	.769	.741
13	2	.907	.826	.756	.694	.640	.592	.549
14	3	.864	.751	.658	.579	.512	.455	.406
15	4	.823	.683	.572	.482	.410	.350	.301
16	5	.784	.621	.497	.402	.328	.269	.223
17	6	.746	.564	.432	.335	.262	.207	.165
18	7	.711	.513	.376	.279	.210	.159	.122
19	8	.677	.467	.327	.233	.168	.123	.091
20	9	.645	.424	.284	.194	.134	.094	.067
21	10	.614	.386	.247	.162	.107	.073	.050
22								
23								
24								
25	\a	{goto}a8~Present Values of £1 at the end of n periods~						
26		{goto}b11~1/((1+b$10)^$a11						
27		/cb11~b12.b21~						
28		/cb11.b21~c11.h21~						

Save your present worksheet with the name *INTABS*, i.e a mnemonic for INTerest TABles.

If you want to continue now, or at some later time, with the activity in paragraph 11 below, please do!

Also you may want to get further practice with the three PRACTICE SESSIONS (11 - 13) which follow this session, before proceeding to Part B of this book (Sessions 14 to 34) where you can apply the skills acquired so far in creating models to solve problems in various areas of financial accounting, management accounting and financial management. The author hopes you will enjoy them and gain confidence and expertise as you work through them.

10. Summary

In this session you should have achieved the objectives set out at the start of this session.

In particular, you should have become acquainted with:

- planning a macro
- positioning a macro (out of the way)
- entering a macro:

  N.B. all labels; one column only; no blank rows

- annotating a macro
- naming a macro (top cell of macro) /RNC\x

`~`	(a tilde) = <Enter>
`^`	(a caret) = to the power of
`{down}`	<↓> moves the cursor down a row
`{up}`	<↑> moves the cursor up a row
`{right}`	<→> moves the cursor one column right
`{left}`	<←> moves the cursor one column left
`{goto}`	<F5> GoTo

11. Activity

Recover your file INTABS which you saved at the end of paragraph 9.

Create three more macros for this worksheet, as follows:

Copy cells A25..B28 to A30..B33, then to A35..B39, and again to A40..B43. Since the four macros contain formulae with similar elements, you can edit each block of macro cells, rather than create them from scratch.

MACRO B

Cell A30: Edit the name to show **\b**

Title: **Present Values of £1 per period for n periods**

[Edit cell B30 to show this revised title.]

Formula: **@PV(1,b$10,$a11)**

[Edit cell B31 to show this revised formula.]

Note: the formula @PV(payments,interest,term) determines the present value of an investment.

The entries in the last two lines of the macro (B32 and B33) stay the same as for macro A. The same applies to macros C and D.

Cell A4 could contain:

Press <Alt>+B for Present Values (Annuities)

[Tip for macros C and D: The copy command can be used to copy formulae from one macro to another before editing. Look for similar formulae.]

MACRO C

Cell A5:	**Press <Alt>+C for Future Values**
Title:	**Future Values of £1 at the end of n periods**
Formula:	**((1+b$10)^$a11)**

MACRO D

Cell A6:	**Press <Alt>+D for Future Values (Annuities)**
Title:	**Future Values of £1 per period for n periods**
Formula:	**@fv(1,b$10,$a11)**

[Tip: Don't forget to NAME the macros.]

Now try out all four of your macros. Keep your fingers crossed!

If your macros do not work, check all your typing meticulously. In addition it may help if you annotate each row of the macro, in a column to the right (e.g. column I, which would not over-write the macros extending from column B). You were recommended to do so (and shown how) in the first part of this session, in the five macros for ZED Bicycle Company. The discipline of doing so usually identifies any error in the macro, such as a missing tilde, comma, bracket, $ sign.

If you feel really energetic, you could move the macros to a safe place on the spreadsheet, and expand the worksheet to show all percentages in stages of 1% from 1% to 50%, and increase the period (year) coverage from 10 to 25 years. Recalculation time when you activate the macro will depend on the speed of your computer.

12. Objective test ☐ A ☐ B ☑ C ☐ D

1. You have planned a macro which will carry out the procedure for naming any macro up to the stage of actually typing in the name, i.e. /RNC. You have decide to give this macro the unique name of N. As a memorandum, you type the name of this macro into cell A20, pressing

   ☐ A '\n

   ☐ B \'n

   ☐ C '/n

   ☐ D /'n

2. Next, you move to cell B20 to type in the macro. You press

☐ A /rnc

☐ B '/rnc

☐ C '/rnc~

☐ D '\rnc~

3. To test the macro at this stage, you press

☐ A <Alt>+N

☐ B <Ctrl>+N

☐ C <Alt> N

☐ D none of these

4. To name the macro you have created in Q2, (with the cursor on cell B20) you press

☐ A /rnc\n<Enter><Enter>

☐ B '/rnc\n<Enter>

☐ C '\rnc/n<Enter><Enter>

☐ D /rnc\n<Enter>

5. You wish to annotate this macro with "Invokes Range, Name, Create". A good place to enter this is in cell

☐ A B21

☐ B B19

☐ C C20

☐ D A20

6. The sign for <Enter> in a macro is

☐ A ~ (a tilde)

☐ B ^ (a caret)

☐ C {~} (a tilde in curly braces)

☐ D {^} (a caret in curly braces)

7. Only one of the following statements is true. It is

- [ ] A {Curly Braces} are optional for macro keywords
- [ ] B a ' must be typed before {curly braces} to make it a label
- [ ] C macros can be split over columns as an alternative to rows
- [ ] D {GOTO} is the macro keyword for <F5>

8. Only one of the following formulae is correct

- [ ] A 1/(1+B$10)^$A11)~
- [ ] B 1/((1+B$10)$^A11)~
- [ ] C 1/((1+B$10)^$A11~
- [ ] D 1/((1+B$10)^$A11)~

9. The figures for periods in column A of a table should be 1, 2, 3 etc. On the worksheet, due to having set a global format, they appear as 1.000, 2.000, 3.000 etc. To correct this for the range, the intitial keystrokes to correct this are

- [ ] A /RFC0<Enter>[range]<Enter>
- [ ] B /RFF.<Enter>[range]<Enter>
- [ ] C /RFF0<Enter>[range]<Enter>
- [ ] D none of these

10. You have planned and created a long and marvellous macro, but, when you try it out, it will not work properly. You have just spent all evening unsuccessfully trying to debug it. The best thing to do is to

- [ ] A try putting tildes at the end of every line
- [ ] B ring up a friend who knows about these things
- [ ] C import the file to a wordprocessor and use the spellchecker
- [ ] D go to bed, and sleep on it.

PRACTICE SESSION 11

Cost Behaviour

1. Introduction

In this session, and in practice sessions 12 and 13, you have an opportunity to attempt to solve some problems, using the skills you have acquired during the previous sessions. The problems are concerned with management accounting.

The problems can, of course, be solved with pencil and paper. However, they can be solved more efficiently on a spreadsheet. The formulae needed are fairly simple. If you get stuck, you can refer to the solution in paragraph 3, which refers you to two figures: the first showing the design of the worksheet, and the second the same worksheet printed out with the formulae used in the corresponding cells.

A suggested approach is:

- ❑ study the problem carefully
- ❑ revise the theory if you cannot recollect it properly
- ❑ plan the layout of the worksheet required for the solution
- ❑ enter the headings on the worksheet as labels
- ❑ fill in the values from the data
- ❑ adjust any column widths to make the worksheet more comfortable to work with
- ❑ enter the first formula required
- ❑ check the results of the formula against the correct figure (use a calculator if necessary)
- ❑ copy the formula to any cells which will benefit
- ❑ test-check the results of the copied formulae against the correct figures
- ❑ if necessary, correct the original formula (e.g. for $ signs)
- ❑ copy the formula again to the appropriate cells
- ❑ repeat the checking, correcting and copying procedure as often as necesary to achieve a satisfactory result
- ❑ enter the next formula, and repeat the previous procedure
- ❑ continue until you are satisfied that the results are satisfactory
- ❑ tidy up the worksheet with lines and general layout, using move and insert commands as necessary

- ❑ compare your results with the suggested solution in figures lla and llb
- ❑ congratulate yourself because yours is better.

2. The problem

A. AUCKLAND

Listed below are total costs at two different levels of activity for the business of Audrey Auckland. Audrey wants to know, for each item of cost, how much is variable and how much is fixed.

Prepare a table for her, showing the costs as shown in the data, and:

- variable costs per unit
- total variable costs at the lower activity level
- total variable costs at the higher activity level
- total fixed costs

Production/sales levels (units)	2,000	5,000
	Total costs	
	£	£
Supervision	20,000	20,000
Direct materials	100,000	250,000
Storage & handling	10,000	17,500
Maintenance	30,000	60,000
Direct wages	90,000	225,000
Eiectricity	10,000	19,000
Rent	26,000	26,000
Insurance	8,000	8,000
Salesmen's salaries (incl. commission)	50,000	65,000
Packaging	27,500	68,750
Staff salaries	80,000	80,000
Distribution	30,000	52,500
Rates	20,000	20,000
Depreciation	40,000	40,000

3. The solution

Reference should be made to figures lla and llb.

An example of the calculations is for Electricity:

	Production/sales units	Cost £s
	5,000	19,000
less:	2,000	10,000
= change:	3,000	9,000

$$\frac{\text{Change in cost (£s)}}{\text{Change in units}} = \frac{£9,000}{3,000} = £3.00 \text{ per unit}$$

If you refer to the figures lla and llb, you will see that the formula in cell D16 reflects this:

(C16-B16)/ ($C$4-$B$4)

Costs which change with levels of activity are variable costs; therefore £3.00 is the variable cost per unit.

The total variable costs in cells E16 and F16 are obtained by multiplying the variable cost per unit (£3 in cell D16) by the number of units (2,000 in cell B4 and 5,000 in cell C4).

The total fixed costs cell G16 are obtained by subtracting the total variable costs in cell F16 from the total costs in cell C16. (Alternatively, the total fixed costs cell G16 could be obtained by subtracting the total variable costs in cell E16 from the total costs in cell B16.)

Comment: This can be a useful table for budgeting fixed costs.

For example, you could take the monthly profit and loss account expenditure figures for the past year, and find two months which had low and high levels of production/sales.

The figures could be entered into the table, and the total of column G would give an indication of the total fixed costs for a typical month. Multiply by 12 and adjust for anticipated inflation and any known changes in fixed costs to arrive at a budgeted figure for fixed costs for next year.

[This problem is an adaptation of an example from the chapter entitled *Cost Behaviour* in AFBIS, to which reference could be made for a more detailed explanation of the principles of cost behaviour.]

Figure 11a

	A	B	C	D	E	F	G
1	A. AUCKLAND						
2	Analysis of Fixed and Variable Costs						
3	----------						
4	Production/Sales (units):-	2,000	5,000	1	2,000	5,000	Any
5	----------						
6				Per Unit	Total	Total	Total
7		Total	Total	Variable	Var.	Var.	Fixed
8		Costs	Costs	Costs	Costs	Costs	Costs
9	Expenditure:	£	£	£	£	£	£
10	----------						
11	Supervision	20,000	20,000	.00	0	0	20,000
12	Direct Materials	100,000	250,000	50.00	100,000	250,000	0
13	Storage & Handling	10,000	17,500	2.50	5,000	12,500	5,000
14	Maintenance	30,000	60,000	10.00	20,000	50,000	10,000
15	Direct Wages	90,000	225,000	45.00	90,000	225,000	0
16	Electricity	10,000	19,000	3.00	6,000	15,000	4,000
17	Rent	26,000	26,000	.00	0	0	26,000
18	Insurance	8,000	8,000	.00	0	0	8,000
19	Salesmen's Sals/Commission	50,000	65,000	5.00	10,000	25,000	40,000
20	Packaging	27,500	68,750	13.75	27,500	68,750	0
21	Staff Salaries	80,000	80,000	.00	0	0	80,000
22	Distribution	30,000	52,500	7.50	15,000	37,500	15,000
23	Rates	20,000	20,000	.00	0	0	20,000
24	Depreciation	40,000	40,000	.00	0	0	40,000
25	==========						

Figure 11b

	A	B	C	D	E	F	G
1	A. Auckland						
2	Analysis of Fixed and Variable Cost						
3	----------						
4	Production/Sales (units)	2,000	5,000	1	+B4	+C4	Any
5	----------						
6				Per Unit	Total	Total	Total
7		Total	Total	Variable	Var.	Var.	Fixed
8		Costs	Costs	Costs	Costs	Costs	Costs
9	Expenditure:	£	£	£	£	£	£
10	----------						
11	Supervision	20,000	20,000	(C11-B11)/($C$4-$B$4)	+$B$4*D11	+$C$4*D11	+C11-F11
12	Direct Materials	100,000	250,000	(C12-B12)/($C$4-$B$4)	+$B$4*D12	+$C$4*D12	+C12-F12
13	Storage & Handling	10,000	17,500	(C13-B13)/($C$4-$B$4)	+$B$4*D13	+$C$4*D13	+C13-F13
14	Maintenance	30,000	60,000	(C14-B14)/($C$4-$B$4)	+$B$4*D14	+$C$4*D14	+C14-F14
15	Direct Wages	90,000	225,000	(C15-B15)/($C$4-$B$4)	+$B$4*D15	+$C$4*D15	+C15-F15
16	Electricity	10,000	19,000	(C16-B16)/($C$4-$B$4)	+$B$4*D16	+$C$4*D16	+C16-F16
17	Rent	26,000	26,000	(C17-B17)/($C$4-$B$4)	+$B$4*D17	+$C$4*D17	+C17-F17
18	Insurance	8,000	8,000	(C18-B18)/($C$4-$B$4)	+$B$4*D18	+$C$4*D18	+C18-F18
19	Salesmen's Sals/Commissi	50,000	65,000	(C19-B19)/($C$4-$B$4)	+$B$4*D19	+$C$4*D19	+C19-F19
20	Packaging	27,500	68,750	(C20-B20)/($C$4-$B$4)	+$B$4*D20	+$C$4*D20	+C20-F20
21	Staff Salaries	80,000	80,000	(C21-B21)/($C$4-$B$4)	+$B$4*D21	+$C$4*D21	+C21-F21
22	Distribution	30,000	52,500	(C22-B22)/($C$4-$B$4)	+$B$4*D22	+$C$4*D22	+C22-F22
23	Rates	20,000	20,000	(C23-B23)/($C$4-$B$4)	+$B$4*D23	+$C$4*D23	+C23-F23
24	Depreciation	40,000	40,000	(C24-B24)/($C$4-$B$4)	+$B$4*D24	+$C$4*D24	+C24-F24
25	==========						

PRACTICE SESSION 12
Overhead Cost Allocation and Apportionment

1. Introduction

In this session you will have an opportunity to solve another problem, using a spreadsheet as a vehicle for entering the data and displaying the solution.

If you have not already attempted practice session 11, please read its introduction before attempting this session. In any case, you may benefit from reading the suggested approach in that introduction again.

2. The problem

L. LORD

Lesley Lord operates a small business manufacturing cricket bats and tennis raquets. There are three production cost centres, namely machining, assembly and finishing departments. The overheads budget for next year is set out below, together with the cost centre details, and Lesley asks you for the annual cost of running each production cost centre.

Annual Overheads Budget:

	£
Rent	20,000
Rates	40,000
Consumables	10,000
Power	4,750
Cleaning	6,000
Light and heat	2,120
Maintenance	10,200
Depreciation – Machinery	8,000
Depreciation – Building	15,900
Indirect wages	19,600
Canteen	23,800
Insurance – Machinery	4,250
Insurance – Building	5,300
Supervision	42,000
Total	211,920

Cost Centre Details:

	Machining	Assembly	Finishing	Total
Area (square metres)	5,000	2,000	3,000	10,000
Volume (cubic metres)	25,000	10,000	18,000	53,000
Capital values (£000s)	70,000	10,000	5,000	85,000
Personnel (number)	10	20	5	35
Machinery (hp/hours)	8,750	350	400	9,500
Maintenance (£s)	9,500	500	200	10,200
Dep'n of machinery (£s)	6,500	1,000	500	8,000
Consumables (£s)	8,000	1,000	1,000	10,000

3. Suggested solution

Reference should be made to figures 12a and 12b.

The total overhead cost of each cost centre may be obtained by constructing an Overhead Cost Analysis Statement, sometimes referred to as an Overhead Cost Distribution Summary. This statement allocates costs to each cost centre if they are cost centre direct costs. If they are cost centre indirect costs, then they are apportioned or shared between the cost centres using a suitable basis of apportionment.

ALLOCATION

The items which have been marked (allocation) in figures 12a and 12b have been allocated to cost centres, since the overhead is directly attributable to those cost centres without apportionment being necessary.

Example: Consumables – the entry in cell D33 is +D17 which means that the figure of £8,000 is taken straight from cell D17 in the Data Entry Block.

APPORTIONMENT

All other items have been charged proportionately to cost centres using a suitable basis of apportionment.

Example: Rent has been apportioned using floor area occupied as a basis. Thus:

$$\text{Total cost to be apportioned x } \frac{\text{Cost centre's share of basis}}{\text{Total apportionment basis}}$$

$$\text{Machining} = \text{£}20{,}000 \text{ x } \frac{5{,}000 \text{ square metres}}{10{,}000 \text{ square metres}}$$

Figure 12a

	A	B	C	D	E	F	G
1	L. LORD						
2	Overhead Cost Allocation and Apportionement						
3	==========	==========	==========	==========	==========	==========	==========
4	DATA ENTRY BLOCK						
5	----------	----------	----------	----------	----------	----------	----------
6	ANNUAL OVERHEADS BUDG	£	COST CENTRE DETAILS:				
7	Rent	20,000	----------	----------	----------	----------	----------
8	Rates	40,000	Description	Mach'g	Ass'y	Fin'g	Total
9	Consumables	10,000	----------	----------	----------	----------	----------
10	Power	4,750	Area sq.m	5,000	2,000	3,000	10,000
11	Cleaning	6,000	Volume cu.m	25,000	10,000	18,000	53,000
12	Light and heat	2,120	Capital vals £k	70,000	10,000	5,000	85,000
13	Maintenance	10,200	Personnel no.	10	20	5	35
14	Depreciation - Machin	8,000	Mach'y hp/hrs	8,750	350	400	9,500
15	Depreciation - Buildi	15,900	Maintenance £s	9,500	500	200	10,200
16	Indirect wages	19,600	Dep'n mach'y £s	6,500	1,000	500	8,000
17	Canteen	23,800	Consumables £s	8,000	1,000	1,000	10,000
18	Insurance - Machienry	4,250					
19	Insurance - Building	5,300					
20	Supervision	42,000					
21		----------					
22		211,920					
23		==========					
24	==========	==========	==========	==========	==========	==========	==========
25	L. LORD: OVERHEAD COST ANALYSIS STATEMENT						
26	----------	----------	----------	----------	----------	----------	----------
27			Basis of		COST CENTRES		
28	ANNUAL OVERHEADS BUDGET:		apportionment	Mach'g	Ass'y	Fin'g	Total
29	----------	----------	----------	----------	----------	----------	----------
30		£		£	£	£	£
31	Rent	20,000	area	10,000	4,000	6,000	20,000
32	Rates	40,000	area	20,000	8,000	12,000	40,000
33	Consumables	10,000	(allocation)	8,000	1,000	1,000	10,000
34	Power	4,750	hp/hrs	4,375	175	200	4,750
35	Cleaning	6,000	area	3,000	1,200	1,800	6,000
36	Light and heat	2,120	volume	1,000	400	720	2,120
37	Maintenance	10,200	(allocation)	9,500	500	200	10,200
38	Depreciation - Machin	8,000	(allocation)	6,500	1,000	500	8,000
39	Depreciation - Buildi	15,900	volume	7,500	3,000	5,400	15,900
40	Indirect wages	19,600	personnel	5,600	11,200	2,800	19,600
41	Canteen	23,800	personnel	6,800	13,600	3,400	23,800
42	Insurance - Machinery	4,250	cap. values	3,500	500	250	4,250
43	Insurance - Building	5,300	volume	2,500	1,000	1,800	5,300
44	Supervision	42,000	personnel	12,000	24,000	6,000	42,000
45		----------		----------	----------	----------	----------
46		211,920		100,275	69,575	42,070	211,920
47		==========		==========	==========	==========	==========

Figure 12b

	A	B	C	D	E	F	G
1	L. LORD						
2	Overhead Cost Allocation and Apportionement						
3	==========	==========	==========	==========	==========	==========	==========
4	DATA ENTRY BLOCK						
5	----------	----------	----------	----------	----------	----------	----------
6	ANNUAL OVERHEADS BUDGET:	£	COST CENTRE DETAILS:				
7	Rent	20,000	----------	----------	----------	----------	----------
8	Rates	40,000	Description	Mach'g	Ass'y	Fin'g	Total
9	Consumables	10,000	----------	----------	----------	----------	----------
10	Power	4,750	Area sq.m	5,000	2,000	3,000	@SUM(D10..F10)
11	Cleaning	6,000	Volume cu.m	25,000	10,000	18,000	@SUM(D11..F11)
12	Light and heat	2,120	Capital vals £k	70,000	10,000	5,000	@SUM(D12..F12)
13	Maintenance	10,200	Personnel no.	10	20	5	@SUM(D13..F13)
14	Depreciation - Machinery	8,000	Mach'y hp/hrs	8,750	350	400	@SUM(D14..F14)
15	Depreciation - Building	15,900	Maintenance £s	9,500	500	200	@SUM(D15..F15)
16	Indirect wages	19,600	Dep'n mach'y £s	6,500	1,000	500	@SUM(D16..F16)
17	Canteen	23,800	Consumables £s	8,000	1,000	1,000	@SUM(D17..F17)
18	Insurance - Machienry	4,250					
19	Insurance - Building	5,300					
20	Supervision	42,000					
21		---------------					
22		@SUM(B7..B20)					
23		===============					
24	==========	==========	==========	==========	==========	==========	==========
25	L. LORD: OVERHEAD COST ANALYSIS STATEMENT						
26	----------	----------	----------	----------	----------	----------	----------
27			Basis of		COST CENTRES		
28	ANNUAL OVERHEADS BUDGET:		apportionment	Mach'g	Ass'y	Fin'g	Total
29	----------	----------	----------	----------	----------	----------	----------
30		£		£	£	£	£
31	Rent	+B7	area	+B31/G10*D10	+B31/G10*E10	+B31/G10*F10	@SUM(D31..F31)
32	Rates	+B8	area	+B32/G10*D10	+B32/G10*E10	+B32/G10*F10	@SUM(D32..F32)
33	Consumables	+B9	(allocation)	+D17	+E17	+F17	@SUM(D33..F33)
34	Power	+B10	hp/hrs	+B34/G14*D14	+B34/G14*E14	+B34/G14*F14	@SUM(D34..F34)
35	Cleaning	+B11	area	+B35/G10*D10	+B35/G10*E10	+B35/G10*F10	@SUM(D35..F35)
36	Light and heat	+B12	volume	+B36/G11*D11	+B36/G11*E11	+B36/G11*F11	@SUM(D36..F36)
37	Maintenance	+B13	(allocation)	+D15	+E15	+F15	@SUM(D37..F37)
38	Depreciation - Machinery	+B14	(allocation)	+D16	+E16	+F16	@SUM(D38..F38)
39	Depreciation - Building	+B15	volume	+B39/G11*D11	+B39/G11*E11	+B39/G11*F11	@SUM(D39..F39)
40	Indirect wages	+B16	personnel	+B40/G13*D13	+B40/G13*E13	+B40/G13*F13	@SUM(D40..F40)
41	Canteen	+B17	personnel	+B41/G13*D13	+B41/G13*E13	+B41/G13*F13	@SUM(D41..F41)
42	Insurance - Machinery	+B18	cap. values	+B42/G12*D12	+B42/G12*E12	+B42/G12*F12	@SUM(D42..F42)
43	Insurance - Building	+B19	volume	+B43/G11*D11	+B43/G11*E11	+B43/G11*F11	@SUM(D43..F43)
44	Supervision	+B20	personnel	+B44/G13*D13	+B44/G13*E13	+B44/G13*F13	@SUM(D44..F44)
45		---------------		----------	----------	----------	----------
46		@SUM(B31..B44)		@SUM(D31..D44)	@SUM(E31..E44)	@SUM(F31..F44)	@SUM(G31..G44
47		===============		==========	==========	==========	==========

Therefore the formula required in cell D31 reflects this:

$$B31 \times \frac{D10}{G10}$$

The formula has been entered in cell D31 as: **B31/G10*D10**

DESIGN OF THE WORKSHEET

It is probably a good idea to keep the main calculation area (A25..G47) away from the data entry area. The ranges B7..B20 and D10..F17 are the only areas where entries of data should be made. These ranges should be unprotected; the remainder of the worksheet should be protected to prevent inadvertant deletion of labels and formulae. Alteration of any figure in the unprotected ranges will result in the Overhead Cost Analysis Statement being recalculated; this is very useful if Lesley Lord decides to amend any of the original budgeted data figures.

ALTERNATIVES

Alternative appropriate bases of apportionment may be used which will give different results from those obtained in figures 12a and 12b. For example, building volume may be just as appropriate for the apportionment of rent, rates and cleaning, whereas building area could have been used for light and heat, building depreciation and building insurance.

The important aspect is to find and use a basis of apportionment most appropriate for the cost being apportioned.

[This problem is an adaptation of an example from the chapter entitled *Cost Allocation and Apportionment* in AFBIS, to which reference could be made for a more detailed explanation of the principles of cost allocation and apportionment.]

PRACTICE SESSION 13
Cost-Volume-Profit Analysis

1. Introduction

This final session is designed to provide you with some additional practice in constructing a spreadsheet to solve a management accounting problem using simple formulae.

If you have not already attempted practice session 11, please read its introduction before attempting this session. In any case, you may benefit from reading the suggested approach in that introduction again.

2. The problem

THE STIRLING BICYCLE COMPANY

The Stirling Bicycle Company are preparing their budgets for next year. They plan to produce and sell four models, ranging from the 'Aberdeen' racing bicycle to the 'Dundee' popular tourer.

(1) The Sales Director provides the following:

Model	Estimated sales demand Number of bicycles	Wholesale selling price per bicycle
Aberdeen	200	£400
Berwick	300	£300
Cairngorm	400	£200
Dundee	600	£100

(2) The budgeted variable costs of production are as follows:

Model	Parts and materials per bicycle	Labour cost per bicycle
Aberdeen	£190	£60
Berwick	£140	£40
Cairngorm	£ 90	£30
Dundee	£ 40	£20

(3) Fixed costs are budgeted at £100,000 for the year.

(4) It is expected that all models produced will be sold immediately.

Required:

As Assistant to the Managing Director, you are asked to prepare a Marginal Costing Statement for him, showing the contribution from each model, and the total budgeted profit for next year.

Figure 13a

	A	B	C	D	E	F	G	H
1	THE STIRLING BICYCLE COMPANY							
2	Marginal Costing Statement showing:							
3	contribution from each model & total budgeted profit for next year							
4	==========	==========	==========	==========	==========	==========	==========	==========
5	Model	Sales	Variable costs per unit			Contrib'n	Prod/Sales	Total
6		price	----------	----------	----------	per unit	(units)	Contrib'r
7			Material	Labour	Total			
8	----------	----------	----------	----------	----------	----------	----------	----------
9		£	£	£	£	£		£
10								
11	Aberdeen	400	190	60	250	150	200	30,000
12	Berwick	300	140	40	180	120	300	36,000
13	Cairngorm	200	90	30	120	80	400	32,000
14	Dundee	100	40	20	60	40	600	24,000
15								---------
16					Total Contributior			122,000
17					less Fixed Costs:			100,000
18								---------
19					Budgeted Profit:			22,000
20								=========
21	==========	==========	==========	==========	==========	==========	==========	==========

Figure 13b

	A	B	C	D	E	F	G	H
1	THE STIRLING BICYCLE COMPANY							
2	Marginal Costing Statement showing:							
3	contribution from each model & total budgeted profit for next year							
4	==========	==========	==========	==========	==========	==========	==========	==========
5	Model	Sales	Variable costs per unit			Contrib'n	Prod/Sales	Total
6		price	----------	----------	----------	per unit	(units)	Contrib'n
7			Material	Labour	Total			
8	----------	----------	----------	----------	----------	----------	----------	----------
9		£	£	£	£	£		£
10								
11	Aberdeen	400	190	60	+C11+D11	+B11-E11	200	+F11*G11
12	Berwick	300	140	40	+C12+D12	+B12-E12	300	+F12*G12
13	Cairngorm	200	90	30	+C13+D13	+B13-E13	400	+F13*G13
14	Dundee	100	40	20	+C14+D14	+B14-E14	600	+F14*G14
15								-------------
16					Total Contribution:			@SUM(H11..H14)
17					less Fixed Costs:			100000
18								-------------
19					Budgeted Profit:			+H16-H17
20								=============
21	==========	==========	==========	==========	==========	==========	==========	==========

3. The solution

Reference should be made to figures 13a and 13b.

The formulae required for the solution to this problem are simple. However, formulae should be used wherever possible, rather than calculated values; the reason for this is that, with formulae, when alternative data are substituted for the existing data, the effect on profit can be ascertained.

For example, you could see the effect on profit of producing 300 Aberdeen bicycles, instead of the present budget figure of 200, by entering 300 in cell G11. If values, based on the existing budget, had been entered in cell H11, instead of the formula multiplying F11 by G11, then the figure in cell H11 would then be incorrect and the correct revised profit figure would not show in cell H19.

Similarly, the effect of an unexpected wage increase could be reflected in revised values entered in cells D11..D14, and the correct revised budgeted profit figure would show in cell H19.

The whole worksheet should be protected, and the ranges B11..D14 and G11..G14 unprotected if revised budget entries are required.

The design of the worksheet shown in figures 13a and 13b is not necessarily the best one. The models (Aberdeen..Dundee) could be positioned horizontally at the head of columns, and the column headings (as shown in figures 13a and 13b) could be listed vertically, e.g. down column A. The important point, however, is that the Total Contribution figure should show at the end with the Fixed Costs deducted to give the Budgeted Profit (perhaps similar to the format shown in cells E16..H19).

[This problem is an example from the chapter entitled *Cost-Volume-Profit Analysis* in AFBIS, to which reference could be made for a more detailed explanation of the principles of cost-volume-profit analysis.]

SESSION 14
Simple Linear Regression Analysis

[Note: the command /DR (Data Regression) is available only for {123} and {AEA}. It is not supported by {VP} or {VPP}. The model in this session was created using {123}, and the descriptions are primarily for {123}. If you are using {AEA}, notes on significant differences are given where appropriate.]

1. Objectives

At the end of this session, you will be able to:

- ❑ understand what is meant by simple linear regression analysis
- ❑ use the command /DR (Data Regression)
- ❑ employ this technique to establish a quantitative relationship between two variables
- ❑ develop this relationship to make budget predictions
- ❑ construct a worksheet incorporating the previous two items

2. Introduction

In this session you will create a model which uses past data to make predictions.

The data relates quantities produced to total production costs. The predictions concerning the total production costs for other quantities are based on these past relationships.

3. The Problem

Poole Perfect Products Ltd. makes a product in batches of 500 units. Details of the number of units produced and the ascertained total production costs for the last seven weeks are as follows:

Week No.	Number of units produced	Actual total production costs (£s)
1	7,500	16,600
2	7,000	15,400
3	6,500	15,100
4	8,500	17,600
5	8,000	17,000
6	9,500	19,600
7	9,000	17,900

The total production costs contain both a variable and fixed element, and costs fluctuate from week to week for both elements.

Demand for the product fluctuates throughout the year, and production tends to follow demand due to storage and other problems. The management wishes to have a rough idea of what total production costs are likely to be at stages of 500 units (i.e. 500 unit batch quantities) for production levels ranging from 500 units to 12,000 units per week.

4. Design of the model

Figure 14a shows:

- the actual data for the past seven weeks (A4..B14)
- the *Regression Output* resulting from the use of the /DR command (D8..G16) [{AEA} (D8..E13)]
- predicted total production costs for the range of output covered by the past seven weeks (C4..C14)
- predicted total production costs for the range required by management (A18..C42)

Figure 14b shows the formulae for Figure 14a. (This printout was obtained by using the command /RFT applied to the range C8..C42.)

5. Notes on creating the model

It is important that you follow these notes in constructing the model, and do not attempt to copy Figure 14a; this is because D8..G14 are produced automatically by the program when you use the Regression command.

Lines 1..7, 17 and 18: Enter the labels as shown in Figure 14a

Enter the values for units and costs as given in paragraph 3 above into cells A8..B14. You will note that week numbers are irrelevant and are not entered on the worksheet.

You will also observe that Figure 14a has sorted the units into an ascending order of magnitude, and you can do the same as follows:

Press `/DSD` (Data, Sort, Data-Range)

Define the data range A8..B14 (preferably by pointing)

Press `P` (Primary-key) and make sure the cursor is in column A

Press `A <Enter>` for Ascending order

Press `G` (Go) to enable the sort

Cells A8..B14 should now appear as in Figure 14a

Next you will produce the *Regression Output* in cells D8..G16.

Move the cursor to cell A8

Press `/DR` (Data, Regression)

Press `X` (for X-range)

Define the range A8..A14

Press `Y` (for Y-range)

Define the range B8..B14

Press `O` (for Output-range)

Type `D8` (to define cell D8 as the top left-hand corner of the range for the regression output)

Press `G` (Go) to produce the *Regression Output* in cells D8..G16.

[{AEA} Cells D8..E13 show the following if you widen column E to 12:

	D	E
8	Intercept	5885.714285
9	Slope	1.392857142
10	R^2	0.952720986
11	Sum X^2	4.55E+08
12	Sum Y^2	2.04406E+09
13	Sum X*Y	9.6335E+08

Cell E8 shows the same value as Constant in {123} cell G9

Cell E9 shows the same value as X Coefficient(s) in {123} cell F15

The {AEA} cell references E8 and E9 should therefore be substituted for the {123} cell references G9 and F15 respectively wherever they occur in the formulae and descriptions which follow.]

An explanation of this output will be given in the next paragraph, but first you will complete the remainder of the model.

Move the cursor to cell A19

Press `/DF` (Data, Fill)

Define the range A19..A42

Enter 500 against the prompt *Start*

Enter 500 against the prompt *Step*

Enter 12000 against the prompt *Stop*

	A	B	C	D	E	F	G
1	POOLE PERFECT PRODUCTS LTD.						
2	PRODUCTION TOTAL COSTS PREDICTION STATEMENT						
3	-------------	-------------	-------------	-------------	-------------	-------------	-------------
4	UNITS	TOTAL PRODUCTION COSTS (£s)					
5	PRODUCED	ACTUAL	PREDICTED				
6	X	Y	Y				
7	-------------	-------------	-------------	-------------	-------------	-------------	-------------
8	6500	15100	14939		Regression Output:		
9	7000	15400	15636	Constant			5885.714
10	7500	16600	16332	Std Err of Y Est			367.132
11	8000	17000	17029	R Squared			0.953
12	8500	17600	17725	No. of Observations			7
13	9000	17900	18421	Degrees of Freedom			5
14	9500	19600	19118				
15				X Coefficient(s)		1.393	
16				Std Err of Coef.		0.139	
17	-------------	-------------	-------------	-------------	-------------	-------------	-------------
18	Table of Predicted Total Costs (£s)						
19	500		6582				
20	1000		7279				
21	1500		7975				
22	2000		8671				
23	2500		9368				
24	3000		10064				
25	3500		10761				
26	4000		11457				
27	4500		12154				
28	5000		12850				
29	5500		13546				
30	6000		14243				
31	6500	15100	14939				
32	7000	15400	15636				
33	7500	16600	16332				
34	8000	17000	17029				
35	8500	17600	17725				
36	9000	17900	18421				
37	9500	19600	19118				
38	10000		19814				
39	10500		20511				
40	11000		21207				
41	11500		21904				
42	12000		22600				

Figure 14a

	A	B	C	D	E	F	G
1	POOLE PERFECT PRODUCTS LTD.						
2	PRODUCTION TOTAL COSTS PREDICTION STATEMENT						
3	-------------	----------	---------------------	---------	------------	--------	------------
4	UNITS	TOTAL PRODUCTION COSTS (£s)					
5	PRODUCED	ACTUAL	PREDICTED				
6	X	Y	Y				
7	-------------	----------	---------------------	---------	------------	--------	------------
8	6500	15100	+$G$9+($F$15*A8)		Regression Output:		
9	7000	15400	+$G$9+($F$15*A9)	Constant			5885.714
10	7500	16600	+$G$9+($F$15*A10)	Std Err of Y Est			367.132
11	8000	17000	+$G$9+($F$15*A11)	R Squared			0.953
12	8500	17600	+$G$9+($F$15*A12)	No. of Observations			7
13	9000	17900	+$G$9+($F$15*A13)	Degrees of Freedom			5
14	9500	19600	+$G$9+($F$15*A14)				
15				X Coefficient(s)		1.393	
16				Std Err of Coef.		0.139	
17	-------------	----------	---------------------	---------	------------	--------	------------
18	Table of Predicted Total Costs (£s)						
19	500		+$G$9+($F$15*A19)				
20	1000		+$G$9+($F$15*A20)				
21	1500		+$G$9+($F$15*A21)				
22	2000		+$G$9+($F$15*A22)				
23	2500		+$G$9+($F$15*A23)				
24	3000		+$G$9+($F$15*A24)				
25	3500		+$G$9+($F$15*A25)				
26	4000		+$G$9+($F$15*A26)				
27	4500		+$G$9+($F$15*A27)				
28	5000		+$G$9+($F$15*A28)				
29	5500		+$G$9+($F$15*A29)				
30	6000		+$G$9+($F$15*A30)				
31	6500	+B8	+$G$9+($F$15*A31)				
32	7000	+B9	+$G$9+($F$15*A32)				
33	7500	+B10	+$G$9+($F$15*A33)				
34	8000	+B11	+$G$9+($F$15*A34)				
35	8500	+B12	+$G$9+($F$15*A35)				
36	9000	+B13	+$G$9+($F$15*A36)				
37	9500	+B14	+$G$9+($F$15*A37)				
38	10000		+$G$9+($F$15*A38)				
39	10500		+$G$9+($F$15*A39)				
40	11000		+$G$9+($F$15*A40)				
41	11500		+$G$9+($F$15*A41)				
42	12000		+$G$9+($F$15*A42)				

Figure 14b

Cells A19..A42 should now agree with Figure 14a

Move the cursor to cell C8

Enter the following formula (carefully!):

$G$9+($F$15*A8)   {AEA} $E$8+($E$9*A8)

[An explanation of this formula will be given in the next paragraph.]

Copy the formula in cell C8 to C9..C14 and to C19..C42

Column C should now contain the numbers shown in Figure 14a, with the underlying formulae as shown in Figure 14b.

Finally, enter **+B8** into cell B31, and copy cell B31 to cells B32..B37.

The underlying formulae for these cells should be as shown in figure 14b. {AEA}: see notes above for the different cell references.

6. An explanation of the model

Simple linear regression analysis establishes a quantitative relationship between two variables and expresses it as an equation.

The variables in the Poole model are:

X (Units) is the *independent* variable

Y (Costs) is the *dependent* variable

If you refer to Figure 14c, you will see the actual data plotted, with X plotted on the horizontal axis and Y on the vertical axis.

The predicted line is the *estimated regression line*. In this model, it is easy to see that the line is probably the *best fit* between the two variables. However, the graphic relationship between the two variables is not always so easy to approximate.

The calculations provided by the /DR command are based on the least-squares method. The assumption is that a linear relationship can be represented by the formula:

$$Y = a + bX$$

where a is the Y intercept (where the predicted line crosses the Y axis) and b is the slope of the line.

In the Poole model, the line intercepts the Y axis at about £5,886, and is shown in the {123} Output in cell G9. This could be regarded as the fixed costs of a typical week's production.

The slope determines the angle of the estimated regression line, i.e the b value shows the amount in £s that the line rises for each unit of production, i.e. the variable production cost. In the Poole model this is £1.39 per unit and is shown in {123} cell F15 as the X coefficient.

This should clarify the significance of the formula, for example, in cell C8, which shows Y as G9+(F15*A8), i.e. $a + bX$. (The dollar signs are purely to keep the cell references absolute rather than relative when the formula is copied to the cells below in column C.)

You may be interested in how the least-squares calculations are performed:

(The figures have been altered to thousands and rounded.

X	Y	X^2	Y^2	XY
6.5	15.1	42.25	228.01	98.15
7.0	15.4	49.00	237.16	107.80
7.5	16.6	56.25	275.56	124.50
8.0	17.0	64.00	289.00	136.00
8.5	17.6	72.25	309.76	149.60
9.0	17.9	81.00	320.41	161.10
9.5	19.6	90.25	384.16	186.20
$\Sigma X = 56.0$	$\Sigma Y = 119.2$	$\Sigma X^2 = 455.00$	$\Sigma Y^2 = 2044.06$	$\Sigma XY = 963.35$

Substitute the above values into the following two simultaneous equations:

$$\Sigma Y = na + b\Sigma X$$

$$\Sigma XY = a\Sigma X + b\Sigma X^2$$

where n is the number of data pairs, i.e. seven.

(a1) $119.2 = 7a + 56b$

(b1) $963.35 = 56a + 455b$ [Multiply (a1) by 8]

(a2) $953.60 = 56a + 448b$ [Subtract (a2) from (b1)]

$9.75 = 7b$

Therefore $b = 1.393$

(a1) $119.2 = 7a + 78$

Therefore $a = 5.885714$ thousand = 5,885.714

You will see that these values for a and b are shown on the worksheet in cells G9 and F15 respectively.

The regression equation is therefore $Y = 5{,}885 + 1.393X$

In the {123} regression output table:

Standard Error of Y Estimate (the average difference between the actual and estimated values) indicates how well the regression equation describes the relationship of the two sets of variables. A small figure should mean that the relationship is good. However, since the measurement is in units of Y, it could be misleading.

***R* Squared** (the coefficient of determination) is a better measure. [For an explanation of the calculations, please refer to a good book on statistics!] In simple words, the figure of 0.953 (cell G11) indicates that you can be approximately 95.3 per cent happy that the predicted total production costs relate to the units of production.

The {AEA} Output shows the Sum figures for X^2, Y^2 and X*Y as shown in the table of explanation above.

[For an explanation of degrees of freedom , please consult a statistics text-book – for example *Business Mathematics and Statistics*, A. Francis, 2nd ed., DP Publications.]

7. Comments and Warnings

{123} The command /DR can also perform multiple linear regression analysis, i.e. using two or more sets of independent variables.

{123} /DRI gives you the option of forcing the intercept on the Y axis to zero, instead of allowing the program to compute it.

{123} When specifying the top left-hand corner of the Output-range (/DRO), remember that the output requires 9 rows and at least 4 columns - additional columns are required for independent variables (Y axis) in excess of two. Any data already in this range will be overwritten.

{AEA} requires 6 rows and two columns.

Remember that the prediction is linear. However, fixed costs may in fact be 'stepped' and variable costs may fluctuate per unit (e.g. with discounts for higher order quantities).

The output produced by /DR can be misleading or worthless if there is a poor relationship between the variables. Interpretation of results requires a sound understanding of statistics. You have been warned!

8. Graphing the Poole model

If you wish to produce a graph similar to that shown in Figure 14c, here is the procedure:

[{AEA} The instructions below are for {123} but the procedure is roughly the same for {AEA}. The main differences are in the number of times you have to press Quit. If you watch the menu headings, you should not get lost. You may wish to alter the scale settings for the X-Axis towards the end to 0 for lower and 12000 for upper.]

First you will create a scatter graph (XY graph) for the actual data:

Press [/GTX] (Graph, Type, XY)

Press [X] (for the horizontal axis), and define the range A19..A42

You require the actual values on the Y axis, so

Type [A] and define the range B19..B42

Type	OFASQ	(Options, Format, A, Symbols, Quit)
Type	C	(Colour) if you want it, and
Type	Q	(Quit) to return to the main Graph menu
Press	V	(View) to see your progress. You should see the plottings for the actual costs, though the scaling needs some adjustment

Press any key to return to the Graph menu.

You now need to produce the regression line for the predicted values.

Press	B	and define the range C19..C42
Press	OFBB	(Options, Format, B, Both)
Press	QQV	(Quit, Quit, View) to view the graph

You will see the regression line, and note that the scaling has altered.

Press any key to return to the Graph menu

Type	OLA	(Options, Legend, A) and *Actual*
Type	OLB	(Options, Legend, B) and *Predicted*

While still in the Options menu,

Type	TF	(Titles, First) and *Poole Perfect Products Ltd.*
Type	TS	(Titles, Second) and *Production Total Costs Predictions*
Type	TX	(Titles, X-Axis) and *Units of Production*
Type	TY	(Titles, Y-Axis) and *Total Production Costs (£000s)*
Press	QV	(Quit, View) to view your graph, and then any key to return to the Graph menu

If you wish to alter the scale of the Y-Axis to start at zero,

Press	OSY	(Options, Scale, Y-Scale)
Press	ML0	(Manual, Lower, and accept zero)

Press `U26000QQV` (Upper, 26000, Quit, Quit, View)

The graph should now resemble Figure 14c.

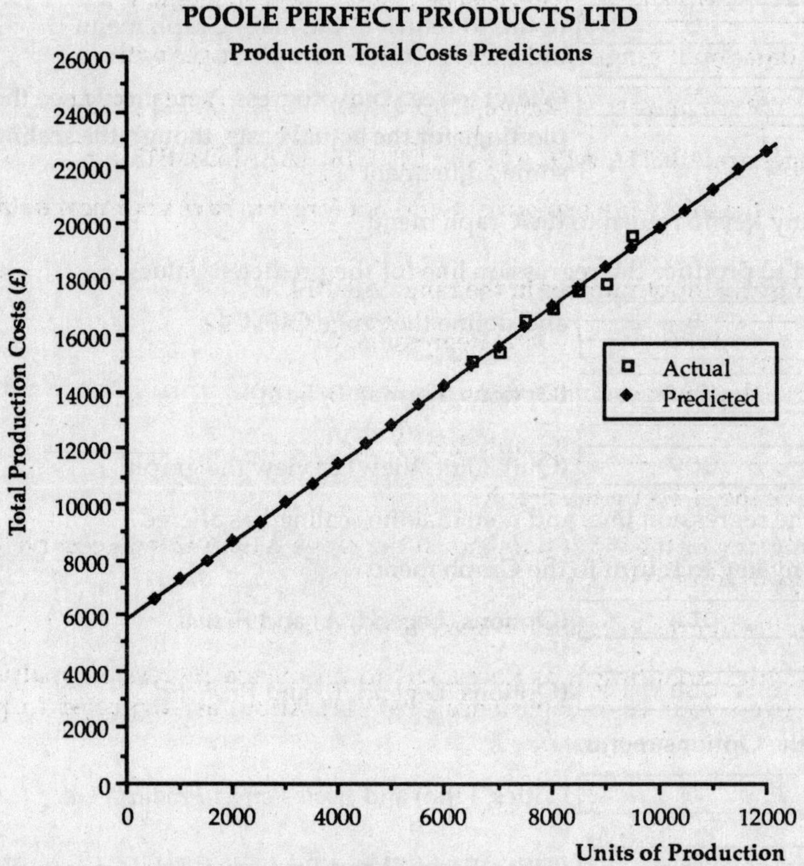

Figure 14c

If you wish to print out your graph, remember to NAME it and {123} SAVE it. Follow the instructions for printing graphs as detailed in session 8. The differences in the procedures for {123} and {AEA} are considerable.

9. Comment

You could use this technique to predict relationships between other sets of variables where there is reasonable expectation that a fair relationship exists. For example, between sales and profits, units of production and profits, advertising and sales. There are dangers, as pointed out above in paragraph 7, but used with discretion and observing such information such as that provided by R^2, the technique can be informative.

10. Activity

Protect the whole worksheet with

Press `/WGPE` (Worksheet, Global, Protect, Enable)

Unprotect the data input ranges and the regression output ranges with

Press `/RU<range>` (Range, Unprotect) {AEA} /RLN

The ranges are A8..B14, A19..A42 and D8..G16 {AEA} D8..E13.

When trying out the following experiments, do not forget to save your new data with a new filename!

(1) Try altering any input number in the range A8..B14.

Press `/DRG` (Data, Regression, Go)

and observe the changes to the outputs.

Press `/GV` (Graph, View)

and observe the effect on the graph.

(2) Try altering any of the input numbers in the range A19..A42, and observe the effect on the outputs in column C.

[Note that the figures in column B become irrelevant.]

(3) Use the model, adapting it as necessary, to produce a regression analysis for some statistics from your own experience or organisation, as suggested in paragraph 8 above.

SESSION 15
Pricing Decisions

1. Objectives

At the end of this session, you will be able to:

- create a pricing decision model which shows the contributions resulting from forecasts of sales volumes at various sales price levels
- adapt the expected results to show minimum and maximum results
- observe the results on a line or XY graph which management can use in making decisions concerning their pricing policy
- understand how to use the <F4> Absolute key to insert $ signs into cell references

2. Introduction

In this session you will create a model which solves a pricing decision problem. This problem concerns a publishing house which has made forecasts concerning the expected sales volumes (with maximum variations around those sales volumes) for a proposed book at various retail prices. It has also forecast variable sales costs and variable and fixed production costs for the book. It wishes to know the price/volume levels at which optimum contributions are likely to be achieved at the expected, as well as the minimum and maximum, levels of sales. Management also requires the model to show the effect of varying any of the forecast volume, price and cost figures on the levels at which optimum contributions can be anticipated.

3. The problem

ROD Publications Ltd. are considering publication of a new title, **Fly Fishing**, by a well-known author. The marketing director has estimated the number of copies which could be sold at various retail net book prices; he has also suggested the maximum variation (+/-) around these numbers, as follows:

Retail price (£)	Expected sales (copies)	Maximum variation (+/-) around expected sales
5	29,000	5,000
6	27,000	5,000
7	25,000	5,000
8	23,000	4,000

9	21,000	4,000
10	19,000	4,000
11	17,000	3,000
12	15,000	3,000
13	14,000	3,000
14	13,000	3,000
15	12,000	2,000
16	10,000	2,000
20	7,000	2,000

The sales director has produced the following sales costs, expressed as percentages of the retail price:

Royalties to the author	10%
Discount to booksellers	30%
Distribution costs	15%

The production director has estimated the fixed production costs as £20,000, and variable production costs as £1.10p per copy.

The managing director wishes to be advised on the print-run and retail price most likely to result in the optimum contribution to all other costs.

4. Design of the model

Figure 15a shows:

- a DATA INPUT BLOCK (A3..F21) where all the data provided in the problem can be entered.
- three output blocks:

  EXPECTED VOLUMES (A23..F41)

  MINIMUM VOLUMES (A43..F61)

  MAXIMUM VOLUMES (A63..F81)

  Each of these three output blocks shows, in column F, the likely contribution to fixed sales costs for each suggested retail price (column A). The highest figure in column F is theoretically the optimum level.

Figure 15b shows the formulae for figure 15a. [This printout was obtained by applying the command /RFT (Range, Format, Text) to the whole worksheet area (A1..F82), and widening the columns as necessary to reveal the whole formulae.]

	A	B	C	D	E	F
1	ROD PUBLICATIONS Limited: Fly Fishing Book					
2	========	============	============	============	=========	============
3	DATA INPUT BLOCK					
4	----------	----------------	----------------	----------------	------------	----------------
5		EXPECTED	QUANTITY	FIXED PROD		
6	PRICE	QUANTITY	MAXIMUM +/-	COSTS		
7	£	(000s)	(000s)	(£000s)		
8						
9	5.00	29.000	5.000	20.000	Sales costs as	
10	6.00	27.000	5.000	20.000	percentage	%
11	7.00	25.000	5.000	20.000	of sales...	55.00
12	8.00	23.000	4.000	20.000		
13	9.00	21.000	4.000	20.000		
14	10.00	19.000	4.000	20.000	Production variable	
15	11.00	17.000	3.000	20.000	costs per	
16	12.00	15.000	3.000	20.000	copy .....£	1.10
17	13.00	14.000	3.000	20.000		
18	14.00	13.000	3.000	20.000		
19	15.00	12.000	2.000	20.000		
20	16.00	10.000	2.000	20.000		
21	20.00	7.000	2.000	20.000		
22	========	============	============	============	=========	============
23		EXPECTED VOLUMES				
24		----------------	------			
25	PRICE	PRICE LESS	QUANTITY	NET REVENUE	PROD'N	CONT'N TO
26		VARIABLE	(000'S)	(£000)	COSTS	FIXED SALES
27		SALES COSTS			(£000)	COSTS (£000)
28						
29	5.00	2.25	29.000	65.250	51.900	13.350
30	6.00	2.70	27.000	72.900	49.700	23.200
31	7.00	3.15	25.000	78.750	47.500	31.250
32	8.00	3.60	23.000	82.800	45.300	37.500
33	9.00	4.05	21.000	85.050	43.100	41.950
34	10.00	4.50	19.000	85.500	40.900	44.600
35	11.00	4.95	17.000	84.150	38.700	45.450
36	12.00	5.40	15.000	81.000	36.500	44.500
37	13.00	5.85	14.000	81.900	35.400	46.500
38	14.00	6.30	13.000	81.900	34.300	47.600
39	15.00	6.75	12.000	81.000	33.200	47.800
40	16.00	7.20	10.000	72.000	31.000	41.000
41	20.00	9.00	7.000	63.000	27.700	35.300
42	----------	----------------	----------------	----------------	------------	----------------

Figure 15a (Part 1)

	A	B	C	D	E	F
43		MINIMUM VOLUMES				
44		---------------				
45	PRICE	PRICE LESS	QUANTITY	NET REVENUE	PROD'N	CONT'N TO
46		VARIABLE	(000'S)	(£000)	COSTS	FIXED COSTS
47		SALES COSTS			(£000)	(£000)
48						
49	5.00	2.25	24.000	54.000	46.400	7.600
50	6.00	2.70	22.000	59.400	44.200	15.200
51	7.00	3.15	20.000	63.000	42.000	21.000
52	8.00	3.60	19.000	68.400	40.900	27.500
53	9.00	4.05	17.000	68.850	38.700	30.150
54	10.00	4.50	15.000	67.500	36.500	31.000
55	11.00	4.95	14.000	69.300	35.400	33.900
56	12.00	5.40	12.000	64.800	33.200	31.600
57	13.00	5.85	11.000	64.350	32.100	32.250
58	14.00	6.30	10.000	63.000	31.000	32.000
59	15.00	6.75	10.000	67.500	31.000	36.500
60	16.00	7.20	8.000	57.600	28.800	28.800
61	20.00	9.00	5.000	45.000	25.500	19.500
62	-----------	----------------	----------------	----------------	-------------	----------------
63		MAXIMUM VOLUMES				
64		---------------				
65	PRICE	PRICE LESS	QUANTITY	NET REVENUE	PROD'N	CONT'N TO
66		VARIABLE	(000s)	(£000)	COSTS	FIXED COSTS
67		SALES COSTS			(£000)	(£000)
68						
69	5.00	2.25	34.000	76.500	57.400	19.100
70	6.00	2.70	32.000	86.400	55.200	31.200
71	7.00	3.15	30.000	94.500	53.000	41.500
72	8.00	3.60	27.000	97.200	49.700	47.500
73	9.00	4.05	25.000	101.250	47.500	53.750
74	10.00	4.50	23.000	103.500	45.300	58.200
75	11.00	4.95	20.000	99.000	42.000	57.000
76	12.00	5.40	18.000	97.200	39.800	57.400
77	13.00	5.85	17.000	99.450	38.700	60.750
78	14.00	6.30	16.000	100.800	37.600	63.200
79	15.00	6.75	14.000	94.500	35.400	59.100
80	16.00	7.20	12.000	86.400	33.200	53.200
81	20.00	9.00	9.000	81.000	29.900	51.100
82	-----------	----------------	----------------	----------------	-------------	----------------

Figure 15a (Part 2)

	A	B	C	D	E	F
1	ROD PUBLICATIONS Limited: Fly Fishing Book					
2	=====	================	===========	==========	================	===========
3	DATA INPUT BLOCK					
4	------	-------------------	------------	-----------	-----------------	------------
5		EXPECTED	QUANTITY	FIXED PROD		
6	PRICE	QUANTITY	MAXIMUM +/-	COSTS		
7	£	(000s)	(000s)	(£000s)		
8						
9	5.00	29.000	5.000	20.000	Sales costs as	
10	6.00	27.000	5.000	20.000	percentage	%
11	7.00	25.000	5.000	20.000	of sales...	55.00
12	8.00	23.000	4.000	20.000		
13	9.00	21.000	4.000	20.000		
14	10.00	19.000	4.000	20.000	Production variable	
15	11.00	17.000	3.000	20.000	costs per	
16	12.00	15.000	3.000	20.000	copy .....£	1.10
17	13.00	14.000	3.000	20.000		
18	14.00	13.000	3.000	20.000		
19	15.00	12.000	2.000	20.000		
20	16.00	10.000	2.000	20.000		
21	20.00	7.000	2.000	20.000		
22	=====	================	===========	==========	================	===========
23		EXPECTED VOLUMES				
24		-------------------	-------			
25	PRICE	PRICE LESS	QUANTITY	NET REVENUE	PROD'N	CONT'N TO
26		VARIABLE	(000'S)	(£000)	COSTS	FIXED SALES
27		SALES COSTS			(£000)	COSTS (£000)
28						
29	+A9	+A29*(1-$F$11/100)	+B9	+C29*B29	+D9+(C29*$F$16)	+D29-E29
30	+A10	+A30*(1-$F$11/100)	+B10	+C30*B30	+D10+(C30*$F$16)	+D30-E30
31	+A11	+A31*(1-$F$11/100)	+B11	+C31*B31	+D11+(C31*$F$16)	+D31-E31
32	+A12	+A32*(1-$F$11/100)	+B12	+C32*B32	+D12+(C32*$F$16)	+D32-E32
33	+A13	+A33*(1-$F$11/100)	+B13	+C33*B33	+D13+(C33*$F$16)	+D33-E33
34	+A14	+A34*(1-$F$11/100)	+B14	+C34*B34	+D14+(C34*$F$16)	+D34-E34
35	+A15	+A35*(1-$F$11/100)	+B15	+C35*B35	+D15+(C35*$F$16)	+D35-E35
36	+A16	+A36*(1-$F$11/100)	+B16	+C36*B36	+D16+(C36*$F$16)	+D36-E36
37	+A17	+A37*(1-$F$11/100)	+B17	+C37*B37	+D17+(C37*$F$16)	+D37-E37
38	+A18	+A38*(1-$F$11/100)	+B18	+C38*B38	+D18+(C38*$F$16)	+D38-E38
39	+A19	+A39*(1-$F$11/100)	+B19	+C39*B39	+D19+(C39*$F$16)	+D39-E39
40	+A20	+A40*(1-$F$11/100)	+B20	+C40*B40	+D20+(C40*$F$16)	+D40-E40
41	+A21	+A41*(1-$F$11/100)	+B21	+C41*B41	+D21+(C41*$F$16)	+D41-E41
42	------	-------------------	------------	-----------	-----------------	------------

Figure 15b (Part 1)

	A	B	C	D	E	F
43		MINIMUM VOLUMES				
44		---------------				
45	PRICE	PRICE LESS	QUANTITY	NET REVENUE	PROD'N	CONT'N TO
46		VARIABLE	(000'S)	(£000)	COSTS	FIXED COSTS
47		SALES COSTS			(£000)	(£000)
48						
49	+A29	+A49*(1-$F$11/100)	+C29-C9	+C49*B49	+D9+(C49*$F$16)	+D49-E49
50	+A30	+A50*(1-$F$11/100)	+C30-C10	+C50*B50	+D10+(C50*$F$16)	+D50-E50
51	+A31	+A51*(1-$F$11/100)	+C31-C11	+C51*B51	+D11+(C51*$F$16)	+D51-E51
52	+A32	+A52*(1-$F$11/100)	+C32-C12	+C52*B52	+D12+(C52*$F$16)	+D52-E52
53	+A33	+A53*(1-$F$11/100)	+C33-C13	+C53*B53	+D13+(C53*$F$16)	+D53-E53
54	+A34	+A54*(1-$F$11/100)	+C34-C14	+C54*B54	+D14+(C54*$F$16)	+D54-E54
55	+A35	+A55*(1-$F$11/100)	+C35-C15	+C55*B55	+D15+(C55*$F$16)	+D55-E55
56	+A36	+A56*(1-$F$11/100)	+C36-C16	+C56*B56	+D16+(C56*$F$16)	+D56-E56
57	+A37	+A57*(1-$F$11/100)	+C37-C17	+C57*B57	+D17+(C57*$F$16)	+D57-E57
58	+A38	+A58*(1-$F$11/100)	+C38-C18	+C58*B58	+D18+(C58*$F$16)	+D58-E58
59	+A39	+A59*(1-$F$11/100)	+C39-C19	+C59*B59	+D19+(C59*$F$16)	+D59-E59
60	+A40	+A60*(1-$F$11/100)	+C40-C20	+C60*B60	+D20+(C60*$F$16)	+D60-E60
61	+A41	+A61*(1-$F$11/100)	+C41-C21	+C61*B61	+D21+(C61*$F$16)	+D61-E61
62	------	--------------------	-------------	------------	------------------	------------
63		MAXIMUM VOLUMES				
64		---------------				
65	PRICE	PRICE LESS	QUANTITY	NET REVENUE	PROD'N	CONT'N TO
66		VARIABLE	(000s)	(£000)	COSTS	FIXED COSTS
67		SALES COSTS			(£000)	(£000)
68						
69	+A49	+A69*(1-$F$11/100)	+C29+C9	+C69*B69	+D9+(C69*$F$16)	+D69-E69
70	+A50	+A70*(1-$F$11/100)	+C30+C10	+C70*B70	+D10+(C70*$F$16)	+D70-E70
71	+A51	+A71*(1-$F$11/100)	+C31+C11	+C71*B71	+D11+(C71*$F$16)	+D71-E71
72	+A52	+A72*(1-$F$11/100)	+C32+C12	+C72*B72	+D12+(C72*$F$16)	+D72-E72
73	+A53	+A73*(1-$F$11/100)	+C33+C13	+C73*B73	+D13+(C73*$F$16)	+D73-E73
74	+A54	+A74*(1-$F$11/100)	+C34+C14	+C74*B74	+D14+(C74*$F$16)	+D74-E74
75	+A55	+A75*(1-$F$11/100)	+C35+C15	+C75*B75	+D15+(C75*$F$16)	+D75-E75
76	+A56	+A76*(1-$F$11/100)	+C36+C16	+C76*B76	+D16+(C76*$F$16)	+D76-E76
77	+A57	+A77*(1-$F$11/100)	+C37+C17	+C77*B77	+D17+(C77*$F$16)	+D77-E77
78	+A58	+A78*(1-$F$11/100)	+C38+C18	+C78*B78	+D18+(C78*$F$16)	+D78-E78
79	+A59	+A79*(1-$F$11/100)	+C39+C19	+C79*B79	+D19+(C79*$F$16)	+D79-E79
80	+A60	+A80*(1-$F$11/100)	+C40+C20	+C80*B80	+D20+(C80*$F$16)	+D80-E80
81	+A61	+A81*(1-$F$11/100)	+C41+C21	+C81*B81	+D21+(C81*$F$16)	+D81-E81
82	------	--------------------	-------------	------------	------------------	------------

Figure 15b (Part 2)

Figure 15c shows a line graph for the three output blocks, and plots the output figures in column F (the contribution to fixed sales costs figures) against the various volume figures in column C.

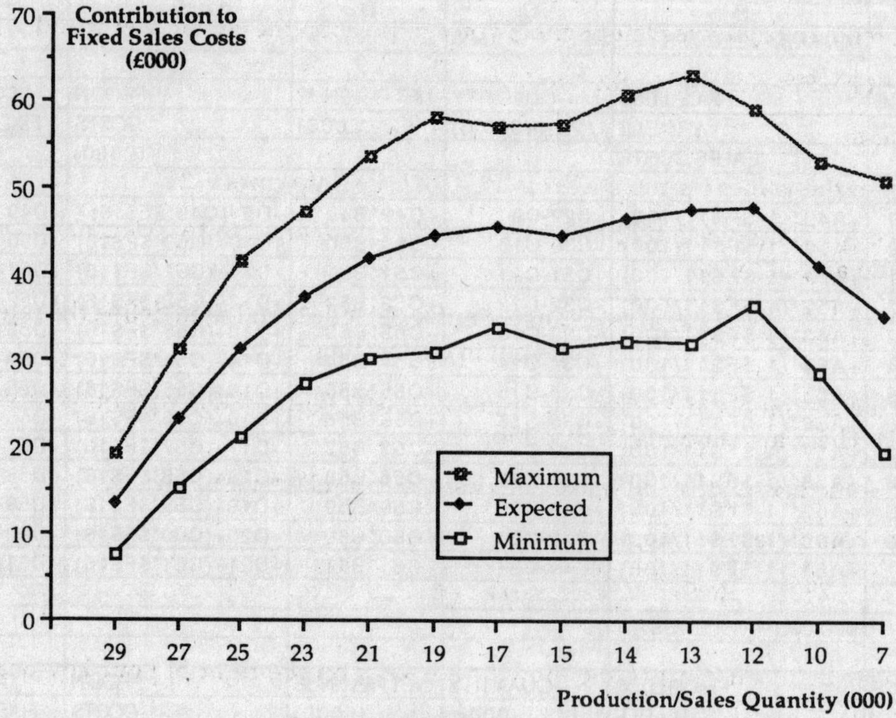

Figure 15c

The three lines peak at different volumes, though it can be seen that volumes of 12,000 or 13,000 would appear best, with the volumes 17,000 to 19,000 following closely behind. Management's decision might depend on whether it took an optimistic (maximum), average (expected), or pessimistic (minimum) view of likely sales volumes, and of the credence it gave to the budgeted data.

When you have created the model, you will be able alter any of the data in the data input block, and observe the effect on the graph simply by pressing /GV (Graph, View).

5. Notes on creating the model

Since most of the labels are to be right-aligned:

Press `/WGLR` (Worksheet, Global, Label-Prefix, Right)

Also most of the values are Formatted to three decimal places:

Press `/WGFF3` (Worksheet, Global, Format, Fixed, 3)

A column-width of twelve is convenient for this worksheet:

Press `/WGC12` (Worksheet, Global, Column-Width, 12)

Enter the labels as shown in Figure 15a for lines 1..7, 22..27, 42..47 and 62..67, and also E9..E11, E14..E16 and F10. Do not forget that you can use /C to copy ranges!

[If you prefer any cell to be left-aligned, you can position the cursor over it and:

either edit it <F2>, (changing the " to '),

or Press `/RLL` (Range, Label, Left)]

Enter the values for the DATA INPUT BLOCK into rows 9..21.

The range A9..20 and cells F11 and F16 should be formatted to two decimal places (rather than the default of three):

Press `/RFF2` (Range, Format, Fixed, 2) and then define the range by typing it in or pointing

Next, enter the labels and formulae into the EXPECTED VOLUMES output block (Cells A29..F41). These are shown in Figure 15b.

Here are some tips which will make entering the formulae more easy:

Enter one complete row first, i.e. row 29:

Cell A29: Press `+A9 <→>`

[Remember that you can use the grey / * - + keys on the right of your key-board, if you have them]

Cell B29: Press `+A29*(1-$F$11/100)`

[The dollar ($) signs make the cell reference F11 absolute (not relative) when this cell (B29) is copied. There is an easier way of entering the $ signs than typing using <Shift>+<4>, and this is to use the <F4> Absolute key. Unfortunately the use of this key varies between programs. If you wish to learn how to use it, please refer to paragraph 9 at the end of this session, either now or at the end of this session.]

Cell C29: Press `+B9`

Cell D29: Press `C29*B29`

Cell E29: Press `+D9+(C29*$F$16)`

Cell F29: Press `+D29-E29`

Check that row 29 is correctly entered, and then copy it (range A29..F29) to the rows below, i.e. rows 30..41.

Next, copy the labels in rows 23..27 to rows 43..47, and alter EXPECTED to MINIMUM in cell B43.

Copy row 29 (Range A29..F29) to row 49. You will have to edit two cells to make them correct:

Cell C49: Alter to read: `+C29-C9` [Type in the new formula]

Cell E49: Alter to read: `+D9+(C49*$F$16)` [Delete the 2 in +D29]

Copy row 49 (Range A49..F49) to the rows below, i.e. rows 50..61.

Next, copy the labels in rows 43..47 to rows 63..67, and alter MINIMUM to MAXIMUM in cell B63.

Copy row 49 (Range A49..F49) to row 69. You will have to edit two cells to make them correct:

Cell C69: Alter to read: `+C29+C9` [Type in the new formula]

Cell E69: Alter to read: `+D9+(C69*$F$16)` [Delete the 2 in +D29]

Copy row 69 (Range A69..F69) to the rows below, i.e. rows 70..81.

If the figures on your screen do not match the figures as shown in Figure 15a, then check your formulae carefully against those shown in Figure 15b.

6. An explanation of the model

You will note that the model contains an input block (A3..F21) where the values can easily be altered to show the effect in the three output blocks.

These output blocks (A23..F82) contain only labels and formulae, and should therefore be protected against change. The whole worksheet should be protected and the input value ranges (A9..D21, F11 and F16) unprotected. The procedure for doing this was demonstrated in Session 5, paragraph 9.

For this particular problem, there is no reason why the fixed production costs as entered in D9..D21 should not have been a single figure, or even omitted, since these fixed costs are the same irrespective of the changes in volume. However, the model is more flexible in its present form, since, if the fixed costs should prove to be 'stepped', the model can accommodate the stepped costs; in any case, it is easy to enter the required figure in cell D9 and copy it to the cells D10..D21.

The formatting of the cells in the data input block is designed to make it easy to enter rounded figures, e.g. the £29,000 in cell B9 can be changed to £30,000 by simply typing in **30**.

7. Graphing the model

The procedure for creating and printing graphs was demonstrated in Sessions 7 and 8.

Figure 15c shows a LINE graph based on the model you have created, and the values entered for ROD Publications Ltd.

The graph settings are as follows:

Type:	Line		
Data ranges:	X	B9..B21	
	A	F29..F41	
	B	F49..F61	
	C	F69..F81	
Legend:	A	Expected	
	B	Minimum	
	C	Maximum	
Titles:	X-Axis		Production/Sales Quantity 000s
	Y-Axis		Contribution to fixed sales costs £000s

You may prefer the graph as an XY type. In which case, once you have named the Line graph as, say, FLY-LINE, you could choose type XY and name it FLY-XY.

Other types of graph (Bar, Stacked-bar, Pie) are not so good for the purpose of decision-making.

8. Activity

(1) Experiment with changing the data in the input block (preferably one item at a time) and seeing the effect on the figures in the output block and the graph (press /GV).

(2) Use or adapt the model to suit any other problem or situation of a type where optimum contribution indications are required from price sensitivity forecasts.

9. Postscript: The <F4> Absolute key

Unfortunately the use of this key varies between programs. Separate descriptions follow for the various programs covered by this book.

{123} only: [See below for other programs.]

<F4> is the Absolute key, and pressing this when you have typed a cell reference results in the $ signs being entered for you. For example, if you type 'F11' in a formula, and press <F4>, the dollar signs $ are inserted before the F and the 11, making the cell reference absolute, i.e. it will not change when you copy all these formulae down to the rows below.

If you keep pressing <F4>, you will see that the cell references become, successively, F$11, $F11, F11, $F$11, F$11, and so on. This is very convenient, since it saves using <Shift>+<4> to type in the dollar signs.

Note also that you can enter a formula without the dollar signs, and then edit it <F2> to insert the dollar signs; in this case, press <F4> while the cursor is over any character of a cell reference (or the mathematical operator or space etc. which follows it) until it is in the form you require. You can, of course, edit cell references in a formula which already contain $ signs, and use <F4> to alter their format.

In addition, you can, when entering a formula, use <F4> when using the pointing mode. To gain some practice in this, follow the instructions for the other programs below. When you have completed that exercise, try out the facility for using the <F4> key while editing <F2> the formula in cell AA5 or AC7.

{AEA} {VP} {VPP}:

The <F4> Absolute key is active only when entering a formula and using point mode. It is not active when editing a cell.

Try this:

Move to an area of the worksheet outside your current working area, say cell AA1.

> Enter 10, 20, 30, 40 in cells AA1, AA2, AA3, AA4 respectively.
>
> Move to cell AA5. Type +AA1+
>
> Move the cursor to cell AA2
>
> Press [<F4>] repeatedly and observe how the cell reference AA2 changes from AA2 to $AA$2, AA$2, $AA2, AA2, $AA$2, and so on
>
> When the input line reads AA$2:
>
> Press [*]
>
> Move the cursor to cell AA3,
>
> Press [<F4>] until the input line reads $AA$3
>
> Type [/]
>
> Move the cursor to cell AA4
>
> Press [<F4>] until the input line reads $AA4
>
> Press [<Enter>]

The cursor should return to cell AA5, which should now contain the answer '25' in the cell and, on the status line, the formula:

+AA1+AA$2*$AA$3/$AA4

The formula contains a mixture of absolute and relative cell references.

Now copy the formula in cell AA5 to cell AC7 (two cells to the right and two cells down). Observe how the formula has changed. The absolute references (preceded by $ signs) have remained as they are in cell AA5, but the relative references (not preceded by $ signs) have changed relatively by two, i.e. AA has changed to AC, 1 has changed to 3, and 4 has changed to 6.

SESSION 16

Investment Appraisal: Simple Pay-Back

1. Objectives

At the end of this session, you will be able to:

- ❑ create a model which calculates simple pay-back period from a set of data;
- ❑ alter the data in the model and see the change in the pay-back period;
- ❑ understand the uses of the @VLOOKUP function.

2. Introduction

There are two main non-discounting methods of investment appraisal: simple pay-back and accounting rate of return.

The model you will create in this session is the first method, simple pay-back, which is the period (usually expressed in years) which it takes the cash inflows from a capital investment project to equal the cash outflows.

When deciding between two or more competing projects, the usual decision is to accept the one with the shortest pay-back. Pay-back is commonly used as a first screening method. It is a rough measure of liquidity and not of profitability. (CIMA Terminology, p.38)

3. The problem

Zeppo Ltd manufacture a wide range of prestigious products for the prestige-conscious businessman. The management are contemplating a new design of brief-case which they hope to sell at £20 per unit wholesale, for subsequent resale at a suitably prestigious retail price.

The necessary manufacturing equipment for this new product will cost £350,000 and have an expected life of ten years.

Variable production and selling costs per unit are costed at £15 per unit, and annual fixed production and selling costs estimated at £20,000, excluding depreciation of the manufacturing equipment.

Relying on experience with other prestigious products which the company has sold since the war, the marketing director estimates unit sales of the brief-case for the next ten years to be as follows:

Year	*Units*
1	5,000
2	10,000
3	20,000
4	30,000
5	30,000
6	25,000
7	22,000
8	15,000
9	8,000
10	3,000

The Managing Director of Zeppo Ltd requires a worksheet on his computer which will show the above data, and the simple payback period. He also requires that the model will allow him to alter any of the input data and see the resulting effect upon the payback period.

4. Design of the model

Figure 16a shows:

- an INPUT TABLE block (A3..D30) into which the data of the problem are entered.
- an OUTPUT TABLE block (E3..H30) where the annual individual and cumulative cash flows (E11..G10) and the payback period (E26..H28) are calculated.

Figure 16b shows the formulae in the range E1..H31 for Figure 16a. You will note that cell E28 contains a very long formula which extends over the adjacent columns to the right. This formula has a rather daunting appearance, but all will be explained in due course (paragraph 6 below).

The first thing for you to do is to create the model, and see if it works!

When you have created the model, you will be able to alter any of the data in the input table and observe the effect on the figures in the output table.

5. Notes on creating the model

The default column-width of 9 is satisfactory for this worksheet.

Enter all the labels as shown in Figure 16a. They can all be entered as left-aligned; however, those in cells C18, D18, C30, E9, F9, G9, and H9 probably look better right-aligned.

Enter the values in cells D5, D7, D9, D11, D13, and D19..D28.

Use /DF (Data, Fill) to enter the values into cells C19..C28.

[**/DF** was demonstrated in session 9, paragraph 5. If you have forgotten, the procedure is:

Position the cursor over cell C19

Press `/DF.` (the full stop anchors the cursor)

Move the cursor to cell D28

Press `<Enter>`

Type `1 <Enter>` against the *Start* prompt

Type `1 <Enter>` against the *Step* prompt

{not AEA} Press `<Enter>` against the *Stop: 8191* prompt

The programs vary slightly in the prompt words and numbers.]

Cell D30: Enter the formula `@SUM(D19..D28)`

Next, format the cells to make them show the figures as can be seen in Figure 16a:

Cells C19..C28 Use `/RFF0<range>`

Cells D5..D30 Use `/RF,0<range>`

Now for the Output Table:

Use `/DF` (Data, Fill) to enter the year numbers in cells E11.E20 and H11..H20

Cell F11: Enter the formula as shown in Figure 16b.

[If your program allows it, use the <F4> Absolute key to enter all the $ signs easily, as described in Session 15, paragraph 9.]

Copy cell F11 to cells F12..F20

Range G11..G12:

Enter the formulae as shown and then copy cell G12 to cells G13..G20

Cells F22, E26, G26 and E28:

Enter the formulae exactly as shown in Figure 16b. Be very careful to type these formulae correctly. If you make a mistake, use the <F2> key to edit them correctly. Be particularly careful about the brackets; there should be the same number of left-brackets as right-brackets! There are seven of each type of bracket in the formula in cell E28. Note that in Figure 16b the formula in row 28 is all in cell E28, even though it spills over across columns F, G and H. If, when you have typed the formula in, you cannot read all of it in the status line when the cursor is on cell E28, press <F2> and you can then use the arrow, <Home> and <End> keys to view all of it, even if you do not want to edit it.

Now format the cells to make them show the figures as shown in Figure 16a:

Cells E11..E20, E26, H11..H20 and G26:	Use `/RFF0<range>`
Cells F11..F22 and G11..G20:	Use `/RF,0<range>`
Cell E28:	Use `/RFF3<range>`

Finally protect the worksheet (global), and unprotect the input cells D5, D9, D11, D13 and D19..D28. [See Session 5, paragraph 9 if you have forgotten how to do this.]

	A	B	C	D	E	F	G	H
1	Session 16: Simple Payback							
2	----------	----------	----------	----------	----------	----------	----------	----------
3	INPUT TABLE				OUTPUT TABLE			
4	----------	----------	----------	----------	----------	----------	----------	----------
5	Initial investment £s......			350,000				
6					----------	----------	----------	----------
7	Expected life: years.......			10	Annual Cash Flows:			
8					----------	----------	----------	----------
9	Selling price per unit £s...			20	Year	£	Cum. £	Year
10								
11	Variable costs per unit £s..			15	1	5,000	5,000	1
12					2	30,000	35,000	2
13	Fixed costs per annum £s..			20,000	3	80,000	115,000	3
14	(excluding depreciation)				4	130,000	245,000	4
15					5	130,000	375,000	5
16		Sales Volumes			6	105,000	480,000	6
17			----------	----------	7	90,000	570,000	7
18			Year	Units	8	55,000	625,000	8
19			1	5,000	9	20,000	645,000	9
20			2	10,000	10	-5,000	640,000	10
21			3	20,000				
22			4	30,000	Total	640,000		
23			5	30,000	----------	----------	----------	----------
24			6	25,000	Payback Period:			
25			7	22,000	----------	----------	----------	----------
26			8	15,000	4	years and	295	days
27			9	8,000				
28			10	3,000	4.808	years		
29								
30			Total	168,000				
31	----------	----------	----------	----------	----------	----------	----------	----------

Figure 16a

	E	F	G	H
1	Session 16: Simple Payback			
2				
3	OUTPUT TABLE			
4				
5				
6				
7	Annual Cash Flows:			
8				
9	Year	£	Cum. £	Year
10				
11	1	+$D19*($D$9-$D$11)-$D$13	+F11	1
12	2	+$D20*($D$9-$D$11)-$D$13	+G11+F12	2
13	3	+$D21*($D$9-$D$11)-$D$13	+G12+F13	3
14	4	+$D22*($D$9-$D$11)-$D$13	+G13+F14	4
15	5	+$D23*($D$9-$D$11)-$D$13	+G14+F15	5
16	6	+$D24*($D$9-$D$11)-$D$13	+G15+F16	6
17	7	+$D25*($D$9-$D$11)-$D$13	+G16+F17	7
18	8	+$D26*($D$9-$D$11)-$D$13	+G17+F18	8
19	9	+$D27*($D$9-$D$11)-$D$13	+G18+F19	9
20	10	+$D28*($D$9-$D$11)-$D$13	+G19+F20	10
21				
22	Total	@SUM(F11:F20)		
23				
24	Payback Period:			
25				
26	@VLOOKUP(D5,G11:H20,1)		(+E28-E26)*365	days
27				
28	+E26+1*((D5-@VLOOKUP(E26,E11:G20,2))/(@VLOOKUP(E26+1,E11:G20,2)-(@VLOOKUP(E26,E11:G20,2))))			
29				
30				
31				

Figure 16b

6. An explanation of the model

Cells F11..F20

The formulae in these cells calculate the contribution per unit (i.e. selling price less variable cost) within the brackets, multiply this by the sales volume (units), and finally deduct the fixed costs for the year.

For example, cell F11 performs the following calculation:

D19	×	(D9	–	D11)	–	D13
5,000 units	×	(£20	–	£15)	–	£20,000

Cells G11..G20

The formulae in these cells calculate the cumulative cash flows by adding the figure to the left to the cumulative figure above.

Cell E26

The formula in this cells *looks up* the figure of £350,000 (from the cell D5) in the cumulative cash flow range G11..G20, and, when it finds the nearest figure *below* £350,000, it prints out the corresponding figure from the range H11..H20; in this case it finds the figure £245,000 (in cell G14) and prints out the figure 4 from cell H14.

The format for @VLOOKUP is: @VLOOKUP(x,range,offset)

In this example:

x is the £350,000

range is G11..H20, which includes both the index column (G) and the value column (H)

offset is the number of columns which the value column (H) is to the right of the index column (G), in this case, 1.

[Note: for further information on how to use @VLOOKUP and @HLOOKUP (Vertical and Horizontal respectively), consult your program manual.]

Cell E28

Cell E26 calculated the payback period in years (rounded down), but the next problem is to calculate the fraction of a year which must be added, and then to convert this fraction to days.

In cell E28, we calculate the fraction and add it to the number in cell E26.

The calculation required is:

4 years plus (350,000 - 245,000) divided by (375,000 - 245,000)

We can substitute the cell references where these figures occur:-

E26 + (D5 - G4) / (G5 - G4)

Although this would work for the present set of figures, it not work when the figure in cell E26 was other than 4 years. What we need is a formula which will find the figure in cell E26, and then look up the relative cells in column G. Fortunately we have the @VLOOKUP function which we used in cell E26.

It may help if we list the above formula vertically, and translate, using the @VLOOKUP function, to the right of it. We can add the brackets and other mathematical symbols later.

E26	+E26
	+1*
D5	D5
G4	@VLOOKUP(E26,E11..G20,2)
	This looks up the 4 (in cell E26) in the left-hand column of the range E11..G20, finds a 4 in cell E14, and then produces the figure 245,000 in cell G14, which is offset 2 columns to the right of column E.)

G5 @VLOOKUP(E26+1,E11..G20,2)

This is the same as the formula for G4, except that we have added 1 to the figure to be looked up, i.e. 4 + 1 = 5. Hence the formula finds 375,000 in cell G15.

G4 @VLOOKUP(E26,E11..G20,2)

This the same as G4 above.

All we have to do now is to insert the brackets and mathematical operators so that the program can understand it, and the model should work for any set of data.

When designing a formula, it is important to remember that the program performs the calculations in the following order:

(1) calculations within parentheses (brackets!) first

(2) exponentiation

(3) multiplication and division from left to right

(4) addition and subtraction from left to right

Brackets are important, and it is very easy to omit one. The author omitted one of the four brackets at the end of cell E28 and the formula failed to work.

7. Activity

(1) Experiment with changing the data in column D, and observe the effect on the payback period.

(2) Alter the model so that it shows the payback period in years and months, rather than years and days.

(3) Alter the model so that it shows the payback period in years and months *as well as* in years and days. You could use the range E27..H27.

(4) Remove all the $ signs from the formulae. Copy the whole range A1..H31 to I1..P31. You will then have two tables to facilitate comparison between two different projects. Head the tables TABLE A and TABLE B in cells A1 and I1. You may be able to hop from one table to the other using <Ctrl> and the left and right arrow keys; this will depend on the monitor display characteristics of your program.

SESSION 17

Investment Appraisal: Discounted Pay-Back

1. Objectives

At the end of this session, you will be able to:

- ❑ add discounted payback to the model you created in Session 16
- ❑ gain further experience in using the @VLOOKUP function
- ❑ alter the data in the expanded model and see the change in the simple and discounted payback periods

2. Introduction

Before you start this session, you should have completed Session 16, and saved the model for simple payback created in that session.

In this session you will add another output table which shows annual discounted cash flows for each of the ten years, and the discounted payback period.

In the next session, you will adapt this model further to calculate the net present values and internal rate of return.

[For comments on the relative merits and significance of these methods of investment appraisal, you are referred to the relevant chapters on Project Appraisal in AFBIS, or to the author's book, *Investment Appraisal*, in the SWOT series, published by CIMA and Financial Training Publications, or to any suitable textbook on management accounting.]

3. The problem

The Managing Director of Zeppo Ltd requires the worksheet which you created for him in Session 16 to calculate the discounted payback period, as well as the simple payback period.

4. Design of the model

Figure 17a shows:

- the model created is Session 16 plus a new range A31..H56 for the addition of discounted payback
- the sole additional item input cell, C34, for data insertion of required discount rate
- an additional output range E32..H56, consisting of outputs for annual discounted cash flows, cumulative totals and the discounted payback period in years and days.

Figure 17b shows the range E31..H56 of Figure 17a in text format, showing the labels and formulae necessary for the calculations.

5. Notes on creating the model

Retrieve the file created in Session 16.

Unprotect the worksheet (if necessary) with /WGPD (Worksheet, Global, Protection, Disable)

Add the labels as shown in Figures 17a and 17b.

Enter the year numbers into the ranges E38..E47 and H38..H47, using /DF (Data Fill) or copying from E11.E20 (or H11..H20).

Enter the formula into cell F38 as shown in Figure 17b. [The $ signs are necessary for the cell reference C34 since this must be absolute when copying cell F38 to the nine cells below.] Be careful to include the caret (^) sign correctly; it designates an exponent.

Copy the formula you have entered into cell F38 down to the range F39..F47.

Enter the formulae into cells G38 and G39.

Copy cell G39 down to the range G40..G47.

Enter the formulae into cell cells F49, E53 and G53.

Copy cell E28 to cell E55, and edit it carefully to produce the new formula as shown in Figure 17b. [Another method of achieving the same objective would have been to edit cell E28, making cell references absolute where necessary. If you want to try this for practice, read the tips in the activity paragraph 7 at the end of this session.]

Format the cells with /RFF0 or /RF,0 as necessary.

Enter 10% or 0.1 (according to your program) into cell C34. Use /RFP0 (Range, Format, Percentage, 0) so that the figure appears as 10%.

Protect the whole worksheet and unprotect cell C34, so that the figure can be altered as necessary.

Check that the correct discounted payback periods are shown on rows 53 and 55. If not, check all your formulae, particularly the one in cell E55.

	A	B	C	D	E	F	G	H
1	Sessions 16 and 17: Simple and Discounted Payback							
2	----------------	-------	--------	------------	------------	----------	-----------	--------
3	INPUT TABLE				OUTPUT TABLE			
4	----------------	-------	--------	------------	------------	----------	-----------	--------
5	Initial investment £s......			350,000	Simple Payback			
6					------------	----------	-----------	--------
7	Expected life: years.......			10	Annual Cash Flows:			
8					------------	----------	-----------	--------
9	Selling price per unit £s...			20	Year	£	Cum. £	Year
10								
11	Variable costs per unit £s...			15	1	5,000	5,000	1
12					2	30,000	35,000	2
13	Fixed costs per annum £s...			20,000	3	80,000	115,000	3
14	(excluding depreciation)				4	130,000	245,000	4
15					5	130,000	375,000	5
16			Sales Volumes		6	105,000	480,000	6
17					7	90,000	570,000	7
18			Year	Units	8	55,000	625,000	8
19			1	5,000	9	20,000	645,000	9
20			2	10,000	10	-5,000	640,000	10
21			3	20,000				
22			4	30,000	Total	640,000		
23			5	30,000	------------	----------	-----------	--------
24			6	25,000	Payback Period:			
25			7	22,000	------------	----------	-----------	--------
26			8	15,000	4	years and	295	days
27			9	8,000				
28			10	3,000	4.808	years		
29								
30			Total	168,000				
31	==============	======	========	==========	============	=========	===========	========
32	Session 17: Discounted Payback				Discounted Payback			
33	----------------	-------	--------	------------	------------	----------	-----------	--------
34	Discount Rate		10%		Annual Discounted Cash Flows:			
35					------------	----------	-----------	--------
36					Year	£	Cum. £	Year
37								
38					1	4,545	4,545	1
39					2	24,793	29,339	2
40					3	60,105	89,444	3
41					4	88,792	178,236	4
42					5	80,720	258,956	5
43					6	59,270	318,225	6
44					7	46,184	364,410	7
45					8	25,658	390,067	8
46					9	8,482	398,549	9
47					10	-1,928	396,622	10
48								
49					Total	396,622		
50					------------	----------	-----------	--------
51					Discounted Payback Period:			
52					------------	----------	-----------	--------
53					6	years and	251	days
54								
55					6.688	years		
56	==============	======	========	==========	============	=========	===========	========

Figure 17a

	E	F	G	H
31	==	=====================	============	========
32	Discounted Payback			
33	--	---------------------	------------	--------
34	Annual Discounted Cash Flows:			
35	--	---------------------	------------	--------
36	Year	£	Cum. £	Year
37				
38	1	+F11/((1+$C$34)^E38)	+F38	1
39	2	+F12/((1+$C$34)^E39)	+G38+F39	2
40	3	+F13/((1+$C$34)^E40)	+G39+F40	3
41	4	+F14/((1+$C$34)^E41)	+G40+F41	4
42	5	+F15/((1+$C$34)^E42)	+G41+F42	5
43	6	+F16/((1+$C$34)^E43)	+G42+F43	6
44	7	+F17/((1+$C$34)^E44)	+G43+F44	7
45	8	+F18/((1+$C$34)^E45)	+G44+F45	8
46	9	+F19/((1+$C$34)^E46)	+G45+F46	9
47	10	+F20/((1+$C$34)^E47)	+G46+F47	10
48				
49	Total	@SUM(F38:F47)		
50	--	---------------------	------------	--------
51	Discounted Payback Period:			
52	--	---------------------	------------	--------
53	@VLOOKUP(D5,G38:H47,1)		(+E55-E53)*365	days
54				
55	+E53+1*((D5-@VLOOKUP(E53,E38:G47,2))/(@VLOOKUP(E53+1,E38:G47,2)-(@VLOOKUP(E53,E38:G47,2))))			
56	==	=====================	============	========

Figure 17b

6. An explanation of the model

Cell F38

The formula used in cell F38 (and in the nine cells below) is the present value formula, which is:

$$P = \frac{A}{(1+r)^t}$$

where P = principal or present value

A = final amount received

r = annual interest rate, expressed as a decimal

t = time in number of years

In this example, for cell F38, the formula (omitting the $ signs) is

+F11/((1+C34)^E38)

where P is the amount we require in cell F38

A is the figure in cell F11 (£5,000)

r is the discount rate in cell C34 (0.1)

t is the year in cell E38 (1)

Cell E53

The explanation of the formula in this cell is similar to that for cell E28, and this can be found in Session 16, paragraph 6.

7. Activity

(1) Experiment with changing the data in column D, and also cell C34, and observe the effect on the simple and discounted payback periods.

(2) Alter the model the model so that it shows the payback periods in years and months *as well as* in years and days. You could use the ranges E27..H27 (unless you did this and saved it in Session 16) and E54..H54 for this.

(3) Remove all the $ signs from the formulae (including any you may have used in the previous activity). Copy the whole range A1..H56 to I1..P56. You will then have two tables to facilitate comparison between two different projects. Head the tables TABLE A and TABLE B in cells H1 and P1. You may be able to hop from one table to the other using <Ctrl> and the left and right arrow keys; this will depend on the monitor display characteristics of your program.

SESSION 18

Investment Appraisal: NPV and IRR

1. Objectives

At the end of this session, you will be able to:

- ❑ create a model which calculates the Net Present Value (NPV) and Internal Rate of Return (IRR) from a set of data;
- ❑ alter the data in the model and see the change to the NPV and IRR;
- ❑ consolidate your appreciation of the present value formula which you used in session 17;
- ❑ understand how to use the @*NPV* and @*IRR* functions.

2. Introduction

For this session it is not essential to have completed sessions 16 and 17, although it may be helpful to have done so, since those sessions covered two other methods of investment appraisal. If you are somewhat rusty on the principles, uses and limitations of investment appraisal, you may find it helpful to read through the relevant chapters on Project Appraisal in AFBIS.

In this session we are concerned with two discounting methods of appraisal, NPV and IRR.

We shall use the same data as we used for payback (simple and discounted) in sessions 16 and 17. The data for the problem is repeated below for the benefit of students who have not worked through those sessions.

3. The problem

Zeppo Ltd manufacture a wide range of prestigious products for the prestige-conscious businessman. The management are contemplating a new design of brief-case which they hope to sell at £20 per unit wholesale, for subsequent resale at a suitably prestigious retail price.

The necessary manufacturing equipment for this new product will cost £350,000 and have an expected life of ten years.

Variable production and selling costs per unit are costed at £15 per unit, and annual fixed production and selling costs estimated at £20,000, excluding depreciation of the manufacturing equipment.

Relying on experience with other prestigious products which the company has sold since the war, the marketing director estimates unit sales of the brief-case for the next ten years to be as follows:

Year	Units
1	5,000
2	10,000
3	20,000
4	30,000
5	30,000
6	25,000
7	22,000
8	15,000
9	8,000
10	3,000

The Managing Director of Zeppo Ltd requires a worksheet on his computer which will show the above data, the Net Present Value of the project, and also the Internal Rate of Return. He also requires that the model will allow him to alter any of the input data and see the resulting effect upon the payback period.

4. Design of the model

Figure 18a shows:

- an INPUT TABLE block (A3..D33) into which the data of the problem are entered.
- an OUTPUT TABLE block (E3..G33) in which:
  - the annual individual cash flows are calculated (F10..F20),
  - the present values are calculated from them (G10..G20),
  - both columns are totalled (F22..G22),
  - the Net Present Value is calculated (E25..G30)
  - the Internal Rate of Return is calculated (E32..G33).

You will see that the figure for Net Present Value (£13,429) appears twice, in cells G22 and G30.

In G22 it is the total of the present values calculated by the present value formulae in cells G10..G20).

In cell G30 it is calculated by using the **@NPV** function in cell G28, applied to years 1..10, and then deducting the original investment for year 0 (in cell G25).

Figure 18b shows all the formulae of the worksheet, and an explanation of these is given below in paragraph 6.

5. Notes on creating the model

[The input table of this model is similar to that created for sessions 16 and 17. If you created one of those models and saved it, you may like to retrieve it and adapt it. You are advised to save the retrieved file immediately with a new name (e.g. SESS18) so that it is preserved. Next erase (/RE) those ranges which do not appear in Figure 18a (E5..H30 and A31..H56). Then move (/M) ranges within the range A5..D14 to agree with Figure 18a.]

The default column-width of 9 is satisfactory for this worksheet, but columns F and G may be widened to, say, 11, if you prefer the appearance.

Enter all the labels as shown in Figure 18a. They can all be entered as left-aligned. However,those in cells B16, B18, B19, B30, E9 and E22 probably look better right-aligned. Also some of the labels in Figure 14a start with spaces. Please feel free to improve the appearance of your worksheet as you wish!

Enter the values in columns C and D as shown in Figure 18b. Note that cell C30 is a formula, not a value.

Format cells D8 and D9 to show as percentages (/RFP0).

Cell F10: Enter `-D5`

Cell F11: Enter the formula as shown in Figure 18b. The $ signs enable this formula to be copied down to F12..F20 with only the cell numbers in C19 changing relative to cells C19..C28. For notes regarding entering $ signs easily using the <F4> function key, see Session 15, paragraph 9. If your program allows use of the <F4> function key only in pointing mode, it is probably quicker in this case simply to type the $ signs in as you enter the formula.

Copy cell F11 down to cells F12..F20.

Cell G10: Enter `+F10`

Cell G11: Enter the formula for present value as shown in Figure 18b.

Copy cell G11 down to cells G12..G20.

Cells F22, G22, G25, G28, G30 and G33:

Enter the formulae as shown in Figure 18b.

Format the cells as necessary:

`/RFF0`	E10..E20
`/RF,0`	C19..C28, C30, D5, D6, D11.D13, F10..G20, F22, G22, G25, G28, G30
`/RFP0`	D8, D9
`/RFP2`	G33

	A	B	C	D	E	F	G
1	Session 18: NPV and IRR						
2	----------	----------	----------	----------	-------	----------	----------
3	INPUT TABLE				OUTPUT TABLE		
4	----------	----------	----------	----------	-------	----------	----------
5	Initial investment ......£s			350,000	Net Present Values		
6	Expected life: ....years			10	-------	----------	----------
7						Cash flows	Present Values
8	Discount rate (NPV).......%			12%	-------	----------	----------
9	Guess rate (IRR)..........%			13%	Year	£	£
10					0	(350,000)	(350,000)
11	Selling price per unit...£s			20	1	5,000	4,464
12	Variable costs per unit .£s			15	2	30,000	23,916
13	Fixed costs per annum ...£s			20,000	3	80,000	56,942
14	(excluding depreciation)				4	130,000	82,617
15					5	130,000	73,765
16		Sales Volumes			6	105,000	53,196
17		----------	----------		7	90,000	40,711
18		Year	Units		8	55,000	22,214
19		1	5,000		9	20,000	7,212
20		2	10,000		10	(5,000)	(1,610)
21		3	20,000		-------	----------	----------
22		4	30,000		Total	290,000	13,429
23		5	30,000		-------	----------	----------
24		6	25,000				£
25		7	22,000		Investment year 0		(350,000)
26		8	15,000				
27		9	8,000		PV of cash flows		
28		10	3,000		years 1 - 10		363,429
29							----------
30		Total	168,000		Net Present Value		13,429
31					-------	----------	----------
32					Internal Rate		
33					of Return (IRR)....		12.88%
34	----------	----------	----------	----------	-------	----------	----------

Figure 18a

Protect the whole worksheet and unprotect the data input cells:

D5, D8, D9, D11..D13, C19..28

Check that the correct NPV figures appear in cells G22 and G30, and that the correct IRR figure appears in cell G33. If not, check all your formulae carefully.

	A	B	C	D	E	F	G
1	Session 18: NPV and IRR						
2	----------	----------	----------	----------	--------	----------	----------
3	INPUT TABLE				OUTPUT TABLE		
4	----------	----------	----------	----------	--------	----------	----------
5	Initial investment ......£s			350,000	Net Present Values		
6	Expected life: ....years			10	--------	----------	----------
7						Cash flows	Present Values
8	Discount rate (NPV).......%			12%	--------	----------	----------
9	Guess rate (IRR)..........%			13%	Year	£	£
10					0	-D5	+F10
11	Selling price per unit...£s			20	1	+$C19*($D$11-$D$12)-$D$13	+F11/((1+$D$8)^E11)
12	Variable costs per unit .£s			15	2	+$C20*($D$11-$D$12)-$D$13	+F12/((1+$D$8)^E12)
13	Fixed costs per annum ...£s			20,000	3	+$C21*($D$11-$D$12)-$D$13	+F13/((1+$D$8)^E13)
14	(excluding depreciation)				4	+$C22*($D$11-$D$12)-$D$13	+F14/((1+$D$8)^E14)
15					5	+$C23*($D$11-$D$12)-$D$13	+F15/((1+$D$8)^E15)
16	Sales Volumes				6	+$C24*($D$11-$D$12)-$D$13	+F16/((1+$D$8)^E16)
17		----------	----------		7	+$C25*($D$11-$D$12)-$D$13	+F17/((1+$D$8)^E17)
18		Year	Units		8	+$C26*($D$11-$D$12)-$D$13	+F18/((1+$D$8)^E18)
19		1	5,000		9	+$C27*($D$11-$D$12)-$D$13	+F19/((1+$D$8)^E19)
20		2	10,000		10	+$C28*($D$11-$D$12)-$D$13	+F20/((1+$D$8)^E20)
21		3	20,000		--------	----------	----------
22		4	30,000		Total	@SUM(F10:F20)	@SUM(G10:G20)
23		5	30,000		--------	----------	----------
24		6	25,000				£
25		7	22,000		Investment year 0		+G10
26		8	15,000				
27		9	8,000		PV of cash flows		
28		10	3,000		years 1 - 10		@NPV(D8,F11:F20)
29							----------
30		Total	@SUM(C19:C28)		Net Present Value		+G28+G25
31					--------		
32					Internal Rate		
33					of Return (IRR)...		@IRR(D9,F10:F20)
34	----------	----------	----------	----------	--------	----------	----------

Figure 18b

6. An explanation of the model

Cells F11..F20

The formulae in these cells calculate the contribution per unit (i.e. selling price less variable cost) within the brackets, multiply this by the sales volume (units), and finally deduct the fixed costs for the year.

For example, cell F11 performs the following calculation:

C19	×	(D11	-	D12)	-	D13
5,000 units	×	(£20	-	£15)	-	£20,000

Cells G11..G20

The formula used in cell G11 (and in the nine cells below) is the present value formula, which is:

$$P = \frac{A}{(1+r)^t}$$

where P = principal or present value

A = final amount received

r = annual interest rate, expressed as a decimal

t = time in number of years

In this example, for cell G11 where the formula (omitting the $ signs)

is

+F11/((1+D8)^E11)

P is the amount we require in cell G11

A is the figure in cell F11 (£5,000)

r is the discount rate in cell D8 (0.12)

t is the year in cell E11 (1)

Cell G28 Formula: @NPV(D8,F11..F20)

The syntax of the @NPV function is:

@NPV(Discount rate,Range)

In this case, the discount rate of 12% (0.12) is in cell D8, and the range of the cash flows is F11..F20. Note that this range does not include cell G10, unlike the formula for IRR in cell G33.

Cell G33 Formula: @IRR(D9,F10..F20)

The syntax of the @IRR function is:

@IRR(Guess discount rate,Range)

In this case, the guess discount rate of 13% (0.13) is in cell D9, and the range of the cash flows is F10..F20. Note that the range here must include the initial investment figure of (350,000) which is referenced in cell F10 (via cell F10) back to the data input figure in cell D5. Unlike @NPV, @IRR presumes the first number in the range is the cash outflow for the initial investment.

The guess rate entered in cell D9 should be your best estimate of what you consider the IRR might be. Usually it should be between 0 (0%) and 1 (100%). Because more than one result is sometimes possible, try another guess if the result shows ERR, or if the result is less than 0 or greater than 1 (100%). The program calculates the IRR using an iterative trial-and -error process; the better the guess, the quicker the calculation; a reasonable guess figure for most practical purposes could be 12%.

7. Activity

(1) Enter **+G33** in cell D8. What is the revised NPV? Why is this so?

(2) Experiment with changing the data in the input table, and observe the effect on the NPV and IRR.

(3) Remove all the $ signs from the formulae (including any you may have used in the previous activity). Copy the whole range A1..G34 to H1..N34. You will then have two tables to facilitate comparison between two different projects. Head the tables TABLE A and TABLE B in cells G1 and N1. You may be able to hop from one table to the other using <Ctrl> and the left and right arrow keys; this will depend on the monitor display characteristics of your program.

SESSION 19
Investment Appraisal: Sensitivity

1. Objectives

At the end of this session, you will be able to:

- ❑ create a model which not only calculates the NPV and IRR of a project, but also measures sensitivity to changes in data input.
- ❑ gain further experience in the uses of the @VLOOKUP function;
- ❑ experiment with the design of the model to accommodate changes to the data inputs.

2. Introduction

For this session, it is assumed that you have completed and saved the model created in session 18.

In this session you will alter the data in the input table and make additions to the model.

These additions will enable the model to produce a sensitivity analysis in addition to the output of NPV and IRR.

3. The problem

[This problem is taken from *Investment Appraisal* by the author, published by CIMA and Financial Training Publications, 1987]

Bobby Shafto runs a fairly profitable business making buckles and braces.

He is planning to expand into making belts.

For this project, his annual budget for the next five years is:

	£
Sales: 40,000 units at £1 each	40,000
Variable costs: 40,000 units at 75p each	30,000
Net cash flows	10,000
Initial outlay	25,000

Life of project	5 years	
Cost of capital	15%	
		£
Annual cash flows: £10,000 x 3.35216		33,522
less: initial outlay		25,000
Therefore NPV is		8,522

Mr. Shafto wishes to know which of the following various sensitive areas is the most sensitive to reducing the NPV of £8,522 to the 'breakeven point' where the NPV is zero in each case:

(a) initial outlay;

(b) cost of capital;

(c) sales volume;

(d) selling price;

(e) variable costs.

4. Design of the model

Figure 19a shows:

- the model which you created in Session 18 in the range A1..G34, with a few slight alterations. The data for the problem in paragraph 3 above replaces the data which you entered for Session 18. The formulae which you entered in the output table (E3..G33) alter the output figures automatically.
- a new range A35..H34 which calculates the answers to the problem in paragraph 3 above.
- another new range H7..H20, which shows cumulative Present Value factors, which are used purely for some of the calculations in the range A35..H34.

Figure 19b shows the formulae for the worksheet, with the exception of the formulae for cells D41 and D42, which are too long to fit into figure 19b.

Figure 19c shows the formulae for cells D41 and D42.

An explanation of these formulae is given below in paragraph 6.

5. Notes on creating the model

Retrieve the worksheet which you created in Session 18.

Rename it (/FS) with a new file name (e.g. SESS19) so that the original file is unaffected by changes made in this current session.

Unprotect the worksheet (/WGPD) if it is already protected.

	A	B	C	D	E	F	G	H
1	Session 19:		Sensitivity					
2	------------	------------	------------	------------	------------	------------	------------	------------
3	INPUT TABLE				OUTPUT TABLE			
4	------------	------------	------------	------------	------------	------------	------------	------------
5	Initial investment ......£s			25,000	Net Present Values			
6	Expected life: ....years			5	----------	----------	---Present	----------
7						Cash flows	Values	Cum. PV
8	Cost of capital (NPV).....%			15%	----------	----------	----------	Factor
9	Guess rate (IRR)..........%			13%	Year	£	£	----------
10					0	(25,000)	(25,000)	
11	Selling price per unit...£s			1.00	1	10,000	8,696	0.86957
12	Variable costs per unit .£s			0.75	2	10,000	7,561	1.62571
13	Fixed costs per annum ...£s			0	3	10,000	6,575	2.28323
14	(excluding depreciation)				4	10,000	5,718	2.85498
15					5	10,000	4,972	3.35216
16		Sales Volumes			6	0	0	3.78448
17		----------	----------		7	0	0	4.16042
18		Year	Units		8	0	0	4.48732
19		1	40,000		9	0	0	4.77158
20		2	40,000		10	0	0	5.01877
21		3	40,000		----------	----------	----------	----------
22		4	40,000		Total	25,000	8,522	
23		5	40,000		----------	----------	----------	----------
24		6	0				£	
25		7	0		Investment year 0		(25,000)	
26		8	0					
27		9	0		PV of cash flows			
28		10	0		years 1 - 10		33,522	
29								
30		Total	200,000		Net Present Value		8,522	
31					----------	----------	----------	----------
32	Total sales £		200,000		Internal Rate			
33					of Return (IRR)...		28.65%	
34	=========	=========	=========	=========	=========	=========	=========	=========
35	The percentage changes which bring NPV of:					8,522	to NIL are:	
36	----------	----------	----------				----------	----------
37				Absolute change			Percentage change	
38	----------	----------	----------	----------	----------		----------	----------
39	(a) Initial outlay			8,522	£ increase		34.09%	
40	(b) Cost of capital			13.65%	point increase		91.00%	
41	(c) Sales volume (units)			10,168	avg. p.a.decrease		25.42%	
42	(d) Selling price			6.355	pence decrease		6.36%	
43	(e) Variable costs			6.355	pence increase		8.47%	
44	=========	=========	=========	=========	=========	=========	=========	=========

Figure 19a

	A	B	C	D	E	F	G	H
1	Session 19:		Sensitivity					
2	-------	-------	----------					
3	INPUT TABLE				OUTPUT TABLE			
4	-------	-------	----------					
5	Initial investment ......£s			25,000	Net Present Values			
6	Expected life: ....years			5			---Present	
7						Cash flows	Values	Cum. PV
8	Cost of capital (NPV).....%			15%				Factor
9	Guess rate (IRR).........%			13%	Year	£	£	
10					0	-D5	+F10	
11	Selling price per unit...£s			1.00	1	+$C19*($D$11-$D$12)-$D$13	+F11/((1+$D$8)^E11)	@PV(1,$D$8,E11)
12	Variable costs per unit .£s			0.75	2	+$C20*($D$11-$D$12)-$D$13	+F12/((1+$D$8)^E12)	@PV(1,$D$8,E12)
13	Fixed costs per annum ...£s			0	3	+$C21*($D$11-$D$12)-$D$13	+F13/((1+$D$8)^E13)	@PV(1,$D$8,E13)
14	(excluding depreciation)				4	+$C22*($D$11-$D$12)-$D$13	+F14/((1+$D$8)^E14)	@PV(1,$D$8,E14)
15					5	+$C23*($D$11-$D$12)-$D$13	+F15/((1+$D$8)^E15)	@PV(1,$D$8,E15)
16	Sales Volumes				6	+$C24*($D$11-$D$12)-$D$13	+F16/((1+$D$8)^E16)	@PV(1,$D$8,E16)
17		-------	----------		7	+$C25*($D$11-$D$12)-$D$13	+F17/((1+$D$8)^E17)	@PV(1,$D$8,E17)
18		Year	Units		8	+$C26*($D$11-$D$12)-$D$13	+F18/((1+$D$8)^E18)	@PV(1,$D$8,E18)
19		1	+$C$19		9	+$C27*($D$11-$D$12)-$D$13	+F19/((1+$D$8)^E19)	@PV(1,$D$8,E19)
20		2	+$C$19		10	+$C28*($D$11-$D$12)-$D$13	+F20/((1+$D$8)^E20)	@PV(1,$D$8,E20)
21		3	+$C$19					
22		4	+$C$19		Total	0	@SUM(G10..G20)	
23		5	+$C$19					
24		6	0				£	
25		7	0		Investment year 0		+G10	
26		8	0					
27		9	0		PV of cash flows			
28		10	0		years 1 - 10		@NPV(D8,F11..F20)	
29								
30		Total	@SUM(C19..C28)		Net Present Value		+G28+G25	
31								
32	Total sales £		+C30*D11		Internal Rate			
33					of Return (IRR)...		@IRR(D9,F10..F15)	
34	=====	====	=======	=======	====	====================	================	============
35	The percentage changes which bring NPV of:					+G30	to NIL are:	
36	-------	-------	----------					
37				Absolute change			Percentage change	
38	-------	-------	----------					
39	(a) Initial outlay			+G30	£ increase		+D39/D5	
40	(b) Cost of capital			+G33-D8	point increase		+D40/D8	
41	(c) Sales volume (units)			[Fig 19c]	avg. p.a.decrease		+D41/(@SUM(C19..C28)/D6)	
42	(d) Selling price			[Fig 19c]	pence decrease		(D42/100)/D11	
43	(e) Variable costs			+D42	pence increase		+D43/(D12*100)	
44	=====	====	=======	=======	====	====================	================	============

Figure 19b

	D
41	((C32/(@SUM(F11..F20)))*((@SUM(F11..F20)/D6)-(D5/(@VLOOKUP(D6,E11..H20,3)))))/D11
42	((D11)-((C32/D6)-((@SUM(F11..F20)/D6)-(D5/(@VLOOKUP(D6,E11..H20,3)))))/(@SUM(C19..C28)/D6))*100

Figure 19c

[For all the following instructions, you could check your entries against Figures 19a, 19b and 19c.]

Alter cell A1 to read `Session 19:`

Alter cell A8 to read `Cost of capital (NPV)...`

Cell C3: Enter `Sensitivity`

Cells D5..D13 and C19 only:
Replace the existing data with the data from the problem, as shown in Figure 19a.

Cell C20: Enter the formula `+$C$19` and copy it to cells C21..C23.

Cells C24..C28: Enter `0` (Zero)

Cells H2..H9: Enter the labels as in Figure 19a.

Cell H11: Enter the formula as shown in Figure 19b and copy it down to cells H12..H20.

Cells A35, G35, D37, G37, A39..A43, E39..E43:
Enter the labels as shown in Figure 19a.

Enter dotted lines as necessary (or as you please!) with \- or \= and using the copy (/C) command.

Cells F35, D39..D43 and G39..G43:
Enter the formulae as shown in Figures 19b and 19c. Note that Figure 19c shows the formulae for cells D41 and D42, because they are too long to show in Figure 19b. Be very careful to enter these formula meticulously. It is very easy to omit a bracket. It is a good idea to count the number of left-hand and right-hand brackets to see if they tally.

Next, format cells D39..D43 and G39..G43 as follows:

D39 and D41 `/RF,0` (Range, Format, Comma, Zero)

D42 and D43 `/RFF3` (Range, Format, Fixed, 3)

D40 and G39..G43 `/RFP2` (Range, Format, Percent, 2)

Finally, protect the whole worksheet and unprotect cells D5, D8, D9, D11..D13 and C19.

6. An explanation of the model

Cells C19..C23

You will have noted that the model is designed to work only with projected sales volumes which are the same each year for the expected life of the project (in this instance for 5 years). Hence the formula '+$C$19' in cells C20..C23.

However, if you were to enter varying sales volume figures into cells C19..C23, the outputs for (a) Inintial Outlay and (b) Cost of capital would work, but those for (c), (d) and (e) would not. At the end of this session you may like to experiment with this. [See paragraph 9. Activity.]

(a) *Initial Outlay*

Row 39 (Cells A39..G39):

The initial outlay can rise by the Net Present Value of £8,522 (cells G22 and G30), i.e. from £25,000 (cell C5) to £33,522 (cell G28) before the NPV becomes nil.

Try it and see! Enter '+G28' into cell D5 and observe the effect on the output tables. Restore £25,000 to cell D5 when you have finished.

The formula in cell D39, '+G30' refers to the value of the NPV shown by that cell.

The formula in cell G39, '+D39/' D5 calculates the percentage increase (34.09%) of the value in cell D39 (£8,522) over the original initial investment figure in cell D5 (£25,000). You formatted (paragraph 5 above) the cell to show the result as a percentage, to two decimal places.

(b) *Cost of Capital*

Row 40 (Cells A40..G40)

The cost of capital can increase from 15% (Cell D8) to 28.65% (Cell G33), which is an increase of 13.65%, before the NPV becomes nil.

Try it and see! Enter **+G33** into cell D8 and observe the effect on the output tables. Restore 15% to cell D8 when you have finished.

The formula in cell D40, **+G33-D8** calculates the increase in the cost of capital before the NPV becomes nil.

The formula in cell G40, **+D40/D8** calculates the percentage increase (91.00%) of the value in cell D40 (13.65%) over the original cost of capital figure in cell D8 (15%). You formatted (paragraph 5 above) the cell to show the result as a percentage, to two decimal places.

(c) *Sales volume (units)*

Row 41 (Cells A41..G41)

This is rather more tricky to calculate.

The present values of annual cash flows will have to fall to £25,000 (the initial outlay) for the NPV to reach nil. Therefore the cumulative PV of five years of cash flows will be £25,000. The discount factor for five years at 15% is 3.35216 (see cell H15). £25,000 divided by 3.35216 = £7,458.

If you want proof, here it is:

	Cash Flows	Discount Factor	Present Values
	£s	(15%)	£
Initial outlay	(25,000)	1.000	(25,000)
Cash flows, years 1 - 5	7,458	3.352	25,000
Net Present Value			nil

Annual net cash flows can therefore decrease by £2,542 (£10,000 – £7,458) before NPV = nil.

The Sales : Cash Flow ratio is £40,000 : £10,000, or 4 : 1.

Therefore sales revenue can decrease by £2,542 × 4 = £10,168.

Selling price per unit is £1; therefore UNIT sales can decrease by 10,168 units per annum (see cell D41 which has worked it out for you).

When constructing the formula for this calculation, we must make sure that it works, whatever the data in the input table. We must therefore be careful to include only references to cells and not to any data in those cells.

The formula is:

```
((C32/(@SUM(F11..F20)))*((@SUM(F11..F20)/D6)
     – (D5/(@VLOOKUP(D6,E11..H20,3)))))/D11
```

It may help to split this down into its components:

C32	Total Sales	£200,000
@SUM(F11..F20)	Total Cash Flows	£50,000
D6	Expected life	5 years
D5	Initial Investment	£25,000
@VLOOKUP(D6,E11..H20,3)	Discount Factor for 5 years at 15%	3.35216

[Note: a description of the @VLOOKUP function was provided in Session 16, paragraph 6. Briefly: this function looks up cell D6 (5 years) in the left-hand column of range E11..H20, finds '5' in cell E15, and then looks up the figure in the 3rd column (offset) to the right, i.e. in cell H15.]

D11	Selling price per unit	£1

So the formula calculates:

$$\frac{£200{,}000}{£50{,}000} \times \left[\frac{£50{,}000}{5 \text{ years}} - \frac{£25{,}000}{3{,}35216} \right] \div £1$$

$$= 4 \times (£10{,}000 - £7{,}458) \div £1$$

$$= 4 \times £2{,}542 \div £1$$

$$= £10{,}168 \div £1$$

$$= 10{,}168 \text{ units}$$

The formula in cell G41, +D41/(@SUM(C19..C28)/D6) calculates the percentage increase (25.42%) of the value in cell D41 (10,168) over the average annual number of units sold, i.e. 40,000. Since the figures for the five years in cells C19..C23 may vary, it is necessary to calculate the average units sold by using the formula @SUM(C19..C28)/D6. You formatted (paragraph 5 above) the cell to show the result as a percentage, to two decimal places.

(d) ***Selling Price***

Row 42 (Cells A42..G42)

This is even more tricky to calculate.

In (c) above we calculated that annual net cash flows can decrease by £2,542 before NPV = nil.

Therefore sales revenue can fall by £2,542 to £37,548 (£40,000 - £2,542).

With units sold remaining at 40,000 units, this gives a selling price of 93.645 pence = (£37,458 ÷ 40,000).

It is important to notice that this is different from the change for sales volume, because we can assume that variable costs will not be affected by the reduction in selling price, i.e. they will remain at 75 pence per unit.

The formula is:

```
((D11)-((C32/D6)-((@SUM(F11..F20)/D6)–
    (D5/(@VLOOKUP(D6,E11..H20,3)))))/(@SUM(C19..C28)/D6))*100
```

It may help to split this down into its components:

D11	Selling price per unit	£1
C32	Total Sales	£200,000
D6	Expected life	5 years
@SUM(F11..F20)	Total Cash Flows	£50,000
D6	Expected life	5 years
D5	Initial Investment	£25,000
@VLOOKUP(D6,E11..H20,3)	Discount Factor for 5 years at 15%	3.35216

[Note: a description of the @VLOOKUP function was provided in Session 16, paragraph 6. Briefly: this function looks up cell D6 (**5** years) in the left-hand column of range E11..H20, finds **5** in cell E15, and then looks up the figure in the 3rd column (offset) to the right, i.e. in cell H15.]

@SUM(C19..C28)	Sales volume (units)	200,000
D6	Expected life	5 years

So the formula calculates as shown on the following page.

$$\left[£1 - \left[\frac{\left[\dfrac{£200,000}{5 \text{ years}} - \left[\dfrac{£50,000}{5 \text{ years}} - \dfrac{£25,000}{3.35216} \right] \right]}{\dfrac{200,000 \text{ units}}{5 \text{ years}}} \right] \right] \times 100$$

Simplifying:

$$\left[£1 - \left[\left[\frac{£40,000 - [£10,000 - £7,458]}{40,000 \text{ units}} \right] \right] \right] \times 100$$

Simplifying again:

$$\left[£1 - \left[\frac{£37,458}{40,000} \right] \right] \times 100$$

and again:

$$(£1 - £0.93645) \times 100$$
$$= 6.355 \text{ pence}$$

The formula in cell G42, (D42/100)/D11 calculates the percentage decrease (6.36%) of the value in cell D42 (6.355 pence) from the selling price per unit as entered in cell D11, i.e. £1. The /100 converts 6.355 pence into a decimal of a £, i.e. £0.06355. You formatted (paragraph 5 above) the cell to show the result as a percentage, to two decimal places.

(e) *Variable Costs*

Row 43 (Cells A43..G43)

Variable costs can rise by £2,542 per annum. £2,542 divided by 40,000 units = 6.355 pence. This is the same result as for (d) Selling Price above. Therefore we can simply refer to cell D42 in cell D43. This is quite a relief.

The formula in cell G43, (D42/100)/D11 calculates the percentage increase (8.47%) of the value in cell D43 (6.355 pence) over the variable costs per unit as entered in cell D12, i.e. £0.75. The *100 converts £0.75 into pence, i.e. 75 pence. You formatted (paragraph 5 above) the cell to show the result as a percentage, to two decimal places.

7. Comments

The percentage changes which bring the NPV of £8,520 to nil are:

		% change	Ranking
(a) Initial outlay	(+)	34.09	4
(b) Cost of capital	(+)	91.00	5
(c) Sales volume	(-)	25.42	3
(d) Selling price	(-)	6.36	1
(e) Variable costs	(+)	8.47	2

Ranking is based on the relative size of the percentage change with the lowest percentage required to eliminate a positive NPV being regarded as representing the most sensitive variable.

The most sensitive (for the data in this particular problem) would therefore appear to be a decrease in selling price, and the least sensitive an increase in the cost of capital.

This is a fairly crude method of assessment. Criticisms may be that, for example, sales volume is much more *likely* to drop than selling price, but sales price may well be a dependent variable relative to sales volume so that the latter should be monitored carefully in spite of its third rank in sensitivity. Also the analysis isolates each variable, where the effect of a combination may be required. However, the model can cope with a variety of changes to the input data, and, provide its limitations are appreciated, the analysis can provide management with useful information.

8. Warning

The model as it stands can cope with changes to most input data *except* Expected Life, which, at present, is five years. The model has been designed to accept input data for up to ten years. However, if you wish to input data for any expected life *other than* five years, you will have to make some alterations. For example, if wanted to input data for 6 years, you should do the following:

(a) Alter cell D6 to read **6** years, and protect the cell;

(b) Adjust the formula in cell G33 for the calculation of IRR. At present this reads:

@IRR(D9,F10..F15)

F10..F15 covers cash flows for years 0..5 in the range F10..F20. Therefore in order to input data for 6 years, you would have edit <F2> cell G33 to read:

@IRR(D9,F10..F16)

(c) Adjust the range C19..C28. C19 should remain unprotected for entry of the sales volume input data (e.g. **40000**). Cells C20..C24 should read **+$C$19**. Cells C25..C28 should read **0** (zero). Cells C20..C28 should be protected.

If you find this model useful, you could create ten separate worksheets, one for each of the ten possible 'Expected Lives', and name them, for example, as follows:

SENS1YR.WKS, SENS2YR.WKS, SENS3YR.WKS, and so on.

If you adjusted each one appropriately for cells D6, G33 and C19..C28, then data could be entered in the data input table without the need for further adjustment.

9. Activity

When trying out the following experiments, do not forget to save any revised worksheets with a new filename!

(1) Using the existing model which you have created for the five-year expected life, experiment with entering revised data in the input tables, one item at a time. For example, alter the initial investment figure in cell D5 from £25,000 to £30,000 and compare the outputs with those in Figure 19a. Reinstate £25,000 to cell D5 before you experiment with:

D8	Cost of capital Enter **+G33**, as you did in session 18, and observe the effect on the outputs.
D11	Selling price per unit
D12	Variable costs per unit
D19	Sales volumes, units

(2) Continue your experiments by combining two changes to the data, and observe the outputs. For example, alter cell D6 to £30,000 and cell D8 (Cost of capital) to 17%.

(3) Enter £2,000 fixed costs into cell D13, and observe the results. How can you correct the present worksheet to correct the outputs which are not required in cells F16..F20 ?

(4) Create a model which will accommodate data for a project with an expected life of 6 years. Read carefully paragraph 8 above (titled 'Warning') before you do so. A good check on whether you have made the alterations correctly is to enter **+G33** into cell D8, and observe the outputs.

(5) Enter data into the model created in the previous activity (4) for the Bobby Shafto problem in paragraph 3 of this session, except that the expected life of the project is now 6 years, instead of five. Compare the NPV, IRR and sensitivity outputs with those for the five year project as shown in Figure 19a.

(6) As mentioned in paragraph 6 (An explanation of the model), you will have noted that the model is designed to work only with projected sales volumes which are the same each year for the expected life of the project (in this instance for 5 years). Hence the formula **+$C$19** in cells C20..C23.

However, if you were to enter varying sales volume figures into cells C19..C23, the outputs for (a) Inintial Outlay and (b) Cost of capital would work, but those for (c), (d) and (e) would not. You may like to experiment with this. Try unprotecting cells C19..C23, copy C19 (40000) to cells C20..C23, and alter cell D8 to read **+G33**. Then enter 39500 in cell C19. Observe the effect on the outputs in lines 39..43.

SESSION 20

Variance analysis: Costs

1. Objectives

At the end of this session, you will be able to:

- ❑ construct a model which produces cost variances from budgeted and actual data
- ❑ test the effect of changes in data input on the variances
- ❑ appreciate the potential of spreadsheets for constructing models of this type.

2. Introduction

In this session you will create a model which is able to produce cost variances (material, labour and fixed overhead) from data given in a typical situation. The variances produced from the data are:

Material:	Price and Usage
Labour:	Rate and Efficiency
Fixed Overhead:	Expenditure, Capacity and Efficiency

3. The Problem

[This problem is taken from *Variance Analysis* by the author, published by CIMA and Financial Training Publications, 1986]

Sparclear Limited bottles and sells sparkling mineral wanters in one-litre bottles.

You have recently been appointed manager of the bottling plant. The cartoning and distribution of the bottles are carried out in other departments, which are not your concern.

The materials costs consist of the mineral water and disposable bottles, which are referred to as 'empties' to distinguish them from the full bottles which are sold. The labour is employed to run and maintain the bottling plant, the depreciation and maintenance costs for which account for a large part of the factory overhead.

Recently, you set standards and standard costs for each litre bottle produced, and these were as follows:

	pence
Mineral water: 1 litre @ 4p per litre	4
Empties: 1 empty @ 3p per empty	3
Labour: the number of employess and hours vary according to demand, but each standard man-hour of £2.24 per hour is expected to produce 28 bottles	8
Fixed factory overhead: the budget, prepared by the accountant, for the year of 48 working weeks, is £108,000, and budgeted production for the year is 720,000 bottles	15
Total standard cost per bottle	30

During the first 14 weeks of this year, things went fairly well in the bottling plant, but last week, ending Friday 13 April, was not a good week.

Production for the week was only 14,000 bottles of mineral water. The accountant has sent you a note of the actual costs for last week, which were:

		£
Mineral water:	14,200 litres	639
Empties:	14,500 empties	493
Labour:	550 hours worked	1,287
Overhead (fixed factory)		2,300
Total costs:		4,719

Your managing director has worked out that 14,000 bottles at 30p per bottle should have cost £4,200, and wants to know exactly where you have managed to lose £519 in one week.

4. Design of the model

Figure 20a shows the solution to this problem:

Columns A..C contain the the INPUT TABLE and show the data given in the problem.

Columns D..H contain the OUTPUT TABLES, and analyse the data in summary and detail formats:

> Rows 5..17 show the actual and standard figures for the two materials, labour and overhead, with the variances in column H.
>
> Rows 19..56 show the above variances, sub-analysed into material price and usage, labour rate and efficiency, and overhead expenditure, capacity and efficiency. The calculations follow the method suggested in *Variance Analysis* for calculation of the variances.

The following abbreviations have been used in the calculations in column D:

AQ = Actual Quantity

AP = Actual Price

SP = Standard Price

AO = Actual Output

SQ = Standard Quantity

AH = Actual Hours

AR = Actual Rate

SR = Standard Rate

SH = Standard Hours

RR = Recovery Rate

There are very many ways of explaining variance analysis calculations, and it is assumed that you understand the basic principles; if not, you are referred to any standard text-book on the subject.

Figure 20b shows the formulae used for Figure 20a; only the range D6..H56 is shown, since the remainder of the worksheet does not use formulae.

5. Notes on creating the model

The labels, values and formulae are all straightforward, and you should refer to Figures 20a and 20b in creating the model.

The $ signs in the formulae in cell G12 are to keep the cell reference G8 absolute (not relative) when copying cell G12 to cells G13..G15. A note on how to use the function key <F4> when entering $ signs in formulae is given in session 15, paragraph 5.

Finally, format the cells as necessary with /RF (Range, Format). [Details were provided in session 18, paragraph 5.]

When you have completed the model, and are satisfied that it is correct, you can protect the whole worksheet, and unprotect the data input range C7..C32. Notes on how to do this were given in session 5, paragraph 9.

This will save accidental changes to labels and formulae.

6. Viewing the model

One of the difficulties of spreadsheets is the relatively small area of the worksheet that is visible on the screen at one time. In the present worksheet, if you are using the standard display of about 72 characters wide and 20 lines deep, you cannot see the input and output ranges at the same time. There are ways round this. You can split the screen into two windows and scroll them independently.

	A	B	C	D	E	F	G	H
1	Session 20: Variance Analysis: Costs							
2	----------	----------	----------	----------	----------	----------	----------	----------
3	INPUT TABLE			OUTPUT TABLES				
4	----------	----------	----------	----------	----------	----------	----------	----------
5	STANDARDS	Description	INPUTS	TOTAL VARIANCES FOR WEEK NO.			15	
6	Material A			----------	----------	----------	----------	----------
7	Quantity per unit	litres	1	ITEM	ACTUAL	STANDARD	STANDARD	VARIANCES
8	Price	pence per litre	4			PER BOTTLE	14000	ADV
9	Material B						BOTTLES	(-)FAV
10	Quantity per unit	empties	1	----------	----------	----------	----------	----------
11	Price	pence per empty	3		£	pence	£	£
12	Labour			Material A	639	4	560	79
13	Bottles per hour	bottles	28	Material B	493	3	420	73
14	Rate	pence per hour	224	Labour	1287	8	1120	167
15	Fixed O'head P.A.:			Fixed O'Head	2300	15	2100	200
16	Budget total p.a.	£	108000	----------	----------	----------	----------	----------
17	Weeks per annum		48	Totals	4719	30	4200	519
18	Budgeted prod'n p.a.	bottles	720000	==========	======	==========	=========	=========
19				DETAILED VARIANCES FOR WEEK NO			15	
20	ACTUAL PRODUCTION	Week No.	15	----------	----------	----------	----------	----------
21	Units	bottles	14000	Calculations		Variance type		VARIANCES
22	ACTUAL COSTS							ADV
23	Material A							(-)FAV
24	Quantity	litres	14200	----------	----------	----------	----------	----------
25	Total cost	£	639	MATERIAL A		MATERIAL A		
26	Material B			M1 AQxAP	639			
27	Quantity	empties	14500			Material A Price		71
28	Total cost	£	493	M2 AQxSP	568			
29	Labour					Material A Usage		8
30	Hours worked	hours worked	550	M3 AOxSQxSP	560			
31	Total cost	£	1287			Material A Total		79
32	Fixed overhead	£	2300	MATERIAL B		MATERIAL B		
33				M1 AQxAP	493			
34						Material B Price		58
35				M2 AQxSP	435			
36						Material B Usage		15
37				M3 AOxSQxSP	420			
38						Material B Total		73
39				LABOUR		LABOUR		
40				L1 AHxAR	1287			
41						Labour Rate		55
42				L2 AHxSR	1232			
43						Labour Efficiency		112
44				L3 AOxSHxSR	1120			
45						Labour Total		167
46				FIXED O'HEAD		FIXED O'HEAD		
47				F1 Actual	2300			
48						Expenditure		50
49				F2 Budget	2250			
50						Capacity		-60
51				F3 AHxRR	2310			
52						Efficiency		210
53				F4 Recovered	2100			
54						F.O'head Total		200
55								
56						TOTAL COST VARIANCE		519

Figure 20a

	D	E	F	G	H
6	----------------	----------------	----------------	----------------	----------------
7	ITEM	ACTUAL	STANDARD	STANDARD	VARIANCES
8			PER BOTTLE	+C21	ADV
9				BOTTLES	(-)FAV
10	----------------	----------------	----------------	----------------	----------------
11		£	pence	£	£
12	Material A	+C25	+C7*C8	+F12*$G$8/100	+E12-G12
13	Material B	+C28	+C10*C11	+F13*$G$8/100	+E13-G13
14	Labour	+C31	+C14/C13	+F14*$G$8/100	+E14-G14
15	Fixed O'Head	+C32	+C16/C18*100	+F15*$G$8/100	+E15-G15
16	----------------	----------------	----------------	----------------	----------------
17	Totals	+C25+C28+C31+C32	@SUM(F12..F15)	@SUM(G12..G15)	@SUM(H12..H15)
18	============	============	============	============	============
19	DETAILED VARIANCES FOR WEEK NO.			+C20	
20	----------------	----------------	----------------	----------------	----------------
21	Calculations		Variance type		VARIANCES
22					ADV
23					(-)FAV
24	----------------	----------------	----------------	----------------	----------------
25	MATERIAL A		MATERIAL A		
26	M1 AQxAP	+C25			
27			Material A Price		+E26-E28
28	M2 AQxSP	+C24*C8/100			
29			Material A Usage		+E28-E30
30	M3 AOxSQxSP	+C21*C7*C8/100			
31			Material A Total		+E26-E30
32	MATERIAL B		MATERIAL B		
33	M1 AQxAP	+C28			
34			Material B Price		+E33-E35
35	M2 AQxSP	+C27*C11/100			
36			Material B Usage		+E35-E37
37	M3 AOxSQxSP	+C21*C10*C11/100			
38			Material B Total		+E33-E37
39	LABOUR		LABOUR		
40	L1 AHxAR	+C31			
41			Labour Rate		+E40-E42
42	L2 AHxSR	+C30*C14/100			
43			Labour Efficiency		+E42-E44
44	L3 AOxSHxSR	+C21/C13*C14/100			
45			Labour Total		+E40-E44
46	FIXED O'HEAD		FIXED O'HEAD		
47	F1 Actual	+C32			
48			Expenditure		+E47-E49
49	F2 Budget	+C16/C17			
50			Capacity		+E49-E51
51	F3 AHxRR	+C30*C16/C18*C13			
52			Efficiency		+E51-E53
53	F4 Recovered	+C21*C16/C18			
54			F.O'head Total		+E47-E53
55					
56			TOTAL COST VARIANCE		+H31+H38+H45+H54

Figure 20b

Move the cursor to row 11

Press `/WWH` (Worksheet, Window, Horizontal)

The screen now has two views of the same worksheet.

The function key <F6> enables you to toggle the cursor between the two windows. You can scroll in each window separately.

The command: `/WWS` (Worksheet, Window, Synch)

synchronises the scrolling of the windows,

whereas: `/WWU` (Worksheet, Window, Unsync)

produces independent scrolling.

Try these commands on the current worksheet until you feel familiar with the procedure.

Scroll each window until those parts of the input and output ranges in which you are interested are conveniently positioned.

If you are using {123} :

you may find it more convenient to use move the cursor to column B, and then:

Press `/WCH` (Worksheet, Column, Hide)

to hide column B (i.e. Columns A and C are now adjacent, and column B is temporarily not visible). Then move the cursor to column D, and

Press `/WWV` (Worksheet, Window, Vertical)

To restore the screen to a single window,

Press `/WWC` (Worksheet, Window, Clear)

7. Activity

(1) Try altering the data inputs and observe the changes of the variances in the total and detailed output tables. When you have finished, do NOT use /FSR (File, Save, Replace) if you wish to preserve the original data in your model. Instead, if you do NOT wish to preserve the altered worksheet, simply quit the program or retrieve a new file (or the same file if you wish to start experimenting with it again). If you DO wish to preserve the altered worksheet, save it with a new filename.

(2) Find a similar variance analysis problem, i.e. one which is restricted to the basic production cost variances. Unprotect the model with /WGPD (Worksheet, Global, Protection, Disable) and adapt the model to suit the new problem. You will need to alter the descriptions in column B. Also, for example, if there are more than two types of material, you will need to make use of the Move and Copy commands, as well as the <F2> Edit key (see session 1, paragraphs 1.7 and 1.8) and <F4> Absolute key (see session 15, paragraph 9), to adjust the cell references.

SESSION 21
Variance analysis: Sales

1. Objectives

At the end of this session, you will be able to:

- ❑ construct a model which produces sales variances from budgeted and actual data
- ❑ integrate that model with that created in session 20
- ❑ add to the model a reconciliation of budgeted with actual profit
- ❑ test the effect of changes in data on the variances

2. Introduction

In session 20 you created a model which produced cost variances from data in a typical situation.

In this session you will add to that model so that sales variances can also be calculated from the previous and some additional data.

In addition, you will create an output table which reconciles budgeted with actual profit from the data inputs of the models created in both this and the previous sessions.

3. The problem

[This problem is taken from *Variance Analysis* by the author, published by CIMA and Financial Training Publications, 1986]

You may remember that you are manager of the *Sparclear Limited* bottling plant. Budgeted sales for the year of 48 weeks are 720,000 bottles (the same as production) at a standard selling price of 50 pence per bottle, i.e. £360,000.

Actual sales for last week were 13,500 bottles, with a revenue of £6,480.

You have already calculated for the managing director the cost variances for last week, and (hopefully) explained them to him to his satisfaction.

Now he wants to know how much profit was actually made last week, how much should have been made, and how much of the difference was due to variances in the selling price and sales volume of the product, ie. not explained by the cost variances.

4. Design of the model

You are going to create this model on the same worksheet as that for session 20, to the right of it, in the range J1..Q38.

Figure 21a shows four main areas:

	J	K	L	M	N	O	P	Q
1	Session 21: Variance Analysis: Sales							
2	----------------	----------------	--------	----------	----------	----------	----------	----------
3	INPUT TABLE			OUTPUT TABLES				
4	----------------	----------------	--------	----------	----------	----------	----------	----------
5	STANDARDS	Description	INPUTS	TOTAL VARIANCES FOR WEEK NO.			15	
6				----------	----------	----------	----------	----------
7	BUDGETED SALES			Calculations		Variance type		VARIANCES
8								ADV
9	Weeks per annum		48					(-)FAV
10	Budgeted Sales p.a.	bottles	720000	----------	----------	----------	----------	----------
11	Budgeted price	pence / bottle	50	SALES				£
12				S1 AQxAP	6480			
13	ACTUAL SALES	Week No.	15			Selling Price		270
14				S2 AQxSP	6750			
15	Units	bottles	13500					
16	Revenue	£	6480	S3 AQxSC	4050			
17								
18				S4 AQxSM	2700			
19						Sales Volume Profit		300
20				S5 SQxSM	3000			
21						TOTAL SALES VARIANCE		570
22	================	============	=======	==========	=======	========	============	==========
23	CALCULATION OF ACTUAL PROFIT			RECONCILIATION OF BUDGETED AND ACTUAL PROFIT				
24	----------------	----------------	--------	----------	----------	----------	----------	----------
25		£	£				£	£
26				Budgeted profit		pence		
27	Actual sales		6480	15000	bottles @	20		3000
28				less: variances				
29	Actual prod'n costs	4719		Selling price			270	
30				Sales volume profit			300	
31	less:						---	
32	increase in stock						570	
33	(at standard cost)	150		Total cost variances			519	
34		----					---	
35			4569	Total variances				1089
36			----------					----------
37			1911	Actual profit				1911
38			=======					==========

Figure 21a

Area 1: J3..L21

This contains the Input Table, where new inputs concerning the sales data are entered. There are also some cells (L9 and L13) which refer to data from the range A1..H56 created in session 20. [These have been included to make the model somewhat more flexible for adapting to accommodate alternative data.]

Area 2: M3..Q21

This area contains the output table for the sales variance calculations. The calculations follow the method suggested in *Variance Analysis* for the calculation of the selling price and sales volume profit variances.

	J	K	L	M	N	O	P	Q
1	Session 21: Variance Analysis: Sales							
2	----------------	----------------	----------	----------	----------------	----------------	----------	----------------
3	INPUT TABLE			OUTPUT TABLES				
4	----------------	----------------	----------	----------	----------------	----------------	----------	----------------
5	STANDARDS	Description	INPUTS	TOTAL VARIANCES FOR WEEK NO.			+L13	
6				----------	----------------	----------------	----------	----------------
7	BUDGETED SALES			Calculations		Variance type		VARIANCES
8								ADV
9	Weeks per annum		+C17					(-)FAV
10	Budgeted Sales p.	bottles	720000	----------	----------------	----------------	----------	----------------
11	Budgeted price	pence/bottle	50	SALES				£
12				S1 AQxAP	+L16			
13	ACTUAL SALES	Week No.	+C20			Selling Price		+N14-N12
14				S2 AQxSP	+L15*L11/100			
15	Units	bottles	13500					
16	Revenue	£	6480	S3 AQxSC	+L15*F17/100			
17								
18				S4 AQxSM	+N14-N16			
19						Sales Volume Profit		+N20-N18
20				S5 SQxSM	+(L10/L9)*(+L11-F17)/100			
21						TOTAL SALES VARIANCE		+Q13+Q19
22	=============	==========	========	========	===========	===========	=========	===========
23	CALCULATION OF ACTUAL PROFIT			RECONCILIATION OF BUDGETED AND ACTUAL PROFIT				
24	----------------	----------------	----------	----------	----------------	----------------	----------	----------------
25		£	£				£	£
26				Budgeted profit		pence		
27	Actual sales		+L16	+L10/L9	bottles @	+L11-F17		+N20
28				less: variances				
29	Actual prod'n cost	+E17		Selling price			+Q13	
30				Sales volume profit			+Q19	
31	less:						---	
32	increase in stock						+P29+P30	
33	(at standard cost	(C21-L15)*F17/100		Total cost variances			+H17	
34		----					---	
35			+K29-K33	Total variances				+P32+P33
36			----------					----------------
37			+L27-L35	Actual profit				+Q27-Q35
38			========					===========

Figure 21b

The following abbreviations have been used in the calculations in column M:

AQ = Actual sales Quantity

AP = Actual selling Price, per unit

SC = Standard Cost, per unit

SQ = Standard sales Quantity

SP = Standard selling Price, per unit

SM = Standard profit or Margin, per unit

There are very many ways of explaining variance analysis calculations, and it is assumed that you understand the basic principles; if not, you are referred to any standard text-book on the subject.

The following may help in understanding the range M11..Q21

	£	Variances Adv (Fav)
S1 Actual sales		
13,500 bottles @ 48p	6,480	
Selling price variance		
13,500 bottles @ 2p		270
S2 Actual units sold at standard selling price		
13,500 bottles @ 50p	6,750	
S3 Actual units sold at standard cost		
13,500 bottles @ 30p	4,050	
S4 Standard profit on actual sales		
13,500 bottles @ 20p	2,700	
Sales volume profit variance		
1,500 bottles @ 20p		300
S5 Standard profit on budgeted sales		
15,000 bottles @ 20p	3,000	

[Note: Line S2 - line S3 = S4, which shows the standard profit (sometimes called *standard margin*) on actual sales. It used to be common practice to calculate the sales volume variance based on selling price, i.e.:

(15,000 - 13,500 bottles =) 1,500 bottles @ 50p = £750

The snag with this is that this figure cannot easily be used in a reconciliation between *actual profit* (or margin) and *standard or budgeted profit* (or margin), which is what we require for the reconciliation statement in the range M23..Q37 referred to below. The reason is that the standard *cost* of 30p per bottle is included in the selling price of 50p per bottle.]

Area 3: M23..Q37

This contains the *Reconciliation of Budgeted and Actual Profit.*

It starts with the budgeted profit (line 26), lists the two sales variances (lines 29 and 30), then the total cost variances (line 33), and ends with the actual profit (line 37) calculated from the preceding figures.

Area 4: J23..L37

This area shows the calculation of the actual profit figure of £1,911, and this is a check on the figure in cell Q37

Figure 20b shows the formulae used for Figure 20a. Note that some of the formulae refer to cells in the range A1..H56; for example, the cell F17 (referred to in cells K33, N16, N20 and O27) is the total standard cost per bottle (£4,719).

5. Notes on creating the model

The labels, values and formulae are all straightforward, and you should refer to Figures 21a and 21b in creating the model.

Finally, format the cells as necessary with /RF (Range, Format). [Details were provided in session 18, paragraph 5.]

When you have completed the model, and are satisfied that it is correct, you can protect the whole worksheet, and unprotect the data input range L10..L11 and L15..L16. Notes on how to do this were given in session 5, paragraph 9. This will save accidental changes to labels and formulae.

6. Viewing the model

One of the difficulties of spreadsheets is the relatively small area of the worksheet that is visible on the screen at one time. In the present worksheet, if you are using the standard display of about 72 characters wide and 20 lines deep, you cannot see the input and output ranges at the same time. There are ways round this. You can split the screen into two windows and scroll them independently. Details of how to do this were provided in session 20, paragraph 6.

7. Activity

(1) Try altering the data inputs in columns C and L and observe the changes of the variances in the output tables. To repeat the note in activity (1) in the previous session, when you have finished, do NOT use /FSR (File, Save, Replace) if you wish to preserve the original data in your model. Instead, if you do NOT wish to preserve the altered worksheet, simply quit the program or retrieve a new file (or the same file if you wish to start experimenting with it again). If you DO wish to preserve the altered worksheet, save it with a new filename.

(2) Find a similar variance analysis problem, i.e. one which is restricted to the basic production cost and sales variances. Unprotect the model with /WGPD (Worksheet, Global, Protection, Disable) and adapt the model to suit the new problem. You will need to alter the descriptions in columns B and K. Also you may need to make use of the Move and Copy commands, as well as the <F2> Edit key (see session 1, paragraphs 1.7 and 1.8) and <F4> Absolute key (see session 15, paragraph 9), to adjust the cell references.

(3) Restructure appropriate parts of the model to achieve the following changes to the *Reconciliation of Budgeted and Actual Profit* table:

(a) start with the actual profit and end with the budgeted profit (instead of the other way round as in the present model); and

(b) show all the cost variances in detail in the body of the reconciliation, instead of simply the total cost variances as at present in cell P33.

SESSION 22

Variance analysis: Material mix and yield

1. Objectives

At the end of this session, you will be able to:

- ❑ construct a model which produces direct material mix and yield variances from budgeted and actual data
- ❑ test the effect of changes in data on the variances
- ❑ appreciate the principles of worksheet construction which enable you to design and construct similar models involving data analysis

2. Introduction

In this session you will create a new model for variance analysis which is independent of the model produced in sessions 20 and 21. This session can therefore be approached independently of those sessions, although you will probably gain from having completed those two sessions first.

Mix variances are subvariances of certain basic variances, and can apply to materials, labour and sales. An understanding of the principles and calculations of these variances can help consolidate your understanding of the basic variances covered in sessions 20 and 21. In this session, we consider a problem which involves direct materials, but the principles of the solutions can be applied to sub-variances of the basic labour and sales variances.

Direct material mix and yield variances are subvariances of the direct material usage variance; together with the price variance they make up the direct material total variance.

3. The problem

[This problem is taken from *Variance Analysis* by the author, published by CIMA and Financial Training Publications, 1986]

Speedigrow Limited manufacture a fertiliser by mixing three chemicals, A, B and C, and the following standards apply:

	Standard proportions	*Standard cost per tonne*
	%	£
A	70	20
B	20	30
C	10	50

During the process of mixing, a process loss of 10% is regarded as the standard.

In week 17, 855 tonnes of the fertiliser were produced, and inputs were as follows:

	Actual inputs (tonnes)	*Actual prices (£ per tonne)*	*Actual cost (£)*
A	660	21	13,860
B	210	32	6,720
C	130	47	6,110
Totals	1,000		26,690

Required: Produce a worksheet into which the above data can be entered, and which calculates the direct material price, mix and yield variances for week 17.

4. Design of the model

Figure 22a shows the solution to this problem:

Lines 3..17 contain the INPUT TABLE and show the data provide by the problem.

Lines 19..62 contain the OUTPUT TABLE which is in two parts:

> Lines 21..25 show a SUMMARY OF VARIANCES which is derived from:
>
> Lines 27..62 which contain the DETAILED CALCULATION OF VARIANCES.

The summary has been placed above the detailed calculations, so that the results of the analysis can be more accessible to the user.

Lines 64..72 contain notes on the abbreviations used in the detailed calculation section.

Only lines 8..10 and 13..16 in the input table contain unprotected cells into which data can be entered. All other lines contain protected labels and formulae.

The calculations follow the method suggested in *Variance Analysis* for the calculation of the variances. Notes and comments on the variances are provided there.

The following abbreviations have been used in the calculations in column A of the detailed calculation section:

	A	B	C	D	E	F
1	Session 22: Variance Analysis: Material Mix and Yield Variances					
2	------------------------	----------	----------	----------	----------	--------
3	INPUT TABLE					
4	------------------------	----------	----------	----------	----------	--------
5	Material Type:-	A	B	C	All	
6	------------------------	----------	----------	----------	----------	--------
7	STANDARDS					
8	Proportions (%)	70%	20%	10%		
9	Cost per tonne (£)	20	30	50		
10	Mix process loss (%)				10%	
11	------------------------	----------	----------	----------	----------	--------
12	ACTUAL					
13	Week Number:-				17	
14	Production (tonnes)				855	
15	Input (tonnes)	660	210	130	1,000	
16	Prices per tonne (£)	21	32	47		
17	Cost (£)	13,860	6,720	6,110	26,690	
18	=====================	==========	==========	==========	==========	=======
19	OUTPUT TABLE					Adv (Fav)
20	------------------------	----------	----------	----------	----------	--------
21	SUMMARY OF VARIANCES:	£	£	£		£
22	Price variance	660	420	-390		690
23	Mix variance	-800	300	1500		1000
24	Yield variance	700	300	250		1250
25	TOTAL MATERIAL VARIANCE	560	1020	1360		2940
26	------------------------	----------	----------	----------	----------	--------
27	DETAILED CALCULATION OF VARIANCES:				£	£
28	M1 Actual cost of direct materials used					
29	AQ x AM (Actual Quant)	660	210	130		
30	@ actual price (£)	21	32	47		
31	= AQ x AM x AP	13860	6720	6110	26,690	
32						
33	PRICE VARIANCE	660	420	-390		690
34						
35	M2 Actual materials used at standard price					
36	AQ x AM (Actual Quant)	660	210	130		
37	@ standard price (£)	20	30	50		
38	= AQ x AM x SP	13200	6300	6500	26,000	
39						
40	MIX VARIANCE	-800	300	1500		1,000
41						
42	M2A Actual usage @ standard proportions @ standard price					
43	AQ (Actual Quantity)	1000	1000	1000		
44	@ proportions (mix)	70%	20%	10%		
45	= AQ x SM	700	200	100		
46	@ standard price (£)	20	30	50		
47	= AQ x SM x SP	14000	6000	5000	25,000	
48						

Figure 22a (Part 1)

	A	B	C	D	E	F
49	YIELD VARIANCE	700	300	250		1,250
50						
51	M3 Std.quant. for act.output in std. prop.@ std.price					
52	AO (Actual output)	855	855	855		
53	x Standard input calc.					
54	1/(1-E10)					
55	= AO x SQ	950	950	950		
56	@ proportions (mix)	70%	20%	10%		
57	= AO x SQ x SM	665	190	95		
58	@ standard price (£)	20	30	50		
59	= AO x SQ x SM x SP	13300	5700	4750	23,750	
60						---------
61	Material Total Variance	560	1020	1360		2940
62						========
63						
64	Notes:					
65	AO = Actual Output	855	tonnes			
66	AQ = Actual Quantity of input (tonnes)					
67	SQ = Standard Quantity of input for output					
68		1/(1-E10)	tonnes			
69	AP = Actual Price					
70	AM = Actual Mix					
71	SM = Standard Mix					
72	SP = Standard Price, per tonne					

Figure 22a (Part 2)

AO = Actual Output (855 tonnes)

AQ = Actual Quantity of input (tonnes)

SQ = Standard Quantity of input for output (100/90)

AP = Actual Price, per tonne

AM = Actual Mix

SM = Standard Mix

SP = Standard Price, per tonne

There are very many ways of explaining variance analysis calculations, and it is assumed that you understand the basic principles; if not, you are referred to any standard text-book on the subject.

5. Notes on creating the model

The labels, values and formulae are all straightforward, and you should refer to Figures 22a and 22b in creating the model.

	A	B	C	D	E	F
1	Session 22: Variance Analysis: Material Mix and Yield Variances					
2	--------------------	--------------------	--------------------	----------	----------	----------
3	INPUT TABLE					
4	--------------------	--------------------	--------------------	----------	----------	----------
5	Material Type:-	A	B	C	All	
6	--------------------	--------------------	--------------------	----------	----------	----------
7	STANDARDS					
8	Proportions (%)	70%	20%	10%		
9	Cost per tonne (£)	20	30	50		
10	Mix process loss (%)				10%	
11	--------------------	--------------------	--------------------	----------	----------	----------
12	ACTUAL					
13	Week Number:-				17	
14	Production (tonnes)				855	
15	Input (tonnes)	660	210	130	+B15+C15+D15	
16	Prices per tonne (£)	21	32	47		
17	Cost (£)	+B15*B16	+C15*C16	+D15*D16	+B17+C17+D17	
18	====================	================	================	=========	=======	============
19	OUTPUT TABLE					Adv (Fav)
20	--------------------	--------------------	--------------------	----------	----------	----------
21	SUMMARY OF VARIANCES:	£	£	£		£
22	Price variance	+B33	+C33	+D33		+F33
23	Mix variance	+B40	+C40	+D40		+F40
24	Yield variance	+B49	+C49	+D49		+F49
25	TOTAL MATERIAL VARIANC	+B61	+C61	+D61		+F61
26	--------------------	--------------------	--------------------	----------	----------	----------
27	DETAILED CALCULATION OF VARIANCES:				£	£
28	M1 Actual cost of direct materials used					
29	AQ x AM (Actual Quant)	+B15	+C15	+D15		
30	@ actual price (£)	+B16	+C16	+D16		
31	= AQ x AM x AP	+B29*B30	+C29*C30	+D29*D30	+B31+C31+D31	
32						
33	PRICE VARIANCE	+B31-B38	+C31-C38	+D31-D38		+B33+C33+D33
34						
35	M2 Actual materials used at standard price					
36	AQ x AM (Actual Quant)	+B15	+C15	+D15		
37	@ standard price (£)	+B9	+C9	+D9		
38	= AQ x AM x SP	+B36*B37	+C36*C37	+D36*D37	+B38+C38+D38	
39						
40	MIX VARIANCE	+B38-B47	+C38-C47	+D38-D47		+B40+C40+D40
41						
42	M2A Actual usage @ standard proportions @ standard price					
43	AQ (Actual Quantity)	+$E$15	+$E$15	+$E$15		
44	@ proportions (mix)	+B8	+C8	+D8		
45	= AQ x SM	+B43*B44	+C43*C44	+D43*D44		
46	@ standard price (£)	+B9	+C9	+D9		
47	= AQ x SM x SP	+B45*B46	+C45*C46	+D45*D46	+B47+C47+D47	
48						

Figure 22b (Part 1)

Tip 1: Complete entering the range B17..B61 before the range C17..D61. Then simply copy B17..B61 to columns C and D. The keystrokes required, after positioning the cursor on cell B17 are:

Press `/C` (Copy)

	A	B	C	D	E	F
49	YIELD VARIANCE	+B47-B59	+C47-C59	+D47-D59		+B49+C49+D49
50						
51	M3 Std.quant. for act.output in std. prop.@ std.price					
52	AO (Actual output)	+$E$14	+$E$14	+$E$14		
53	x Standard input calc.					
54	1/(1-E10)					
55	= A0 x SQ	+B52*(1/(1-$E$10))	+C52*(1/(1-$E$10))	+D52*(1/(1-$E$10))		
56	@ proportions (mix)	+B8	+C8	+D8		
57	= AO x SQ x SM	+B55*B56	+C55*C56	+D55*D56		
58	@ standard price (£)	+B9	+C9	+D9		
59	= AO x SQ x SM x SP	+B57*B58	+C57*C58	+D57*D58	+B59+C59+D59	
60						------------------
61	Material Total Variance	+B31-B59	+C31-C59	+D31-D59		+E31-E59
62						============
63						
64	Notes:					
65	AO = Actual Output	+E14	tonnes			
66	AQ = Actual Quantity of input (tonnes)					
67	SQ = Standard Quantity of input for output					
68		1/(1-E10)	tonnes			
69	AP = Actual Price					
70	AM = Actual Mix					
71	SM = Standard Mix					
72	SP = Standard Price, per tonne					

Figure 22b (Part 2)

Move the cursor to B61 (highlighting B17..B61)

Press `<Enter>`

Press `<→>.<→>` (Right-arrow, Full Stop, Right-arrow)

Press `<Enter>`

Tip 2: The formula in cell E15 can be copied to cells E17, E31, E38, E47 and E59.

It can also be copied to E33 and then moved (/M) from E33 to F33.

Similarly for cells F40 and F49. This is because /C retains relativity (unless made absolute with $ signs) and /M retains the absolute figures.

E15 (+B15+C15+D15) becomes (+B33+C33+D33) when copied to E33, and stays that way when moved to F33.

Finally, format the cells as necessary with /RF (Range, Format). [Details were provided in session 18, paragraph 5.]

When you have completed the model, and are satisfied that it is correct, you can protect the whole worksheet, and unprotect the data input range B8..D9, E10, E13..E14, B15..D16. Notes on how to do this were given in session 5, paragraph 9. This will save accidental changes to labels and formulae.

6. Viewing the model

One of the difficulties of spreadsheets is the relatively small area of the worksheet that is visible on the screen at one time. In the present worksheet, if you are using the standard display of about 72 characters wide and 20 lines deep, you cannot see the input and output ranges at the same time. There are ways round this. You can split the screen into two windows and scroll them independently. Details of how to do this were provided in session 20, paragraph 6.

7. Activity

(1) Try altering the data inputs in the unprotected cells of the input table and observe the changes of the variances in the output tables. To repeat the note in activity (1) of session 20, when you have finished, do NOT use /FSR (File, Save, Replace) if you wish to preserve the original data in your model. Instead, if you do NOT wish to preserve the altered worksheet, simply quit the program or retrieve a new file (or the same file if you wish to start experimenting with it again). If you DO wish to preserve the altered worksheet, save it with a new filename.

(2) Find a similar direct material mix and yield variance analysis problem. Unprotect the model with /WGPD (Worksheet, Global, Protection, Disable) and adapt the model to suit the new problem. You will need to alter some of the labels in column A. Also you may need to make use of the Move and Copy commands, as well as the <F2> Edit key (see session 1, paragraphs 1.7 and 1.8) and <F4> Absolute key (see session 15, paragraph 9), to adjust the cell references.

(3) Practise using the move command. For example, move (/M) the range A27..F72 to the right of the range A1..F26.

SESSION 23
VAT registration numbers

1. Objectives

At the end of this session, you will be able to:

- ❑ construct a simple model which checks the validity of VAT registration numbers
- ❑ check the validity of any VAT registration number by simply entering it in the worksheet
- ❑ understand the potential of the @IF logical function
- ❑ know how to hide columns and cells

2. Introduction

It is to be hoped that you have not found the previous sessions too heavy going! Before we turn to financial accounting in the following sessions, you could (by way of light relief ?) create this small model which checks the validity of VAT registration numbers. It is fairly easy to enter, and the one long formula (in cell C6) introduces you to the @IF logical function. In addition you will be invited to try out the HIDE command, which hides display of ranges or columns.

3. The problem

The VAT registration number consists of nine digits, 345 6789 12, for example. To check the validity, the procedure is as follows:

(a) List the first seven digits in one column.

(b) List the digits 8,7,6,5,4,3,2 against them in a second column.

(c) Multiply the digits in the first column by those in the second column, and list the results in a third column.

(d) Total the third column.

(e) Keep deducting 97 from the total of the third column until a negative figure is obtained.

(f) The first negative figure obtained should be the same as the last two digits of the VAT number.

Refer to figure 23a for an example. Under the heading CALCULATIONS, in the range D7..F20, you will see the above procedure carried out for the VAT number given at the start of this paragraph. The first negative result in in cell F18, i.e. -12. This is the same as the last two digits of the VAT number, which is therefore valid.

	A	B	C	D	E	F
1	Session 23: VAT Registration Numbers					
2	------------------	--------	------------	----	----------	---------
3	INPUT TABLE		OUTPUT TABLE	CALCULATIONS		
4	------------------	--------	------------	----	----------	---------
5	Enter digits		------------			
6	in column B:		| Valid |			
7	Digit 1:	3	------------	3	x 8 =	24
8	Digit 2:	4		4	x 7 =	28
9	Digit 3:	5		5	x 6 =	30
10	Digit 4:	6		6	x 5 =	30
11	Digit 5:	7		7	x 4 =	28
12	Digit 6:	8		8	x 3 =	24
13	Digit 7:	9		9	x 2 =	18
14						---------
15	Digits 8 & 9:	12			Total:	182
16						=======
17					- 97 =	85
18					- 97 =	-12
19					- 97 =	-109
20					- 97 =	-206

Figure 23a

	A	B	C	D	E	F
1	Session 23: VAT Registration Numbers					
2	------------------	------	------------------------------------	--------	--------	------------
3	INPUT TABLE		OUTPUT TABLE	CALCULATIONS		
4	------------------	------	------------------------------------	--------	--------	------------
5	Enter digits		------------			
6	in column B:		@IF(B15=-F17#OR#B15=-F18#OR#B15=-F19#OR#B15=-F20,"| Valid |","| Invalid |")			
7	Digit 1:	3	------------	+B7	x 8 =	+B7*8
8	Digit 2:	4		+B8	x 7 =	+B8*7
9	Digit 3:	5		+B9	x 6 =	+B9*6
10	Digit 4:	6		+B10	x 5 =	+B10*5
11	Digit 5:	7		+B11	x 4 =	+B11*4
12	Digit 6:	8		+B12	x 3 =	+B12*3
13	Digit 7:	9		+B13	x 2 =	+B13*2
14						------------
15	Digits 8 & 9:	12			Total:	@SUM(F7..F13)
16						============
17					- 97 =	+F15-97
18					- 97 =	+F17-97
19					- 97 =	+F18-97
20					- 97 =	+F19-97

Figure 23b

The problem is to translate this procedure into spreadsheet format, so that entry of the VAT number into an input table will automatically show whether the VAT number is valid or invalid in an output table.

4. Design of the model

Figure 23a contains three areas:

Columns A and B are the input range, column C is the output range, and Columns D, E and F is a range where the calculations are performed.

Columns D and E are included for explanatory purposes only.

Figure 23b shows the calculations in formulae format in column F.

The formula in cell C6 checks cell B15 (the last two digits of the Vat number) against any of the outputs in the four cells F17..F20.

There is only need for the four lines of calculation in cells F17..F20. This is because the highest VAT number possible (first 7 digits only) is 9999999, and when multiplied by the digits in column E, this results in a total of 315 in cell F15. Four deductions of 97 is adequate to produce a negative result (-73). You can check this when you have created the model.

The formula as shown in Figure 23b for cell C6 shows **Valid** or **Invalid**.

However some programs (e.g. {VP}) will not print words. Details of this are provided in the next paragraph.

5. Notes on creating the model

The labels, values and formulae (with the exception of cell C6) are all straightforward, and you should refer to Figures 23a and 23b in creating the model.

Cell C6: An explanation of the formula in this cell is given below in paragraph 6.

The formula to be entered in cell C6 depends on which program you are using. Figure 23b shows the formula for {123}, {AEA} or {VPP} only. The formula for {VP} is given later on below.

If you are using {123} {AEA} or {VPP}, you can enter the formula as shown in Figure 23b, i.e.:

@IF(B15=-F17#OR#B15=-F18#OR#B15=-F19#OR#B15=-F20,"¦ Valid ¦","¦ Invalid ¦")

There are 3 spaces before **Valid** and 2 spaces after it.

There is one space before **Invalid** and 2 spaces after it.

The spaces and broken vertical bars are purely cosmetic (to complete the border and position the words **Valid** and **Invalid** centrally in the box). You could omit them if you prefer.

If you are using {VP}, the formula should be:

@IF(B15=-F17#OR#B15=-F18#OR#B15=-F19#OR#B15=-F20,@TRUE,@FALSE)

In addition {VP only}, enter the following labels:

In cell C8: **'1 = Valid**

In cell C9: **'0 = Invalid**

{All programs}:

Finally, adjust the width of the cells (/WCS) as appropriate.

When you have completed the model, and are satisfied that it is correct, you can protect the whole worksheet, and unprotect the data input range B8..D9, E10, E13..E14, B15..D16. Notes on how to do this were given in session 5, paragraph 9. This will save accidental changes to labels and formulae.

6. An explanation of the @IF formula in cell C6

For {123} {AEA} or {VPP}:

@IF	If
(B15	the contents of cell B15 (the number 12)
=-F17	are the same as the negative of the contents of cell F17,
#OR#B15=-F18	or the negative of the contents of cell F18,
#OR#B15=-F19	or the negative of the contents of cell F19,
#OR#B15=-F20	or the negative of the contents of cell F20,
,	either, if this is TRUE,
"| Valid |"	print out the letters etc. between the inverted commas,
,	or, if this is false,
"| Invalid |")	print out the letters etc. between the inverted commas.

For {VP} only:

@IF	If
(B15	the contents of cell B15 (the number 12)
=-F17	are the same as the negative of the contents of cell F17,
#OR#B15=-F18	or the negative of the contents of cell F18,
#OR#B15=-F19	or the negative of the contents of cell F19,
#OR#B15=-F20	or the negative of the contents of cell F20,
,	either, if this is TRUE,
@TRUE	print out the number 1,
,	or, if this is false,
@FALSE)	print out the number 0.

7. General Explanation of the @IF function:

The syntax is: @IF(condition,x,y)

There are three arguments within the brackets, each separated by a comma.

Condition:	is a conditional statement in the form of a logical formula or statement which results in a logical value (1 for true or 0 for false);
x:	is the value returned if the conditional value is true;
y:	is the value returned if the conditional value is false.

x and y can be values, or formulas, or {not VP} character strings between inverted commas.

@TRUE (no arguments) returns the logical value of 1.

@FALSE (no arguments) returns the logical value of 0.

@TRUE and @FALSE could be used with {123}, {AEA} or {VPP} instead of the character strings shown in Figure 23b, though this would be less informative.

Instead of **,@TRUE,@FALSE)** you could type in **,1,0)** as the second and third arguments.

The formula in cell C6 uses:

= which is a *logical operator*

and

#OR#~ which is a *Boolean operator*.

Further examples of these operators are given below:

Logical Operators

Symbol	*Definition*	*For example*
=	equal to	B15=F17
<>	not equal to	B15<>F17
>	greater than	B15>F17
<	less than	B15<F17
>=	greater than or equal to	B15>=F17
<=	less than or equal to	B15<=F17

Boolean operators

[Note the use of the hash (#) sign before and after each word.]

Symbol	*Definition*	*For example*
#AND#	both condition 1 AND condition 2	B15=F17#AND#B15=F18
#OR#	either condition 1 OR condition 2	B15=F17#OR#B15=F18
#NOT#	NOT condition 1	#NOT#B15=F17
#AND##NOT#	both cond. 1 AND NOT cond. 2	B15=F17#AND##NOT#B15=F18
#OR##NOT#	either cond. 1 OR NOT cond. 2	B15=F17#AND##NOT#B15=F18

8. Hiding ranges and columns

Since only columns A..C are relevant to the user of this model, there is no reason why the range D1..F20, or the whole of columns D..F should not be hidden from the monitor display.

8a. Hiding ranges

One way of achieving this is to use **/RFH** (Range, Format, Hidden)

Move the cursor to cell D1

Press `/RFH`

Define the range D1..F20 by pointing, and press <Enter>

The contents of the hidden cells are still operational, though not displayed on the worksheet area. If you move the cursor over the hidden cells you will see (H) (or [H... {AEA}) in the control panel.

[Note: {AEA}{123} The data also appears in the control panel.]

You can narrow the cells (/WCS) to a width of 1 {123} or 0 {VP}{VPP}{AEA} if you wish.

To redisplay the hidden range,

Move the cursor to cell D1

Press `/RFR` (Range, Format, Reset)

Define the hidden range D1..F20 by pointing, and press <Enter>

The range D1..F20 reappears as before it was hidden.

8b. Hiding columns

The programs vary in the procedure required. Follow the instructions below which are appropriate to your program.

{123 only}

You can also use **/WCH** (Worksheet, Column, Hide)

Move the cursor to column D (any row will do)

Press `/WCH`

Define the columns D..F by pressing . (full stop) and right-arrow twice

Press `<Enter>`

The column letters in the top border now omit D..F.

Note that the *whole* of the columns are hidden, right to the bottom row of the spreadsheet; this command should therefore be used with care in the case of large worksheets.

To redisplay the hidden columns,

Press `/WCD`

Columns D..F reappear with an asterisk against their column letters

Move the cursor to column D, press . (full-stop) and right-arrow twice

Press `<Enter>`

Columns D..F reappear as before they were hidden.

{VP}{VPP}{AEA}

You can hide a column by using /WCS (Worksheet, Col-Wid, Set) to set the column width to 0 (zero). The column letter disappears from the top border, but if you move the cursor across the hidden column, the cell reference of the hidden column appears in the control panel. To display the column again, move the cursor until the column reference required appears in the control panel, and use /WCS to widen the column to its previous width.

9. Activity

(1) Use the model to check the validity of some VAT registration numbers which you can find on invoices etc.

(2) Practise using the methods described in paragraph 8 above for hiding ranges or columns, using one of the models created in one of the previous sessions. For example, column H in Figure 19a (Session 19 on Investment Appraisal - Sensitivity) could well be hidden, because it is used in the model purely as a means to an end. Using the Hide and Move commands (and any others which are appropriate), you should be able to improve the appearance of a worksheet. It is obviously very convenient for the user if the data input section of a worksheet and the output table are both visible on the monitor at the same time, without the need for scrolling. This is not always possible, but it is worth a try.

SESSION 24
The accounting worksheet

1. Objectives

At the end of this session, you will be able to:

- ❑ construct a fairly large model which creates an accounting worksheet into which data can be entered and from which a Profit & Loss Account and a Balance Sheet are prepared automatically;
- ❑ gain more experience in viewing a large worksheet on your monitor;
- ❑ have the opportunity to adapt the model for future years and to adapt it for similar data;
- ❑ use /WGRM (Worksheet, Global, Recalculation, Manual) and <F9> to cut down on waiting time (if necessary).

2. Introduction

As promised in the last session, we now turn to financial accounting, and if you glance briefly at figures 24a and 24b you will see that there is some hard work to be done. The task is not as daunting as it may appear. A lot of the formulae to be entered can take advantage of the copy command, and tips to help make the task more easy are given below in paragraph 5. Your practice with the previous sessions should have given you enough confidence to tackle this rather larger enterprise.

Once you get the idea of how to construct a model of this type, you will find that it could help you in your understanding of the principles of account preparation as well as solving accounting problems without resorting to large sheets of analysis paper.

As you enter the formulae, try to trace the cell references and understand the logic of the calculations which the formulae are meant to calculate.

3. The problem

George Nettlerash has for several years traded as the *G.K.Nettlerash Company*. He specialises in pre-packaged nuts and bolts for the DIY market. He buys his nuts and bolts from a wholesaler, and the semi-mechanised operation of sorting, counting and packing the nuts and bolts takes several days; hence at any time his stocks consist of a unprocessed goods, packed goods, and, to a small extent, work-in-progress. He owns an estate car which is used for local deliveries.

You are required to prepare, for the year ended 31st December 19x1, an accounting worksheet, starting with the opening trial balance, entering the year's figures from his bank account, petty cash book, sales and purchase ledgers and wages summary, adjusting for depreciation, accruals and prepayments, and ending with the basic figures for a Profit & Loss Account for the period ended 31st December 19x1 and a Balance Sheet as at that date.

In previous years, the accounting worksheet has been prepared manually, but now you are to prepare it using a spreadsheet.

The closing trial balance for last year is as follows:

	Dr	Cr
	£	£
Bank Account		28,596
Petty Cash	19	
No. 2 Account	348	
VAT		6,725
PAYE		2,320
Sales Ledger	97,917	
Purchase Ledger		95,468
Capital Account		45,279
Plant and Machinery	32,500	
Dep'n Provision		9,009
Office Equipment	7,325	
Dep'n Provision		2,033
Car 1	16,953	
Dep'n Provision		7,417
Stock	40,068	
Work-in-Progress	2,602	
Motor Expenses	350	462
Rent and Rates	2,500	1,554
Light and Heat		300
Telephone		450
Accountancy		975
Insurance	1,040	
Bank Charges		343
Bank Interest		691
Totals	201,622	201,622

The analysed Cash Book (Bank Account) for the year to 31st December, 19x1, showed the following:

	Payments	Receipts
	£	£
Petty Cash	12,300	
VAT	26,144	
PAYE	13,920	
Sales Ledger		601,062
Purchase Ledger	398,621	
Capital introduced		5,000
Drawings	24,000	
Car No. 2	12,000	
Sub-Contract	1,346	
Consumables	896	
Wages and Nat.Ins.	43,164	
Motor Expenses	6,895	
Transport and Storage	900	
Rent and rates	25,069	
Light and Heat	1,498	
Telephone	2,365	
Printing and Stationery	986	
Advertising	720	
Cleaning and Sundries	1,691	
Repairs and renewals	875	
Leases	1,056	
Legal & Professional	650	
Accountancy	975	
Insurance	5,600	
Sale of Car No. 1		10,000
Bank Charges	1,465	
Bank Interest	5,425	
Total Payments/Receipts	588,561	616,062

The analysed Petty Cash Book for the year to 31st December, 19x1, showed the following payments:

	£
VAT	445
Purchases	599
Wages and Nat.Ins.	8,236
Light and Heat	256
Telephone	52
Printing and Stationery	752
Cleaning and Sundries	1,458
Repairs and renewals	489
	12,287

Ascertained accruals and prepayments at 31st December 19x1 were:

	Accrued	Prepaid
	£	£
Motor Expenses	546	375
Rent and Rates	1,743	2,500
Light and Heat	325	
Telephone	475	
Accountancy	1,050	
Insurance		1,172
Bank Charges	396	
Totals	4,535	4,047

The Sales Ledger Control Account showed the following for the year:

	£	£
Debtors at 1 January 19x1 b/fwd	97,917	
Sales	513,850	
VAT	89,924	
Cash received		601,062
Debtors at 31 December 19x1 c/fwd		100,629
	701,691	701,691
Debtors at 1 January 19x2 b/fwd	100,629	

The Purchase Ledger Control Account showed the following for the year:

	£	£
Creditors at 1 January 19x1 b/fwd		95,468
Purchases		344,003
VAT		60,200
Cash paid	398,621	
Creditors at 31 December 19x1 c/fwd	101,050	
	499,671	499,671
Creditors at 1 January 19x2 b/fwd		101,050

Depreciation is calculated using the reduced balance method, and employing the following percentage rates:

Plant and Machinery	15%
Office Equipment	15%
Cars	25%

Depreciation is applied for a full year for assets purchased during a financial year, but is not applied during the year of their disposal.

4. Design of the model

Figure 24a shows the worksheet as it will appear on your monitor, with the exception of the top four rows, which can be used for your own customised headings.

Figure 24b shows the underlying formulae required for the calculations in the worksheet.

The worksheet consists of two main areas:

Lines 5..61:

This is the input table area for all the data apart from the opening trial balance. Line 6 shows the column headings:

Columns B and C	Bank Account
Columns D and E	Petty Cash
Columns F and G	Sales and Purchase Ledgers
Columns H and I	Accruals and Prepayments
Columns J and K	Journal Entries

Columns L and M are used for entries such as the depreciation rates for fixed assets, and items such as PAYE and NI deducted and closing values of stocks and work-in-progress.

[These latter items could be entered as journal entries, but it is easier to make the entries here and let formulae in the journal entries columns (J and K) do the work for you.]

	A	B	C	D	E	F	G	H	I	J	K	L	M
5		£	£	£	£	£	£	£	£	£	£	PAYE,NI deducted	
6	INPUT TABLE	BANK ACCOUNT		PETTY CASH		SALES/PUR LEDG.		ACCRUED/PREPAY		JOURNAL ENTRIES		DEPRECIATION (Red.Bal.)	
7		Debit	Credit	Debit	Credit	Debit	Credit	Debit	Credit	Debit	Credit	CLOSING STOCK & WIP	
8													
9	TOTALS:-	1204623	1204623	12287	12287							Type	Rate %
10													
11	Bank Account	616062	588561										
12	Petty Cash	12300		0	12287								
13	No. 2 Account												
14	VAT	26144		445		60200	89924					PAYE & NI	
15	PAYE	13920									13970	deducted:...	13970
16	Sales Ledger		601062			603774							
17	Purchase Ledger	398621					404203						
18	Capital Account												
19	Capital introduced		5000										
20	Drawings	24000											
21	Plant and Machinery										B76	Plant & M/c	15%
22	Dep'n provision									C77			
23	P & L A/c												
24	Office Equipment										B79	Off. Equip.:	15%
25	Dep'n provision									C80			
26	P & L A/c												
27	Car 1										16953	Car 1 :.....	25%
28	Dep'n provision									7417			
29	P & L A/c												
30	Car 2	12000									B85	Car 2 :.....	25%
31	Dep'n provision									C86			
32	P & L A/c												
33	Stock - opening											Closing	
34	Stock - closing									46321	46321	Stock:......	46321
35	W.I.P.-opening											Closing	
36	W.I.P.-closing									2752	2752	W.I.P.:.....	2752
37	Sales						513850						
38	Purchases			599		344003							
39	Sub-Contract	1346											
40	Consumables	896											
41	Wages & Nat Ins	43164		8236						13970			
42	Motor Expenses	6895						546	375				
43	Transport & Storage	900											
44	Rent & Rates	25069						1743	2500				
45	Light & Heat	1498		256				325					
46	Telephone	2365		52				475					
47	Printing & Stat'y	986		752									
48	Advertising	720											
49	Cleaning & Sundries	1691		1458									
50	Repairs & Renewals	875		489									
51	Leases	1056											
52	Legal & Prof'nal	650											
53	Accountancy	975						1050					
54	Insurance	5600							1172				
55	Sale of assets		10000							16953	7417		
56	Bank Charges	1465						396					
57	Bank Interest	5425											
58	Accrued/Prepaid							4047	4535				
59													
60	TOTALS:-	1204623	1204623	12287	12287	1007977	1007977	8582	8582	87413	87413		
61	==============	=======	=======	=======	=======	=======	=======	=======	=====	======	======	========	=======

Figure 24a (Part 1)

Lines 62..118:

This area contains the opening trial balance (on the left) and all the calculations required to produce the Profit & Loss Account and Balance Sheet in columnar Debit and Credit form on the right.

[From this area a set of accounts suitable for presentation to the client can be produced. We shall leave doing so until the session 25.]

Line 62 shows the column headings:

Columns B and C   Opening Trial Balance

	A	B	C	D	E	F	G	H	I	J	K
62	EXTENDED	Opening T.B.		Current Year		Adjusted T.B.		Profit & Loss		Balance Sheet	
63	TRIAL	----------	----------	----------	----------	----------	----------	----------	----------	----------	----------
64	BALANCE	Debit	Credit	Debit	Credit	Debit	Credit	Debit	Credit	Debit	Credit
65	----------------	----------	----------	----------	----------	----------	----------	----------	----------	----------	----------
66	Bank Account		28596	616062	588561	0	1095			0	1095
67	Petty Cash	19		12300	12287	32	0			32	0
68	No. 2 Account	348		0	0	348	0			348	0
69	VAT		6725	86789	89924	0	9860			0	9860
70	PAYE		2320	13920	13970	0	2370			0	2370
71	Sales Ledger	97917		603774	601062	100629	0			100629	0
72	Purchase Ledger		95468	398621	404203	0	101050			0	101050
73	Capital Account		45279	0	0	0	45279			0	45279
74	Capital introduced			0	5000	0	5000			0	5000
75	Drawings			24000	0	24000	0			24000	0
76	Plant and Machinery	32500		0	0	32500	0			32500	0
77	Dep'n provision		9009	0	3524	0	12533				12533
78	P & L A/c			3524	0	3524	0	3524			
79	Office Equipment	7325		0	0	7325	0			7325	0
80	Dep'n provision		2033	0	794	0	2827				2827
81	P & L A/c			794	0	794	0	794			
82	Car 1	16953		0	16953	0	0			0	0
83	Dep'n provision		7417	7417	0	0	0				0
84	P & L A/c			0	0	0	0	0			
85	Car 2			12000	0	12000	0			12000	0
86	Dep'n provision			0	3000	0	3000				3000
87	P & L A/c			3000	0	3000	0	3000			
88	Stock - opening	40068		0	0	40068	0	40068			0
89	Stock - closing			46321	46321	46321	46321		46321	46321	
90	W.I.P.-opening	2602		0	0	2602	0	2602			0
91	W.I.P.-closing			2752	2752	2752	2752		2752	2752	
92	Sales			0	513850	0	513850	0	513850		
93	Purchases			344602	0	344602	0	344602	0	0	0
94	Sub-Contract			1346	0	1346	0	1346	0	0	0
95	Consumables			896	0	896	0	896	0	0	0
96	Wages & Nat Ins			65370	0	65370	0	65370	0	0	0
97	Motor Expenses	350	462	7441	375	6954	0	6954	0	375	546
98	Transport & Storage			900	0	900	0	900	0	0	0
99	Rent & Rates	2500	1554	26812	2500	25258	0	25258	0	2500	1743
100	Light & Heat		300	2079	0	1779	0	1779	0	0	325
101	Telephone		450	2892	0	2442	0	2442	0	0	475
102	Printing & Stat'y			1738	0	1738	0	1738	0	0	0
103	Advertising			720	0	720	0	720	0	0	0
104	Cleaning & Sundries			3149	0	3149	0	3149	0	0	0
105	Repairs & Renewals			1364	0	1364	0	1364	0	0	0
106	Lease rentals			1056	0	1056	0	1056	0	0	0
107	Legal & Prof'nal			650	0	650	0	650	0	0	0
108	Accountancy		975	2025	0	1050	0	1050	0	0	1050
109	Insurance	1040		5600	1172	5468	0	5468	0	1172	0
110	Sale of assets			16953	17417	0	464	0	464	0	0
111	Bank Charges		343	1861	0	1518	0	1518	0	0	396
112	Bank Interest		691	5425	0	4734	0	4734	0	0	0
113	Accrued/Prepaid			4047	4535	4047	4535				
114	----------------	----------	----------	----------	----------	----------	----------	----------	----------	----------	----------
115	Totals	201622	201622	2328199	2328199	750935	750935	520981	563387	229954	187548
116	==============	=======	=======	========	========	=======	=======	42406	0	0	42406
117								563387	563387	229954	229954
118								======	======	======	======

Figure 24a (Part 2)

[Note: In this session, you will enter the figures from the data here. However, for subsequent years, the cells can be referenced to the closing figures of the previous year. This means that the only data entry area would be lines 5..61.]

Columns D..K contain only formulae.

	A	B	C	D	E	F	G
5		£	£	£	£	£	£
6	INPUT TABLE	BANK ACCOUNT		PETTY CASH		SALES/PUR LEDG.	
7		Debit	Credit	Debit	Credit	Debit	Credit
8	------------	------------	------------	------------	------------	------------	------------
9	TOTALS :-	@SUM(B11:B58)	@SUM(C11:C58)	@SUM(D11:D58)	@SUM(E11:E58)		
10	------------	------------	------------	------------	------------	------------	------------
11	Bank Account	@SUM(C12:C57)	@SUM(B12:B57)				
12	Petty Cash	12300		@SUM(E13:E57)+E11	@SUM(D13:D57)+D11		
13	No. 2 Account						
14	VAT	26144		445		60200	89924
15	PAYE	13920					
16	Sales Ledger		601062			+G37+G14	
17	Purchase Ledger	398621					+F38+F14
18	Capital Account						
19	Capital introduced		5000				
20	Drawings	24000					
21	Plant and Machinery						
22	Dep'n provision						
23	P & L A/c						
24	Office Equipment						
25	Dep'n provision						
26	P & L A/c						
27	Car 1						
28	Dep'n provision						
29	P & L A/c						
30	Car 2	12000					
31	Dep'n provision						
32	P & L A/c						
33	Stock - opening						
34	Stock - closing						
35	W.I.P.-opening						
36	W.I.P.-closing						
37	Sales						513850
38	Purchases			599		344003	
39	Sub-Contract	1346					
40	Consumables	896					
41	Wages & Nat Ins	43164		8236			
42	Motor Expenses	6895					
43	Transport & Storage	900					
44	Rent & Rates	25069					
45	Light & Heat	1498		256			
46	Telephone	2365		52			
47	Printing & Stat'y	986		752			
48	Advertising	720					
49	Cleaning & Sundries	1691		1458			
50	Repairs & Renewals	875		489			
51	Leases	1056					
52	Legal & Prof'nal	650					
53	Accountancy	975					
54	Insurance	5600					
55	Sale of assets		10000				
56	Bank Charges	1465					
57	Bank Interest	5425					
58	Accrued/Prepaid						
59	------------	------------	------------	------------	------------	------------	------------
60	TOTALS :-	@SUM(B11:B58)	@SUM(C11:C58)	@SUM(D11:D58)	@SUM(E11:E58)	@SUM(F11:F58)	@SUM(G11:G58)
61	============	============	============	============	============	============	============

Figure 24b (Part 1)

Columns D and E　　　Current Year

Columns D and E contain formulae which amalgamate the data entries in the data input table (lines 5..61)

Columns F and G　　　Adjusted Trial Balance

Columns F and G adjust columns B and C by the current year's entries in columns D and E.

	H	I	J	K	L	M
5	£	£	£	£	PAYE,NI deducted	
6	ACCRUED/PREPAY		JOURNAL ENTRIES		DEPRECIATION (Red.Bal.)	
7	Debit	Credit	Debit	Credit	CLOSING STOCK & WIP	
8	--------	--------	--------	--------	--------	--------
9					Type	Rate %
10						
11						
12						
13						
14					PAYE & NI	
15				+M15	deducted:...	13970
16						
17						
18						
19						
20						
21				B76	Plant & M/c:	15%
22			C77			
23						
24				B79	Off. Equip.:	15%
25			C80			
26						
27				+B82	Car 1 :.....	25%
28			+C83			
29						
30				B85	Car 2 :.....	25%
31			C86			
32						
33					Closing	
34			+M34	+M34	Stock:......	46321
35					Closing	
36			+M36	+M36	W.I.P.:.....	2752
37						
38						
39						
40						
41			+M15			
42	546	375				
43						
44	1743	2500				
45	325					
46	475					
47						
48						
49						
50						
51						
52						
53	1050					
54		1172				
55			+K21+K24+K27+K30	+J22+J25+J28+J31		
56	396					
57						
58	@SUM(I11:I57)	@SUM(H11:H57)				
59	--------	--------	--------	--------	--------	--------
60	@SUM(H11:H58)	@SUM(I11:I58)	@SUM(J11:J58)	@SUM(K11:K58)		
61	==========	==========	==========	==========	==========	==========

Figure 24b (Part 2)

Columns H and I	Profit & Loss Account
Columns J and K	Balance Sheet

Columns H..K analyse the adjusted trial balance into either the Profit & Loss Account or the Balance Sheet.

	A	B	C	D
62	EXTENDED	Opening T.B.		Current Year
63	TRIAL	------------------	------------------	--
64	BALANCE	Debit	Credit	Debit
65	------------------	------------------	------------------	--
66	Bank Account		28596	+B11+D11+F11+H11+J11
67	Petty Cash	19		+B12+D12+F12+H12+J12
68	No. 2 Account	348		+B13+D13+F13+H13+J13
69	VAT		6725	+B14+D14+F14+H14+J14
70	PAYE		2320	+B15+D15+F15+H15+J15
71	Sales Ledger	97917		+B16+D16+F16+H16+J16
72	Purchase Ledger		95468	+B17+D17+F17+H17+J17
73	Capital Account		45279	+B18+D18+F18+H18+J18
74	Capital introduced			+B19+D19+F19+H19+J19
75	Drawings			+B20+D20+F20+H20+J20
76	Plant and Machinery	32500		+B21+D21+F21+H21+J21
77	Dep'n provision		9009	+B22+D22+F22+H22+J22
78	P & L A/c			+(B21+D21+F21+H21+J21+J22+B76-C22-E22-G22-I22-K21-K22-C77)*M21
79	Office Equipment	7325		+B24+D24+F24+H24+J24
80	Dep'n provision		2033	+B25+D25+F25+H25+J25
81	P & L A/c			+(B24+D24+F24+H24+J24+J25+B79-C25-E25-G25-I25-K24-K25-C80)*M24
82	Car 1	16953		+B27+D27+F27+H27+J27
83	Dep'n provision		7417	+B28+D28+F28+H28+J28
84	P & L A/c			+(B27+D27+F27+H27+J27+J28+B82-C28-E28-G28-I28-K27-K28-C83)*M27
85	Car 2			+B30+D30+F30+H30+J30
86	Dep'n provision			+B31+D31+F31+H31+J31
87	P & L A/c			+(B30+D30+F30+H30+J30+J31+B85-C31-E31-G31-I31-K30-K31-C86)*M30
88	Stock - opening	40068		+B33+D33+F33+H33+J33
89	Stock - closing			+B34+D34+F34+H34+J34
90	W.I.P.-opening	2602		+B35+D35+F35+H35+J35
91	W.I.P.-closing			+B36+D36+F36+H36+J36
92	Sales			+B37+D37+F37+H37+J37
93	Purchases			+B38+D38+F38+H38+J38
94	Sub-Contract			+B39+D39+F39+H39+J39
95	Consumables			+B40+D40+F40+H40+J40
96	Wages & Nat Ins			+B41+D41+F41+H41+J41
97	Motor Expenses	350	462	+B42+D42+F42+H42+J42
98	Transport & Storage			+B43+D43+F43+H43+J43
99	Rent & Rates	2500	1554	+B44+D44+F44+H44+J44
100	Light & Heat		300	+B45+D45+F45+H45+J45
101	Telephone		450	+B46+D46+F46+H46+J46
102	Printing & Stat'y			+B47+D47+F47+H47+J47
103	Advertising			+B48+D48+F48+H48+J48
104	Cleaning & Sundries			+B49+D49+F49+H49+J49
105	Repairs & Renewals			+B50+D50+F50+H50+J50
106	Lease rentals			+B51+D51+F51+H51+J51
107	Legal & Prof'nal			+B52+D52+F52+H52+J52
108	Accountancy		975	+B53+D53+F53+H53+J53
109	Insurance	1040		+B54+D54+F54+H54+J54
110	Sale of assets			+B55+D55+F55+H55+J55
111	Bank Charges		343	+B56+D56+F56+H56+J56
112	Bank Interest		691	+B57+D57+F57+H57+J57
113	Accrued/Prepaid			+B58+D58+F58+H58+J58
114	------------------	------------------	------------------	--
115	Totals	@SUM(B66:B113)	@SUM(C66:C113)	@SUM(D66:D113)
116	==============	==============	==============	==

Figure 24b (Part 3)

5. Notes on creating the model

This is probably the most formidable-looking model so far. However, your practice in previous sessions should stand you in good stead. In any case, most of the long formulae can be typed in and copied to the cells below, with minor editing for a few lines. Tips on doing so are provided below in this paragraph. If you get tired, save your worksheet (as I hope you do frequently) and continue later. Your efforts should be rewarded by increased confidence in spreadsheet modelling in addition to a model which could be adapted and used for the preparation of other sets of accounts.

	E	F
62		Adjusted T.B.
63	------------------------------------	--
64	Credit	Debit
65	------------------------------------	--
66	+C11+E11+G11+I11+K11	@IF(B66+D66-C66-E66<=0,0,B66+D66-C66-E66)
67	+C12+E12+G12+I12+K12	@IF(B67+D67-C67-E67<=0,0,B67+D67-C67-E67)
68	+C13+E13+G13+I13+K13	@IF(B68+D68-C68-E68<=0,0,B68+D68-C68-E68)
69	+C14+E14+G14+I14+K14	@IF(B69+D69-C69-E69<=0,0,B69+D69-C69-E69)
70	+C15+E15+G15+I15+K15	@IF(B70+D70-C70-E70<=0,0,B70+D70-C70-E70)
71	+C16+E16+G16+I16+K16	@IF(B71+D71-C71-E71<=0,0,B71+D71-C71-E71)
72	+C17+E17+G17+I17+K17	@IF(B72+D72-C72-E72<=0,0,B72+D72-C72-E72)
73	+C18+E18+G18+I18+K18	@IF(B73+D73-C73-E73<=0,0,B73+D73-C73-E73)
74	+C19+E19+G19+I19+K19	@IF(B74+D74-C74-E74<=0,0,B74+D74-C74-E74)
75	+C20+E20+G20+I20+K20	@IF(B75+D75-C75-E75<=0,0,B75+D75-C75-E75)
76	+C21+E21+G21+I21+K21	@IF(B76+D76-C76-E76<=0,0,B76+D76-C76-E76)
77	+C22+E22+G22+I22+K22+D78	@IF(B77+D77-C77-E77<=0,0,B77+D77-C77-E77)
78	+C23+E23+G23+I23+K23	@IF(B78+D78-C78-E78<=0,0,B78+D78-C78-E78)
79	+C24+E24+G24+I24+K24	@IF(B79+D79-C79-E79<=0,0,B79+D79-C79-E79)
80	+C25+E25+G25+I25+K25+D81	@IF(B80+D80-C80-E80<=0,0,B80+D80-C80-E80)
81	+C26+E26+G26+I26+K26	@IF(B81+D81-C81-E81<=0,0,B81+D81-C81-E81)
82	+C27+E27+G27+I27+K27	@IF(B82+D82-C82-E82<=0,0,B82+D82-C82-E82)
83	+C28+E28+G28+I28+K28+D84	@IF(B83+D83-C83-E83<=0,0,B83+D83-C83-E83)
84	+C29+E29+G29+I29+K29	@IF(B84+D84-C84-E84<=0,0,B84+D84-C84-E84)
85	+C30+E30+G30+I30+K30	@IF(B85+D85-C85-E85<=0,0,B85+D85-C85-E85)
86	+C31+E31+G31+I31+K31+D87	@IF(B86+D86-C86-E86<=0,0,B86+D86-C86-E86)
87	+C32+E32+G32+I32+K32	@IF(B87+D87-C87-E87<=0,0,B87+D87-C87-E87)
88	+C33+E33+G33+I33+K33	@IF(B88+D88-C88-E88<=0,0,B88+D88-C88-E88)
89	+C34+E34+G34+I34+K34	+D89
90	+C35+E35+G35+I35+K35	@IF(B90+D90-C90-E90<=0,0,B90+D90-C90-E90)
91	+C36+E36+G36+I36+K36	+D91
92	+C37+E37+G37+I37+K37	@IF(B92+D92-C92-E92<=0,0,B92+D92-C92-E92)
93	+C38+E38+G38+I38+K38	@IF(B93+D93-C93-E93<=0,0,B93+D93-C93-E93)
94	+C39+E39+G39+I39+K39	@IF(B94+D94-C94-E94<=0,0,B94+D94-C94-E94)
95	+C40+E40+G40+I40+K40	@IF(B95+D95-C95-E95<=0,0,B95+D95-C95-E95)
96	+C41+E41+G41+I41+K41	@IF(B96+D96-C96-E96<=0,0,B96+D96-C96-E96)
97	+C42+E42+G42+I42+K42	@IF(B97+D97-C97-E97<=0,0,B97+D97-C97-E97)
98	+C43+E43+G43+I43+K43	@IF(B98+D98-C98-E98<=0,0,B98+D98-C98-E98)
99	+C44+E44+G44+I44+K44	@IF(B99+D99-C99-E99<=0,0,B99+D99-C99-E99)
100	+C45+E45+G45+I45+K45	@IF(B100+D100-C100-E100<=0,0,B100+D100-C100-E100)
101	+C46+E46+G46+I46+K46	@IF(B101+D101-C101-E101<=0,0,B101+D101-C101-E101)
102	+C47+E47+G47+I47+K47	@IF(B102+D102-C102-E102<=0,0,B102+D102-C102-E102)
103	+C48+E48+G48+I48+K48	@IF(B103+D103-C103-E103<=0,0,B103+D103-C103-E103)
104	+C49+E49+G49+I49+K49	@IF(B104+D104-C104-E104<=0,0,B104+D104-C104-E104)
105	+C50+E50+G50+I50+K50	@IF(B105+D105-C105-E105<=0,0,B105+D105-C105-E105)
106	+C51+E51+G51+I51+K51	@IF(B106+D106-C106-E106<=0,0,B106+D106-C106-E106)
107	+C52+E52+G52+I52+K52	@IF(B107+D107-C107-E107<=0,0,B107+D107-C107-E107)
108	+C53+E53+G53+I53+K53	@IF(B108+D108-C108-E108<=0,0,B108+D108-C108-E108)
109	+C54+E54+G54+I54+K54	@IF(B109+D109-C109-E109<=0,0,B109+D109-C109-E109)
110	+C55+E55+G55+I55+K55	@IF(B110+D110-C110-E110<=0,0,B110+D110-C110-E110)
111	+C56+E56+G56+I56+K56	@IF(B111+D111-C111-E111<=0,0,B111+D111-C111-E111)
112	+C57+E57+G57+I57+K57	@IF(B112+D112-C112-E112<=0,0,B112+D112-C112-E112)
113	+C58+E58+G58+I58+K58	+D113
114	------------------------------------	--
115	@SUM(E66:E113)	@SUM(F66:F113)
116	============================	==
117		
118		

Figure 24b (Part 4)

The labels, values and formulae are all straightforward, and you should refer to Figures 24a and 24b in creating the model.

	G	H	I
62		Profit & Loss	
63	------------------------------	------------------------------	------------------------------
64	Credit	Debit	Credit
65	------------------------------	------------------------------	------------------------------
66	@IF(C66+E66-B66-D66<=0,0,C66+E66-B66-D66)		
67	@IF(C67+E67-B67-D67<=0,0,C67+E67-B67-D67)		
68	@IF(C68+E68-B68-D68<=0,0,C68+E68-B68-D68)		
69	@IF(C69+E69-B69-D69<=0,0,C69+E69-B69-D69)		
70	@IF(C70+E70-B70-D70<=0,0,C70+E70-B70-D70)		
71	@IF(C71+E71-B71-D71<=0,0,C71+E71-B71-D71)		
72	@IF(C72+E72-B72-D72<=0,0,C72+E72-B72-D72)		
73	@IF(C73+E73-B73-D73<=0,0,C73+E73-B73-D73)		
74	@IF(C74+E74-B74-D74<=0,0,C74+E74-B74-D74)		
75	@IF(C75+E75-B75-D75<=0,0,C75+E75-B75-D75)		
76	@IF(C76+E76-B76-D76<=0,0,C76+E76-B76-D76)		
77	@IF(C77+E77-B77-D77<=0,0,C77+E77-B77-D77)		
78	@IF(C78+E78-B78-D78<=0,0,C78+E78-B78-D78)	+F78	
79	@IF(C79+E79-B79-D79<=0,0,C79+E79-B79-D79)		
80	@IF(C80+E80-B80-D80<=0,0,C80+E80-B80-D80)		
81	@IF(C81+E81-B81-D81<=0,0,C81+E81-B81-D81)	+F81	
82	@IF(C82+E82-B82-D82<=0,0,C82+E82-B82-D82)		
83	@IF(C83+E83-B83-D83<=0,0,C83+E83-B83-D83)		
84	@IF(C84+E84-B84-D84<=0,0,C84+E84-B84-D84)	+F84	
85	@IF(C85+E85-B85-D85<=0,0,C85+E85-B85-D85)		
86	@IF(C86+E86-B86-D86<=0,0,C86+E86-B86-D86)		
87	@IF(C87+E87-B87-D87<=0,0,C87+E87-B87-D87)	+F87	
88	@IF(C88+E88-B88-D88<=0,0,C88+E88-B88-D88)	+F88	
89	+E89		+G89
90	@IF(C90+E90-B90-D90<=0,0,C90+E90-B90-D90)	+F90	
91	+E91		+G91
92	@IF(C92+E92-B92-D92<=0,0,C92+E92-B92-D92)	+F92	+G92
93	@IF(C93+E93-B93-D93<=0,0,C93+E93-B93-D93)	+F93	+G93
94	@IF(C94+E94-B94-D94<=0,0,C94+E94-B94-D94)	+F94	+G94
95	@IF(C95+E95-B95-D95<=0,0,C95+E95-B95-D95)	+F95	+G95
96	@IF(C96+E96-B96-D96<=0,0,C96+E96-B96-D96)	+F96	+G96
97	@IF(C97+E97-B97-D97<=0,0,C97+E97-B97-D97)	+F97	+G97
98	@IF(C98+E98-B98-D98<=0,0,C98+E98-B98-D98)	+F98	+G98
99	@IF(C99+E99-B99-D99<=0,0,C99+E99-B99-D99)	+F99	+G99
100	@IF(C100+E100-B100-D100<=0,0,C100+E100-B100-D100)	+F100	+G100
101	@IF(C101+E101-B101-D101<=0,0,C101+E101-B101-D101)	+F101	+G101
102	@IF(C102+E102-B102-D102<=0,0,C102+E102-B102-D102)	+F102	+G102
103	@IF(C103+E103-B103-D103<=0,0,C103+E103-B103-D103)	+F103	+G103
104	@IF(C104+E104-B104-D104<=0,0,C104+E104-B104-D104)	+F104	+G104
105	@IF(C105+E105-B105-D105<=0,0,C105+E105-B105-D105)	+F105	+G105
106	@IF(C106+E106-B106-D106<=0,0,C106+E106-B106-D106)	+F106	+G106
107	@IF(C107+E107-B107-D107<=0,0,C107+E107-B107-D107)	+F107	+G107
108	@IF(C108+E108-B108-D108<=0,0,C108+E108-B108-D108)	+F108	+G108
109	@IF(C109+E109-B109-D109<=0,0,C109+E109-B109-D109)	+F109	+G109
110	@IF(C110+E110-B110-D110<=0,0,C110+E110-B110-D110)	+F110	+G110
111	@IF(C111+E111-B111-D111<=0,0,C111+E111-B111-D111)	+F111	+G111
112	@IF(C112+E112-B112-D112<=0,0,C112+E112-B112-D112)	+F112	+G112
113	+E113		
114	------------------------------	------------------------------	------------------------------
115	@SUM(G66:G113)	@SUM(H66:H113)	@SUM(I66:I113)
116	==============================	@IF(I115>=H115,I115-H115,0)	@IF(H115>=I115,H115-I115,0)
117		+H115+H116	+I115+I116
118		==============================	==============================

Figure 24b (Part 5)

The top four rows are not shown in these figures, and they can be used for your own customised headings.

	J	K
62	Balance Sheet	
63	------------------------------------	------------------------------------
64	Debit	Credit
65	------------------------------------	------------------------------------
66	+F66	+G66
67	+F67	+G67
68	+F68	+G68
69	+F69	+G69
70	+F70	+G70
71	+F71	+G71
72	+F72	+G72
73	+F73	+G73
74	+F74	+G74
75	+F75	+G75
76	+F76	+G76
77		+G77
78		
79	+F79	+G79
80		+G80
81		
82	+F82	+G82
83		+G83
84		
85	+F85	+G85
86		+G86
87		
88		+G88
89	+F89	
90		+G90
91	+F91	
92		
93	+I38	+H38
94	+I39	+H39
95	+I40	+H40
96	+I41	+H41
97	+I42	+H42
98	+I43	+H43
99	+I44	+H44
100	+I45	+H45
101	+I46	+H46
102	+I47	+H47
103	+I48	+H48
104	+I49	+H49
105	+I50	+H50
106	+I51	+H51
107	+I52	+H52
108	+I53	+H53
109	+I54	+H54
110	+I55	+H55
111	+I56	+H56
112	+I57	+H57
113		
114	------------------------------------	------------------------------------
115	@SUM(J66:J113)	@SUM(K66:K113)
116	@IF(K115>=J115,K115-J115,0)	@IF(J115>=K115,J115-K115,0)
117	+J115+J116	+K115+K116
118	=========================	=========================

Figure 24b (Part 6)

SOME TIPS:

Recalculation:

This is a fairly large model, particularly if you increase it to cope with year 2, as suggested in paragraph 8 below. In addition you will add to it in sessions 25 and 26. If you have rather slow hardware and a slow program, you will almost certainly have to wait for recalculation after each entry which activates it. Try using /WGRM (Worksheet, Global, Recalculation, Manual) and then pressing <F9> only when you need a recalculation.

Shortcuts:

The labels in column A, rows 11..58 are repeated exactly in rows 66..113 and can be copied down.

The formulae in row 60 are the same for columns B..K, and therefore the formula in B60: **@SUM(B11..B58)** can be copied to C60..K60.

The same applies to rows in the range B115..K115.

D66..D113: The formula in D66 can be copied down to D67..D113. Then edit <F2> cell D78 to add the additional cell references (don't forget the bracket at the beginning) and copy D78 (individually) to D81, D84 and D87.

F66..F113: The formula in F66 can be copied down to F67..F112. Then move to cells F89, F91 and F113 and type in the correct formulae.

G66..G113: The formula in G66 can be copied down to F67..F112. Then move to cells G89, G91 and G113 and type in the correct formulae.

Protection:

The whole worksheet should be protected, and the following cells unprotected:

B12..C58, D11..E12, D13..E58, F11..G15, F18..G58, H11..I57, J11..K14,
J16..K33, J35..K35, J37..K40, J42..K54, J56..K58, M11..M58, B66..C112.

Column Widths:

A global column-width of 8 is suggested (/WGC), with column A widened to 19 (/WCS). On some monitors, this shows columns A..G (after pressing <Home>), and columns H..M after pressing <Tab> or <Ctrl>+<→>. <Shift>+<Tab> or <Ctrl>+<←> returns to columns A..G. This is obviously convenient, and the actual settings and key presses depend on your monitor and program. Experiment with column-widths until you produce the most convenient setting.

6. Viewing the worksheet

Use /WT (Worksheet, Titles) [/WB for {AEA}] to help you view the worksheet more easily. Details of how to use these commands were given in session 6, paragraph 8.

For example, if you want rows 62..64 frozen at the top of the monitor and column A frozen at the left of the monitor, move the cursor until row 62 is at the top of the monitor, then move the cursor to cell B65 and press /WTB [/WBB for {AEA}].

Alternatively, you can also use /WW (Worksheet, Window). Details of how to use this command were given in session 20, paragraph 6.

For example, if you want rows 62..64 frozen at the top of the monitor , move the cursor until row 62 is at the top of the monitor, then move the cursor to cell B65 and press /WWH (Worksheet, Windows, Horizontal). Use <F6> to toggle between the windows. This method has the advantage that you can scroll the top window to show rows 6 and 7 instead of 62..64.

If you also want column A frozen at the left of the monitor, use <F6> to go to column B in each window and use /WTV (Worksheet, Titles, Vertical) [/WBV for {AEA}]

Try these commands out and experiment with them, until you find the settings which are most convenient for you.

7. An explanation of the model

The worksheet has been designed as a relatively simple model to produce the accounts for a small business.

It should be possible to adapt it fairly easily to accommodate other types of business. For example, there are four classes of assets, and the labels for these could be altered as required.

The data input table should be able to cope with many unusual accounting items, perhaps mainly through the Journal Entries columns.

Columns J and K (rows 21..32) contain some cell references as labels which can help with adjustments necessary when there is a disposal of assets. For example, for plant and machinery, cell K21 contains the label **"B76** and cell J22 contains the label **"C77**. If the *whole* of the asset is disposed of, it is necessary only to edit <F2> the cell to read **+B76** and **+C77** respectively to achieve the elimination of the original cost and cumulative depreciation for that asset. This has already been done for Car 1 in cells K27 and J28, since it was sold for £10,000 (see cell C55). If an asset category sustains a *part* disposal, then the actual original cost and cumulative depreciation figures relating to the *part* disposal must be entered.

***Important note** re the above-mentioned labels in the range J21..K32:*

*Some programs show **ERR** in formulae which include references to cells which contain labels. If this happens to you, simply erase these labels.*

The formulae in rows 66..113, columns D..G are perhaps more comprehensive in their referral to the data input table than they need be, but it was considered better to allow for too many eventualities rather than too few. If, after use of the model you find it useful, you could prune the formulae in D66..G113 to what is necessary for the requirements of your particular application.

The range F66..G113 makes extensive use of the **@IF** function. A detailed explanation of this function was give in session 23, paragraphs 6 and 7.

The duplication of the TOTALS in cells B9..E9 may seem to be a curiosity; however, you may find it useful to have a visual record of totals as the data is being entered. These totals could be extended to F9..K9 if found useful, or erased if they are felt to be surplus to your requirements.

As mentioned in paragraph 4 above, you will, in the next session, be invited to extend this present model to produce a set of accounts suitable for presentation to the client.

8. Year 2 and subsequent years

The present model can be used to produce similar accounts for a second and subsequent years.

First, make sure that you have not included any absolute ($) cell references in any of the formulae. If you have, remove them with <F2> and the <Del> key (or <F4> if your program permits it), as described in session 15, paragraph 9.

Then copy the whole range A1..M118 to the right, to the range with cell Q1 in the top left corner. [Columns N..P can be narrowed to a small number, so that shifting two screens to the right from the year 1 work area (A1..M118) has column Q at the left of the screen.]

Next, you will have to enter formulae in the range R66..S113 which refer to the range J66..K113, so that the closing balances of year 1 become the opening balances of year 2, as follows:

Enter **+J66** in cell R66, and **+K66** in cell S66.

Copy cells R66..J66 down to R67..S113.

Some editing is now necessary to deal with the Capital Account, and also stocks and work-in-progress brought forward:

Cell A29: Enter `+K73-J73+K74-J74+K75-J75+K116-J116`

Cells R73, R74, S74, R75, S75: Enter `0` (Zero)

Cell R88: Alter J88 to read `J89`

Cell R90: Alter J90 to read `J91`

Cells R89 and R91: Enter `0` (Zero)

Finally, the labels in the range Z22..AA31 (to help entry of adjustments for disposal of assets, and assuming they do not result in **ERR** messages in formulae which refer to them - see **Important note** in paragraph 7 above) must be adjusted, as follows:

Cell	to read
Z22	S77
Z25	S80
Z28	S83
Z31	S84
AA21	R76
AA24	R79
AA27	R82
AA30	R85

[It might be a good idea to protect these cells temporarily, before carrying out the following operation:]

The data entries in year 2 are, of course, still those for year 1. Protect the whole worksheet and either erase the unprotected cells where there are year 1 figures, or replace them with 0s (zeros). If you create a worksheet for year 3 (in anticipation that it will still be in business) before making data entries for year 2, you will not have to make any of these adjustments again, apart from the labels in the range Z22..AA31.

It may be helpful to enter **Year 1** and **Year 2** etc. as appropriate in some of the spare cells (rows 1..4) at the head of the worksheet as a guide to which year is on view. Another precaution against entering year 2 data into year 1 might be to protect all the cells in the year 1 range, once that year has been finalised.

9. Activity

Retrieve the file for this model and rename it! Then take a question from an accounting text-book where the situation is similar to the problem set out in paragraph 3 above (George Nettlerash), and adapt the worksheet model to suit the new data. You will almost certainly have to alter the labels for expenses, classes of fixed assets etc. Replace the data for George Nettlerash with the new data. Compare the outputs from the revised worksheet with those from your handwritten answer. If they differ, find out why. Is it the fault of the worksheet formulae etc. or is it due to mistakes in your handwritten calculations?

SESSION 25

Financial accounts

1. Objectives

At the end of this session, you will be able to:

- ❑ construct a model which extracts information from the accounting worksheet created in session 24 and produces and prints the financial accounts for a small business;
- ❑ use the File, Combine (Merge) command.

2. Introduction

In this session you will retrieve the model you created in session 24, and expand it with additional formulae. These will produce a Profit & Loss Account, Balance Sheet with Notes to the Accounts, ready for printing.

The accounts so produced will reflect any entries to the data input table in the original model. It will also be possible to copy the additional work of this session and adapt it for subsequent years, as was the case with the original model.

3. The problem

In session 24, you met George Nettlerash and, from the data provided there, produced a worksheet which took his accounting data for the year to 31st December 19x1 and produced a columnar Profit & Loss Account and Balance Sheet for that year.

George Nettlerash now requires a printed copy of his accounts for the year.

4. Design of the model

Figure 24a (Session 24) used the range A1..M118 for the Accounting Worksheet.

Reference to Figures 25a and 25b will show that the accounting statements are located below A1..M118 in the range A123..G283.

A123..G178 contains the Trading and Profit & Loss Account.

A179..G227 contains the Balance Sheet.

A228..G283 contains the Notes to the Accounts.

Figure 25a shows the accounts as it appears on the screen, and as will be printed out.

	A	B	C	D	E	F	G
123							
124		G.K. Nettlerash Company					
125							
126		TRADING AND PROFIT & LOSS ACCOUNT					
127							
128		for the year ended 31st December 19x1					
129							
130					£	£	£
131	SALES						513,850
132							
133	LESS: COST OF SALES						
134							
135	Opening Stock and Work-in-progress					42,670	
136	add Purchases					344,602	
137						------------	
138						387,272	
139	less Closing Stock and Work-in-progress					49,073	
140						------------	
141							338,199
142							------------
143	GROSS PROFIT	34.18%	of Sales				175,651
144							
145	LESS: EXPENSES						
146							
147	Sub-Contract					1,346	
148	Consumables					896	
149	Wages and NI					65,370	
150	Motor Expenses					6,954	
151	Transport & Storage					900	
152	Rent & Rates					25,258	
153	Light & Heat					1,779	
154	Telephone					2,442	
155	Printing & Stationery					1,738	
156	Advertising					720	
157	Cleaning & Sundries					3,149	
158	Repairs & Renewals					1,364	
159	Lease Rentals					1,056	
160	Legal & Professional					650	
161	Accountancy					1,050	
162	Insurance					5,468	
163	Bank Charges					1,518	
164	Bank Interest					4,734	
165	Depreciation:						
166	Plant & Machinery				3,524		
167	Office Equipment				794		
168	Car 1				0		
169	Car 2				3,000		
170					------------	7,317	
171						------------	133,709
172							------------
173							41,942
174	ADD: Profit (Loss) on sale of asset						464
175							------------
176	NET PROFIT (LOSS) FOR YEAR						42,406
177							=========

Figure 25a (Part 1)

	A	B	C	D	E	F	G
179							
180							
181							
182		G.K. Nettlerash Company					
183							
184		BALANCE SHEET					
185							
186		at 31st December, 19x1					
187							
188				19x1		19x0	
189							
190			£	£	£	£	
191							
192	TANGIBLE ASSETS (Note 1)			33,466		38,319	
193							
194							
195	CURRENT ASSETS						
196	Stock		46,321		40,068		
197	Work-in-progress		2,752		2,602		
198	Debtors		100,629		97,917		
199	Prepayments		4,047		3,890		
200	No. 2 Account		348		348		
201	Cash at Bank		0		0		
202	Cash-in-hand		32		19		
203			-------------		-------------		
204			154,129		144,844		
205			-------------		-------------		
206							
207							
208	CURRENT LIABILITIES						
209	Creditors		101,050		95,468		
210	Accruals		4,535		4,775		
211	PAYE		2,370		2,320		
212	VAT		9,860		6,725		
213	Overdraft		1,095		28,596		
214			-------------		-------------		
215			118,910		137,884		
216			-------------		-------------		
217							
218	Net Current Assets			35,219		6,960	
219				-------------		-------------	
220				68,685		45,279	
221				=========		=========	
222	Represented by:						
223							
224	CAPITAL ACCOUNT (Note 2)			68,685		45,279	
225				=========		=========	
226							
227							

Figure 25a (Part 2)

Figure 25b shows the labels and underlying formulae, for entry in the cells. You will note (probably with some relief after session 24) that the formulae are all very simple.

	A	B	C	D	E	F	G
228							
229		G.K. Nettlerash Company					
230							
231		NOTES TO THE ACCOUNTS					
232							
233		at 31st December, 19x1					
234							
235							
236	Note 1						
237	------						
238	FIXED ASSETS		Plant	Office	Car 1	Car 2	TOTAL
239			and	Equip.			
240			Mach'y				
241			------------	------------	------------	------------	------------
242	Cost		£	£	£	£	£
243							
244	at 31st December 1990		32,500	7,325	16,953	0	56,778
245	Additions		0	0	0	12,000	12,000
246	Disposals		0	0	-16,953	0	-16,953
247			------------	------------	------------	------------	------------
248	at 31st December 1991		32,500	7,325	0	12,000	51,825
249			------------	------------	------------	------------	------------
250							
251	Depreciation						
252							
253	at 31st December 1990		9,009	2,033	7,417	0	18,459
254	re disposals		0	0	-7,417	0	-7,417
255	charge for year		3,524	794	0	3,000	7,317
256			------------	------------	------------	------------	------------
257	at 31st December 1991		12,533	2,827	0	3,000	18,359
258			------------	------------	------------	------------	------------
259							
260	Net Book Value						
261							
262	at 31st December 1990		23,491	5,292	9,536	0	38,319
263			------------	------------	------------	------------	------------
264	at 31st December 1991		19,967	4,498	0	9,000	33,466
265			------------	------------	------------	------------	------------
266							
267	Note 2						
268	------						
269	CAPITAL ACCOUNT						£
270							
271	Balance at 31st December 19x0						45,279
272							
273	add: Capital introduced						5,000
274							------------
275							50,279
276	Net Profit / Loss for year						42,406
277							------------
278							92,685
279	less: Drawings						24,000
280							------------
281	Balance at 31st December 19x1						68,685
282							=========
283							

Figure 25a (Part 3)

	A	B	C	D	E	F	G
123							
124		G.K. Nettlerash Company					
125							
126		TRADING AND PROFIT & LOSS ACCOUNT					
127							
128		for the year ended 31st December 19x1					
129							
130					£	£	£
131	SALES						+I92
132							
133	LESS: COST OF SALES						
134							
135	Opening Stock and Work-in-progress					+H88+H90	
136	add Purchases					+H93	
137						----------------------	
138						+F135+F136	
139	less Closing Stock and Work-in-progress					+I89+I91	
140						----------------------	
141							+F138-F139
142							----------------------
143	GROSS PRO(	+G143	of Sales				+G131-G141
144							
145	LESS: EXPENSES						
146							
147	Sub-Contract					+H94	
148	Consumables					+H95	
149	Wages and NI					+H96	
150	Motor Expenses					+H97	
151	Transport & Storage					+H98	
152	Rent & Rates					+H99	
153	Light & Heat					+H100	
154	Telephone					+H101	
155	Printing & Stationery					+H102	
156	Advertising					+H103	
157	Cleaning & Sundries					+H104	
158	Repairs & Renewals					+H105	
159	Lease Rentals					+H106	
160	Legal & Professional					+H107	
161	Accountancy					+H108	
162	Insurance					+H109	
163	Bank Charges					+H111	
164	Bank Interest					+H112	
165	Depreciation:						
166	Plant & Machinery				+H78		
167	Office Equipment				+H81		
168	Car 1				+H84		
169	Car 2				+H87		
170					----------------------	@SUM(E166..E169)	
171						----------------------	@SUM(F147..F170)
172							----------------------
173							+G143-G171
174	ADD: Profit (Loss) on sale of asset						+I110-H110
175							----------------------
176	NET PROFIT (LOSS) FOR YEAR						+G173+G174
177							==============
178							

Figure 25b (Part 1)

	A	B	C	D	E	F	G
179							
180							
181							
182		G.K. Nettlerash Company					
183							
184		BALANCE SHEET					
185							
186		at 31st December, 19x1					
187							
188				19x1		19x0	
189							
190			£	£	£	£	
191							
192	TANGIBLE ASSETS (Note 1)			+G264		+G262	
193							
194							
195	CURRENT ASSETS						
196	Stock		+J89		+B88		
197	Work-in-progress		+J91		+B90		
198	Debtors		+J71		+B71		
199	Prepayments		+F113		@SUM(B92..B112)		
200	No. 2 Account		+J68		+B68		
201	Cash at Bank		+J66		+B66		
202	Cash-in-hand		+J67		+B67		
203			-----------------------		-----------------------		
204			@SUM(C196..C202)		@SUM(E196..E202)		
205			-----------------------		-----------------------		
206							
207							
208	CURRENT LIABILITIES						
209	Creditors		+K72		+C72		
210	Accruals		+G113		@SUM(C92..C112)		
211	PAYE		+K70		+C70		
212	VAT		+K69		+C69		
213	Overdraft		+K66		+C66		
214			-----------------------		-----------------------		
215			@SUM(C209..C213)		@SUM(E209..E213)		
216			-----------------------		-----------------------		
217							
218	Net Current Assets			+C204-C215		+E204-E215	
219				-----------------------		-----------------------	
220				+D192+D218		+F192+F218	
221				===============		===============	
222	Represented by:						
223							
224	CAPITAL ACCOUNT (Note 2)			+G281		+C73	
225				===============		===============	
226							
227							

Figure 25b (Part 2)

5. Notes on creating the model

[The model is now rather large, particularly if you already have increased the model by adding year 2. As suggested in session 24, paragraph 5, if you have rather slow hardware and a slow program, you will almost certainly have to wait for recalculation after each entry which activates it. Try using /WGRM (Worksheet, Global, Recalculation, Manual) and then pressing <F9> only when you need a recalculation.]

	A	B	C	D	E	F	G
228							
229		G.K. Nettlerash Company					
230							
231		NOTES TO THE ACCOUNTS					
232							
233		at 31st December, 19x1					
234							
235							
236	Note 1						
237	------						
238	FIXED ASSETS		Plant	Office	Car 1	Car 2	TOTAL
239			and	Equip.			
240			Mach'y				
241			----------	----------	----------	----------	----------
242	Cost		£	£	£	£	£
243							
244	at 31st December		+B76	+B79	+B82	+B85	@SUM(C244..F244)
245	Additions		+B21	+B24	+B27	+B30	@SUM(C245..F245)
246	Disposals		-K21	-K24	-K27	-K30	@SUM(C246..F246)
247			----------	----------	----------	----------	----------
248	at 31st December		@SUM(C244..C246)	@SUM(D244..D246)	@SUM(E244..E246)	@SUM(F244..F246)	@SUM(C248..F248)
249			----------	----------	----------	----------	----------
250							
251	Depreciation						
252							
253	at 31st December		+C77	+C80	+C83	+C86	@SUM(C253..F253)
254	re disposals		-J22	-J25	-J28	-J31	@SUM(C254..F254)
255	charge for year		+H78	+H81	+H84	+H87	@SUM(C255..F255)
256			----------	----------	----------	----------	----------
257	at 31st December		@SUM(C253..C255)	@SUM(D253..D255)	@SUM(E253..E255)	@SUM(F253..F255)	@SUM(C257..F257)
258			----------	----------	----------	----------	----------
259							
260	Net Book Value						
261							
262	at 31st December		+C244-C253	+D244-D253	+E244-E253	+F244-F253	@SUM(C262..F262)
263			----------	----------	----------	----------	----------
264	at 31st December		+C248-C257	+D248-D257	+E248-E257	+F248-F257	@SUM(C264..F264)
265			----------	----------	----------	----------	----------
266							
267	Note 2						
268	------						
269	CAPITAL ACCOUNT						£
270							
271	Balance at 31st December 19x0						+C73
272							
273	add: Capital introduced						+K74
274							----------
275							+G271+G273
276	Net Profit / Loss for year						+G176
277							----------
278							+G275+G276
279	less: Drawings						+J75
280							----------
281	Balance at 31st December 19x1						+G278-G279
282							==============
283							

Figure 25b (Part 3)

You should by now find no difficulty in entering the labels and formulae with careful reference to figures 25a and 25b.

Tips:

A39..A54 can be copied down to A147..A162.

F147 can be copied own to F148..F164

G244 can be copied down to G245..G246, G248, G253..G255, G257, G262 and G264.

C248, C257, C262 and C264 can all be copied to columns D..F.

6. An explanation of the model

The layout of the accounts is fairly traditional.

If you feel that some of the Current Assets and Current Liabilities should be grouped, with details in the notes, please feel free to alter the model to do this.

Also you may prefer to substitute the wording: **CREDITORS: amounts due within one year** for "CURRENT LIABILITIES" in cell A208.

7. Printing the accounts

Details of how to print were provided in session 4.

The accounts prepared here are designed to be printed out on three pages of A4 size paper.

You can print each page separately, redefining the range for each page before printing. The ranges could be:

A123..G178 containing the Trading and Profit & Loss Account.

A179..G227 containing the Balance Sheet.

A228..G283 containing the Notes to the Accounts.

An alternative [not {AEA}] is to enter page breaks, using the command

`/WP` (Worksheet, Page)

Place the cursor in cell A179, i.e. the first cell of the second page containing the Balance Sheet.

Press `/WP`

A blank row (179) is inserted by the program, and what was row 179 now becomes row 180.

Row 179 now contains double colons (::) and if you move the cursor to cell A179 you will see | :: in the control panel. This is a page break line, and it is not printed out. The whole row 179 should be left empty.

Note that all the row references below the page break line have increased by one. The formulae etc. are unaffected.

A similar page break can be made at cell A228.

With both page breaks entered, you can define the whole range A123..G283 for printing.

If you want to remove a page break, delete it with /RE (Range, Erase).

If you want to delete a page break *and* the whole row, you can use /WDR (Worksheet, Delete, Row).

If you have a more sophisticated spreadsheet publishing program, you may like to try out your artistic skills with various fonts and trimmings.

8. Activity

(1) **Accuracy**

Check the accuracy of this session by comparing the accounts in columnar form (range H62..K118) with the printed accounts.

(2) **Combining or Merging Files**

If you completed the activity at the end of session 24 (paragraph 9) where you entered your own data into the model produced in session 24, you can copy the range created in this session (session 25) into your own data file.

Suppose the files are named as follows:

NETTRASH.WK1	The file created in session 25 for Nettlerash.
ACTIVITY.WK1	The file created for your own data.

Retrieve ACTIVITY.WK1 and move the cursor to cell A123

The next steps depend on your program.

[Note: Some of these operations may take some time in calculation, depending on your machine and program. This is a fairly large worksheet.]

If you are using {123}{VP}{VPP}

Press `/FCC` (File, Combine, Copy)

Choose Named/Specified-Range

Press `<Enter>`

Type `A123..G283`

Press `<Enter>`

Respond to **Enter name of file to combine** by typing in `NETTRASH.WK1`

or highlight the file name (press <F3> if you have many files to view)

Press `<Enter>`

and the range A123..G283 should be copied in correctly.

If you are using {AEA}

Press `/FMR` (File, Merge, Range)

Type `A123..G283`

Press `<Enter>`

Press `F` (Formula)

Press `R` (Replace)

Respond to **Name of file ?** by typing in `NETTRASH.WK1`

or highlight the file name.

Press `<Enter>`

and the range A123..G283 should be copied in correctly.

(3) Year 2 range

If you have created a year 2 range for your model (as described in session 24, paragraph 8), you can copy (/C) this range (A123..G283) to the same rows under the accounting worksheet for year 2. You will then have to alter the labels to refer to the year 2 dates.

(4) Depreciation

The depreciation in this model uses the reduced balance method of depreciation, and the formulae in cells D78, D81, D83 and D86 reflect this.

If the straight-line method is required, the formulae in those cells must be altered. For example, the formula in cell D78 should be altered to

(B21+D21+F21+H21+J21+B76-K21)*M21

which eliminates reference to depreciation provision. Compare the new formula with the original in Figure 24b.

This formula can be copied down to the other three cells.

Experiment with this, and check that the new calculations are correct by referring to the altered values in Note 1 in the NOTES TO THE ACCOUNTS (range A236..G265).

[Remember not to save the file, unless you wish to preserve the straight-line calculations; in which case, save the file under a new name.]

There are other depreciation methods. Three other methods can be achieved using financial @functions. These are:

@SLN	Straight-line method with salvage value
@SYD	Sum-of-years method
@DDB	Double-declining balance method

[@SLN could be used in the Nettlerash model, but would be difficult to adapt to cope with journal entries etc., e.g. with regard to additions and disposals.]

Details and examples of these functions can be found in appendix D.

SESSION 26

Cashflow statement: FRS1

1. Objectives

At the end of this session, you will be able to:

- ❑ construct a model which extracts information from the accounting worksheet created in session 24 and the financial accounts created in session 25, and produce and print a cashflow statement which follows the format required by FRS1 (*Financial Reporting Standard No 1*);
- ❑ point (or refer) to cells when using mathematical operators in formulae;
- ❑ name a range with the purpose of making that range easier to remember and refer to.

2. Introduction

In this session you will retrieve the file which you created in sessions 24 and 25, the worksheet and financial accounts for George Nettlerash, and add to it a range which will print out a cashflow statement.

This cashflow statement for the G.K. Nettlerash Company follows the format required by FRS1 (*Financial Reporting Standard No 1*), which applies to financial statements relating to periods after 23 March 1992. The FRS exempts most small reporting entities from the requirement to include this cashflow statement as part of their financial statements. However, some accountants may well provide such a statement for companies or individuals where the standard statement is not obligatory. Some adaptation of the standard is necessary for a sole trader, particularly in respect of the capital structure (note 4: analysis of changes in financing), but the adapted cashflow statement which you will create is essentially the same as that for a single company, as shown in the illustrative example 1 of the FRS1. If you have adapted the Nettlerash file (sessions 24 and 25) to cope with, say, the accounts of a limited liability company, you should not find it too difficult to alter this additional cashflow statement to accommodate any necessary changes.

3. The problem

In sessions 24, you met George Nettlerash and, from the data provided there, produced a worksheet which took his accounting data for the year to 31st December 19x1 and produced a columnar Profit & Loss Account and Balance Sheet for that year. In session 25 you added a printed copy of his accounts for the year.

Now George requires a printed copy of a cashflow statement for the same period.

	A	B	C	D	E	F	G
284		G.K. Nettlerash Company					
285		CASH FLOW STATEMENT					
286		for the year ended 31st December 19x1					
287						£	£
288	Net cash flow from operating activities (see note 1)						53,248
289	Returns on investments and servicing of finance						
290	Interest received					0	
291	Interest paid					(4,734)	
292	Drawings					(24,000)	
293	Net cash outflow from returns on investments						
294	and servicing of finance						(28,734)
295							
296	Investing Activities						
297	Payments to acquire fixed assets					(12,000)	
298	Receipts from sale of tangible fixed assets					10,000	
299							
300	Net cash outflow from investing Activities						(2,000)
301							------------
302	Net cash inflow before financing						22,514
303	Financing						
304	New capital introduced					5,000	
305	Net cash inflow from financing						5,000
306							------------
307	Increase in cash and cash equivalents						27,514
308	(see notes 2 and 3)						==========
309	------------	------------	------------	------------	------------	------------	------------
310	Notes to the Cash Flow Statement						
311	------------	------------	------------	------------	------------	------------	------------
312	(1) Reconciliation of operating profit to net cash inflow from						
313	operating activities						
314						£	£
315	Operating profit						42,406
316	Add back						
317	Loss on sale of assets					0	
318	Interest paid					4,734	
319	Depreciation					7,317	
320						------------	12,051
321							------------
322							54,457
323	Deduct:	Profit on sale of assets				464	
324		Interest received				0	
325						------------	464
326							------------
327							53,993
328	Deduct:	Increase (Decrease) in stocks and WIP				6,403	
329		Increase (Decrease) in debtors				2,869	
330						------------	9,272
331							------------
332							44,721
333	Add:	Increase (Decrease) in creditors				8,527	
334						------------	8,527
335							------------
336	Net cash flow from operating activities						53,248
337							==========
338	------------	------------	------------	------------	------------	------------	------------

Figure 26a (Part 1)

	A	B	C	D	E	F	G
339	(2) Analysis of changes in cash and cash equivalents during the year						
340							£
341	Balance at 1st January 19x1						(28,229)
342	Net cash inflow (see note 3)						27,514
343							------------
344	Balance at 31 December 19x1						(715)
345							=========
346	------------	------------	------------	------------	------------	------------	------------
347	(3) Analysis of the balances of cash and cash equivalents as shown						
348	in the balance sheet						
349			19x1		19x0		Change
350							in year
351			£		£		£
352	No. 2 Account		348		348		0
353	Cash at Bank		0		0		0
354	Cash-in-hand		32		19		13
355	Bank overdraft		(1,095)		(28,596)		27,501
356			------------		------------		------------
357			(715)		(28,229)		27,514
358			=========		=========		=========
359	------------	------------	------------	------------	------------	------------	------------
360	(4) Analysis of changes in financing during the year						
361	See Note 2 under NOTES TO THE ACCOUNTS						
362	------------	------------	------------	------------	------------	------------	------------

Figure 26a (Part 2)

4. Design of the model

Figure 24a (Session 24) used the range A1..M118 for the Accounting Worksheet.

Figures 25a (Session 25) used the range A123..G283 for the Financial Accounts.

The cashflow statement for this session uses the range A284..G362.

Figure 26a shows the statement as it appears on the screen, and as will be printed out.

Figure 26b shows the labels and underlying formulae, for entry in the cells. As in session 25, the formulae are all very simple.

5. Notes on creating the model

[The model is now rather large, particularly if you already have increased the model by adding year 2. As suggested in the previous sessions, if you have rather slow hardware and a slow program, you will almost certainly have to wait for recalculation after each entry which activates it. Try using /WGRM (Worksheet, Global, Recalculation, Manual) and then pressing <F9> only when you need a recalculation.]

You should by now find no difficulty in entering the labels and formulae with careful reference to figures 26a and 26b.

	A	B	C	D	E	F	G
284		G.K. Nettlerash Company					
285		CASH FLOW STATEMENT					
286		for the year ended 31st December 19x1					
287						£	£
288	Net cash flow from operating activities (see note 1)						+G336
289	Returns on investments and servicing of finance						
290	Interest received					+I112	
291	Interest paid					-H112	
292	Drawings					-G279	
293	Net cash outflow from returns on investments						
294	and servicing of finance						@SUM(F291..F292)
295							
296	Investing Activities						
297	Payments to acquire fixed assets					-G245	
298	Receipts from sale of tangible fixed assets					+C55	
299							
300	Net cash outflow from investing Activities						@SUM(F297..F298)
301							---------------
302	Net cash inflow before financing						+G288+G294+G300
303	Financing						
304	New capital introduced					+C19	
305	Net cash inflow from financing						+F304
306							---------------
307	Increase in cash and cash equivalents						+G302+G305
308	(see notes 2 and 3)						===============
309	-----------	-----------	-----------	-----------	-----------	-----------	-----------
310	Notes to the Cash Flow Statement						
311	-----------	-----------	-----------	-----------	-----------	-----------	-----------
312	(1) Reconciliation of operating profit to net cash inflow from						
313	operating activities						
314						£	£
315	Operating profit						+H116
316	Add back						
317	Loss on sale of assets					+H110	
318	Interest paid					+H112	
319	Depreciation					+F170	
320						-----------	@SUM(F317..F319)
321							---------------
322							+G315+G320
323	Deduct:	Profit on sale of assets				+I110	
324		Interest received				+I112	
325						-----------	+F323+F324
326							---------------
327							+G322-G325
328	Deduct:	Increase (Decrease) in stocks and WIP				+C196-E196+C197-E197	
329		Increase (Decrease) in debtors				+C198-E198+C199-E199	
330						-----------	+F328+F329
331							---------------
332							+G327-G330
333	Add:	Increase (Decrease) in creditors				@SUM(C209..C212)-@SUM(E209..E212)	
334						-----------	+F333
335							---------------
336	Net cash flow from operating activities						+G332+G334
337							===============
338	-----------	-----------	-----------	-----------	-----------	-----------	-----------

Figure 26b (Part 1)

	A	B	C	D	E	F	G
339	(2) Analysis of changes in cash and cash equivalents during the year						
340							£
341	Balance at 1st January 19x1						+E357
342	Net cash inflow (see note 3)						+G357
343							------------------------
344	Balance at 31 December 19x1						+C357
345							===============
346	------------	------------------	-----------------	---------	-------------	-------------------------------	------------------------
347	(3) Analysis of the balances of cash and cash equivalents as shown						
348	in the balance sheet						
349			19x1		19x0		Change
350							in year
351			£		£		£
352	No. 2 Account		+C200		+E200		+C352-E352
353	Cash at Bank		+C201		+E201		+C353-E353
354	Cash-in-hand		+C202		+E202		+C354-E354
355	Bank overdraft		-C213		-E213		+C355-E355
356			-----------------		-------------		------------------------
357			@SUM(C352..C355)		@SUM(E352..E355)		@SUM(G352..G355)
358			==========		========		===============
359	------------	------------------	-----------------	---------	-------------	-------------------------------	------------------------
360	(4) Analysis of changes in financing during the year						
361	See Note 2 under NOTES TO THE ACCOUNTS						
362	------------	------------------	-----------------	---------	-------------	-------------------------------	------------------------

Figure 26b (Part 2)

Tip on pointing (or referring):

There are quite a number of formulae in figure 26b which use the operators + and - . If you are simply copying from figures 26a and 26b, this causes no problem. However, if you were composing the worksheet yourself and were trying to find the cell reference to enter after the operator, you might have difficulty if it was far away. You can *point* after entering the operator, just as you can after using @SUM(, as you learnt in session 3, paragraph 8. For example, in cell G327 is the formula +G322-G325. To enter this using pointing ({AEA} calls it *referring*):

Move the cursor to cell G327

Press [+]

Move the cursor to cell G322 (You are now in *point* or *refer* mode)

DO *NOT* PRESS <Enter> !

Press [–]

The cursor moves back to cell G327

Move the cursor to cell G325

Press [<Enter>]

The formula +G322-G325 should now be in cell G327.

If the cell references can be seen (as in this example), it may be quicker simply to type them in. But if the cell reference is far away, and you have to move there to see what it is, then pointing after typing the operator can save time.

6. An explanation of the model

Some of the cell references refer back to the worksheet, rather than references in the accounts. This is always a rather difficult decision to make. Perhaps using the source cell is the best policy, in case the chain is broken by later alterations.

For example, interest paid (£4,734) in cells F291 and F318 both refer back to cell H112. These cells could have referred to F164 in the Profit & Loss Account (which itself refers to H112), or back further to F112 (to which H112 refers).

If you do alter or adapt a worksheet, be careful that chained references are not broken.

Note that cell G288 refers to cell G336, because Note (1) of the statement works out the *Net cash flow from operating activities*.

7. Activity

(1) **Presentation**

Print out the Cashflow Statement, and criticise its presentation. Improve the layout, particulary with regard to such aspects as column-widths and page-breaks. If you are fortunate enough to have access to a good printer, or have a spreadsheet publishing program (such as ALLWAYS, which is a Lotus 1-2-3 add-in), experiment with fonts and layouts to achieve a professional-looking presentation. If not, do the best you can!

(2) **Naming Ranges**

If you completed the activity at the end of session 25, paragraph 8 (2), where you used the combine or merge commands to copy the NETTRASH range A123..G283 into your ACTIVITY file, you can now do the same for this new range A284..G362.

However, you may like to experiment with *naming* the range while doing so. The purpose of naming a range is to make that range easier to remember and refer to. When you are in the ACTIVITY file, and want to copy the range A284..G362 from the NETTRASH file, you may well have forgotten to make a note of the cell references before you retrieved the ACTIVITY file. If you name the range A284..G362 with the name CASHFLOW before saving NETTRASH and retrieving ACTIVITY, you should find the name easier to remember.

To save you having to refer back to session 25, here are the full instructions for copying the range A284..G362 from NETTRASH to ACTIVITY files, using CASHFLOW as the name for that range:

Suppose the files are named as follows:

NETTRASH.WK1	The file created in sessions 24 and 25 for Nettlerash.
ACTIVITY.WK1	The file created for your own data.

Retrieve the NETTRASH.WK1 file.

Move the cursor to cell A284 (the start of the Cashflow Statement).

Press `/RNC` (Range, Name, Create)

Type `CASHFLOW`

Define the range by typing in A284..G362 or by pointing, and press <Enter>.

Save the NETTRASH file with /FSR (File, Save, Replace)

Retrieve ACTIVITY.WK1 and move the cursor to cell A284.

The next steps depend on your program.

[Note: Some of these operations may take some time in calculation, depending on your machine and program. This is a fairly large worksheet.]

If you are using {123}{VP}{VPP}

Press `/FCC` (File, Combine, Copy)

Choose Named/Specified-Range

Press `<Enter>`

Press `CASHFLOW`

Press `<Enter>`

Respond to **Enter name of file to combine** by typing in `NETTRASH.WK1`

or highlight the file name (press <F3> if you have many files to view)

Press `<Enter>`

and the range A284..G362 should be copied in correctly.

If you are using {AEA}

Press `/FMR` (File, Merge, Range)

Press `CASHFLOW`

Press `<Enter>`

Press `F` (Formula)

Press `R` (Replace)

Respond to **Name of file ?** by typing in `NETTRASH.WK1`

or highlight the file name.

Press `<Enter>`

and the range A284..G362 should be copied in correctly.

(3) **Year 2 range**

If you have created a year 2 range for your model, as suggested in session 24, paragraph 8, and session 25, paragraph 8 (3), you can copy (/C) this range (A284..G362) to the same rows under year 2's worksheet and accounts. You will then have to alter the labels to refer to the year 2 dates.

SESSION 27
Analysed cash book

1. Objectives

At the end of this session, you will be able to:

- ❑ construct an analysed cash book (bank account)
- ❑ understand further uses for the @IF function
- ❑ use the @DSUM function (not {AEA})

2. Introduction

Note: The @ function **@DSUM** is used for the analysis part of the model, and this function is not available in {AEA}, at least in version 4.00Q. However, an alternative method for the analysis part of this model for {AEA} users is provided in detail below in paragraph 8. [Session 28 extends this model to produce a bank reconciliation, and this is not affected by the method used for the analysis, and is therefore possible for all programs covered by this book.]

In this session you will construct a model which keeps a cash book with cumulative balances and the facility for separating VAT. In addition, a cash book analysis, using accounts codes, is added.

This is a completely separate worksheet from that created in the previous three sessions (Nettlerash), although the same expense headings are used for the analysis codes. If you have a program which can link cells between worksheets (Lotus 1-2-3 releases 2.2 and higher, and major Windows programs have this facility), the totals produced by the analysis codes of this model can be automatically posted to the cash book analysis columns of the Nettlerash model. It is beyond the scope of this present book to explain the procedure, but you can easily refer to the manual for your particular program. Alternatively, (in theory) the model produced in this session can be copied (using the techniques described in sessions 25 and 26) into an area of the Nettlerash worksheet; in which case the "linking" can be effected by internal cell references. However, unless you have fast hardware and a fast program, you may find the resulting worksheet too large and slow to be practicable.

3. The problem

George Nettlerash wants a simple spreadsheet model on which he can record his bank transactions and which will produce a running balance of his bank balance. He would like his VAT payments separated out, and, if possible a cumulative analysis of his payments etc. under his usual expenses classifications.

	A	B	C	D	E	F	G	H	I	J	K	L	M
1	Session 27: Analysed Cash Book (Bank Account)												
2	------	------	------	------	------	------	------	------	------	------	------	------	------
3			£	£	£		£	£					£
4	------	------	------	------	------	------	------	------	------	------	------	------	------
5	Cumulative Running Balances:			13,241.98	(15,354.02)		(562.97)	13,804.95		Cumulative Cash Book Analysis			13,241.98
6	------	------	------	------	------	------	------	------	------	------	------	------	------
7	Starting balance:				(28,596.00)					Code	Account Headings		
8	------	------	------	------	------	------	------	------	------	------	------	------	------
9	19x1								Bank	Code			
10	Date	Number	Details	Amount	Cum.Bal.	Code	VAT	Excl.VAT	Rec	112	Petty Cash		(800.00)
11	Jan 3	100576	Mr. Sowerberry	(11.75)	(28,607.75)	143	(1.75)	(10.00)		Code			
12	Jan 4	100577	Crackit & Co	(2,000.00)	(30,607.75)	144		(2,000.00)		113	Deposit Account		0.00
13	Jan 6	100578	Fagin & Co	(29.37)	(30,637.12)	140	(4.37)	(25.00)		Code			
14	Jan 6	100579	Gamfield Repairs	(57.13)	(30,694.25)	150	(8.51)	(48.62)		114	VAT		(562.97)
15	Jan 6	100580	Fagin & Co	(52.87)	(30,747.12)	140	(7.87)	(45.00)		Code			
16	Jan 7	311216	Lively DIY Store	11,243.98	(19,503.14)	116		11,243.98		115	PAYE		(986.81)
17	Jan 7	100581	Sikes Supplies	(7,302.66)	(26,805.80)	117		(7,302.66)		Code			
18	Jan 7	100582	Wages	(830.60)	(27,636.40)	141		(830.60)		116	Sales Ledger		45,098.18
19	Jan 10	100583	Gamfield Repairs	(22.58)	(27,658.98)	150	(3.36)	(19.22)		Code			
20	Jan 11	100584	Fagin & Co	(16.40)	(27,675.38)	140	(2.44)	(13.96)		117	Purchase Ledger		(29,444.41)
21	Jan 12	100585	Brownlow Brokers	(798.00)	(28,473.38)	154		(798.00)		Code			
22	Jan 13	100586	Limbkins Oil	(249.70)	(28,723.08)	145	(37.19)	(212.51)		119	Capital		0.00
23	Jan 13	100587	PAYE	(1,159.50)	(29,882.58)	115	(172.69)	(986.81)		Code			
24	Jan 14	311217	Fang's DIY Store	12,976.78	(16,905.80)	116		12,976.78		120	Drawings		(2,000.00)
25	Jan 14	100588	Sikes Supplies	(7,416.22)	(24,322.02)	117		(7,416.22)		Code			
26	Jan 14	100589	Petty Cash	(400.00)	(24,722.02)	112		(400.00)		121	Plant & M/c		0.00
27	Jan 14	311218	Sale of Car 1	10,000.00	(14,722.02)	155		10,000.00		Code			
28	Jan 14	100590	Wages	(825.35)	(15,547.37)	141	(122.92)	(702.43)		124	Office Eqpt		0.00
29	Jan 17	100591	Mr. Sowerberry	(22.36)	(15,569.73)	143	(3.33)	(19.03)		Code			
30	Jan 18	100592	Fagin & Co	(72.13)	(15,641.86)	140	(10.74)	(61.39)		127	Car 1		0.00
31	Jan 18	100593	Dodger Motors	(432.65)	(16,074.51)	142	(64.44)	(368.21)		Code			
32	Jan 19	100594	Grimwig PR Co.	(42.12)	(16,116.63)	148	(6.27)	(35.85)		130	Car 2		0.00
33	Jan 19	100595	Duff Stationers	(67.50)	(16,184.13)	147	(10.05)	(57.45)		Code			
34	Jan 20	100596	Bates Solicitors	(105.00)	(16,289.13)	152	(15.64)	(89.36)		139	Sub-Contract		0.00
35	Jan 21	311219	Lively DIY Store	10,143.87	(6,145.26)	116		10,143.87		Code			
36	Jan 21	100597	Sikes Supplies	(7,234.65)	(13,379.91)	117		(7,234.65)		140	Consumables		(154.06)
37	Jan 21	100598	Wages	(810.75)	(14,190.66)	141		(810.75)		Code			
38	Jan 24	100599	Fagin & Co	(10.23)	(14,200.89)	140	(1.52)	(8.71)		141	Wages & Nat Ins		(3,174.43)
39	Jan 24	100600	Mr. Sowerberry	(15.80)	(14,216.69)	143	(2.35)	(13.45)		Code			
40	Jan 26	100601	Twist Telephones	(587.68)	(14,804.37)	146	(87.53)	(500.15)		142	Motor Expenses		(368.21)
41	Jan 26		Dawkins Bank-Chs	(110.00)	(14,914.37)	156		(110.00)		Code			
42	Jan 26		Dawkins Bank-Int	(451.67)	(15,366.04)	157		(451.67)		143	Transport & Storage		(42.48)
43	Jan 28	100602	Petty Cash	(400.00)	(15,766.04)	112		(400.00)		Code			
44	Jan 28	100603	Kags' DIY Store	10,733.55	(5,032.49)	116		10,733.55		144	Rent & Rates		(2,000.00)
45	Jan 28	311220	Sikes Supplies	(7,490.88)	(12,523.37)	117		(7,490.88)		Code			
46	Jan 28	100604	Drawings	(2,000.00)	(14,523.37)	120		(2,000.00)		145	Light & Heat		(212.51)
47	Jan 28	100605	Wages	(830.65)	(15,354.02)	141		(830.65)		Code			
48					0.00			0.00		146	Telephone		(500.15)

Figure 27a (Part 1)

4. Design of the model

A study of Figure 27a will reveal the overall structure of the model.

Column A: shows the date of the cheque or paying-in.

Column B: is for the cheque or paying-in slip reference.

Column C: is the space for payee or payer.

Column D: records the amount paid out as a *negative* or paid in as *positive* value. Cell D5 contains a formula which keeps a running total of column D.

	A	B	C	D	E	F	G	H	I	J	K	L	M
49					0.00			0.00		Code			
50					0.00			0.00		147	Printing & Stat'y		(57.45)
51					0.00			0.00		Code			
52					0.00			0.00		148	Advertising		(35.85)
53					0.00			0.00		Code			
54					0.00			0.00		149	Cleaning & Sundries		0.00
55					0.00			0.00		Code			
56					0.00			0.00		150	Repairs & Renewals		(67.84)
57					0.00			0.00		Code			
58					0.00			0.00		151	Leases		0.00
59					0.00			0.00		Code			
60					0.00			0.00		152	Legal & Prof'nal		(89.36)
61					0.00			0.00		Code			
62					0.00			0.00		153	Accountancy		0.00
63					0.00			0.00		Code			
64					0.00			0.00		154	Insurance		(798.00)
65					0.00			0.00		Code			
66					0.00			0.00		155	Sale of assets		10,000.00
67					0.00			0.00		Code			
68					0.00			0.00		156	Bank Charges		(110.00)
69					0.00			0.00		Code			
70					0.00			0.00		157	Bank Interest		(451.67)
71					0.00			0.00					
72					0.00			0.00					
73					0.00			0.00					------------
74					0.00			0.00		Total Receipts less Payments			13,241.98
75					0.00			0.00					========
76	Alter formulae at D5,G5,H5 and M10..M70.............				Copy E75 down..............			Copy H75 down					

Figure 27a (Part 2)

Column E: contains formulae which (see Figure 27b) calculate the cumulative balance, after taking into account the opening balance which is in cell E7. Cell E5 calculates the cumulative running balance, i.e the opening balance (E7) plus the current total of column D.

Column F: records the expenses or other code. For a list of the codes, you can refer to columns J and K. These conform to the headings in the Nettlerash model (sessions 24, 25 and 26).

Column G: is for entry of the VAT amount of the payment. Cell G5 maintains a cumulative running balance which is used in cell M14 for code 114.

Column H: calculates the non-VAT element of the payment, i.e. column D less column G. Cell H5 maintains a cumulative running balance.

Column I: is unused in this session, but will be used in session 28 for recording cleared and uncleared items against the bank statement, so that a bank reconciliation can be effected.

Columns J..M: contain labels and formulae which perform running balances of an analysis of column H (not column D), i.e. amounts exclusive of VAT, analysed from the accounts codes entered in column F. You will note that the VAT element is accumulated under code 114. Cells M5 and M74 both record the cumulative running total of the analysis. The formulae in column M make use of the @DSUM function. This function is not available for {AEA}, as explained in paragraph 2 above, but an alternative method to that employed in columns J..M is described in paragraph 8.

	A	B	C	D	E	F	G	H	I
1	Session 27: Analysed Cash Book (Bank Account)								
2									
3			£	£	£		£	£	
4									
5	Cumulative Running Balances:			@SUM(D11..D75)	@SUM(D11..D75)+E7		@SUM(G11..G75)	@SUM(H11..H75)	
6									
7	Starting balance:				(28,596.00)				
8									
9	19x1								Bank
10	Date	Number	Details	Amount	Cum.Bal.	Code	VAT	Excl.VAT	Rec
11	Jan 3	100576	Mr. Sowerberry	(11.75)	+E7+D11	143	(1.75)	+D11-G11	
12	Jan 4	100577	Crackit & Co	(2,000.00)	@IF(D12=0,0,+D12+E11)	144		+D12-G12	
13	Jan 6	100578	Fagin & Co	(29.37)	@IF(D13=0,0,+D13+E12)	140	(4.37)	+D13-G13	
14	Jan 6	100579	Gamfield Repairs	(57.13)	@IF(D14=0,0,+D14+E13)	150	(8.51)	+D14-G14	
15	Jan 6	100580	Fagin & Co	(52.87)	@IF(D15=0,0,+D15+E14)	140	(7.87)	+D15-G15	
16	Jan 7	311216	Lively DIY Store	11,243.98	@IF(D16=0,0,+D16+E15)	116		+D16-G16	
17	Jan 7	100581	Sikes Supplies	(7,302.66)	@IF(D17=0,0,+D17+E16)	117		+D17-G17	
18	Jan 7	100582	Wages	(830.60)	@IF(D18=0,0,+D18+E17)	141		+D18-G18	
19	Jan 10	100583	Gamfield Repairs	(22.58)	@IF(D19=0,0,+D19+E18)	150	(3.36)	+D19-G19	
20	Jan 11	100584	Fagin & Co	(16.40)	@IF(D20=0,0,+D20+E19)	140	(2.44)	+D20-G20	
21	Jan 12	100585	Brownlow Brokers	(798.00)	@IF(D21=0,0,+D21+E20)	154		+D21-G21	
22	Jan 13	100586	Limbkins Oil	(249.70)	@IF(D22=0,0,+D22+E21)	145	(37.19)	+D22-G22	
23	Jan 13	100587	PAYE	(1,159.50)	@IF(D23=0,0,+D23+E22)	115	(172.69)	+D23-G23	
24	Jan 14	311217	Fang's DIY Store	12,976.78	@IF(D24=0,0,+D24+E23)	116		+D24-G24	
25	Jan 14	100588	Sikes Supplies	(7,416.22)	@IF(D25=0,0,+D25+E24)	117		+D25-G25	
26	Jan 14	100589	Petty Cash	(400.00)	@IF(D26=0,0,+D26+E25)	112		+D26-G26	
27	Jan 14	311218	Sale of Car 1	10,000.00	@IF(D27=0,0,+D27+E26)	155		+D27-G27	
28	Jan 14	100590	Wages	(825.35)	@IF(D28=0,0,+D28+E27)	141	(122.92)	+D28-G28	
29	Jan 17	100591	Mr. Sowerberry	(22.36)	@IF(D29=0,0,+D29+E28)	143	(3.33)	+D29-G29	
30	Jan 18	100592	Fagin & Co	(72.13)	@IF(D30=0,0,+D30+E29)	140	(10.74)	+D30-G30	
31	Jan 18	100593	Dodger Motors	(432.65)	@IF(D31=0,0,+D31+E30)	142	(64.44)	+D31-G31	
32	Jan 19	100594	Grimwig PR Co.	(42.12)	@IF(D32=0,0,+D32+E31)	148	(6.27)	+D32-G32	
33	Jan 19	100595	Duff Stationers	(67.50)	@IF(D33=0,0,+D33+E32)	147	(10.05)	+D33-G33	
34	Jan 20	100596	Bates Solicitors	(105.00)	@IF(D34=0,0,+D34+E33)	152	(15.64)	+D34-G34	
35	Jan 21	311219	Lively DIY Store	10,143.87	@IF(D35=0,0,+D35+E34)	116		+D35-G35	
36	Jan 21	100597	Sikes Supplies	(7,234.65)	@IF(D36=0,0,+D36+E35)	117		+D36-G36	
37	Jan 21	100598	Wages	(810.75)	@IF(D37=0,0,+D37+E36)	141		+D37-G37	
38	Jan 24	100599	Fagin & Co	(10.23)	@IF(D38=0,0,+D38+E37)	140	(1.52)	+D38-G38	
39	Jan 24	100600	Mr. Sowerberry	(15.80)	@IF(D39=0,0,+D39+E38)	143	(2.35)	+D39-G39	
40	Jan 26	100601	Twist Telephones	(587.68)	@IF(D40=0,0,+D40+E39)	146	(87.53)	+D40-G40	
41	Jan 26		Dawkins Bank-Chs	(110.00)	@IF(D41=0,0,+D41+E40)	156		+D41-G41	
42	Jan 26		Dawkins Bank-Int	(451.67)	@IF(D42=0,0,+D42+E41)	157		+D42-G42	
43	Jan 28	100602	Petty Cash	(400.00)	@IF(D43=0,0,+D43+E42)	112		+D43-G43	
44	Jan 28	100603	Kags' DIY Store	10,733.55	@IF(D44=0,0,+D44+E43)	116		+D44-G44	
45	Jan 28	311220	Sikes Supplies	(7,490.88)	@IF(D45=0,0,+D45+E44)	117		+D45-G45	
46	Jan 28	100604	Drawings	(2,000.00)	@IF(D46=0,0,+D46+E45)	120		+D46-G46	
47	Jan 28	100605	Wages	(830.65)	@IF(D47=0,0,+D47+E46)	141		+D47-G47	
48					@IF(D48=0,0,+D48+E47)			+D48-G48	

Figure 27b (Part 1)

You will also note that space has been allocated on the worksheet for entries down to and including row 75. This limitation is purely in order to keep the Figures 27a and 27b to a reasonable size for reproduction. Notes have been added in row 76, as a warning that more space (and formulae) are required for further entries. Session 28 uses space below row 76 for the bank reconciliation range, and this range would have to be moved down if necessary (a simple matter of using /M (Move).

5. Notes on creating the model

The model can be created by reference to Figures 27a and 27b, with the following exceptions:

	J	K	L	M
1				
2				
3				£
4				
5	Cumulative Cash Book Analysis			@SUM(M10..M72)
6				
7	Code	Account Headings		
8				
9	Code			
10	112	Petty Cash		@DSUM($F$10..$H$75,2,J9..J10)
11	Code			
12	113	Deposit Account		@DSUM($F$10..$H$75,2,J11..J12)
13	Code			
14	114	VAT		@DSUM($F$10..$H$75,2,J13..J14)+G5
15	Code			
16	115	PAYE		@DSUM($F$10..$H$75,2,J15..J16)
17	Code			
18	116	Sales Ledger		@DSUM($F$10..$H$75,2,J17..J18)
19	Code			
20	117	Purchase Ledger		@DSUM($F$10..$H$75,2,J19..J20)
21	Code			
22	119	Capital		@DSUM($F$10..$H$75,2,J21..J22)
23	Code			
24	120	Drawings		@DSUM($F$10..$H$75,2,J23..J24)
25	Code			
26	121	Plant & M/c		@DSUM($F$10..$H$75,2,J25..J26)
27	Code			
28	124	Office Eqpt		@DSUM($F$10..$H$75,2,J27..J28)
29	Code			
30	127	Car 1		@DSUM($F$10..$H$75,2,J29..J30)
31	Code			
32	130	Car 2		@DSUM($F$10..$H$75,2,J31..J32)
33	Code			
34	139	Sub-Contract		@DSUM($F$10..$H$75,2,J33..J34)
35	Code			
36	140	Consumables		@DSUM($F$10..$H$75,2,J35..J36)
37	Code			
38	141	Wages & Nat Ins		@DSUM($F$10..$H$75,2,J37..J38)
39	Code			
40	142	Motor Expenses		@DSUM($F$10..$H$75,2,J39..J40)
41	Code			
42	143	Transport & Storage		@DSUM($F$10..$H$75,2,J41..J42)
43	Code			
44	144	Rent & Rates		@DSUM($F$10..$H$75,2,J43..J44)
45	Code			
46	145	Light & Heat		@DSUM($F$10..$H$75,2,J45..J46)
47	Code			
48	146	Telephone		@DSUM($F$10..$H$75,2,J47..J48)

Figure 27b (Part 2)

If you are using {AEA}

Do not create columns J..M, but create all the other columns (including the codes in column F) as described in this paragraph. Then refer to paragraph 8 for specific instructions to replace those for columns J..M.

If you are using {VP or {VPP}

The formula in cell M14 should read:

+G5+(@DSUM($F$10..$H$75,2,J13..J14))

This is most easily entered by editing the cell after it has been copied down (like most of the other formulae in this column) from the initial formula in cell M10).

	A	B	C	D	E	F	G	H	I
49					@IF(D49=0,0,+D49+E48)			+D49-G49	
50					@IF(D50=0,0,+D50+E49)			+D50-G50	
51					@IF(D51=0,0,+D51+E50)			+D51-G51	
52					@IF(D52=0,0,+D52+E51)			+D52-G52	
53					@IF(D53=0,0,+D53+E52)			+D53-G53	
54					@IF(D54=0,0,+D54+E53)			+D54-G54	
55					@IF(D55=0,0,+D55+E54)			+D55-G55	
56					@IF(D56=0,0,+D56+E55)			+D56-G56	
57					@IF(D57=0,0,+D57+E56)			+D57-G57	
58					@IF(D58=0,0,+D58+E57)			+D58-G58	
59					@IF(D59=0,0,+D59+E58)			+D59-G59	
60					@IF(D60=0,0,+D60+E59)			+D60-G60	
61					@IF(D61=0,0,+D61+E60)			+D61-G61	
62					@IF(D62=0,0,+D62+E61)			+D62-G62	
63					@IF(D63=0,0,+D63+E62)			+D63-G63	
64					@IF(D64=0,0,+D64+E63)			+D64-G64	
65					@IF(D65=0,0,+D65+E64)			+D65-G65	
66					@IF(D66=0,0,+D66+E65)			+D66-G66	
67					@IF(D67=0,0,+D67+E66)			+D67-G67	
68					@IF(D68=0,0,+D68+E67)			+D68-G68	
69					@IF(D69=0,0,+D69+E68)			+D69-G69	
70					@IF(D70=0,0,+D70+E69)			+D70-G70	
71					@IF(D71=0,0,+D71+E70)			+D71-G71	
72					@IF(D72=0,0,+D72+E71)			+D72-G72	
73					@IF(D73=0,0,+D73+E72)			+D73-G73	
74					@IF(D74=0,0,+D74+E73)			+D74-G74	
75					@IF(D75=0,0,+D75+E74)			+D75-G75	
76	Alter formulae at D5,G5,H5 and M10..M70................				Copy E75 down..............			Copy H75 down	

Figure 27b (Part 3)

	J	K	L	M
49	Code			
50	147	Printing & Stat'y		@DSUM($F$10..$H$75,2,J49..J50)
51	Code			
52	148	Advertising		@DSUM($F$10..$H$75,2,J51..J52)
53	Code			
54	149	Cleaning & Sundries		@DSUM($F$10..$H$75,2,J53..J54)
55	Code			
56	150	Repairs & Renewals		@DSUM($F$10..$H$75,2,J55..J56)
57	Code			
58	151	Leases		@DSUM($F$10..$H$75,2,J57..J58)
59	Code			
60	152	Legal & Prof'nal		@DSUM($F$10..$H$75,2,J59..J60)
61	Code			
62	153	Accountancy		@DSUM($F$10..$H$75,2,J61..J62)
63	Code			
64	154	Insurance		@DSUM($F$10..$H$75,2,J63..J64)
65	Code			
66	155	Sale of assets		@DSUM($F$10..$H$75,2,J65..J66)
67	Code			
68	156	Bank Charges		@DSUM($F$10..$H$75,2,J67..J68)
69	Code			
70	157	Bank Interest		@DSUM($F$10..$H$75,2,J69..J70)
71				
72				
73				------------------------------
74	Total Receipts less Payments			@SUM(M10..M72)
75				==============================
76				

Figure 27b (Part 4)

All programs:

Make use of the /C (copy) command for the formulae in columns E, H and M.

Column M causes a slight problem: either copy M10 down to M70 and erase (/RE<Enter>) alternate cells down this column, or copy M10 to M12, M12 to M14 and so on. Do not forget to edit cell M14 for the extra reference to cell G5 [{123} as Figure 27b, {VP} and {VPP} as note above].

The dates in column A are simply labels and are not used for any analysis.

The labels in row 10 are used later in this session (and in session 28) as database column designations (field names), and should therefore be copied carefully. For example **Rec** in cell I10 is used in the database, and the word **Bank** in cell I9 above it is purely for clarity. [This layout is designed this way to keep the column thin.]

Adjust column-widths as necessary.

The worksheet should be protected, and the following ranges unprotected:

A11..D75, F11..G75, I11..I75.

6. An explanation of the model

Column E: The @IF formulae produce a zero if there is no corresponding entry in column D, otherwise they add the corresponding figure in column D to the previous cumulative balance in column E. For a general explanation of the @IF function, see session 23, paragraph 7.

Column M: For an explanation of the @DSUM function used in this column see paragraph 7 below.

7. The @DSUM database function

Column M: the **@DSUM** function is a database @ function, similar to @SUM except that it is selective. The argument is

@DSUM(input,offset,criterion)

For example, the formula in cell M10, omitting the absolute ($) signs, is:

@DSUM(F10..H75,2,J9..J10)

It may help to refer to Figure 27a in following the explanation. It may also help you (but this is not absolutely necessary) to have worked through session 9 (A Simple Database), which explained such terms as *Input* and *Criterion*.

Input range: F10..H75. Note that the top row of this range includes the single row of column designations (field names), i.e.

F10	G10	H10
Code	VAT	Excl.VAT

It is essential to include these designations in the input range.

Offset: Here it is 2, i.e. column H, which is the second column to the right from the left-most column of the range F10..H75. [Column F has the offset of 0 (zero) and column G has the offset of 1.]

Criterion: Here the range is J9..J10, i.e. **Code** in J9 and **112** in cell J10. Note that this criterion range must include an exact duplicate of the column designation in cell F10 (Code) and the criterion (112) directly beneath it.

What the formula does is to look in the *input* range for all the values in the *offset* column (the one headed Excl.VAT) which meet the *criterion* of having the number **112** in the column headed **Code** (which is the field name in the input range). It adds them up, and produces the result in the cell containing the formula, cell M10. In this particular instance, it finds (£400) in cell H26 and (£400) in cell H43 and gives the total (£800) in cell M10.

8. An alternative analysis

The following method of analysing the cash book can be used by users of programs which do not have the @DSUM function. It may also be used by those who do have programs with this function, but prefer a more traditional layout.

The range which you will create is to the right of the model created so far, because you will need the area beneath the present model for the bank reconciliation in session 28.

Copy the dotted lines in rows 2,4,6 and 8 across to column AW.

Cell S1:	Type	`Petty`
Cell S3:	Type	`Cash`
Cell S5:	Type	`112`
Cell S7:	Type	`@sum(S11..S75)`
Cell S11:	Type	`@IF(F11=112,H11,0)`

Copy cell S11 to the range S12..S75.

What you have done is to analyse all the Petty Cash (code 112) amounts in column H (the Excl.VAT column) to column S with a total in cell S7. Cell S7 now reads the same as appears in Figure 27a, cell M10, i.e. (£800).

Now do the same for all the other headings/codes which appear in Figure 27a columns J and K.

There are 31 of them, and this will need columns S..AW.

For rows 1 and 3, you will have to type in the heading names. When you have done so, centre all the labels in the range S1..AW3 (/Range, Label (or Prefix), Centre) to improve the appearance.

For row 5, you will have to type in the codes individually, since they are not consecutive.

For row 7, you can copy S7 across to the range T7..AW7, since the formula is relative.

For row 11, the formula in cell S11 has to be adjusted for the individual code numbers. For example, T11 should read: **@IF(F11=113,H11,0)**

You might save some time if you do as follows:

Make the cell references absolute in cell S11: **@IF($F$11=112,$H$11,0)**

Copy S11 across to T11..AW11.

Then edit <F2> each cell to alter the code number appropriately, *and also* delete the four absolute ($) signs. When you have completed S11..AW11, you could check your accuracy by moving the cursor along the row over the cells and observe the formulae in the control panel: only the code numbers should change.

Next, copy the whole range S11..AW11 down to S12..AW75.

The formula in cell U7 should be edited to add cell G5 to the @sum total: **@SUM(U11..U75)+G5**

or (if that does not work): **+G5+(@SUM(U11..U75))**

The reason for this is that you are analysing the Excl.VAT figures in column H, and the total VAT from column G must be added to complete the analysis.

Format the whole range S7..AW75 with /Range, Format, Comma, 2.

You will have to widen columns with large figures in row 7.

Finally you could place a total **@SUM(S7..AW7)** somewhere as a check with the total in cell D5.

9. Activity

(1) Make a few extra entries in rows 48 and below and observe the effects on the worksheet.

(2) If you have used the @DSUM method (columns K..M of Figure 27a), create the more traditional-type of analysis described in paragraph 8 above, and compare the two methods. (This is all good practice!)

(3) If you have completed sessions 24, 25 and perhaps 26, and have (or can create) a worksheet which has a 'blank' year 2, post the totals from the analysis of this present session (which covers the month of January) to the Bank Account input section of year 2, and observe the results. If you are using a program which can link worksheets, try linking these totals, instead of posting them.

SESSION 28

Bank reconciliation

1. Objectives

At the end of this session, you will be able to:

- ❑ construct a model which extracts information from the analysed cash book model created in session 27 and from which you can produce a bank reconciliation and a list of outstanding (uncleared) items in the cash book.
- ❑ appreciate further the usefulness of the database facilities of your program

2. Introduction

In this session you will add a small range below the worksheet created in session 27.

Figure 28a shows (subject to minor variations for the various programs) the results of your work in this session.

	A	B	C	D	J	K	L	M
76	Alter formulae at D5,G5,H5 and M10..M70..................							
77		Also move (/M) range below down.						
78								
79	---------	-----------	--------------------	-------------		-----------------	-------	---------------
80	ITEMS OUTSTANDING					BANK RECONCILIATION		£
81	Rec		Total					
82	os		Outstanding:	(8,277.09)		Cash Book Balance:		(15,354.02)
83								
84						less Items		
85						Outstanding:		(8,277.09)
86	Details of outstanding items:							---------------
87	Date	Number	Details	Amount				(7,076.93)
88	Jan 19	100595	Duff Stationers	(67.50)				
89	Jan 20	100596	Bates Solicitors	(105.00)		less Adjustments:		0.00
90	Jan 24	100599	Fagin & Co	(10.23)				---------------
91	Jan 24	100600	Mr. Sowerberry	(15.80)		Bank Statement		
92	Jan 26	100601	Twist Telephones	(587.68)		Balance:		(7,076.93)
93	Jan 28	311220	Sikes Supplies	(7,490.88)				===========
94								
95								

Figure 28a

	A	B	C	D	K	L	M
76	Alter formulae at D5,G5,H5 and M10..M70..................						
77		Also move (/M) range below down.					
78							
79	---------	-----------	-------------------	----------------------------------	-------------------	-------	-------------
80	ITEMS OUTSTANDING				BANK RECONCILIATION		£
81	Rec		Total				
82	os		Outstanding:	@DSUM(A10..I75,3,A81..A82)	Cash Book Balance:		+E5
83							
84					less Items		
85					Outstanding:		+D82
86	Details of outstanding items:						-------------
87	Date	Number	Details	Amount			+M82-M85
88	Jan 19	100595	Duff Stationers	(67.50)			
89	Jan 20	100596	Bates Solicitors	(105.00)	less Adjustments:		0.00
90	Jan 24	100599	Fagin & Co	(10.23)			-------------
91	Jan 24	100600	Mr. Sowerberry	(15.80)	Bank Statement		
92	Jan 26	100601	Twist Telephones	(587.68)	Balance:		+M87-M89
93	Jan 28	311220	Sikes Supplies	(7,490.88)			=========
94							
95							

Figure 28b

Do NOT attempt to reproduce this model by duplicating the entries shown in Figures 28a and 28b. The range A80..D93 is produced mainly by using the database *Extract* command. The procedure for using this command has been covered in session 9. If you worked through that session you may feel confident that you can create this model without further help; if so, please feel free to do so.

However, you may feel you want to refresh your skills again. Therefore full instructions are provided below in paragraph 5 (*Notes on creating the model*), with separate instructions for each program. If you worked through session 9, you will realise that the programs vary considerably in the procedures required.

3. The problem

George Nettlerash wants to be able to use the analysed cash book model to reconcile his cash book with his bank statements, and to have a list of uncleared items to which he can refer.

4. Design of the model

If you refer to Figure 28c, you will note that column I now contains the entries:

- **c** for "cleared"
- **os** for "outstanding"

There is no reason why other letters or numbers should not be used. However, for the purposes of this exercise, keep to these letters since the database uses the *os* letters later. The procedure in the reconciliation is to enter *c* against items appearing on the bank statement, and, when finished, enter *os* against the remaining items.

	A	B	C	D	I
1	Session 28: Bank Reconciliation				
2	--------------	--------------	--------------	--------------	--------------
3			£	£	
4	--------------	--------------	--------------	--------------	--------------
5	Cumulative Running Balances:			13,241.98	
6	--------------	--------------	--------------	--------------	--------------
7	Starting balance:				c/os
8	--------------	--------------	--------------	--------------	--------------
9	19x1				Bank
10	Date	Number	Details	Amount	Rec
11	Jan 3	100576	Mr. Sowerberry	(11.75)	c
12	Jan 4	100577	Crackit & Co	(2,000.00)	c
13	Jan 6	100578	Fagin & Co	(29.37)	c
14	Jan 6	100579	Gamfield Repairs	(57.13)	c
15	Jan 6	100580	Fagin & Co	(52.87)	c
16	Jan 7	311216	Lively DIY Store	11,243.98	c
17	Jan 7	100581	Sikes Supplies	(7,302.66)	c
18	Jan 7	100582	Wages	(830.60)	c
19	Jan 10	100583	Gamfield Repairs	(22.58)	c
20	Jan 11	100584	Fagin & Co	(16.40)	c
21	Jan 12	100585	Brownlow Brokers	(798.00)	c
22	Jan 13	100586	Limbkins Oil	(249.70)	c
23	Jan 13	100587	PAYE	(1,159.50)	c
24	Jan 14	311217	Fang's DIY Store	12,976.78	c
25	Jan 14	100588	Sikes Supplies	(7,416.22)	c
26	Jan 14	100589	Petty Cash	(400.00)	c
27	Jan 14	311218	Sale of Car 1	10,000.00	c
28	Jan 14	100590	Wages	(825.35)	c
29	Jan 17	100591	Mr. Sowerberry	(22.36)	c
30	Jan 18	100592	Fagin & Co	(72.13)	c
31	Jan 18	100593	Dodger Motors	(432.65)	c
32	Jan 19	100594	Grimwig PR Co.	(42.12)	c
33	Jan 19	100595	Duff Stationers	(67.50)	os
34	Jan 20	100596	Bates Solicitors	(105.00)	os
35	Jan 21	311219	Lively DIY Store	10,143.87	c
36	Jan 21	100597	Sikes Supplies	(7,234.65)	c
37	Jan 21	100598	Wages	(810.75)	c
38	Jan 24	100599	Fagin & Co	(10.23)	os
39	Jan 24	100600	Mr. Sowerberry	(15.80)	os
40	Jan 26	100601	Twist Telephones	(587.68)	os
41	Jan 26		Dawkins Bank-Chs	(110.00)	c
42	Jan 26		Dawkins Bank-Int	(451.67)	c
43	Jan 28	100602	Petty Cash	(400.00)	c
44	Jan 28	100603	Kags' DIY Store	10,733.55	c
45	Jan 28	311220	Sikes Supplies	(7,490.88)	os
46	Jan 28	100604	Drawings	(2,000.00)	c
47	Jan 28	100605	Wages	(830.65)	c

Figure 28c

You will find it easier to do this if you hide columns E..H. Columns D and I are then adjacent, as in Figure 28c. [The procedure for hiding columns and ranges was covered in session 23, paragraph 8. Use the procedure appropriate to your program.]

The model then uses the entries in column I to produce the information as shown in Figure 28a, rows 80..93, using facilities available in each program.

5. Notes on creating the model

First: enter the label **ITEMS OUTSTANDING** in cell A80, **Total** in cell C81, **Outstanding** in cell C82, and **Details of outstanding items:** in cell A86.

Second: enter the range K80..M93 as shown in Figures 28a and 28b. The entries in column M are formulae, except M89.

Third: follow the instructions below, as appropriate to your program.

If you are using {123}

Cell A81: Enter `Rec`

Cell A82: Enter `os`

Cell D82: Enter `@DSUM(A10..I75,3,A81..A82)`

Copy A10..D10 to A87..D87. [It is best to *copy* this range, because the output range A87..D87 has to be an exact duplicate of the column designations of the Input range.]

Next, use /DQ (Data, Query) and define the ranges as follows:

Input: A10..I75

Criteria: A81..A82

Output: A87..D87

If (from READY) you then press `/DQE` (Data, Query, Extract)

the range A88..D93 (containing the outstanding items) will appear.

Format the cells appropriately, protect the worksheet and unprotect the cells I11..I75, M89 and A88..D187 in the usual manner.

[Note: A88..D187 allows for 100 uncleared items in the data extract range; adjust this range as required.]

If you are using {VP}

Do *NOT* make entries in cells A81 and A82

Cell D82: Enter `@DSUM(A10..I75,3,A84..F85)`

Copy A10..D10 to A84..D84. [This is part of the Criterion range.]

Copy A10..D10 to A87..D87. [This is part of the Output range.]

[It is best to *copy* this range, because the entries in the criterion and output ranges have to be exact duplicates of the column designations of the Input range.]

Copy I10 to E84 (the label **Rec**)

Cell E85: Enter `os`

Next, use /DQ (Data, Query) and define the ranges as follows:

Input: A10..I75

Criteria: A84..E85

Output: A87..D87

If (from READY) you then press `/DQE` (Data, Query, Extract)

the range A88..D93 (containing the outstanding items) will appear.

Format the cells appropriately, protect the worksheet and unprotect the cells I11..I75, M89 and A88..D187 in the usual manner.

[Note: A88..D187 allows for 100 uncleared items in the data extract range; adjust this range as required.]

If you are using {AEA}

Do *NOT* make entries in cells A81 and A82

Cell D82: Enter `@SUM(D88..D187)`

[Note: this allows for 100 uncleared items when listed in the data extract range below; adjust the range as required.]

Copy A10..I10 to A84..I84. [This is part of the Criterion range.]

Copy A10..I10 to A87..I87. [This is part of the Output range.]

[It is best to copy this range, because the entries in the criterion and output ranges have to be exact duplicates of the column designations of the Input range.]

Cell I85: Enter `os`

Cell A85: Enter `*` (an asterisk)

Next, use /DQ (Data, Question) and define the ranges as follows:

Input: A10..I75

Criteria: A84..I85

Output: A87..D87

If (from READY) you then press `/DQE` (Data, Question, Extract)

the range A88..D93 (containing the outstanding items) will appear.

Format the cells appropriately, protect the worksheet and unprotect the cells I11..I75, M89 and A88..D187 in the usual manner.

[Note: A88..D187 allows for 100 uncleared items in the data extract range; adjust this range as required.]

6. An explanation of the model

{123}{VP} An explanation of the @DSUM formula in cell D82 can be found in session 27, paragraph 7. This cell is referred to in cell M85 in the *BANK RECONCILIATION* range.

{AEA} The @SUM formula in cell D82 refers to the range D88..D187 in the data Extract range, and this Extract operation must be performed before the correct figure can be calculated. This cell is referred to in cell M85 in the *BANK RECONCILIATION* range.

The *BANK RECONCILIATION* range has been positioned in columns K..M to avoid conflict with the data Criterion and Output ranges. It should be easy to view this range by moving 'whole screen' from the *ITEMS OUTSTANDING* area. However, you may prefer to move (/M) it nearer.

When you come to do another Bank Reconciliation, say one month later, you could use a different letter (say **d** instead of **c**) in column I. This would overwrite most, if not all, of the **os** entries. Then, once again, any blank uncleared items could be marked **os**. This method ensures that old **os** items remain marked as such and are listed in the Extract listing.

If you wish to keep a copy of the Bank Reconciliation at any particular date, it is perhaps easiest to print out a hard copy of rows 80 and below.

Note that it is essential to use the /DQE command each time you require the Extract listing to be updated after any changes in the data Input range.

7. Activity

(1) Create a separate 'blank' file from this model; leave the codes and headings which can be adapted when required.

(2) If you have access to a cash book for which this model could be suitably employed, retrieve the template created in the previous activity and adapt it appropriately. Headings and codes should be changed as necessary. Try to devise a good coding system, with a logical grouping of code numbers. When a suitable bank statement is received, perform a reconciliation, and print it out.

(3) Use the template model for your own personal cash book. If you have more than one account, e.g. bank and building society, create a file for each. If you find the thought of doing this to be too depressing, forget it and do something more enjoyable.

SESSION 29

Budgets: Product and absorption costing

1. Objectives

At the end of this session, you will be able to:

- ❑ create a model which, from budgeted data, can prepare a variety of budgets such as materials,labour, production costs (using absorption costing), stocks of raw materials and finished goods, production costs of goods sold.
- ❑ continue to expand this model in sessions 30 and 31 to produce an analysed budgeted cost and profit statement and a table which can calculate product contribution for various budget restraints (limiting factors);

2. Introduction

The model created in this session is independent of those created in previous sessions. It can be expanded in sessions 30 and 31.

[Session 31 can be tackled independently of sessions 29 and 30, provided the input data are entered as values and not as formulae referring to cells in the preceding sessions.]

This session is concerned with budgets, and covers four different products produced in three departments. Absorption costing is employed in the calculation of product costs.

If you have worked through all (or most) of the sessions in this book, you may by now feel confident enough to tackle the creation of the model, perhaps referring to Figure 29a, but without reference to the Figure 29b (which shows the underlying formulae) and the notes on creating the model in paragraph 5 later. Why not try it anyway? If you get stuck, you can always refer to Figure 29b. You may find that your formulae are different from those in Figure 29b. There can be many different ways of arriving at the same result; make sure that your method produces the correct figures!

3. The problem

Nelson and Hardy Ltd., an old-established firm specialising in nautical supplies, have decided to set up a separate unit for the manufacture of life-jackets.

They have decided to produce and sell four different types of jacket, coded types W, X, Y and Z.

	A	B	C	D	E	F	G	H
1	Session 29: Nelson and Hardy Budgets							
2	---------	---------	---------	---------	---------	---------	---------	---------
3	INPUT TABLE		Budgeted Data for the month of January					
4	---------	---------	---------	---------	---------	---------	---------	---------
5	Product	Prod'n	Sales	Selling	Material	Direct Wages Costs p.u. £p		
6	Type	Units	Units	Price £p	Costs £p	---------	---------	---------
7				per unit	per unit	Dept P	Dept Q	Dept R
8	---------	---------	---------	---------	---------	---------	---------	---------
9	W	400	350	100.00	11.00	3.00	4.50	6.00
10	X	400	320	75.00	9.50	2.00	3.00	4.00
11	Y	300	230	50.00	8.00	1.00	1.50	2.00
12	Z	200	170	50.00	8.00	1.00	1.50	2.00
13	---------	---------	---------	---------	---------	---------	---------	---------
14					All Depts	Dept P	Dept Q	Dept R
15					£	£	£	£
16	Material purchases				14,400			
17	Allocable production overheads				4,250	1,000	2,250	1,000
18	General production overheads				5,625			
19	Administration overheads				8,480			
20	Selling & distribution overheads				9,334			
21	========	========	========	========	========	========	========	========
22	TABLE A: Material cost of production							
23	---------	---------	---------	---------	---------	---------	---------	---------
24	Product	Prod'n	Cost per	Total				
25	type	units	unit £p	cost £				
26								
27	W	400	11.00	4,400				
28	X	400	9.50	3,800				
29	Y	300	8.00	2,400				
30	Z	200	8.00	1,600				
31				---------				
32				12,200				
33				========				
34	========	========	========	========	========	========	========	========
35	TABLE B: Direct Wages, per product type and per department							
36	---------	---------	---------	---------	---------	---------	---------	---------
37	Product	Prod'n			Dept P	Dept Q	Dept R	Total
38	type	units			£	£	£	£
39								
40	W	400			1,200	1,800	2,400	5,400
41	X	400			800	1,200	1,600	3,600
42	Y	300			300	450	600	1,350
43	Z	200			200	300	400	900
44					---------	---------	---------	---------
45					2,500	3,750	5,000	11,250
46					========	========	========	========
47	========	========	========	========	========	========	========	========

Figure 29a (Part 1)

	A	B	C	D	E	F	G	H
48	TABLE C: Departmental overhead absorption rates							
49	---------	---------	---------	---------	---------	---------	---------	---------
50					Dept P	Dept Q	Dept R	Total
51					£	£	£	£
52	Allocable production overheads							
53		(allocation)			1,000	2,250	1,000	4,250
54	General production overheads							
55		(apportionment)			1,250	1,875	2,500	5,625
56					---------	---------	---------	---------
57	Totals				2,250	4,125	3,500	9,875
58					========	========	========	========
59	Totals as % of departmental wages				90.00%	110.00%	70.00%	
60	========	========	========	========	========	========	========	========
61	TABLE D: Production costs PER UNIT							£p
62	---------	---------	---------	---------	---------	---------	---------	---------
63					W	X	Y	Z
64	---------	---------	---------	---------	---------	---------	---------	---------
65	Materials			(All £p)	11.00	9.50	8.00	8.00
66	---------	---------	---------	---------	---------	---------	---------	---------
67	Direct wages:		Dept P		3.00	2.00	1.00	1.00
68			Dept Q		4.50	3.00	1.50	1.50
69			Dept R		6.00	4.00	2.00	2.00
70					---------	---------	---------	---------
71			Total		13.50	9.00	4.50	4.50
72	---------	---------	---------	---------	---------	---------	---------	---------
73		Prime Cost			24.50	18.50	12.50	12.50
74	---------	---------	---------	---------	---------	---------	---------	---------
75	Prod'n	}	Dept P		2.70	1.80	0.90	0.90
76	overhead	}	Dept Q		4.95	3.30	1.65	1.65
77	recovery:	}	Dept R		4.20	2.80	1.40	1.40
78					---------	---------	---------	---------
79			Total		11.85	7.90	3.95	3.95
80	---------	---------	---------	---------	---------	---------	---------	---------
81	Total production cost per unit				36.35	26.40	16.45	16.45
82	========	========	========	========	========	========	========	========
83	TABLE E: Overhead absorption, per product type							
84	---------	---------	---------	---------	---------	---------	---------	---------
85	Product	Prod'n	O'head	Total		Total production overheads		
86	type	units	Rate £p	£				£
87								
88	W	400	11.85	4,740		Allocable:		4,250
89	X	400	7.90	3,160				
90	Y	300	3.95	1,185		General:		5,625
91	Z	200	3.95	790				
92				---------				---------
93				9,875				9,875
94				========				========
95	========	========	========	========	========	========	========	========

Figure 29a (Part 2)

	A	B	C	D	E	F	G	H
96	TABLE F: Closing stocks of raw materials							
97	---------	---------	--------	---------	---------	---------	--------	---------
98	Product	Prod'n			R.M. cost	Total		
99	type	units			per unit	£		
100					£.p			
101	W	400			11.00	4,400		
102	X	400			9.50	3,800		
103	Y	300			8.00	2,400		
104	Z	200			8.00	1,600		
105						---------		
106	Cost of raw material used in production					12200		
107	Raw material purchases					14400		
108						---------		
109	Stock of raw material at purchase price					2200		
110						========		
111	========	========	========	========	========	========	========	========
112	TABLE G: Finished goods stock at production cost							
113	---------	---------	--------	---------	---------	---------	--------	---------
114	Product	FG stock			Prod.cost	Total		
115	type	(units)			per unit	£		
116					£.p			
117	W	50			36.35	1,818		
118	X	80			26.40	2,112		
119	Y	70			16.45	1,152		
120	Z	30			16.45	494		
121						---------		
122	Stock of finished goods at production cost					5,575		
123						========		
124	========	========	========	========	========	========	========	========
125	TABLE H: Calculation of sales value							
126	---------	---------	--------	---------	---------	---------	--------	---------
127	Product	Sales			S. price	Total		
128	type	(units)			per unit	£		
129					£.p			
130	W	350			100.00	35,000		
131	X	320			75.00	24,000		
132	Y	230			50.00	11,500		
133	Z	170			50.00	8,500		
134						---------		
135	Total sales value					79,000		
136						========		
137	========	========	========	========	========	========	========	========
138	TABLE I: Production cost of goods sold							
139	---------	---------	--------	---------	---------	---------	--------	---------
140	Product	Sales			Prod.cost	Total		
141	type	(units)			per unit	£		
142					£.p			
143	W	350			36.35	12,723		
144	X	320			26.40	8,448		
145	Y	230			16.45	3,784		
146	Z	170			16.45	2,797		
147						---------		
148	Total production cost of goods sold					27,751		
149						========		

Figure 29a (Part 3)

	A	B	C	D	E	F	G	H
1	Session 29: Nelson and Hardy Budgets							
2								
3	INPUT TABLE		Budgeted Data for the month of January					
4								
5	Product	Prod'n	Sales	Selling	Material	Direct Wages Costs p.u. £p		
6	Type	Units	Units	Price £p	Costs £p			
7				per unit	per unit	Dept P	Dept Q	Dept R
8								
9	W	400	350	100.00	11.00	3.00	4.50	6.00
10	X	400	320	75.00	9.50	2.00	3.00	4.00
11	Y	300	230	50.00	8.00	1.00	1.50	2.00
12	Z	200	170	50.00	8.00	1.00	1.50	2.00
13								
14					All Depts	Dept P	Dept Q	Dept R
15					£	£	£	£
16	Material purchases				14,400			
17	Allocable production overheads				+F17+G17+H17	1,000	2,250	1,000
18	General production overheads				5,625			
19	Administration overheads				8,480			
20	Selling & distribution overheads				9,334			
21	=====	======	=====	============	==============	==============	==============	============
22	TABLE A: Material cost of production							
23								
24	Product	Prod'n	Cost per	Total				
25	type	units	unit £p	cost £				
26								
27	W	+$B$9	+E9	+B27*C27				
28	X	+$B$10	+E10	+B28*C28				
29	Y	+$B$11	+E11	+B29*C29				
30	Z	+$B$12	+E12	+B30*C30				
31								
32				@SUM(D27..D30)				
33				============				
34	=====	======	=====	============	==============	==============	==============	============
35	TABLE B: Direct Wages, per product type and per department							
36								
37	Product	Prod'n			Dept P	Dept Q	Dept R	Total
38	type	units			£	£	£	£
39								
40	W	+$B$9			+$B40*F9	+$B40*G9	+$B40*H9	@SUM(E40..G40)
41	X	+$B$10			+$B41*F10	+$B41*G10	+$B41*H10	@SUM(E41..G41)
42	Y	+$B$11			+$B42*F11	+$B42*G11	+$B42*H11	@SUM(E42..G42)
43	Z	+$B$12			+$B43*F12	+$B43*G12	+$B43*H12	@SUM(E43..G43)
44								
45					@SUM(E40..E43)	@SUM(F40..F43)	@SUM(G40..G43)	@SUM(H40..H43)
46					==============	==============	==============	============
47	=====	======	=====	============	==============	==============	==============	============

Figure 29b (Part 1)

Manufacture will take place in three departments:

- Department P: Cutting
- Department Q: Sewing
- Department R: Packing

	A	B	C	D	E	F	G	H
48	TABLE C: Departmental overhead absorption rates:							
49	--------	--------	--------	--------	--------	--------	--------	--------
50					Dept P	Dept Q	Dept R	Total
51					£	£	£	£
52	Allocable production overheads							
53		(allocation)			+F17	+G17	+H17	+E17
54	General production overheads:							
55		(apportionment)			+$H$55*E45/$H$45	+$H$55*F45/$H$45	+$H$55*G45/$H$45	+E18
56					--------	--------	--------	--------
57	Totals				+E53+E55	+F53+F55	+G53+G55	+H53+H55
58					========	========	========	========
59	Totals as % of departmental wages				+E57/E45	+F57/F45	+G57/G45	
60	========	========	========	========	========	========	========	========
61	TABLE D: Production costs PER UNIT							£p
62	--------	--------	--------	--------	--------	--------	--------	--------
63					W	X	Y	Z
64	--------	--------	--------	--------	--------	--------	--------	--------
65	Materials			(All £p)	+E9	+E10	+E11	+E12
66	--------	--------	--------	--------	--------	--------	--------	--------
67	Direct wages:		Dept P		+F9	+F10	+F11	+F12
68			Dept Q		+G9	+G10	+G11	+G12
69			Dept R		+H9	+H10	+H11	+H12
70					--------	--------	--------	--------
71			Total		@SUM(E67..E69)	@SUM(F67..F69)	@SUM(G67..G69)	@SUM(H67..H69)
72	--------	--------	--------	--------	--------	--------	--------	--------
73		Prime Cost			+E65+E71	+F65+F71	+G65+G71	+H65+H71
74	--------	--------	--------	--------	--------	--------	--------	--------
75	Prod'n	}	Dept P		+E67*E59	+F67*E59	+G67*E59	+H67*E59
76	overheac	}	Dept Q		+E68*F59	+F68*F59	+G68*F59	+H68*F59
77	recovery:	}	Dept R		+E69*G59	+F69*G59	+G69*G59	+H69*G59
78					--------	--------	--------	--------
79			Total		@SUM(E75..E77)	@SUM(F75..F77)	@SUM(G75..G77)	@SUM(H75..H77)
80	--------	--------	--------	--------	--------	--------	--------	--------
81	Total production cost per unit:				+E73+E79	+F73+F79	+G73+G79	+H73+H79
82	========	========	========	========	========	========	========	========
83	TABLE E: Overhead absorption, per product type							
84	--------	--------	--------	--------	--------	--------	--------	--------
85	Product	Prod'n	O'head	Total		Total production overheads		
86	type	units	Rate £p	£				£
87								
88	W	+$B$9	+E79	+B88*C88		Allocable:		+E17
89	X	+$B$10	+F79	+B89*C89				
90	Y	+$B$11	+G79	+B90*C90		General:		+E18
91	Z	+$B$12	+H79	+B91*C91				
92				--------				--------
93				@SUM(D88..D91)				+H88+H90
94				========				========
95	========	========	========	========	========	========	========	========

Figure 29b (Part 2)

The selling-prices of the four product types are given below, together with the budgeted production and sales quantities of each type, for the coming month of January.

	Selling Price (£)	Production (units)	Sales (units)
Type W	100	400	350
Type X	75	400	320
Type Y	50	300	230
Type Z	50	200	170

	A	B	C	D	E	F	G	H
96	TABLE F: Closing stocks of raw materials							
97	--------	--------	--------	--------	--------	--------	--------	--------
98	Product	Prod'n			R.M. cost	Total		
99	type	units			per unit	£		
100					£.p			
101	W	+$B$9			+E9	+B101*E101		
102	X	+$B$10			+E10	+B102*E102		
103	Y	+$B$11			+E11	+B103*E103		
104	Z	+$B$12			+E12	+B104*E104		
105						--------		
106	Cost of raw material used in production					@SUM(F101..F104)		
107	Raw material purchases					+E16		
108						--------		
109	Stock of raw material at purchase price					+F107-F106		
110						========		
111	========	========	========	========	========	========	========	========
112	TABLE G: Finished goods stock at production cost							
113	--------	--------	--------	--------	--------	--------	--------	--------
114	Product	FG stock			Prod.cost	Total		
115	type	(units)			per unit	£		
116					£.p			
117	W	+B9-C9			+$E$81	+B117*E117		
118	X	+B10-C10			+$F$81	+B118*E118		
119	Y	+B11-C11			+$G$81	+B119*E119		
120	Z	+B12-C12			+$H$81	+B120*E120		
121						--------		
122	Stock of finished goods at production cost					@SUM(F117..F120)		
123						========		
124	========	========	========	========	========	========	========	========
125	TABLE H: Calculation of sales value							
126	--------	--------	--------	--------	--------	--------	--------	--------
127	Product	Sales			S. price	Total		
128	type	(units)			per unit	£		
129					£.p			
130	W	+C9			+D9	+B130*E130		
131	X	+C10			+D10	+B131*E131		
132	Y	+C11			+D11	+B132*E132		
133	Z	+C12			+D12	+B133*E133		
134						--------		
135	Total sales value					@SUM(F130..F133)		
136						========		
137	========	========	========	========	========	========	========	========
138	TABLE I: Production cost of goods sold							
139	--------	--------	--------	--------	--------	--------	--------	--------
140	Product	Sales			Prod.cost	Total		
141	type	(units)			per unit	£		
142					£.p			
143	W	+C9			+$E$81	+B143*E143		
144	X	+C10			+$F$81	+B144*E144		
145	Y	+C11			+$G$81	+B145*E145		
146	Z	+C12			+$H$81	+B146*E146		
147						--------		
148	Total production cost of goods sold					@SUM(F143..F146)		
149						========		

Figure 29b (Part 3)

The company accountant has produced the following budgeted figures for the month of January, after consultation with his colleagues:

		£	£
Material purchases			14,400
Allocable production expenses:	Dept. P	1,000	
	Dept. Q	2,250	
	Dept. R	1,000	4,250
General production expenses			5,625
Administration costs		8,480	
Selling and distribution costs		9,334	17,814

Costs per life-jacket are budgeted as follows:

	Materials Costs	*Direct Wages Costs*		
		Dept. P	*Dept. Q*	*Dept. R*
	£.p	£.p	£.p	£.p
Type W	11.00	3.00	4.50	6.00
Type X	9.50	2.00	3.00	4.00
Type Y	8.00	1.00	1.50	2.00
Type Z	8.00	1.00	1.50	2.00

It is the practice of the company to:

(a) value finished goods stock using the full production cost method (materials, direct wages, allocable and general production expenses);

(b) apportion general production expenses to departments on the basis of total direct departmental wages;

(c) recover all production expenses as a percentage of direct departmental wages;

(d) charge administration, selling and distribution costs to product lines on the basis of the full production cost of goods sold;

(e) ignore work-in-progress, which is expected to be negligible.

You have been requested to prepare the following budgets for the month of January:

A. Material cost of production, per product type;

B. Direct wages, per product type and per department;

C. Departmental production overhead absorption rates;

D. Production costs per unit for each product type;

E. Overhead absorption, per product type;

F. Closing stocks of raw material;

G. Finished goods stock at production cost, per product type;

H. Sales, per product type;

I. Production cost of goods sold, per product type.

4. Design of the model

The model has been planned vertically, with each budget, referenced with the above budget letter, following sequentially downwards.

Reference to Figure 29a will show:

A1..H21: an INPUT TABLE for entry of all the data provided in the problem.

A22..H149: the various OUTPUT tables, one for each budget, where all the entries are labels or formulae.

5. Notes on creating the model

This is a straightforward model, with no complicated formulae.

Time can be saved in creating the model by making some cell references absolute where necessary to copy them. For example, the range B88..B91 can be copied to B101..B104 without change.

Note that cell E17 in the INPUT TABLE is a formula. This adds the data in cells F17..H17.

Format the cells appropriately. Figure 29a can be a guide.

The worksheet should be protected when complete. Unprotected cells are those in the INPUT TABLE which are not labels, formulae or empty, i.e. B9..H12, E16, E18..20 and F17..H17.

6. An explanation of the model

The model should be easy to understand if you remember that the "practices" of the company, as detailed (a)..(e) in paragraph 3 are adhered to in the construction of the formulae.

For example, production overhead recovery for life-jacket type W is effected in respect of department P in cell E75 by multiplying cell E67 (direct wage cost) by cell E59 (percentage departmental overhead absorption rate based on direct departmental wages). This conforms with the "practice" of: (c) recovering all production expenses as a percentage of direct departmental wages.

7. Activity

Alter the data in the Input Table and observe the changes to the budgets.

SESSION 30

Analysed cost and profit statement

1. Objectives

At the end of this session, you will be able to:

- ❑ extend the model created in session 29 to include an analysed cost and profit statement and a budgeted production cost and income statement.

2. Introduction

The model created in this session builds on that created in session 29. It uses the data and the output produced there to consolidate the product cost and income information into a summary table and also produces an overall profit statement in financial accounting format.

As suggested in the previous session, you may by now feel confident enough to tackle the creation of the model, perhaps referring to Figure 30a, but without reference to Figure 30b (which shows the underlying formulae) and the notes on creating the model in paragraph 5 below. If you get stuck, you can always refer to Figure 30b. You may find that your formulae are different from those in Figure 30b. There can be many different ways of arriving at the same result; make sure that your method produces the correct figures!

3. The problem

Nelson and Hardy Ltd. now require a summary budget statement which shows the detailed production cost, cost of sales, gross and net profits for each product type for the month of January.

They also would like an overall budgeted financial profit statement.

4. Design of the model

Reference to Figure 30a will show the two statements placed on the worksheet in cells below those for the budget tables produced in session 29.

Cells A150..O175 contain Table J: Analysed cost and profit statement.

Cells A176..H206 contain Table K: Budgeted production cost and income statement

All the cells are labels or formulae which reflect any relevant changes to data entered in the Input Table.

	A	B	C	D	E	F	G	H
150	==========	==========	==========	==========	==========	==========	==========	==========
151	TABLE J: Analysed cost and profit statement							
152	--------------	--------------	--------------	--------------	--------------	--------------	--------------	--------------
153		Product:-	W	W	W	X	X	X
154			Units	Rate £p	£	Units	Rate £p	£
155	--------------	--------------	--------------	--------------	--------------	--------------	--------------	--------------
156	Materials		400	11.00	4,400	400	9.50	3,800
157	Direct wages		400	13.50	5,400	400	9.00	3,600
158	Prod'n Overhead		400	11.85	4,740	400	7.90	3,160
159	--------------	--------------	--------------	--------------	--------------	--------------	--------------	--------------
160	PRODUCTION COST		400	36.35	14,540	400	26.40	10,560
161	less: Finished							
162	goods stock		50	36.35	1,818	80	26.40	2,112
163	--------------	--------------	--------------	--------------	--------------	--------------	--------------	--------------
164	PRODUCTION COST							
165	OF GOODS SOLD:		350	36.35	12,723	320	26.40	8,448
166	--------------	--------------	--------------	--------------	--------------	--------------	--------------	--------------
167	Sales		350	100.00	35,000	320	75.00	24,000
168	--------------	--------------	--------------	--------------	--------------	--------------	--------------	--------------
169	GROSS PROFIT		350	63.65	22,278	320	48.60	15,552
170	--------------	--------------	--------------	--------------	--------------	--------------	--------------	--------------
171	LESS: Admin,sales,							
172	& dist'b'n costs		350	23.33	8,167	320	16.95	5,423
173	--------------	--------------	--------------	--------------	--------------	--------------	--------------	--------------
174	NET PROFIT		350	40.32	14,110	320	31.65	10,129
175	==========	==========	==========	==========	==========	==========	==========	==========
176	TABLE K: Budgeted production cost and income statement for January							
177	--------------	--------------	--------------	--------------	--------------	--------------	--------------	--------------
178					£	£	£	
179	Sales						79,000	
180								
181	Production cost:							
182		Materials: purchases			14,400			
183		less closing stock			2,200			
184		=Materials used			--------------	12,200		
185		Direct wages				11,250		
186						--------------		
187		Prime cost				23,450		
188		Production overheads:						
189			Allocable		4,250			
190			General		5,625			
191					--------------	9,875		
192						--------------		
193		Production cost				33,325		
194		less stock of finished goods				5,575		
195						--------------		
196	Production cost of goods sold						27,751	
197							--------------	
198	Gross profit						51,250	
199								
200	less:	Administration overheads				8,480		
201		Selling & distribution overheads				9,334		
202						--------------		
203							17,814	
204							--------------	
205							33,436	
206							=========	

Figure 30a (Part 1)

	I	J	K	L	M	N	O
150	===========	===========	===========	===========	===========	===========	===========
151							
152	-----------	-----------	-----------	-----------	-----------	-----------	-----------
153	Y	Y	Y	Z	Z	Z	TOTAL
154	Units	Rate £p	£	Units	Rate £p	£	£
155	-----------	-----------	-----------	-----------	-----------	-----------	-----------
156	300	8.00	2,400	200	8.00	1,600	12,200
157	300	4.50	1,350	200	4.50	900	11,250
158	300	3.95	1,185	200	3.95	790	9,875
159	-----------	-----------	-----------	-----------	-----------	-----------	-----------
160	300	16.45	4,935	200	16.45	3,290	33,325
161							
162	70	16.45	1,152	30	16.45	494	5,575
163	-----------	-----------	-----------	-----------	-----------	-----------	-----------
164							
165	230	16.45	3,784	170	16.45	2,797	27,751
166	-----------	-----------	-----------	-----------	-----------	-----------	-----------
167	230	50.00	11,500	170	50.00	8,500	79,000
168	-----------	-----------	-----------	-----------	-----------	-----------	-----------
169	230	33.55	7,717	170	33.55	5,704	51,250
170	-----------	-----------	-----------	-----------	-----------	-----------	-----------
171							
172	230	10.56	2,429	170	10.56	1,795	17,814
173	-----------	-----------	-----------	-----------	-----------	-----------	-----------
174	230	22.99	5,288	170	22.99	3,908	33,436
175	===========	===========	===========	===========	===========	===========	===========
176							
177							
178							
179							
180							
181							
182							
183							
184							
185							
186							
187							
188							
189							
190							
191							
192							
193							
194							
195							
196							
197							
198							
199							
200							
201							
202							
203							
204							
205							
206							

Figure 30a (Part 2)

	A	B	C	D	E	F	G	H
150	=========	======	=======	==========	===================	==========	==========	===================
151	TABLE J: Analysed cost and profit statement							
152	-------------	---------	---------	------------	----------------------	------------		----------------------
153		Product:	W	W	W	X	X	X
154			Units	Rate £p	£	Units	Rate £p	£
155	-------------	---------	---------	------------	----------------------	------------	------------	----------------------
156	Materials		+$B$9	+E65	+C156*D156	+$B$10	+F65	+F156*G156
157	Direct wages		+$B$9	+E71	+C157*D157	+$B$10	+F71	+F157*G157
158	Prod'n Overhead		+$B$9	+E79	+C158*D158	+$B$10	+F79	+F158*G158
159	-------------	---------	---------	------------	----------------------	------------	------------	----------------------
160	PRODUCTION COST		+$B$9	+$E$81	+C160*D160	+$B$10	+$F$81	+F160*G160
161	less: Finished							
162	goods stock		+B9-C9	+$E$81	+C162*D162	+B10-C10	+$F$81	+F162*G162
163	-------------	---------	---------	------------	----------------------	------------	------------	----------------------
164	PRODUCTION COST							
165	OF GOODS SOLD:		+$C$9	+$E$81	+C165*D165	+$C$10	+$F$81	+F165*G165
166	-------------	---------	---------	------------	----------------------	------------	------------	----------------------
167	Sales		+$C$9	+D9	+C167*D167	+$C$10	+D10	+F167*G167
168	-------------	---------	---------	------------	----------------------	------------	------------	----------------------
169	GROSS PROFIT		+$C$9	+D167-D165	+C169*D169	+$C$10	+G167-G165	+F169*G169
170	-------------	---------	---------	------------	----------------------	------------	------------	----------------------
171	LESS: Admin,sales,							
172	& dist'b'n costs		+$C$9	+E172/C172	+$O$172/$O$165*E165	+$C$10	+H172/F172	+$O$172/$O$165*H165
173	-------------	---------	---------	------------	----------------------	------------	------------	----------------------
174	NET PROFIT		+$C$9	+D169-D172	+E169-E172	+$C$10	+G169-G172	+H169-H172
175	=========	======	=======	==========	===================	==========	==========	===================
176	TABLE K: Budgeted production cost and income statement for January							
177	-------------	---------	---------	------------	----------------------	------------	------------	----------------------
178					£	£	£	
179	Sales						+O167	
180								
181	Production cost:							
182		Materials: purchases			+E16			
183		less closing stock			+F109			
184		=Materials used			----------------------------	+E182-E183		
185		Direct wages				+H45		
186						------------		
187		Prime cost				+F184+F185		
188		Production overheads:						
189			Allocable		+E17			
190			General		+E18			
191					----------------------------	+E189+E190		
192						------------		
193		Production cost				+F187+F191		
194		less stock of finished goods				+F122		
195						------------		
196	Production cost of goods sold						+F193-F194	
197							------------	
198	Gross profit						+G179-G196	
199								
200	less:	Administration overheads				+E19		
201		Selling & distribution overheads				+E20		
202						------------		
203							+F200+F201	
204							------------	
205							+G198-G203	
206							==========	

Figure 30b (Part 1)

	I	J	K	L	M	N	O
150	--------	--------	--------	--------	--------	--------	--------
151							
152	--------	--------	--------	--------	--------	--------	--------
153	Y	Y	Y	Z	Z	Z	TOTAL
154	Units	Rate £p	£	Units	Rate £p	£	£
155	--------	--------	--------	--------	--------	--------	--------
156	+$B$11	+G65	+I156*J156	+$B$12	+H65	+L156*M156	+D32
157	+$B$11	+G71	+I157*J157	+$B$12	+H71	+L157*M157	+H45
158	+$B$11	+G79	+I158*J158	+$B$12	+H79	+L158*M158	+H93
159	--------	--------	--------	--------	--------	--------	--------
160	+$B$11	+$G$81	+I160*J160	+$B$12	+$H$81	+L160*M160	+O156+O157+O158
161							
162	+B11-C11	+$G$81	+I162*J162	+B12-C12	+$H$81	+L162*M162	+F122
163	--------	--------	--------	--------	--------	--------	--------
164							
165	+$C$11	+$G$81	+I165*J165	+$C$12	+$H$81	+L165*M165	+F148
166	--------	--------	--------	--------	--------	--------	--------
167	+$C$11	+D11	+I167*J167	+$C$12	+D12	+L167*M167	+F135
168	--------	--------	--------	--------	--------	--------	--------
169	+$C$11	+J167-J165	+I169*J169	+$C$12	+M167-M165	+L169*M169	+O167-O165
170	--------	--------	--------	--------	--------	--------	--------
171							
172	+$C$11	+K172/I172	+$O$172/$O$165*K165	+$C$12	+N172/L172	+$O$172/$O$165*N165	+E19+E20
173	--------	--------	--------	--------	--------	--------	--------
174	+$C$11	+J169-J172	+K169-K172	+$C$12	+M169-M172	+N169-N172	+O169-O172
175	--------	--------	--------	--------	--------	--------	--------
176							
177							
178							
179							
180							
181							
182							
183							
184							
185							
186							
187							
188							
189							
190							
191							
192							
193							
194							
195							
196							
197							
198							
199							
200							
201							
202							
203							
204							
205							
206							

Figure 30b (Part 2)

5. Notes on creating the model

As for session 29, this is a straightforward model, with no complicated formulae.

Time can be saved in creating the model by making some cell references absolute where necessary to copy them. For example, the cell E172 can be copied to cells H172, K172 and N172 without change.

Format the cells appropriately. Figure 30a can be a guide.

The worksheet should be protected when complete. There should be no unprotected cells in this new section of the worksheet.

6. An explanation of the model

The model should be easy to understand if you remember that the "practices" of the company, as detailed (a)..(e) in paragraph 3 are adhered to in the construction of the formulae.

For example, cell O172 totals the administration, selling and distribution costs from cells E19 and E20. These are then charged to each product type in cells E172, H172, K172 and N172 by apportioning them according to the production cost of goods sold in row 165. For example, cell E172 divides cell O172 by O165 and multiplies it by E165. This conforms with the "practice" of: (d) charging administration, selling and distribution costs to product lines on the basis of the full production cost of goods sold;

The budgets in this model are selective, and do not include, for example, a budgeted balance sheet or cash flow forecast. To do so would require additional data in the Input Table block, and would require a much larger and more complicated model. A budgeted profit and loss account, balance sheet and cashflow statement could be produced by adapting the Nettlerash model from sessions 24, 25 and 26.

7. Activity

Alter the data in the Input Table and observe the changes to all the budget tables and statements produced in sessions 29 and 30. Models of this type are useful for answering "What if?" questions.

SESSION 31
Limiting factors

1. Objectives

At the end of this session, you will be able to:

- ❑ create a model which calculates contribution per unit of limiting factor from data and outputs arising from the Nelson and Hardy worksheet created in sessions 29 and 30, using a variety of limiting factors;
- ❑ have gained further experience of the uses of the @IF logical function

2. Introduction

Although this model expands on the Nelson and Hardy model created in sessions 29 and 30, you can produce this model independently of those sessions by entering data instead of formulae in rows 213..217.

Absorption costing was employed in the budgets created in the model so far. This session shows how ad hoc management accounting information using contribution costing theory can be derived from existing costing data and budgets.

3. The problem

Nelson and Hardy Ltd. wish to know, with respect to the budgets produced in the previous two sessions, which product types produce the highest contributions subject to each of the following limiting factors or principal budget factors:

(1) shortage of materials
(2) shortage of direct labour
(3) shortage of both materials and labour
(4) pressure on sales turnover

The assumption is that materials and direct labour are the only variable costs.

4. Design of the model

The data necessary for the calculations appear in the range A207..H222, as shown in Figure 31a. These figures are produced by formulae, referring to the existing worksheet above this range, and the formulae are shown in Figure 31b. However, if you wish to enter data in this range, rather than in the Input Table (range A3..H20), you can do so, bearing in mind that you will overwrite the formulae if you have previously entered them. If you want to do both, create two separate worksheets, one for formulae and one for data entry.

	A	B	C	D	E	F	G	H
207	===========	===========	========	=========	===========	===========	===========	===========
208	TABLE L: Product type ranking by budget restraint							
209	-------------	-------------	----------	----------	-------------	-------------	-------------	-------------
210	Product:-				W	X	Y	Z
211					£.p	£.p	£.p	£.p
212	-------------	-------------	----------	----------	-------------	-------------	-------------	-------------
213	Selling price per unit				100.00	75.00	50.00	50.00
214	-------------	-------------	----------	----------	-------------	-------------	-------------	-------------
215	less assumed variable costs:							
216		Materials			11.00	9.50	8.00	8.00
217		Direct wages			13.50	9.00	4.50	4.50
218	-------------	-------------	----------	----------	-------------	-------------	-------------	-------------
219	Assumed variable cost per unit				24.50	18.50	12.50	12.50
220	-------------	-------------	----------	----------	-------------	-------------	-------------	-------------
221	Contribution per unit				75.50	56.50	37.50	37.50
222	===========	===========	========	=========	===========	===========	===========	===========
223	Budget restraints (Limiting factors)							
224	-------------	-------------	----------	----------	-------------	-------------	-------------	-------------
225	(1) Materials							
226		Material cost per unit			11.00	9.50	8.00	8.00
227								
228	Contribution per £1 of material cost				6.86	5.95	4.69	4.69
229					Best			
230	-------------	-------------	----------	----------	-------------	-------------	-------------	-------------
231	(2) Direct labour							
232		Labour cost per unit			13.50	9.00	4.50	4.50
233								
234	Contribution per £1 of labour cost				5.59	6.28	8.33	8.33
235							Best	Best
236	-------------	-------------	----------	----------	-------------	-------------	-------------	-------------
237	(3) Prime cost							
238		Prime cost per unit			24.50	18.50	12.50	12.50
239								
240	Contribution per £1 of prime cost				3.08	3.05	3.00	3.00
241					Best			
242	-------------	-------------	----------	----------	-------------	-------------	-------------	-------------
243	(4) Sales price							
244		Sales price per unit			100.00	75.00	50.00	50.00
245								
246	Contribution per £1 of sales price				0.76	0.75	0.75	0.75
247					Best			
248	===========	===========	========	=========	===========	===========	===========	===========

Figure 31a

5. Notes on creating the model

This is a straightforward model, with no complicated formulae except those in rows 229, 235, 241 and 247.

Important Note for users of VP-Planner:

Do *NOT* enter the formulae as shown in Figure 31b. The formulae should be entered with 1 and 0 as the second and third arguments. For example, cell E229 should read:

@IF(E228>=F228#AND#E228>=G228#AND#E228>=H228,1,0)

	A	B	C	D	E
207	===========	==========	=====	==	==
208	TABLE L: Product type ranking by budget restraint				
209	----------------	--------------	--------	---	--
210	Product:-				W
211					£.p
212	----------------	--------------	--------	---	--
213	Selling price per unit				+D9
214	----------------	--------------	--------	---	--
215	less assumed variable costs:				
216		Materials			+E9
217		Direct wages			+E71
218	----------------	--------------	--------	---	--
219	Assumed variable cost per unit				+E216+E217
220	----------------	--------------	--------	---	--
221	Contribution per unit				+E213-E219
222	===========	==========	=====	==	==
223	Budget restraints (Limiting factors)				
224	----------------	--------------	--------	---	--
225	(1) Materials				
226		Material cost per unit			+E216
227					
228	Contribution per £1 of material cost				+E221/E226
229					@IF(E228>=F228#AND#E228>=G228#AND#E228>=H228," Best"," ")
230	----------------	--------------	--------	---	--
231	(2) Direct labour				
232		Labour cost per unit			+E217
233					
234	Contribution per £1 of labour cost				+E221/E232
235					@IF(E234>=F234#AND#E234>=G234#AND#E234>=H234," Best"," ")
236	----------------	--------------	--------	---	--
237	(3) Prime cost				
238		Prime cost per unit			+E219
239					
240	Contribution per £1 of prime cost				+E221/E238
241					@IF(E240>=F240#AND#E240>=G240#AND#E240>=H240," Best"," ")
242	----------------	--------------	--------	---	--
243	(4) Sales price				
244		Sales price per unit			+E213
245					
246	Contribution per £1 of sales price				+E221/E244
247					@IF(E246>=F246#AND#E246>=G246#AND#E246>=H246s," Best"," ")
248	===========	==========	=====	==	==

Figure 31b (Part 1)

This applies to all 16 cells in rows 229, 235, 241 and 247 for columns E, F G and H. The result of this is that **1** will be shown in the cell instead of the word **Best**, and **0** will show in the cell instead of nothing.

ALL users now read on!

The @IF formulae in rows 229, 235, 241 and 247 (columns E, F G and H) perform the following:

If the figure in the row above is greater than the figures in the corresponding cells of the other three columns, print the word **Best**, otherwise print nothing.

	F	G
207	================================	================================
208		
209		
210	X	Y
211	£.p	£.p
212		
213	+D10	+D11
214		
215		
216	+E10	+E11
217	+F71	+G71
218		
219	+F216+F217	+G216+G217
220		
221	+F213-F219	+G213-G219
222	================================	================================
223		
224		
225		
226	+F216	+G216
227		
228	+F221/F226	+G221/G226
229	@IF(F228>=E228#AND#F228>=G228#AND#F228>=H228," Best"," ")	@IF(G228>=E228#AND#G228>=F228#AND#G228>=H228," Best"," ")
230		
231		
232	+F217	+G217
233		
234	+F221/F232	+G221/G232
235	@IF(F234>=E234#AND#F234>=G234#AND#F234>=H234," Best"," ")	@IF(G234>=E234#AND#G234>=F234#AND#G234>=H234," Best"," ")
236		
237		
238	+F219	+G219
239		
240	+F221/F238	+G221/G238
241	@IF(F240>=E240#AND#F240>=G240#AND#F240>=H240," Best"," ")	@IF(G240>=E240#AND#G240>=F240#AND#G240>=H240," Best"," ")
242		
243		
244	+F213	+G213
245		
246	+F221/F244	+G221/G244
247	@IF(F246>=E246#AND#F246>=G246#AND#F246>=H246," Best"," ")	@IF(G246>=E246#AND#G246>=F246#AND#G246>=H246," Best"," ")
248	================================	================================

Figure 31b (Part 2)

For a fuller explanation of the @IF function, please refer to session 23, paragraphs 6 and 7.

Format the cells appropriately. Figure 31a can be a guide.

The worksheet should be protected when complete. Unprotected cells are only necessary if you are using E213..H213 and E216..H217 for data entry.

6. An explanation of the model

The calculations of this model are straightforward. The interpretation of the results is a different matter, and beyond the scope of this book.

Unless you are already acquainted with the principles involved, you should refer to any good text book or manual on cost and management accounting. [There is a chapter on Limiting Factors in AFBIS.]

	H
207	==
208	
209	--
210	Z
211	£.p
212	--
213	+D12
214	--
215	
216	+E12
217	+H71
218	--
219	+H216+H217
220	--
221	+H213-H219
222	==
223	
224	--
225	
226	+H216
227	
228	+H221/H226
229	@IF(H228>=E228#AND#H228>=F228#AND#H228>=G228," Best"," ")
230	--
231	
232	+H217
233	
234	+H221/H232
235	@IF(H234>=E234#AND#H234>=F234#AND#H234>=G234," Best"," ")
236	--
237	
238	+H219
239	
240	+H221/H238
241	@IF(H240>=E240#AND#H240>=F240#AND#H240>=G240," Best"," ")
242	--
243	
244	+H213
245	
246	+H221/H244
247	@IF(H246>=E246#AND#H246>=F246#AND#H246>=G246," Best"," ")
248	==

Figure 31b (Part 3)

7. Activity

Alter the data in the Input Table and observe the changes to the limiting factor contributions. For example, double the material cost of the W type life-jacket (from £11 to £22 in cell E9); how does this affect the ranking of the product types in the event of material shortages?

SESSION 32
Cost-volume-profit

1. Objectives

At the end of this session, you will be able to:

- ❑ understand how a cost-volume-profit analysis can be created in a worksheet;
- ❑ enter data into the worksheet and observe the following:
  - unit contribution to fixed costs,
  - breakeven point in terms of units and sales values,
  - sales and net profit at budgeted level of activity, and
  - sales units and values required to achieve a predetermined net profit;
- ❑ create a contribution and break-even graph;
- ❑ test the sensitivity of the above to changes in the data.

2. Introduction

In the previous session you saw how the concept of contribution, when applied to limiting factors, can provide useful management accounting information. The same concept will be used in this session to calculate, from budgeted data, more useful information such as breakeven-points and unit sales required to achieve target levels of profit.

Separating costs into their variable and fixed elements, according to whether they are considered to vary or not to vary with a defined type of activity (in this case sales units), is an essential part of this process.

In Practice Session 13, you carried out a simple cost-volume-profit exercise. In this current session you will perform a rather fuller analysis.

3. The problem

Drake and Ralegh Ltd., a competitor of Nelson and Hardy, make, among other nautical products, an inflatable dinghy.

Their present budget for next year is to produce 20,000 units (mainly for export) at an average selling price of £350.

Costs per unit, which can be regarded as variable costs, are budgeted as follows:

Direct material	£97.50
Direct labour	£78.30
Direct expense	£24.90
Salesmen's commissions	£35.00
Distribution costs	£23.60

Annual budgeted overheads, which can be regarded as fixed costs, are as follows:

Production indirect labour	£235,000
Production indirect expense	£365,700
Salesmen's salaries	£ 45,800
Distribution costs	£ 84,500
Other selling & distribution overhead	£ 49,850
Administration salaries and wages	£123,500
Other administration overhead	£234,000

The management wish to know:

- what contribution each unit of production/sales (stocks can be ignored) will make to the fixed overhead,
- what their present (possibly inadequate) budgeted level of activity will produce by way of net profit,
- at what level of activity (in terms of both units and turnover) they would break-even, and
- how many units and what level of sales would have to be budgeted for to achieve a target level of £1,000,000 net profit.

4. Design of the model

As usual, you will create a data input table, where the above data can be entered, and, if required, altered. This is the range A3..F29 in Figure 32a.

The output table is shown in the range A31..F44.

The range A78..F94 contains figures (formulae referring to cells in the ranges above) to calculate the graph which appears in the range A46..F76.

The reason for including the graph here is that you may have a program which can print out a graph included in the actual worksheet. For example, Figure 32a (perhaps altered slightly by the typesetter) was produced using Lotus 1-2-3 release 2.2 which comes (unless you have the students' edition) with *ALLWAYS*, an excellent Add-in spreadsheet publishing program (no mice, icons or egg-timers!) which can be attached to Lotus 1-2-3. There are many other spreadsheet publishing programs, and if you are fortunate enough to have access to one, you may be able to include the graph in your print-out. If not, you can print out the graph separately; printing graphs was covered fairly fully in session 8. Creating graphs was covered in session 7, but brief details of the procedure required to produce this break-even graph will be given below in paragraph 7.

	A	B	C	D	E	F
1	Session 32: Cost-Volume-Profit Analysis: Drake and Ralegh Ltd.					
2	-------------	-------------	-------------	-------------	-------------	-------------
3	DATA INPUT TABLE					
4	-------------	-------------	-------------	-------------	-------------	-------------
5				Units	£ per annum	Graph
6	Budgeted unit sales:		Units:	20,000		Steps
7				£.p	* * *	Units
8	Selling Price per Unit:		£.p:	£350.00	* * *	2,500
9	Target net profit:			* * *	£1,000,000	
10						
11	Costs:			Variable	Fixed	
12				£p per unit	£ per annum	
13	Production costs:					
14		Direct Material		£97.50		
15		Direct Labour		£78.30		
16		Direct Expense		£24.90		
17	Production Overhead:					
18		Indirect Labour			£235,000	
19		Indirect Expense			£365,700	
20	Selling & Distribution Overhead:					
21		Salesmen's Salaries			£45,800	
22		Salesmen's Commissions		£35.00		
23		Distribution Costs		£23.60	£84,500	
24		Other S & D Overhead			£49,850	
25	Administration Overhead:					
26		Salaries & Wages			£123,500	
27		Other Overhead			£234,000	
28				-------------	-------------	
29				£259.30	£1,138,350	
30	===========	===========	===========	===========	===========	===========
31	OUTPUT TABLES				Units	£/£.p
32	-------------	-------------	-------------	-------------	-------------	-------------
33	CONTRIBUTION		Margin per unit			£90.70
34	-------------	-------------	-------------	-------------	-------------	-------------
35	BREAK-EVEN POINT		Unit sales		12,551	
36			£ sales			£4,392,751
37	-------------	-------------	-------------	-------------	-------------	-------------
38	BUDGETED LEVEL		Unit sales		20,000	
39			£ sales			£7,000,000
40			Net profit			£675,650
41	-------------	-------------	-------------	-------------	-------------	-------------
42	TARGET LEVEL		Unit sales to achieve:		23,576	
43	OF NET PROFIT		£ Sales to achieve:			£8,251,626
44			Net Profit required of			£1,000,000
45	===========	===========	===========	===========	===========	===========

Figure 32a (Part 1)

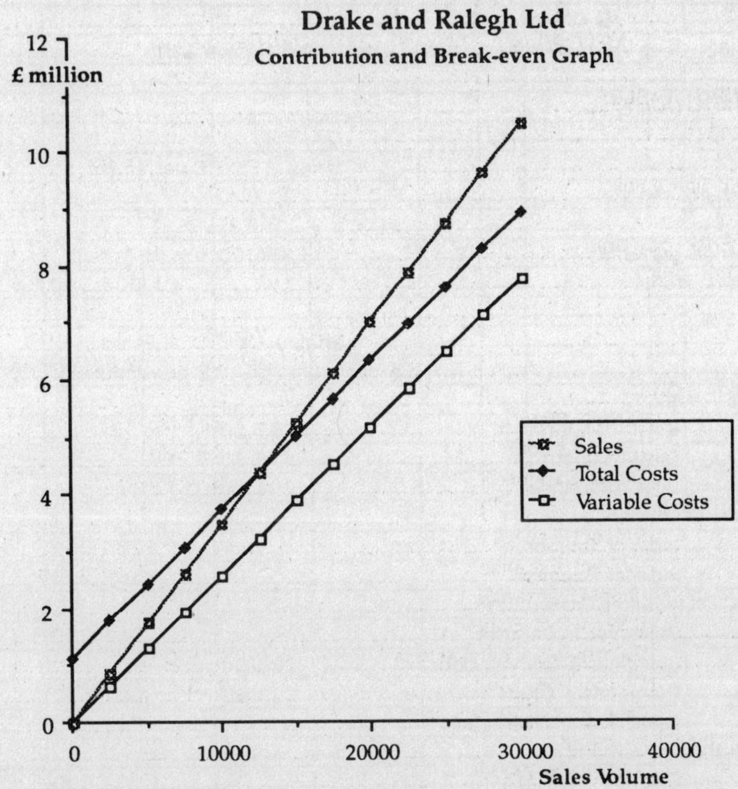

	A	B	C	D	E	F
77	===========	===========	===========	===========	===========	===========
78	Data for break-even graph					
79		£	£	£	£	£
80		Costs:	Costs:	Costs:		
81	Units	Variable	Fixed	Total	Sales	Net Profit
82	0	0	1,138,350	1,138,350	0	-1,138,350
83	2,500	648,250	1,138,350	1,786,600	875,000	-911,600
84	5,000	1,296,500	1,138,350	2,434,850	1,750,000	-684,850
85	7,500	1,944,750	1,138,350	3,083,100	2,625,000	-458,100
86	10,000	2,593,000	1,138,350	3,731,350	3,500,000	-231,350
87	12,500	3,241,250	1,138,350	4,379,600	4,375,000	-4,600
88	15,000	3,889,500	1,138,350	5,027,850	5,250,000	222,150
89	17,500	4,537,750	1,138,350	5,676,100	6,125,000	448,900
90	20,000	5,186,000	1,138,350	6,324,350	7,000,000	675,650
91	22,500	5,834,250	1,138,350	6,972,600	7,875,000	902,400
92	25,000	6,482,500	1,138,350	7,620,850	8,750,000	1,129,150
93	27,500	7,130,750	1,138,350	8,269,100	9,625,000	1,355,900
94	30,000	7,779,000	1,138,350	8,917,350	10,500,000	1,582,650
95	===========	===========	===========	===========	===========	===========

Figure 32a (Part 2)

	A	B	C	D	E	F
1	Session 32: Cost-Volume-Profit Analysis: Drake and Ralegh Ltd.					
2	-----------	------------	--------	----------------	-------------	------------------
3	DATA INPUT TABLE					
4	-----------	------------	--------	----------------	-------------	------------------
5				Units	£ per annum	Graph
6	Budgeted unit sales:		Units:	20,000		Steps
7				£.p	* * *	Units
8	Selling Price per Unit:		£.p:	£350.00	* * *	2,500
9	Target net profit:			* * *	£1,000,000	
10						
11	Costs:			Variable	Fixed	
12				£p per unit	£ per annum	
13	Production costs:					
14		Direct Material		£97.50		
15		Direct Labour		£78.30		
16		Direct Expense		£24.90		
17	Production Overhead:					
18		Indirect Labour			£235,000	
19		Indirect Expense			£365,700	
20	Selling & Distribution Overhead:					
21		Salesmen's Salaries			£45,800	
22		Salesmen's Commissions		£35.00		
23		Distribution Costs		£23.60	£84,500	
24		Other S & D Overhead			£49,850	
25	Administration Overhead:					
26		Salaries & Wages			£123,500	
27		Other Overhead			£234,000	
28				----------------	-------------	
29				@SUM(D14..D27)	@SUM(E14..E27)	
30	=========	===========	=======	==============	===========	================
31	OUTPUT TABLES				Units	£/£.p
32	-----------	------------	--------	----------------	-------------	------------------
33	CONTRIBUTION		Margin per unit			+D8-D29
34	-----------	------------	--------	----------------	-------------	------------------
35	BREAK-EVEN POINT		Unit sales		+E29/F33	
36			£ sales			+D8*E35
37	-----------	------------	--------	----------------	-------------	------------------
38	BUDGETED LEVEL		Unit sales		+D6	
39			£ sales			+E38*D8
40			Net profit			+F39-E29-D29*E38
41	-----------	------------	--------	----------------	-------------	------------------
42	TARGET LEVEL		Unit sales to achieve:		(+F44+E29)/F33	
43	OF NET PROFIT		£ Sales to achieve:			+E42*D8
44			Net Profit required of			+E9
45	=========	===========	=======	==============	===========	================

Figure 32b (Part 1)

	A	B	C	D	E	F
77	=========	===========	=======	==============	===========	================
78	Data for break-even graph					
79		£	£	£	£	£
80		Costs:	Costs:	Costs:		
81	Units	Variable	Fixed	Total	Sales	Net Profit
82	0	+$D$29*A82	+$E$29	+B82+C82	+$D$8*A82	+E82-D82
83	+$F$8+A82	+$D$29*A83	+$E$29	+B83+C83	+$D$8*A83	+E83-D83
84	+$F$8+A83	+$D$29*A84	+$E$29	+B84+C84	+$D$8*A84	+E84-D84
85	+$F$8+A84	+$D$29*A85	+$E$29	+B85+C85	+$D$8*A85	+E85-D85
86	+$F$8+A85	+$D$29*A86	+$E$29	+B86+C86	+$D$8*A86	+E86-D86
87	+$F$8+A86	+$D$29*A87	+$E$29	+B87+C87	+$D$8*A87	+E87-D87
88	+$F$8+A87	+$D$29*A88	+$E$29	+B88+C88	+$D$8*A88	+E88-D88
89	+$F$8+A88	+$D$29*A89	+$E$29	+B89+C89	+$D$8*A89	+E89-D89
90	+$F$8+A89	+$D$29*A90	+$E$29	+B90+C90	+$D$8*A90	+E90-D90
91	+$F$8+A90	+$D$29*A91	+$E$29	+B91+C91	+$D$8*A91	+E91-D91
92	+$F$8+A91	+$D$29*A92	+$E$29	+B92+C92	+$D$8*A92	+E92-D92
93	+$F$8+A92	+$D$29*A93	+$E$29	+B93+C93	+$D$8*A93	+E93-D93
94	+$F$8+A93	+$D$29*A94	+$E$29	+B94+C94	+$D$8*A94	+E94-D94
95	=========	===========	=======	==============	===========	================

Figure 32b (Part 2)

It is suggested that you create and retain the *Data for break-even graph* in the range A78..F94, since it is not part of the output requirement. However, having created it, you may feel (unless you have positioned a graph in the range A46..F76) that it is of sufficient interest to move up (/M) nearer the Output Tables.

5. Notes on creating the model

The formulae required for this model have been kept as simple as possible, and you should have no trouble entering them, particularly if you refer to Figure 32b. As suggested in the previous sessions, try the formulae on your own, referring to Figure 32b if you get stuck.

Format the cells appropriately. Figure 32a can be a guide.

The worksheet should be protected when complete. Unprotected cells are in the ranges D6, D8, E9, D14..E27.

6. An explanation of the model

A few reminders of marginal costing formulae may help:

SALES – VARIABLE COSTS = CONTRIBUTION – FIXED COSTS = PROFIT

CONTRIBUTION PER UNIT = SELLING PRICE PER UNIT – VARIABLE COST PER UNIT

F33 = D8 – D29

BREAKEVEN POINT (UNITS) = FIXED COSTS / CONTRIBUTION PER UNIT

E35 = E29 / F33

TARGET UNIT SALES = [REQU'D NET PROFIT + FIXED COSTS] / CONT'B'N PER UNIT

E42 = [F44 or E9 + E29] / F33

The graph in Figure 32a (range A46..F76) is a contribution type of breakeven graph. The contribution wedge is formed by the sales and variable cost lines. The total cost line is formed by adding fixed costs above the variable costs, and where it crosses the sales line is the breakeven point.

7. Graphing the model

It is to be hoped that the following notes will help refresh the skills you acquired by working through session 7. Since the procedures vary between programs, only key points are provided:

/G (Graph or Graphics)

Type: Line

X: A82..A94

A: E82..E94

B: B82..B94

C: D82..D94

Options, Legend:	A:	Sales
	B:	Variable Costs
	C:	Total Costs
Options, Titles:	First:	Drake and Ralegh Ltd.
	Second:	Contribution and Break-even Graph
	X axis:	Sales Volume (Units)
	Y axis:	£s

Name the graph and Save (or Plot) as necessary.

8. Activity

(1) As usual with models of this type, try altering the data and observe the effects on the output tables and graph. What happens when you alter the targeted net profit in cell E9 to £0 (zero)? How sensitive is the breakeven point to the level of the fixed costs? You can observe this by altering the formula in cell E29 to @SUM(E14..E27)***1.5** or any other factor. If you want to try a number of other factors, alter the formula to @SUM(E14..E27)***F29** and try out various factors in cell F29. Leave a factor of **1** in cell F29 when you have finished. Experiment with this kind of sensitivity test in any other interesting area.

(2) Alter the graph to the more orthodox (non-contribution) type of break-even graph where the variable costs are on top of the fixed costs. Give it a different name if you want to keep both types.

(3) Adapt the whole model to produce similar information for another suitable organisation, or for part of another suitable organisation.

SESSION 33

Budgets: Cashflow forecast with profit & loss account

1. Objectives

At the end of this session, you will be able to:

- ❑ create a model which will produce a detailed month-by-month cashflow forecast and profit and loss account for next year;
- ❑ expand this model in session 34 to produce outline balance sheets for the same period;
- ❑ appreciate further uses for the @IF function;
- ❑ understand the significance of circular references introduced into formulae.

2. Introduction

In sessions 3 and 4, you learnt how to create and print out a simple cash flow forecast for Mr. B. Bristol.

Now that you have gained more experience in tackling rather larger worksheets, you will, in this session, create a more detailed forecast for a full year, using data input areas and leaving other areas to perform the calculations.

This session is independent of, but follows on from, sessions 24, 25 and 26, where you created a worksheet for the accounts of George Nettlerash, resulting in printed financial accounts and FRS1 cashflow statement for the year ended 31.12.19x1.

This current session creates a separate worksheet. You will enter data from the closing balances of session 24, and proceed from there.

[However, having created it, you could later combine or merge (see session 25, paragraph 8(2)) the two worksheets and replace the data entries with cell references, or you could link the separate worksheets if you have a program which can do this. The trouble with the first alternative is that the worksheet would then be quite large, and you may suffer from the limitations imposed by the speed of your hardware and software.]

3. The problem

You have completed the accounts for George Nettlerash for 19x1, and now George wants a model which will produce a detailed month-by-month cashflow forecast for the current year ended 31.12.19x2.

His specification contains the following requirements and information:

- He will provide his month-by-month forecast of sales turnover for each of the months of 19x2, since sales are subject to seasonal fluctuations.
- He then wants to see the effect on the forecast of changes to his budgeted sales if he specifies a percentage change to his original budgeted sales, in the event of likely changes in demand.
- Initially, to simplify the model, the expenses are assumed to be spread evenly over the year but he wants to be able to alter some of them at some future time for the uneven incidence of payments for such items as rent, rates, light & heat, telephone, accountancy charges and insurance.
- As far as gross profit and purchases are concerned, he is happy if these are calculated by providing an overall gross profit percentage margin to the monthly sales figures, provided he can specify a different percentage in order to observe the effect on the forecasts.
- He considers that some of his expenses vary with turnvover, and he would like the model to take this into account if he applies a percentage change to the original monthly budgeted sales figures.
- Since some of his customers are slow payers, he would like to supply his estimate of the separate percentages of those who are likely to pay within 1, 2 and 3 months of invoice date, and to alter these percentages if necessary, again in order to observe the effects on the forecast.
- George regularly pays his suppliers within two months after invoice date, and hopes that they will continue to allow him to do so.
- VAT is paid in the normal manner, and not under cash accounting or any other VAT scheme.
- George suggests that his drawings are allowed for at £2,000 per month (with the facility to adjust this monthly figure), purely to see how this works out. He realises that schedule D tax for last year will be payable in January and July, but says that adjustment for this can be made when the position is clearer.
- He would also like to see the effect of all the above on his monthly gross and net profit figures.
- He would also like to see simple monthly forecast balance sheets which reflect these budgets and any changes to them, but, being a considerate individual, agrees that you can leave this problem until session 34.

	A	B	C	D	E	F	G	H	I	J	K
1	G.K.Nettlerash Company										
2	Projected Profit & Loss Account & CASH FLOW FORECAST										
3	For the year ended 31st December 19x2										
4	-----	-----	-----	-----	-----	-----	-----	-----	-----	-----	-----
5	DATA INPUT TABLE										
6	-----	-----	-----	-----	-----	-----	-----	-----	-----	-----	-----
7	SALES: % OF ORIGINAL BUDGET		95.0%								
8											
9	GROSS PROFIT MARGIN ON SALES		34.0%								
10											
11	BANK INTEREST RATE		18.5%								
12											
13	VAT RATE		17.5%								
14											
15	SALES RECEIPTS: within:	1 month	50%								
16		2 months	30%								
17		3 months	20%								
18											
19	DRAWINGS PER MONTH:		£2,000								
20											
21	ESTIMATED DEPRECIATION FOR YEAR		£5,987								
22											
23	BALANCES B/FWD AT 31.12.19X1:-										
24											
25	BANK ACCOUNT BALANCE		£(1,095)								
26	DEBTORS		£100,629								
27	PURCHASE LEDGER CREDITORS		£101,050	Paid Jan:	63,000						
28	V.A.T. OUTSTANDING		£9,860								
29											
30	=====	=====	=====	=====	=====	=====	=====	=====	=====	=====	=====
31	G.K.Nettlerash Company										
32	Projected Profit & Loss Account										
33	For the year ended 31st December 19x2										
34	-----	-----	-----	-----	-----	-----	-----	-----	-----	-----	-----
35				JAN	FEB	MAR	APR	MAY	JUN	JUL	AUG
36	-----	-----	-----	-----	-----	-----	-----	-----	-----	-----	-----
37	ORIGINAL SALES BUDGET	DATA INPUTS:......		35,000	32,750	37,900	39,600	40,500	44,750	44,750	45,500
38	-----	-----	-----	-----	-----	-----	-----	-----	-----	-----	-----
39	REVISED SALES BUDGET:			33,250	31,113	36,005	37,620	38,475	42,513	42,513	43,225
40		CELLS C46..C62									
41	Purchases	DATA INPUTS:		21,945	20,534	23,763	24,829	25,394	28,058	28,058	28,529
42		ENTER BELOW									
43	GROSS PROFIT	ORIGINAL BUDGET		11,305	10,578	12,242	12,791	13,082	14,454	14,454	14,697
44		MONTHLY AMOUNTS:-									
45	LESS EXPENSES:										
46	Sub-Contract	Variable	112	106	106	106	106	106	106	106	106
47	Consumables	Variable	75	71	71	71	71	71	71	71	71
48	Wages & NI	Fixed	5,447	5,447	5,447	5,447	5,447	5,447	5,447	5,447	5,447
49	Motor Expenses	Variable	579	550	550	550	550	550	550	550	550
50	Transport & Storage	Variable	75	71	71	71	71	71	71	71	71
51	Rent & Rates	Fixed	2,105	2,105	2,105	2,105	2,105	2,105	2,105	2,105	2,105
52	Light & Heat	Fixed	148	148	148	148	148	148	148	148	148
53	Telephone	Variable	194	184	184	184	184	184	184	184	184
54	Printing & Stationery	Fixed	145	145	145	145	145	145	145	145	145
55	Advertising	Fixed	60	60	60	60	60	60	60	60	60
56	Cleaning & Sundries	Fixed	263	263	263	263	263	263	263	263	263
57	Repairs & Renewals	Fixed	114	114	114	114	114	114	114	114	114
58	Lease Rentals	Fixed	88	88	88	88	88	88	88	88	88
59	Legal & Professional	Fixed	55	55	55	55	55	55	55	55	55
60	Accountancy	Fixed	88	88	88	88	88	88	88	88	88
61	Insurance	Fixed	433	433	433	433	433	433	433	433	433
62	Bank Charges	Fixed	121	121	121	121	121	121	121	121	121
63	Bank Interest	Fixed	Calcs.	417	435	402	423	394	373	385	327
64	Depreciation	Fixed	499	499	499	499	499	499	499	499	499
65	-----	-----	-----	-----	-----	-----	-----	-----	-----	-----	-----
66	Total Expenses:			10,966	10,984	10,950	10,972	10,943	10,922	10,934	10,876
67	-----	-----	-----	-----	-----	-----	-----	-----	-----	-----	-----
68	NET PROFIT FOR PERIOD			339	-406	1,291	1,819	2,139	3,532	3,520	3,821
69	=====	=====	=====	=====	=====	=====	=====	=====	=====	=====	=====

Figure 33a (Part 1)

	L	M	N	O	P	Q	R	S
1								
2								
3								
4	---------	---------	---------	---------	---------			
5								
6	---------	---------	---------	---------	---------			
7								
8								
9								
10								
11								
12								
13								
14								
15								
16								
17								
18								
19								
20								
21								
22								
23								
24								
25								
26								
27								
28								
29								
30	=======	=======	=======	=======	=======			
31								
32								
33								
34	---------	---------	---------	---------	---------			
35	SEP	OCT	NOV	DEC	TOTAL			
36	---------	---------	---------	---------	---------			
37	47,400	47,950	48,750	49,000	513,850			
38	---------	---------	---------	---------	---------			
39	45,030	45,553	46,313	46,550	488,158			
40								
41	29,720	30,065	30,566	30,723	322,184			
42								
43	15,310	15,488	15,746	15,827	165,974			
44								
45								
46	106	106	106	106	1,277			
47	71	71	71	71	855			
48	5,447	5,447	5,447	5,447	65,364			
49	550	550	550	550	6,601			
50	71	71	71	71	855			
51	2,105	2,105	2,105	2,105	25,260			
52	148	148	148	148	1,776			
53	184	184	184	184	2,212			
54	145	145	145	145	1,740			
55	60	60	60	60	720			
56	263	263	263	263	3,156			
57	114	114	114	114	1,368			
58	88	88	88	88	1,056			
59	55	55	55	55	660			
60	88	88	88	88	1,056			
61	433	433	433	433	5,196			
62	121	121	121	121	1,448			
63	269	282	196	114	4,017			
64	499	499	499	499	5,987			
65	---------	---------	---------	---------	---------			
66	10,818	10,831	10,745	10,663	130,603			
67	---------	---------	---------	---------	---------			
68	4,493	4,657	5,002	5,164	35,370			
69	=======	=======	=======	=======	=======			

Figure 33a (Part 2)

	A	B	C	D	E	F	G	H	I	J	K
70	G.K.Nettlerash Company										
71	CASH FLOW FORECAST										
72	For the year ended 31st December 19x2										
73	----------	----------	----------	----------	----------	----------	----------	----------	----------	----------	----------
74	ADJUSTED SALES BUDGET (FROM P&L A/c) + VAT			39,069	36,557	42,306	44,204	45,208	49,952	49,952	50,789
75	----------	----------	----------	----------	----------	----------	----------	----------	----------	----------	----------
76	Debtors at 31st December 19x1	100,629		JAN	FEB	MAR	APR	MAY	JUN	JUL	AUG
77	----------	----------	----------	----------	----------	----------	----------	----------	----------	----------	----------
78	SALES LEDGER RECEIPTS										
79	FROM SALES 3 MONTHS AGO			11,839	11,839	11,839	7,814	7,311	8,461	8,841	9,042
80	FROM SALES 2 MONTHS AGO			17,758	17,758	11,721	10,967	12,692	13,261	13,562	14,986
81	FROM SALES 1 MONTH AGO			29,597	19,534	18,279	21,153	22,102	22,604	24,976	24,976
82	Other receipts/loans & H.P										
83	----------	----------	----------	----------	----------	----------	----------	----------	----------	----------	----------
84	TOTAL INFLOWS			59,194	49,131	41,838	39,934	42,105	44,326	47,379	49,003
85	----------	----------	----------	----------	----------	----------	----------	----------	----------	----------	----------
86	PURCHASE LEDGER PAYMENTS	incl.VAT		63,000	38,050	25,785	24,128	27,922	29,174	29,837	32,968
87	Sub-Contract	incl.VAT		125	125	125	125	125	125	125	125
88	Consumables	incl.VAT		84	84	84	84	84	84	84	84
89	Gross Wages & N.I.			5,447	5,447	5,447	5,447	5,447	5,447	5,447	5,447
90	Motor Expenses	incl.VAT		646	646	646	646	646	646	646	646
91	Transport & Storage	incl.VAT		84	84	84	84	84	84	84	84
92	Rent & Rates			2,105	2,105	2,105	2,105	2,105	2,105	2,105	2,105
93	Light & Heat	incl.VAT		174	174	174	174	174	174	174	174
94	Telephone	incl.VAT		217	217	217	217	217	217	217	217
95	Printing & Stationery	incl.VAT		170	170	170	170	170	170	170	170
96	Advertising	incl.VAT		71	71	71	71	71	71	71	71
97	Cleaning & Sundries	incl.VAT		309	309	309	309	309	309	309	309
98	Repairs & Renewals	incl.VAT		134	134	134	134	134	134	134	134
99	Lease Rentals	incl.VAT		103	103	103	103	103	103	103	103
100	Legal & Professional	incl.VAT		65	65	65	65	65	65	65	65
101	Accountancy	incl.VAT		103	103	103	103	103	103	103	103
102	Insurance			433	433	433	433	433	433	433	433
103	Bank Charges					362			362		
104	Bank Interest					1,253			1,191		
105	Drawings			2,000	2,000	2,000	2,000	2,000	2,000	2,000	2,000
106	Capital Expenditure	incl.VAT									
107	Loan & H.P. Payments										
108	VAT payments			9,860			4,951			6,036	
109	----------	----------	----------	----------	----------	----------	----------	----------	----------	----------	----------
110	TOTAL OUTFLOWS			85,129	50,319	39,670	41,348	40,191	42,997	48,143	45,238
111	----------	----------	----------	----------	----------	----------	----------	----------	----------	----------	----------
112	NET INFLOW/(OUTFLOW)			-25,936	-1,188	2,168	-1,415	1,914	1,330	-764	3,765
113	----------	----------	----------	----------	----------	----------	----------	----------	----------	----------	----------
114	BANK ACCOUNT BALANCE	(1,095)		-27,031	-28,219	-26,052	-27,466	-25,553	-24,223	-24,987	-21,221
115		at 31.12.19x1									
116	==========	==========	==========	==========	==========	==========	==========	==========	==========	==========	==========
117	VAT CALCULATIONS:										
118	VAT on sales (revised budget)			5,819	5,445	6,301	6,584	6,733	7,440	7,440	7,564
119	VAT on purchases (revised budget)			3,840	3,593	4,159	4,345	4,444	4,910	4,910	4,992
120				----------	----------	----------	----------	----------	----------	----------	----------
121				1,978	1,851	2,142	2,238	2,289	2,529	2,529	2,572
122	VAT on expenses paid			340	340	340	340	340	340	340	340
123				----------	----------	----------	----------	----------	----------	----------	----------
124	VAT due re current month			1,638	1,511	1,802	1,898	1,949	2,189	2,189	2,232
125	==========	==========	==========	==========	==========	==========	==========	==========	==========	==========	==========

Figure 33a (Part 3)

	L	M	N	O	P	Q	R	S
70								
71								
72								
73	---------	---------	---------	---------	---------	---------	---------	---------
74	52,910	53,524	54,417	54,696				
75	---------	---------	---------	---------	---------	---------	---------	---------
76	SEP	OCT	NOV	DEC	TOTAL	Jan 93	Feb 93	Mar 93
77	---------	---------	---------	---------	---------	---------	---------	---------
78								
79	9,990	9,990	10,158	10,582	117,706	10,705	10,883	10,939
80	14,986	15,237	15,873	16,057	174,858	16,325	16,409	0
81	25,395	26,455	26,762	27,209	289,041	27,348	0	0
82								
83	---------	---------	---------	---------	---------	---------	---------	---------
84	50,371	51,682	52,793	53,848	581,604	Drs. at 31.12.92:-		92,610
85	---------	---------	---------	---------	---------	---------	---------	---------
86	32,968	33,521	34,921	35,326	407,601			
87	125	125	125	125	1,500			
88	84	84	84	84	1,005			
89	5,447	5,447	5,447	5,447	65,364			
90	646	646	646	646	7,756			
91	84	84	84	84	1,005			
92	2,105	2,105	2,105	2,105	25,260			
93	174	174	174	174	2,087			
94	217	217	217	217	2,599			
95	170	170	170	170	2,045			
96	71	71	71	71	846			
97	309	309	309	309	3,708			
98	134	134	134	134	1,607			
99	103	103	103	103	1,241			
100	65	65	65	65	776			
101	103	103	103	103	1,241			
102	433	433	433	433	5,196			
103	362			362	1,448			
104	981			592	4,017			
105	2,000	2,000	2,000	2,000	24,000			
106					0			
107					0			
108		6,760			27,607			
109	---------	---------	---------	---------	---------			
110	46,581	52,550	47,190	48,549	587,908			
111	---------	---------	---------	---------	---------			
112	3,790	-868	5,603	5,299	-6,303			
113	---------	---------	---------	---------	---------			
114	-17,432	-18,300	-12,697	-7,398	-7,398			
115								
116	=======	=======	=======	=======	=======			
117								
118	7,880	7,972	8,105	8,146				
119	5,201	5,261	5,349	5,377				
120	---------	---------	---------	---------				
121	2,679	2,710	2,756	2,770				
122	340	340	340	340				
123	---------	---------	---------	---------				
124	2,339	2,370	2,415	2,429				
125	=======	=======	=======	=======				

Figure 33a (Part 4)

	A	B	C	D
31	G.K.Nettlerash Company			
32	Projected Profit & Loss Account			
33	For the year ended 31st December 19x2			
34	------------------------------	--------	----------	------------------------------
35				JAN
36	------------------------------	--------	----------	------------------------------
37	ORIGINAL SALES BUDGET	DATA INPUTS:......		35,000
38	------------------------------	--------	----------	------------------------------
39	REVISED SALES BUDGET:			+D37*$C$7
40		CELLS C46..C62		
41	Purchases	DATA INPUTS:		+D39*(1-$C$9)
42		ENTER BELOW		
43	GROSS PROFIT	ORIGINAL BUDGET		+D39-D41
44		MONTHLY AMOUNTS:-		
45	LESS EXPENSES:			
46	Sub-Contract	Variable	112	+$C46*$C$7
47	Consumables	Variable	75	+$C47*$C$7
48	Wages & NI	Fixed	5,447	+$C48
49	Motor Expenses	Variable	579	+$C49*$C$7
50	Transport & Storage	Variable	75	+$C50*$C$7
51	Rent & Rates	Fixed	2,105	+$C51
52	Light & Heat	Fixed	148	+$C52
53	Telephone	Variable	194	+$C53*$C$7
54	Printing & Stationery	Fixed	145	+$C54
55	Advertising	Fixed	60	+$C55
56	Cleaning & Sundries	Fixed	263	+$C56
57	Repairs & Renewals	Fixed	114	+$C57
58	Lease Rentals	Fixed	88	+$C58
59	Legal & Professional	Fixed	55	+$C59
60	Accountancy	Fixed	88	+$C60
61	Insurance	Fixed	433	+$C61
62	Bank Charges	Fixed	121	+$C62
63	Bank Interest	Fixed	Calcs.	@IF(D114<0,-D114*$C$11/12,0)
64	Depreciation	Fixed	+$C$21/12	+$C64
65	------------------------------	--------	----------	------------------------------
66	Total Expenses:			@SUM(D46..D64)
67	------------------------------	--------	----------	------------------------------
68	NET PROFIT FOR PERIOD			+D43-D66
69	======================	=======	=========	==

Figure 33b (Part 1)

4. Design of the model

The design of the model can best be understood by reference to Figures 33a and 33b. Note that columns J,K,L,M,N and O are not shown, since the formulae for July..December (columns J..O) are similar to those for January..June (columns D..I).

There is the usual data input table in rows 5..28. The percentage entries in rows 7..17 can be altered as required, and changes will be reflected in the output tables.

The model is not elaborate enough to calculate depreciation which reflects additions to or disposal of fixed assets. The figure in cell C21 must therefore be estimated, and changed as necessary.

The figures in cells C25..28 must be entered as data (unless referenced as suggested at the end of paragraph 2 above).

	E	F
31		
32		
33		
34	------------------------------	------------------------------
35	FEB	MAR
36	------------------------------	------------------------------
37	32,750	37,900
38	------------------------------	------------------------------
39	+E37*$C$7	+F37*$C$7
40		
41	+E39*(1-$C$9)	+F39*(1-$C$9)
42		
43	+E39-E41	+F39-F41
44		
45		
46	+$C46*$C$7	+$C46*$C$7
47	+$C47*$C$7	+$C47*$C$7
48	+$C48	+$C48
49	+$C49*$C$7	+$C49*$C$7
50	+$C50*$C$7	+$C50*$C$7
51	+$C51	+$C51
52	+$C52	+$C52
53	+$C53*$C$7	+$C53*$C$7
54	+$C54	+$C54
55	+$C55	+$C55
56	+$C56	+$C56
57	+$C57	+$C57
58	+$C58	+$C58
59	+$C59	+$C59
60	+$C60	+$C60
61	+$C61	+$C61
62	+$C62	+$C62
63	@IF(E114<0,-E114*$C$11/12,0)	@IF(F114<0,-F114*$C$11/12,0)
64	+$C64	+$C64
65	------------------------------	------------------------------
66	@SUM(E46..E64)	@SUM(F46..F64)
67	------------------------------	------------------------------
68	+E43-E66	+F43-F66
69	==============================	==============================

Figure 33b (Part 2)

Rows 31..68 contain the projected *profit & loss account*. This section contains more data input ranges, i.e. row 37, for George's budgeted monthly sales figures, and C46..C62, where estimated monthly budget figures for expenses must be entered. Note that C63 and C64 contain formulae.

Rows 70..115 contain the *cashflow forecast*, and there are no data inputs in this section. Note that rows 79..81 extend beyond column P to column S. This could be avoided by more complicated formulae, but this layout is, perhaps, more easy to understand.

Rows 117..124 contain formulae for VAT calculations. These are for calculation and reference purposes only; other formulae are based on them and are therefore less complicated. This section could be hidden unless it is felt that George might be interested in the information. [Hiding ranges and columns was described in session 23, paragraph 8.]

	G	H
31		
32		
33		
34	--------------------	--------------------
35	APR	MAY
36	--------------------	--------------------
37	39,600	40,500
38	--------------------	--------------------
39	+G37*$C$7	+H37*$C$7
40		
41	+G39*(1-$C$9)	+H39*(1-$C$9)
42		
43	+G39-G41	+H39-H41
44		
45		
46	+$C46*$C$7	+$C46*$C$7
47	+$C47*$C$7	+$C47*$C$7
48	+$C48	+$C48
49	+$C49*$C$7	+$C49*$C$7
50	+$C50*$C$7	+$C50*$C$7
51	+$C51	+$C51
52	+$C52	+$C52
53	+$C53*$C$7	+$C53*$C$7
54	+$C54	+$C54
55	+$C55	+$C55
56	+$C56	+$C56
57	+$C57	+$C57
58	+$C58	+$C58
59	+$C59	+$C59
60	+$C60	+$C60
61	+$C61	+$C61
62	+$C62	+$C62
63	@IF(G114<0,-G114*$C$11/12,0)	@IF(H114<0,-H114*$C$11/12,0)
64	+$C64	+$C64
65	--------------------	--------------------
66	@SUM(G46..G64)	@SUM(H46..H64)
67	--------------------	--------------------
68	+G43-G66	+H43-H66
69	====================	====================

Figure 33b (Part 3)

5. Notes on creating the model

If you have worked through all (or most) of the previous sessions, you should find no difficulty in creating this model from Figures 33a and 33b.

[Note again that columns J,K,L,M,N and O are not shown, since the formulae for July..December (columns J..O) are similar to those for January..June (columns D..I).]

The Copy command can be used extensively, since absolute cell references (with the $ signs) are included in Figure 33b. For example cell D63, which contains a long formula, can be copied across to D63..O63. Similarly cell F104 (quarterly bank interest) - an even longer formula - can be copied to cells I104, L104 and O104.

	I	P	Q	R	S
31					
32					
33					
34	----------	----------			
35	JUN	TOTAL			
36	----------	----------			
37	44,750	@SUM(B37..O37)			
38	----------	----------			
39	+I37*$C$7	@SUM(B39..O39)			
40					
41	+I39*(1-$C$9)	@SUM(B41..O41)			
42					
43	+I39-I41	+P39-P41			
44					
45					
46	+$C46*$C$7	@SUM(D46..O46)			
47	+$C47*$C$7	@SUM(D47..O47)			
48	+$C48	@SUM(D48..O48)			
49	+$C49*$C$7	@SUM(D49..O49)			
50	+$C50*$C$7	@SUM(D50..O50)			
51	+$C51	@SUM(D51..O51)			
52	+$C52	@SUM(D52..O52)			
53	+$C53*$C$7	@SUM(D53..O53)			
54	+$C54	@SUM(D54..O54)			
55	+$C55	@SUM(D55..O55)			
56	+$C56	@SUM(D56..O56)			
57	+$C57	@SUM(D57..O57)			
58	+$C58	@SUM(D58..O58)			
59	+$C59	@SUM(D59..O59)			
60	+$C60	@SUM(D60..O60)			
61	+$C61	@SUM(D61..O61)			
62	+$C62	@SUM(D62..O62)			
63	@IF(I114<0,-I114*$C$11/12,0)	@SUM(D63..O63)			
64	+$C64	@SUM(D64..O64)			
65	----------	----------			
66	@SUM(I46..I64)	@SUM(D66..O66)			
67	----------	----------			
68	+I43-I66	@SUM(D68..O68)			
69	==========	==========			

Figure 33b (Part 4)

6. An explanation of the model

If you examine each of the formulae carefully, you should be able to trace the logic of the calculations which they perform.

Extensive use is made of the @IF function, as in some previous sessions. If you wish to revise your understanding of this function, please refer to the general explanation provided in session 23, paragraph 7.

The VAT calculations in row 124 are calculated on expenses *paid* which include VAT. The formulae therefore require the VAT element to be 17.5/117.5 of each item (C13/(1+C13)).

	A	B	C	D
70	G.K.Nettlerash Company			
71	CASH FLOW FORECAST			
72	For the year ended 31st December 19x2			
73	------------------	----------	----------	------------------------------
74	ADJUSTED SALES BUDGET (FROM P&L A/c) + VA			+D39*(1+$C$13)
75	------------------	----------	----------	------------------------------
76	Debtors at 31st December	+C26		JAN
77	------------------	----------	----------	------------------------------
78	SALES LEDGER RECEIPTS			
79	FROM SALES 3 MONTHS AGO			+$B$76*($C$17)/($C$17*3+$C$16*2+$C$15)
80	FROM SALES 2 MONTHS AGO			+$B$76*($C$16)/($C$17*3+$C$16*2+$C$15)
81	FROM SALES 1 MONTH AGO			+$B$76*($C$15)/($C$17*3+$C$16*2+$C$15)
82	Other receipts/loans & H.P			
83	------------------	----------	----------	------------------------------
84	TOTAL INFLOWS			@SUM(D79..D82)
85	------------------	----------	----------	------------------------------
86	PURCHASE LEDGER PAYMEN	incl.VAT		+E27
87	Sub-Contract	incl.VAT		+D46*(1+$C$13)
88	Consumables	incl.VAT		+D47*(1+$C$13)
89	Gross Wages & N.I.			+D48
90	Motor Expenses	incl.VAT		+D49*(1+$C$13)
91	Transport & Storage	incl.VAT		+D50*(1+$C$13)
92	Rent & Rates			+D51
93	Light & Heat	incl.VAT		+D52*(1+$C$13)
94	Telephone	incl.VAT		+D53*(1+$C$13)
95	Printing & Stationery	incl.VAT		+D54*(1+$C$13)
96	Advertising	incl.VAT		+D55*(1+$C$13)
97	Cleaning & Sundries	incl.VAT		+D56*(1+$C$13)
98	Repairs & Renewals	incl.VAT		+D57*(1+$C$13)
99	Lease Rentals	incl.VAT		+D58*(1+$C$13)
100	Legal & Professional	incl.VAT		+D59*(1+$C$13)
101	Accountancy	incl.VAT		+D60*(1+$C$13)
102	Insurance			+D61
103	Bank Charges			
104	Bank Interest			
105	Drawings			+$C$19
106	Capital Expenditure	incl.VAT		
107	Loan & H.P. Payments			
108	VAT payments			+C28
109	------------------	----------	----------	------------------------------
110	TOTAL OUTFLOWS			@SUM(D86..D108)
111	------------------	----------	----------	------------------------------
112	NET INFLOW/(OUTFLOW)			+D84-D110
113	------------------	----------	----------	------------------------------
114	BANK ACCOUNT BALANCE	+C25		+B114+D112
115		at 31.12.19x1		
116	==================	=======	=======	==============================
117	VAT CALCULATIONS:			
118	VAT on sales (revised budget)			+D39*$C$13
119	VAT on purchases (revised budget)			+D41*$C$13
120				------------------------------
121				+D118-D119
122	VAT on expenses paid			(+D87+D88+D90+D91+@SUM(D93:D101)+D106)*($C$13/(1+$C$13))
123				------------------------------
124	VAT due re current month			+D121-D122
125	==================	=======	=======	==============================

Figure 33b (Part 5)

	E	F
70		
71		
72		
73		
74	+E39*(1+$C$13)	+F39*(1+$C$13)
75		
76	FEB	MAR
77		
78		
79	+$B$76*($C$17)/($C$17*3+$C$16*2+$C$15)	+$B$76*($C$17)/($C$17*3+$C$16*2+$C$15)
80	+$B$76*($C$16)/($C$17*3+$C$16*2+$C$15)	+D$74*$C$16
81	+D$74*$C$15	+E$74*$C$15
82		
83		
84	@SUM(E79..E82)	@SUM(F79..F82)
85		
86	+C27-D86	+D41*(1+$C$13)
87	+E46*(1+$C$13)	+F46*(1+$C$13)
88	+E47*(1+$C$13)	+F47*(1+$C$13)
89	+E48	+F48
90	+E49*(1+$C$13)	+F49*(1+$C$13)
91	+E50*(1+$C$13)	+F50*(1+$C$13)
92	+E51	+F51
93	+E52*(1+$C$13)	+F52*(1+$C$13)
94	+E53*(1+$C$13)	+F53*(1+$C$13)
95	+E54*(1+$C$13)	+F54*(1+$C$13)
96	+E55*(1+$C$13)	+F55*(1+$C$13)
97	+E56*(1+$C$13)	+F56*(1+$C$13)
98	+E57*(1+$C$13)	+F57*(1+$C$13)
99	+E58*(1+$C$13)	+F58*(1+$C$13)
100	+E59*(1+$C$13)	+F59*(1+$C$13)
101	+E60*(1+$C$13)	+F60*(1+$C$13)
102	+E61	+F61
103		+D62+E62+F62
104		((@IF(D114<0,-D114,0))+(@IF(E114<0,-E114,0))+(@IF(F114<0,-F114,0)))*$C$11/12
105	+$C$19	+$C$19
106		
107		
108		
109		
110	@SUM(E86..E108)	@SUM(F86..F108)
111		
112	+E84-E110	+F84-F110
113		
114	+D114+E112	+E114+F112
115		
116	==========	==========
117		
118	+E39*$C$13	+F39*$C$13
119	+E41*$C$13	+F41*$C$13
120		
121	+E118-E119	+F118-F119
122	(+E87+E88+E90+E91+@SUM(E93:E101)+E106)*($C$13/(1+$C$13))	(+F87+F88+F90+F91+@SUM(F93:F101)+F106)*($C$13/(1+$C$13))
123		
124	+E121-E122	+F121-F122
125	==========	==========

Figure 33b (Part 6)

Bank interest is charged to the profit and loss account monthly (row 63) but to the cashflow forecast at the end of each quarter (row 104). The formula in cell D63 instructs the program, if the bank balance in cell D114 is negative (overdrawn), to take the positive value of this figure and calculate interest on it at a rate of one-twelfth of the interest rate entered in cell C11 (in the data input table). Similarly for cells E63..O63. This causes no problem.

Circular References

However, the formula in cell F104 causes a *circular reference,* which some programs indicate by showing **CIRC** in the status indicator. This is deliberate, so don't worry. The cause is, in the formula in cell F104, the third @IF argument refers to cell F114 (bank balance) which refers to cell F112 which refers to cell F110 which sums cells F86..F108. This latter range includes cell F104 which has not yet been calculated! Each time the worksheet is recalculated, the results change by smaller and smaller amounts until the error is insignificant.

You can force recalculation by pressing <F9>, say, five times, which should be enough in this instance. If your program includes **/WGRI** (Worksheet, Global, Recalculation, Iteration) you can specify 5 times, which means that the program will recalculate the worksheet 5 times on each recalculation. This is not recommended in this instance, particularly if your hardware and software are slow. In any case, you will probably have caused at least 5 recalculations in the normal course of events before long.

	G	H
70		
71		
72		
73	----------------	----------------
74	+G39*(1+$C$13)	+H39*(1+$C$13)
75	----------------	----------------
76	APR	MAY
77	----------------	----------------
78		
79	+D$74*$C$17	+E$74*$C$17
80	+E$74*$C$16	+F$74*$C$16
81	+F$74*$C$15	+G$74*$C$15
82		
83	----------------	----------------
84	@SUM(G79..G82)	@SUM(H79..H82)
85	----------------	----------------
86	+E41*(1+$C$13)	+F41*(1+$C$13)
87	+G46*(1+$C$13)	+H46*(1+$C$13)
88	+G47*(1+$C$13)	+H47*(1+$C$13)
89	+G48	+H48
90	+G49*(1+$C$13)	+H49*(1+$C$13)
91	+G50*(1+$C$13)	+H50*(1+$C$13)
92	+G51	+H51
93	+G52*(1+$C$13)	+H52*(1+$C$13)
94	+G53*(1+$C$13)	+H53*(1+$C$13)
95	+G54*(1+$C$13)	+H54*(1+$C$13)
96	+G55*(1+$C$13)	+H55*(1+$C$13)
97	+G56*(1+$C$13)	+H56*(1+$C$13)
98	+G57*(1+$C$13)	+H57*(1+$C$13)
99	+G58*(1+$C$13)	+H58*(1+$C$13)
100	+G59*(1+$C$13)	+H59*(1+$C$13)
101	+G60*(1+$C$13)	+H60*(1+$C$13)
102	+G61	+H61
103		
104		
105	+$C$19	+$C$19
106		
107		
108	@SUM(D124..F124)	
109	----------------	
110	@SUM(G86..G108)	@SUM(H86..H108)
111	----------------	----------------
112	+G84-G110	+H84-H110
113	----------------	----------------
114	+F114+G112	+G114+H112
115		
116	================	================
117		
118	+G39*$C$13	+H39*$C$13
119	+G41*$C$13	+H41*$C$13
120	----------------	----------------
121	+G118-G119	+H118-H119
122	(+G87+G88+G90+G91+@SUM(G93:G101)+G106)*($C$13/(1+$C$13))	(+H87+H88+H90+H91+@SUM(H93:H101)+H106)*($C$13/(1+$C$13))
123	----------------	----------------
124	+G121-G122	+H121-H122
125	================	================

Figure 33b (Part 7)

	I	P	Q	R	S
70					
71					
72					
73					
74	+I39*(1+$C$13)				
75					
76	JUN	TOTAL	Jan 93	Feb 93	Mar 93
77					
78					
79	+F$74*$C$17	@SUM(D79..O79)	+M$74*$C$17	+N$74*$C$17	+O$74*$C$17
80	+G$74*$C$16	@SUM(D80..O80)	+N$74*$C$16	+O$74*$C$16	+P$74*$C$16
81	+H$74*$C$15	@SUM(D81..O81)	+O$74*$C$15	+P$74*$C$15	+Q$74*$C$15
82					
83					
84	@SUM(I79..I82)	@SUM(D84..O84)	Drs. at 31.12.92..-		@SUM(Q79..S81)
85					
86	+G41*(1+$C$13)	@SUM(D86..O86)			
87	+I46*(1+$C$13)	@SUM(D87..O87)			
88	+I47*(1+$C$13)	@SUM(D88..O88)			
89	+I48	@SUM(D89..O89)			
90	+I49*(1+$C$13)	@SUM(D90..O90)			
91	+I50*(1+$C$13)	@SUM(D91..O91)			
92	+I51	@SUM(D92..O92)			
93	+I52*(1+$C$13)	@SUM(D93..O93)			
94	+I53*(1+$C$13)	@SUM(D94..O94)			
95	+I54*(1+$C$13)	@SUM(D95..O95)			
96	+I55*(1+$C$13)	@SUM(D96..O96)			
97	+I56*(1+$C$13)	@SUM(D97..O97)			
98	+I57*(1+$C$13)	@SUM(D98..O98)			
99	+I58*(1+$C$13)	@SUM(D99..O99)			
100	+I59*(1+$C$13)	@SUM(D100..O100)			
101	+I60*(1+$C$13)	@SUM(D101..O101)			
102	+I61	@SUM(D102..O102)			
103	+G62+H62+I62	@SUM(D103..O103)			
104	((@IF(G114<0,-G114,0))+(@IF(H114<0,-H114,0))+(@IF(I114<0,-I114,0)))*$C$11/12	@SUM(D104..O104)			
105	+$C$19	@SUM(D105..O105)			
106		@SUM(D106..O106)			
107		@SUM(D107..O107)			
108		@SUM(D108..O108)			
109					
110	@SUM(I86..I108)	@SUM(D110..O110)			
111					
112	+I84-I110	@SUM(D112..O112)			
113					
114	+H114+I112	+B114+P112			
115					
116	==	================			
117					
118	+I39*$C$13				
119	+I41*$C$13				
120					
121	+I118-I119				
122	(+I87+I88+I90+I91+@SUM(I93:I101)+I106)*($C$13/(1+$C$13))				
123					
124	+I121-I122				
125	==				

Figure 33b (Part 8)

The command /WS (Worksheet, Status or Summary) provides a lot of useful information, including possibly the location of the last circular reference entered in the worksheet (depending on your program).

The formula in cell F104 is repeated in cells I104, L104, and O104. If you wish to see recalculation in action (assuming the worksheet has not been recalculated), move to cells O114 and P114 (which should be the same figures). Format the cells temporarily with /Range, Format, Fixed and specify 15 decimals places; also widen (/WCS) the columns O and P until all the ***s change to figures. The figures should differ. Press <F9> and observe the convergence.

As stated above, in this case the inclusion of circular references in the formulae is deliberate. It could have been avoided by placing the row for bank interest below the bank account balance row (114) and then adding another revised bank account balance row below that. The formula for bank interest need not then have included itself. In fact, this would be more realistic, since banks do not calculate interest on the interest. However, the error is small for a forecast, and the remedy rather cumbersome.

Note: Most circular references are unintentional. Not all circular references converge like this. Some diverge, and that is a bad thing. Also some converging circular references need a lot of iterations before resolution. So they should only be used when it is deliberate and convenient and unavoidable if the desired results are to be obtained.

7. Activity

(1) Test the model for sensitivity. Changes to the percentages in the data input table can have appreciable results on the profits and cashflows.

(2) If you wish to adapt or improve the model, you are, as usual, advised to save it with a new name before you start, so that the original is still available for retrieval if things go wrong. Also, as you progress, assuming the progress of the alterations are satisfactory, save and replace (or backup) at frequent intervals. Sometimes it is a good idea to save each stage with a new name, e.g. Nettle1, Nettle 2, Nettle3, and so on. When you achieve the final masterpiece (say Nettle7), you can carefully delete all the earlier, unwanted, files (i.e Nettle1..Nettle 6). If you are saving to hard disk, do not forget to backup to floppy. Hard disks have been known to crash. The author recommends this from personal experience!

SESSION 34
Budgets: Balance sheets

1. Objectives

At the end of this session, you will be able to:

- ❑ extend the model created in session 33 to produce simple outline budgeted monthly balance sheets corresponding to the monthly profit and loss account budgets and cashflow forecast;
- ❑ appreciate still further uses for the @IF function;
- ❑ have a rest, because this is the last session.

2. Introduction

In session 33 you created for George Nettlerash a model which produced budgeted monthly profit and loss accounts and a monthly cashflow forecast for 19x2. In this final session, you will extend it to produce simple outline budgeted monthly balance sheets corresponding to those monthly profit and loss account budgets and cashflow forecast.

This model is so dependent on the previous model that it is pointless trying to create it on its own; it is essential that you complete session 33 first.

The model is fairly simplistic. It reflects changes made to the data inputs of session 33, but other changes are not catered for.

3. The problem

George is reasonably happy with the previous model, though he finds the results of decreasing profit margins and the possibility of reduced turnovers somewhat depressing. However, while he appreciates that the cashflow forecast is, perhaps, the most important document of all, he would also like to get a rough idea of the sensitivity of budgeted monthly balance sheets to changes in budgeted activity.

He has no immediate plans for changes in fixed assets, but would like the model to allow him to include these if necessary.

He would also like space for inclusion of bank and H.P. loans, just in case he needs to see the effect of including them.

Items which can 'stay the same' each month (in order to keep the model simple) are stocks and work-in-progress, deposit account, prepayments and PAYE.

4. Design of the model

You should refer to Figures 34a and 34b.

The layout is traditional, with net assets (row 163) represented by capital account (row 171). There are no data inputs; all the cells are labels and formulae. The formulae are all fairly short and simple.

5. Notes on creating the model

As usual, the Copy command will be found useful. Most of the formulae can be copied across from January to December. Accruals (row 155) tends to repeat itself every three months, due to quarterly entries in the cashflow forecast reflecting monthly entries in the forecast profit & loss account for bank charges and bank interest.

6. An explanation of the model

You will notice in row 174 that there is a row labelled ***Balance Sheet difference***. The author used this for his own peace of mind while entering the formulae. Rather than eliminate it, he decided to include it, since you may find it useful if you decide to amend and improve the model for your own requirements. You can always hide it if you want to; hiding ranges and columns was described in session 23, paragraph 8.

7. Activity

All the models in this book have been kept deliberately fairly simple. The idea is that by *active learning* you gain confidence and experience in creating models to solve particular problems. You may then feel inspired to adapt and improve the models created in this book and perhaps create your own tailor-made models.

The model in these last two sessions (33 and 34) is, perhaps, particulary suitable for adaptation and improvement.

8. Happy Ending

Some of my students have suggested that this book should have a happy ending. This is it. I hope you have (on the whole) enjoyed working through most, if not all, of these 34 sessions, and now feel more at ease about using spreadsheets. They have enormous potential, but can still be used for solving relatively small and interesting problems. One of the joys is to alter a single figure in a data input block and see the effect on a large output block - a definite improvement since the days of pencils and rubbers!

And now for some final advice:

- experiment,
- explore your manuals and, above all,
- **Enjoy yourself!**

	A	B	D	E	F	G	H	I	J	K	L	M	N	O
126	G.K.Nettlerash Company													
127	Projected Balance Sheet													
128	as at the 31st December 19x2													
129														
130		BROUGHT												
131		FORWARD	JAN	FEB	MAR	APR	MAY	JUN	JUL	AUG	SEP	OCT	NOV	DEC
132														
133	FIXED ASSETS													
134	Plant & Machinery	32500	32500	32500	32500	32500	32500	32500	32500	32500	32500	32500	32500	32500
135	Office Equipment	7325	7325	7325	7325	7325	7325	7325	7325	7325	7325	7325	7325	7325
136	Motor Car 1	0	0	0	0	0	0	0	0	0	0	0	0	0
137	Motor Car 2	12000	12000	12000	12000	12000	12000	12000	12000	12000	12000	12000	12000	12000
138	Capital Additions		0	0	0	0	0	0	0	0	0	0	0	0
139	Cumulative Dep'n	18359	18858	19357	19856	20355	20854	21353	21851	22350	22849	23348	23847	24346
140		-------	-------	-------	-------	-------	-------	-------	-------	-------	-------	-------	-------	-------
141		33466	32967	32468	31969	31470	30971	30472	29974	29475	28976	28477	27978	27479
142		-------	-------	-------	-------	-------	-------	-------	-------	-------	-------	-------	-------	-------
143	CURRENT ASSETS													
144	Debtors	100629	80504	67930	68398	72668	75771	81397	83970	85756	88295	90137	91761	92610
145	Stock & WIP	49073	49073	49073	49073	49073	49073	49073	49073	49073	49073	49073	49073	49073
146	Bank Current A/c	0	0	0	0	0	0	0	0	0	0	0	0	0
147	No. 2 Account	348	348	348	348	348	348	348	348	348	348	348	348	348
148	Prepayments	4047	4047	4047	4047	4047	4047	4047	4047	4047	4047	4047	4047	4047
149	Cash In Hand	32	32	32	32	32	32	32	32	32	32	32	32	32
150		-------	-------	-------	-------	-------	-------	-------	-------	-------	-------	-------	-------	-------
151		154129	134004	121430	121898	126168	129271	134897	137470	139256	141795	143637	145261	146110
152		-------	-------	-------	-------	-------	-------	-------	-------	-------	-------	-------	-------	-------
153	CURRENT LIABILITIES													
154	Purchase Ledger	101050	63835	49913	52050	57096	59012	62806	65937	66489	68442	70247	71241	72015
155	Accruals	4535	5072	5628	4535	5079	5594	4535	5041	5489	4535	4938	5254	4535
156	P.A.Y.E	2370	2370	2370	2370	2370	2370	2370	2370	2370	2370	2370	2370	2370
157	V.A.T	9860	1638	3149	4951	1898	3847	6037	2189	4421	6760	2370	4786	7215
158	Bank & H.P Loans	0	0	0	0	0	0	0	0	0	0	0	0	0
159	Bank Overdraft	1095	27031	28219	26052	27466	25553	24223	24987	21221	17432	18300	12697	7398
160		-------	-------	-------	-------	-------	-------	-------	-------	-------	-------	-------	-------	-------
161		118910	99947	89280	89957	93910	96375	99970	100524	99991	99538	98224	96348	93533
162		-------	-------	-------	-------	-------	-------	-------	-------	-------	-------	-------	-------	-------
163	NET ASSETS	68685	67024	64619	63910	63729	63867	65399	66920	68740	71233	73890	76891	80055
164		======	======	======	======	======	======	======	======	======	======	======	======	======
165														
166	REPRESENTED BY													
167	Capital A/c B/F		68685	67024	64619	63910	63729	63867	65399	66920	68740	71233	73890	76891
168	Profit for Period		339	-406	1291	1819	2139	3532	3520	3821	4493	4657	5002	5164
169	Drawings		2000	2000	2000	2000	2000	2000	2000	2000	2000	2000	2000	2000
170		-------	-------	-------	-------	-------	-------	-------	-------	-------	-------	-------	-------	-------
171		68685	67024	64619	63910	63729	63867	65399	66920	68740	71233	73890	76891	80055
172		======	======	======	======	======	======	======	======	======	======	======	======	======
173														
174	Balance Sheet diff	0	0	0	0	0	0	0	0	0	0	0	0	0
175														
176														
177	============	======	======	======	======	======	======	======	======	======	======	======	======	======

Figure 34a

	A	B	D	E	F
126	G.K.Nettlerash Company				
127	Projected Balance Sheet				
128	as at the 31st December 19x2				
129	------------	------------	------------	------------	------------
130		BROUGHT			
131		FORWARD	JAN	FEB	MAR
132	------------	------------	------------	------------	------------
133	FIXED ASSETS				
134	Plant & Machinery	32500	+$B$134	+$B$134	+$B$134
135	Office Equipment	7325	+$B$135	+$B$135	+$B$135
136	Motor Car 1	0	+$B$136	+$B$136	+$B$136
137	Motor Car 2	12000	+$B$137	+$B$137	+$B$137
138	Capital Additions		+D106	+E106	+F106
139	Cumulative Dep'n	18359	+B139+D64	+D139+E64	+E139+F64
140		-------	-------	-------	-------
141		@SUM(B134:B138)-B139	@SUM(D134:D138)-D139	@SUM(E134:E138)-E139	@SUM(F134:F138)-F139
142		-------	-------	-------	-------
143	CURRENT ASSETS				
144	Debtors	100629	+D74+E79+F79+E80	+E74+F79+G79+F80	+F74+G79+H79+G80
145	Stock & WIP	49073	+$B$145	+$B$145	+$B$145
146	Bank Current A/c	0	@IF(D114>=0,D114,0)	@IF(E114>=0,E114,0)	@IF(F114>=0,F114,0)
147	No. 2 Account	348	+$B$147	+$B$147	+$B$147
148	Prepayments	4047	+$B$148	+$B$148	+$B$148
149	Cash In Hand	32	+$B$149	+$B$149	+$B$149
150		-------	-------	-------	-------
151		@SUM(B144..B150)	@SUM(D144..D150)	@SUM(E144..E150)	@SUM(F144..F150)
152		-------	-------	-------	-------
153	CURRENT LIABILITIES				
154	Purchase Ledger	101050	+B154+(D41*(1+$C$13))-D86	(+D41+E41)*(1+$C$13)	(+E41+F41)*(1+$C$13)
155	Accruals	4535	+$B$155+D62+D63	+$B$155+D62+D63+E62+E63	+$B$155
156	P.A.Y.E	2370	+$B$156	+$B$156	+$B$156
157	V.A.T	9860	+D124	+D124+E124	+D124+E124+F124
158	Bank & H.P.Loans	0	+$B$158	+$B$158	+$B$158
159	Bank Overdraft	1095	@IF(D114<0,-D114,0)	@IF(E114<0,-E114,0)	@IF(F114<0,-F114,0)
160		-------	-------	-------	-------
161		@SUM(B154..B159)	@SUM(D154..D159)	@SUM(E154..E159)	@SUM(F154..F159)
162		-------	-------	-------	-------
163	NET ASSETS	+B141+B151-B161	+D141+D151-D161	+E141+E151-E161	+F141+F151-F161
164		=======	=======	=======	=======
165					
166	REPRESENTED BY				
167	Capital A/c B/F		+B171	+D171	+E171
168	Profit for Period		+D68	+E68	+F68
169	Drawings		+$C$19	+$C$19	+$C$19
170			-------	-------	-------
171		68685	+D167+D168-D169	+E167+E168-E169	+F167+F168-F169
172		=======	=======	=======	=======
173					
174	Balance Sheet diff	+B163-B171	+D163-D171	+E163-E171	+F163-F171
175					
176					
177	============	=================	=====================	=====================	==================

Figure 34b (Part 1)

	G	H	I	J	K
126					
127					
128					
129					
130					
131	APR	MAY	JUN	JUL	AUG
132					
133					
134	+$B$134	+$B$134	+$B$134	+$B$134	+$B$134
135	+$B$135	+$B$135	+$B$135	+$B$135	+$B$135
136	+$B$136	+$B$136	+$B$136	+$B$136	+$B$136
137	+$B$137	+$B$137	+$B$137	+$B$137	+$B$137
138	+G106	+H106	+I106	+J106	+K106
139	+F139+G64	+G139+H64	+H139+I64	+I139+J64	+J139+K64
140	-------	-------	-------	-------	-------
141	@SUM(G134:G138)-G139	@SUM(H134:H138)-H139	@SUM(I134:I138)-I139	@SUM(J134:J138)-J139	@SUM(K134:K138)-K139
142	-------	-------	-------	-------	-------
143					
144	+G74+H79+I79+H80	+H74+I79+J79+I80	+I74+J79+K79+J80	+J74+K79+L79+K80	+K74+L79+M79+L80
145	+$B$145	+$B$145	+$B$145	+$B$145	+$B$145
146	@IF(G114>=0,G114,0)	@IF(H114>=0,H114,0)	@IF(I114>=0,I114,0)	@IF(J114>=0,J114,0)	@IF(K114>=0,K114,0)
147	+$B$147	+$B$147	+$B$147	+$B$147	+$B$147
148	+$B$148	+$B$148	+$B$148	+$B$148	+$B$148
149	+$B$149	+$B$149	+$B$149	+$B$149	+$B$149
150	-------	-------	-------	-------	-------
151	@SUM(G144..G150)	@SUM(H144..H150)	@SUM(I144..I150)	@SUM(J144..J150)	@SUM(K144..K150)
152	-------	-------	-------	-------	-------
153					
154	(+F41+G41)*(1+$C$13)	(+G41+H41)*(1+$C$13)	(+H41+I41)*(1+$C$13)	(+I41+J41)*(1+$C$13)	(+J41+K41)*(1+$C$13)
155	+$B$155+G62+G63	+$B$155+G62+G63+H62+H63	+$B$155	+$B$155+J62+J63	+$B$155+J62+J63+K62+K63
156	+$B$156	+$B$156	+$B$156	+$B$156	+$B$156
157	+G124	+G124+H124	+G124+H124+I124	+J124	+J124+K124
158	+$B$158	+$B$158	+$B$158	+$B$158	+$B$158
159	@IF(G114<0,-G114,0)	@IF(H114<0,-H114,0)	@IF(I114<0,-I114,0)	@IF(J114<0,-J114,0)	@IF(K114<0,-K114,0)
160	-------	-------	-------	-------	-------
161	@SUM(G154..G159)	@SUM(H154..H159)	@SUM(I154..I159)	@SUM(J154..J159)	@SUM(K154..K159)
162	-------	-------	-------	-------	-------
163	+G141+G151-G161	+H141+H151-H161	+I141+I151-I161	+J141+J151-J161	+K141+K151-K161
164	=======	=======	=======	=======	=======
165					
166					
167	+F171	+G171	+H171	+I171	+J171
168	+G68	+H68	+I68	+J68	+K68
169	+$C$19	+$C$19	+$C$19	+$C$19	+$C$19
170	-------	-------	-------	-------	-------
171	+G167+G168-G169	+H167+H168-H169	+I167+I168-I169	+J167+J168-J169	+K167+K168-K169
172	=======	=======	=======	=======	=======
173					
174	+G163-G171	+H163-H171	+I163-I171	+J163-J171	+K163-K171
175					
176					
177	==================	======================	==================	==================	=====================

Figure 34b (Part 2)

	L	M	N	O
126				
127				
128				
129	------------------	------------------	------------------	------------------
130				
131	SEP	OCT	NOV	DEC
132	------------------	------------------	------------------	------------------
133				
134	+$B$134	+$B$134	+$B$134	+$B$134
135	+$B$135	+$B$135	+$B$135	+$B$135
136	+$B$136	+$B$136	+$B$136	+$B$136
137	+$B$137	+$B$137	+$B$137	+$B$137
138	+L106	+M106	+N106	+O106
139	+K139+L64	+L139+M64	+M139+N64	+N139+O64
140	-------	-------	-------	-------
141	@SUM(L134:L138)-L139	@SUM(M134:M138)-M139	@SUM(N134:N138)-N139	@SUM(O134:O138)-O139
142	-------	-------	-------	-------
143				
144	+L74+M79+N79+M80	+M74+N79+O79+N80	+N74+O79+Q79+O80	+O74+Q79+R79+Q80
145	+$B$145	+$B$145	+$B$145	+$B$145
146	@IF(L114>=0,L114,0)	@IF(M114>=0,M114,0)	@IF(N114>=0,N114,0)	@IF(O114>=0,O114,0)
147	+$B$147	+$B$147	+$B$147	+$B$147
148	+$B$148	+$B$148	+$B$148	+$B$148
149	+$B$149	+$B$149	+$B$149	+$B$149
150	-------	-------	-------	-------
151	@SUM(L144..L150)	@SUM(M144..M150)	@SUM(N144..N150)	@SUM(O144..O150)
152	-------	-------	-------	-------
153				
154	(+K41+L41)*(1+$C$13)	(+L41+M41)*(1+$C$13)	(+M41+N41)*(1+$C$13)	(+N41+O41)*(1+$C$13)
155	+$B$155	+$B$155+M62+M63	+$B$155+M62+M63+N62+N63	+$B$155
156	+$B$156	+$B$156	+$B$156	+$B$156
157	+J124+K124+L124	+M124	+M124+N124	+M124+N124+O124
158	+$B$158	+$B$158	+$B$158	+$B$158
159	@IF(L114<0,-L114,0)	@IF(M114<0,-M114,0)	@IF(N114<0,-N114,0)	@IF(O114<0,-O114,0)
160	-------	-------	-------	-------
161	@SUM(L154..L159)	@SUM(M154..M159)	@SUM(N154..N159)	@SUM(O154..O159)
162	-------	-------	-------	-------
163	+L141+L151-L161	+M141+M151-M161	+N141+N151-N161	+O141+O151-O161
164	=======	=======	=======	=======
165				
166				
167	+K171	+L171	+M171	+N171
168	+L68	+M68	+N68	+O68
169	+$C$19	+$C$19	+$C$19	+$C$19
170	-------	-------	-------	-------
171	+L167+L168-L169	+M167+M168-M169	+N167+N168-N169	+O167+O168-O169
172	=======	=======	=======	=======
173				
174	+L163-L171	+M163-M171	+N163-N171	+O163-O171
175				
176				
177	==================	==================	==================	==================

Figure 34b (Part 3)

APPENDIX A
Help Screens

1. Introduction

During the course of the first ten sessions, you have gained experience of the basics of worksheet creation and design. You have also obtained glimpses of some of the powerful potential of spreadsheets. On your way, you have used or seen a few of the following:

Movement keys	e.g. <Home> in READY mode to return to cell A1
Function keys	e.g <F5> for GoTo
Mode Indicators	e.g. READY
Statistical Functions	e.g. @SUM
Financial Functions	e.g @PV
Date Functions	e.g. @DATE
Logical Functions	e.g. @IF
Macro keystrokes	e.g. {UP}

There are, of course, many more keystrokes, indicators and functions under each of the above headings which you may want to use in your future spreadsheet explorations.

How to find them and learn how to use them?

There are two approaches:

(1) Refer to the excellent manuals that came with your program. In particular, practise using the table of contents and the index to find what you want and, most important, try it out on a worksheet. (Save the worksheet before you experiment.)

(2) Use the Help Screens which are lurking behind your screen, ready to spring into life if only you will let them. Many students spend valuable time desperately trying to find somebody to help them solve a problem when the answer is only a few keystrokes away.

Each program has its own helpscreen system. In the following paragraphs, you will learn how to use the system appropriate to your particular program.

Paragraph 2 for Lotus 1-2-3 Release 2.0

Paragraph 3 for Lotus 1-2-3 Release 2.2

Paragraph 4 for VP-Planner and VP-Planner PLUS

Paragraph 5 for As-Easy-As

For practice, you will suppose that you want to remember what the financial function @PV does and how to enter it.

At the same time you will get the feel of moving round the help screens.

Load a blank (or any other saved worksheet), check that you are in READY mode, and carry out the following:

2. Help screens {123} Release 2.0

Press `<F1>`

A screen replaces your worksheet (temporarily), and tells you about READY mode, which is the mode you were in when you asked for Help.

Press `<End>`

The cursor moves to *How to Use Help* in the bottom right-hand corner of the screen.

Press `<Enter>`

This screen tells you how to use the Help Facility. Read it and try out pressing <End> and <Home>.

Move the cursor to *Help Index.*

Press `<Enter>`

You are now at the Help Index screen. You are looking for help with an @ function, so

Move the cursor to *@Functions.*

Press `<Enter>`

Read the screen about @Functions. Since PV (Present Value) is a Financial function,

Move the cursor to *Financial.*

Press `<Enter>`

A screen appears with details of various financial functions, but @PV is not one of them. However, the cursor is over the word *Continued*, so

Press `<Enter>` and details of @PV appear to refresh your memory.

Press `<Esc>` to return to your worksheet.

Now you have made a preliminary skirmish into help screens, why not get some practice in using them by simply pressing <F1> and exploring?

When you have finished, please read paragraph 6 below.

3. Help screens {123} Release 2.2

Press `<F1>`

A screen replaces your worksheet (temorarily), and is the Lotus 1-2-3 Help Index. The cursor should be on *About 1-2-3 Help.*

Press `<Enter>`

This screen tells you how to use the Help Facility. Read it and try out pressing <End> and <Home>.

Move the cursor to *Help Index.*

Press `<Enter>`

You are now at the Help Index screen. You are looking for help with an @ function, so

Move the cursor to *@Function Index.*

Press `<Enter>`

An @Function Index screen appears. However, @PV is not listed. However, move the cursor to the word *Continued* at the foot of the screen, and

Press `<Enter>`

@PV is in the second column. Move the cursor there and press <Enter>

Details of @PV appear to refresh your memory.

Press `<Esc>` to return to your worksheet.

Now you have made a preliminary skirmish into help screens, why not get some practice in using them by simply pressing <F1> and exploring?

When you have finished, please read paragraph 6 below.

4. Help screens {VP} and {VPP}

Press `<F1>`

A screen replaces your worksheet (temporarily), and tells you about *Using Help.* Read this screen, and then

Press `<F1>` again.

You are now at the Help Index screen. You are looking for help with a Financial Function, which is page 18; so

Press `<F5>` Type `18` <Enter>

Details of @PV appear to refresh your memory.

Press `<Esc>` to return to your worksheet.

Now you have made a preliminary skirmish into help screens, why not get some practice in using them by simply pressing <F1> and exploring?

When you have finished, please read paragraph 6 below.

5. Help screens {AEA}

Press `<F1>`

A screen replaces your worksheet (temporarily), which is an index of the help screens.

You are looking for an @Financial function. You can either press the down arrow until you come to it, or

Press `<Shift> + @`

The cursor moves down to @Date/Time.

Press `<↓>` to highlight @Finance.

You will see the window to the right displaying FINANCIAL FUNCTIONS.

Press `<→>` to move the cursor to the heading FINANCIAL FUNCTIONS.

Press `<PgDn>` three times

and details of @PV appear to refresh your memory.

Press `<Esc>` to return to your worksheet.

Now you have made a preliminary skirmish into help screens, why not get some practice in using them by simply pressing <F1> and exploring?

When you have finished, please read paragraph 6 below.

6. Menu maps

Some students find "maps" of the menu system useful, particularly in the early stages of acquaintance with spreadsheets.

Lotus 1-2-3 Help Facility covers all the commands under the topic *1-2-3 Commands* and *Command Menus* (1-2-3 Main Menu in release 2.2) in the Help Index. The manual has individual menu maps, e.g. in *Quick Reference* and at the start of Chapter 12 for Worksheet

Commands in the Reference Manual (Release 2.2). However, there is no "at-a-glance" chart showing an overall annotated view, and this is provided in Appendix B.

VP-Planner Help Facility covers all the commands under screens 30-49 in the Help Index. The screen numbers in VP-Panner Plus are arranged differently. The VP-Planner Plus manual has individual menu charts at the start of each section under Command Reference. However, there is no "at-a-glance" chart showing an overall annotated view, and this is provided in Appendix B.

As-Easy-As Help Facility has separate windows e.g. for Worksheet commands under ComWSheet which show clear individual menu maps. The manual has a clear Menu Command Summary section. However, there is no "at-a-glance" chart showing an overall view, and this is provided in Appendix C.

[These notes are repeated at the start of Appendices B and C.]

APPENDIX B

Menu Map

for 1-2-3 and VP-Planner Plus

LOTUS 1-2-3 (R 2.0) and VP-PLANNER PLUS

[Note for As-Easy-As users: A separate abbreviated menu map is provided in Appendix C.]

Some students find "maps" of the menu system useful, particularly in the early stages of acquaintance with spreadsheets.

Lotus 1-2-3 Help Facility covers all the commands under the topic *1-2-3 Commands* and *Command Menus (1-2-3 Main Menu* in release 2.2) in the Help Index. The manual has individual menu maps, e.g. in *Quick Reference* and at the start of Chapter 12 for Worksheet Commands in the Reference Manual (Release 2.2). However, there is no "at-a-glance" chart showing an overall annotated view, and this is provided in this appendix.

VP-Planner Help Facility covers all the commands under screens 30-49 in the Help Index. The screen numbers in VP-Planner Plus are arranged differently. The VP-Planner Plus manual has individual menu charts at the start of each section under Command Reference. However, there is no "at-a-glance" chart showing an overall annotated view, and this is provided in Appendix B.

Menu maps such this are small-scale maps, help screens are medium-scale maps, and the manuals are large-scale maps. Each type is suitable for its own particlar purpose. For exploring the hills, small-scale maps are useless and can be dangerous.

This menu-map is designed to help you find your way around the menu structure of 123 and VPP. It is not a complete map of either program's menus; selections have been made of the most useful menu items.

If you look at the complete menu maps in the program manuals, you will see that some menus descend through many levels; for example, in 123,

/Worksheet, Global, Default, Other, International, Date, A (MM/DD/YY)

The lower levels are mainly self-explanatory, though you would be well advised to look up the manual for guidance; you will also learn more thoroughly by doing so.

Tip 1: You may find it helpful to consult the help screens. Press <F1> and follow the instructions on the screen. See Appendix A on how to use the help screens.

Tip 2: As you press each menu command, look for and read the explanation or list of submenus on the screen in the control panel or drop-down menu.

Tip 3: The index at the end of this book shows key sequences, where appropriate, against the entry, as well as referring you to the session and paragraph number where further guidance is given.

MENU MAP

/ WORKSHEET

Global			Controls overall worksheet settings
	Format		Sets standard for numeric displays
		Fixed	Fixed number of decimal places
		Scientific	Exponential format
		Currency	Currency format e.g £1,000.00
		, (Comma)	Comma format e.g 1,000.00
		General	Standard format e.g 1000.00
		+/-	Horizontal bar graph
		Percent	Percent format e.g 1.00%
		Date	Date and time formats; various options
		Text	Displays formulae
	Label-Prefix		Choice of alignments
	Column-Width		Sets global column-width for entire worksheet
	Recalculation		Various options: Natural, Columnwise, Rowwise, Automatic, Manual, Iteration
	Protection		Choices: Enable, Disable
	Default		Establishes initial (default) printer, disk and display settings. {123} has choices for Printer, Directory, Status, Update, and "Other": International (including currency sign), Help, Clock {VPP} displays a screen where all the choices can be seen, and includes Printer, Directory, External-path, Hardware, Custom, Status, Update and Other.
Insert			Inserts blank Columns or Rows
Delete			Deletes Columns or Rows
Column			Changes width of current column Includes Set, Reset and {123} Hide and Display
Erase			Erases the entire worksheet from memory Prompt: Yes or No
Titles			Freezes rows and columns above and to the left of the cell pointer Choices: Both, Horizontal, Vertical, Clear

Window	Controls split screen and synchronized scrolling Choices: Horizontal, Vertical,Sync, Unsync, Clear
Status	Displays current settings
Page	Inserts a row containing a page-break symbol above the cell pointer
/ RANGE	
Format	See under /Worksheet, Global, Format above Also: Reset and Hide (Hidden)
Label	Changes alignment for a label or range of labels
Erase	Erases a cell or range of cells
Name	
Create	Creates or changes a range name
Delete	Deletes a range name
Labels	Creates range names from a range of labels
Reset	Deletes all range names
Table	Creates a table of range names
Justify	Reformats a column of label cells
Protect	Prevents changes to a range of cells
Unprotect	Unprotects globally protected cells
Input	Limits cursor movement to unprotected cells
/ COPY	Copies a cell or range of cells
/ MOVE	Moves a cell or range of cells
/ FILE	
Retrieve	Erases the current worksheet from memory and loads a file from disk
Save	Saves the entire worksheet in a worksheet file Choices: Cancel, Replace, Backup
Combine	Incorporates all or part of a worksheet file into the current worksheet Choices: Copy, Add, Subtract
Xtract	Saves a range of cells in a worksheet file Choices: Formulas, Values
Erase	Erases a file from disk Choices: Worksheet, Print, Graph, Other
List	Lists files in current directory Choices: Worksheet, Print, Graph, Other
Import	Superimposes print file on current file at cursor position Choices: Text, Numbers

Directory			Displays or resets the current directory
/ PRINT			Prints current worksheet or stores it in a text file
File			Stores current worksheet in a text file
			Enter file name; then choices as for Printer
Printer			Prints current worksheet
	Range		Defines cells to be printed
	Line		Advances paper by one line
	Page		Advances paper to top of next page
	Options		
		Header	Text line at top of each page
		Footer	Text line at bottom of each page
		Margins	Set margins, Left, Right, Top, Bottom
		Borders	Columns (left)/Rows (top) for each page
		Set-up	String e.g. \027\015 for condensed print
			Leave blank if printer controlled
		Page-length	Lines per page: e.g. 66 (11"), 70 (A4)
		Other	
		As-displayed	Prints as displayed on screen
		Cell-Formulas	One cell per line; prints control panel display for each cell
		Formatted	Standard printing including Options
		Unformatted	Does not print Options
		{VP} Page#	Prints page number at top right-hand corner
		{VP} No-Page#	Turns off Page# [Note: Page numbers can be included in headers and footers {123}{VP}.]
		{VP} R/C#s	Prints row and column references (numbers and letters) as shown by most of Figures in this book
		{VP} Stop-R/C#s	Turns off R/C#s
		{VP} Background	Printing On/Off
		{VP} Wide-print	Sideways printing On/Off
	Clear		Cancels choice of print settings
			Choices: All, Range, Borders, Format
	Align		Tells program that printer is at top of page

Go	Prints worksheet as instructed in settings
Quit	Returns to READY mode
/ GRAPH	
Type	Selects type of graph Choices: Line, Bar, XY, Stacked-bar, Pie
X	Sets range of cells for horizontal axis (slice for Pie)
A, B, C, D, E, F	Sets up to six (A..F) ranges for vertical axis
Reset	Cancels all or individual range settings Choices: Graph X A B C D E F Quit
View	Displays current graph
Print {VP}	Prints current graph on a graphics printer [{123} prints using Printgraph program]
Save	Saves graph as a .PIC file
Options	
Legend	Defines legends for symbols or patterns Choices: A..F
Format	Specifies way lines drawn in line or XY graph Choices: Graph, A B C D E F Choices: Lines, Symbols, Both, Neither
Titles	Specifies titles for: Choices: First, Second, X-axis, Y-axis
Grid	Include or exclude grid lines (not for pie graphs) Choices: Horizontal, Vertical, Both, Clear
Scale	Sets scales on X and Y axes Choices: Y-scale, X-scale, Skip Choices: Automatic, Manual, Lower, Upper, Format, Indicator (Format has choices: see under /WGF or /RF)
Colour	Displays graph in colour; see manual for details
B&W	Displays in Black and White; see manual for details
Data-Labels	Uses contents of a range as labels; for example values may be printed at top of bars Choices: A B C D E F Choices: Centre, Left, Above, Right, Below
Quit	Returns to the Graph menu
Name	Performs the following:
Use	Makes a previously named graph the current graph
Create	Names the current graph with current settings
Delete	Deletes a named graph

	Reset	Deletes all named graphs
/ DATA		
Fill		Fills a range with a sequence of values, equally spaced, top to bottom, left to right
Table		Performs sensitivity (What if?) analyses Choices: 1-variable, 2-variable, Reset
Sort		Arranges data in specified order
	Data-range	Specifies range to be sorted
	Primary-key	Specifies first field to sort
	Secondary-key	Specifies second field to sort
	Reset	Clears data-range and sort keys
	Go	Carries out the specified sort
	Quit	Returns to READY mode
Query		Locates and edits selected records
	Input	Specifies range of records to search
	Criterion	Specifies criteria range for selection criteria
	Output	Specifies range to which selected records are copied
	Find	Highlights selected records in input range
	Extract	Copies selected records to specified output range
	Unique	As Extract, omitting duplicate records
	Delete	Deletes selected records from input range
	Reset	Clears input, criterion and output ranges
	Quit	Returns to READY mode
Distribution		Calculates frequency distribution of specified range of values

[Note: {VP}{VPP}{123} have additional (different) Data commands]

/ TOOLS {VPP}	For details, see manual
/ SYSTEM	Leave program temporarily to run a DOS program Caution: Save your worksheet first before using this command Refer to your manual for details To return to program, type at DOS prompt: exit<return>
/ QUIT	Quits the spreadsheet program

APPENDIX C

Menu Map

for As-Easy-As (version 4.00Q)

AS-EASY-AS (Version 4.00Q)

Some students find "maps" of the menu system useful, particularly in the early stages of acquaintance with spreadsheets. This menu-map is designed to help you find your way around the menu structure.

There are useful menu maps in the program's 'Help' facility which can be accessed using the <F1> Help key. Choose the topic you want, and press <→> to move to the window; scroll if needed, using the keys indicated at the foot of the screen. See Appendix A for further details.

This As-Easy-As Help Facility has separate windows e.g. for Worksheet commands under ComWSheet which show clear individual menu maps. The manual has a detailed Menu Command Summary section. However, there is no "at-a-glance" chart showing an overall view, and this is provided by this Appendix.

Menu maps such as this are small-scale maps, help screens are medium-scale maps, and the manuals are large-scale maps. Each type is suitable for its own particular purpose. For exploring the hills, small scale maps are useless and can be dangerous.

Tip 1: You may find it helpful to consult the help screens. Press <F1> and follow the instructions on the screen. See Appendix A on how to use the help screens.

Tip 2: As you press each menu command, look for and read the explanation or list of sub-menus on the screen in the control panel or drop-down menu.

Tip 3: The index at the end of this book shows key sequences, where appropriate, against the entry, as well as referring you to the session and paragraph number where further guidance is given.

/ WORKSHEET

ColWidth	Set / Reset	
Delete	Column / Row	
Erase	No/Yes	
Border	Horizon / Vertical / Both / Suppress / Clear	
Insert	Column / Row / Page	
General	Format	Fixed / Science / , (comma) / Currency / General / Date: (various choices) / Percent / +/- / Text / Hide / Reset

	Label	Left / Right / Centre	
	Column		
	Recalc	Manual / Auto	
	Protect	Enable / Disable	
	Zeros	No / Yes	
	Negative	No / Yes	
	INSTALL	Colors	Text / MenuBk / MenuFr / Csr / Ptr / Bord / Bot / Top / Neg / UnPr / Quit
		Punctuate	Decimal / Argument / Currency / Thousand / MenuKey / Quit
		Dimension	
		Ega43	
		Addin	Create / Delete / Reset
		SAVE	
		Quit	
Macro	Compose / Execute / Step / Quit		
Summary			
Window	Horizon / Vertical / Sync / UnSync / Clear		
Text	Find / Replace / Justify / Word		

/ RANGE

Audit	Trace / CrossRef / OverView / Quit
Copy	Value / Transpose / Scale / Invert
Erase	
Format	Fixed / Science / , (comma) / Currency / General / / Date (various choices) / Percent / +/- / Text / Hide / Reset
Lock	Yes / No
Name	Create / Delete / Reset / Table / Build
Prefix	Left / Center / Right
Quit	

/ COPYCELL

/ MOVECELL

/ ARRAY Add / Subtract / Multiply / Invert / Transpose / E-Solve / Quit

/DATA

Fill	
Parse	
Question	InpRange / OutRange / Criteria / FindRec / Extract / Reset / Quit
Sort	D-Range / P(1)-key / S(2)-key / Reset / Go / Quit
Table	1-Column / 2-Column

GoalSeek	Input / Output / Desire / Quit	
Regress	XData / Ydata / Output / Quit	
Bin		
Input	Form / Criteria / Range / Quit	
/ FILE		
Retrieve		
Store	Cancel / Replace / Backup	
Merge	All / Range	
	↓ ↓	
	Value / Formula	
	↓ ↓	
	Replace / Sum / Diff	
Xport	Wks / DbIII	
Import	Values / Text / DbIII / List	
Erase	W?? / P?? / Other	
List	W?? / P?? / Other	
Dir		
UpLink		
Option		
/ GRAPHICS		
Type	X-Y / Bar / Pie / Stack / Line / Cume / Hloc / Radar / Area / Delta	
X A..F		
Labels	A / B / C / D / E / F / Reset	
Options	Legend:	A / B / C / D / E / F / Line / Table / None
	Format:	Graph / A / B / C / D / E / F
		↓ ↓ ↓ ↓ ↓ ↓ ↓
		None / Line / Symbols / Both / Depth
	Titles:	First / Second / X / Y / Quit
	Scale:	X-Scale / Y-Scale / Quit
		↓ ↓
		Auto / Manual / Upper / Lower /
		/ Format (usual choices) / Step / Exp / Normal / Quit
	Grid	Horizon / Vertical / Both / Clear / Dot / Solid
	Color	No / Yes
	Quit	
Reset	Graph / X / A / B / C / D / E / F	
Name	Use / Create / Delete / Merge / Split / Reset	
View		
Plot	Image:	High / Wide / Top / Bottom / Left / Quit
	Density	Low / High

	Hardware	PIC / LASER / FX/MX / 24-PIN	
	Paper	Height / Width / Quit	
	Orient	Portrait / Landscape	
	Eject		
	GO		
	Quit		
Quit			

/ PRINTTO

Printer	Range		
	Border:	Rows / Columns / None	
	LineFeed		
	PageAdv		
	Options	Margins:	Left / Right / PgLen / Top / Bot
		Setup	
		PgLength	
		Header	
		Footer	
		Type:	As-Seen / Contents / NoForm
		Quit	
	Adjust		
	Go		
	Quit		
File			
Append			

/ USER

Shell	Leave program temporarily to run a DOS program Caution: Save your worksheet first before using this command Refer to your manual for details To return to program, type at DOS prompt: exit<return>
LndScape	[Executable AddIn] Range / LineFeed / PageAdv / Option (Margin / LineSpace / CharSpace / / Pglength / Width / SkipPerf / Quit) / Type (Expanded / Normal / / Condensed) / Go / Quit

/ EXIT

APPENDIX D

Financial DEPRECIATION @ Functions

@SLN

Syntax: @SLN(Cost, Salvage, Life)

Cost = Cost of the purchase
Salvage = Estimated value at end of depreciated life
Life = Number of periods for depreciation

Use: Calculates the depreciation of an asset, per period, using the straight-line method

Formula: [Cost-Salvage]/Life

Example

	A	B	C	D	E	F
18	Example	Asset	Cost	Salvage	Life	Dep'n
19						
20		Machine	20000	2400	4	4400
21						
22		Fittings	15000	0	10	1500
23						
24		Car	18000	6000	2	6000

Example showing formulae

	A	B	C	D	E	F	G
26	Example	Asset	Cost	Salvage	Life	Dep'n	
27	showing						
28	formulae	Machine	20000	2400	4	@SLN(C28,D28,E28)	
29							
30		Fittings	15000	0	10	@SLN(C30,D30,E30)	
31							
32		Car	18000	6000	2	@SLN(C32,D32,E32)	

@SYD

Syntax: @SYD(Cost, Salvage, Life, Period)

Cost = Cost of the purchase
Salvage = Estimated value at end of depreciated life
Life = Number of periods for depreciation
Period = Current period, i.e. period of the asset's life for which the calculated depreciation is required

Use: Calculates the depreciation of an asset for a specified period, using the using the Sum-of-Years depreciation method

Formula: [[Cost-Salvage]*[Life-Period+1]]/[Life*[Life+1]/2]

Example

	A	B	C	D	E	F	G	H
51	Example:	Asset	Cost	Salvage	Life	Period	Dep'n	Cum.Dep/n
52								
53		Machine	20000	2400	4	1	7040.00	7040.00
54		Machine	20000	2400	4	2	5280.00	12320.00
55		Machine	20000	2400	4	3	3520.00	15840.00
56		Machine	20000	2400	4	4	1760.00	17600.00
57								
58		Fittings	15000	0	10	5	1636.36	
59								
60		Car	18000	6000	2	1	8000.00	8000.00
61		Car	18000	6000	2	2	4000.00	12000.00

Example showing formulae

	A	B	C	D	E	F	G	H
63	Example	Asset	Cost	Salvage	Life	Period	Dep'n	Cum.Dep/n
64	showing							
65	formulae:	Machine	20000	2400	4	1	@SYD(C65,D65,E65,F65)	+G65
66		Machine	20000	2400	4	2	@SYD(C66,D66,E66,F66)	+G66+H65
67		Machine	20000	2400	4	3	@SYD(C67,D67,E67,F67)	+G67+H66
68		Machine	20000	2400	4	4	@SYD(C68,D68,E68,F68)	+G68+H67
69								
70		Fittings	15000	0	10	5	@SYD(C70,D70,E70,F70)	
71								
72		Car	18000	6000	2	1	@SYD(C72,D72,E72,F72)	+G72
73		Car	18000	6000	2	2	@SYD(C73,D73,E73,F73)	+G73+H72

@DDB

Syntax: @DDB(Cost, Salvage, Life, Period)

Cost = Cost of the purchase

Salvage = Estimated value at end of depreciated life

Life = Number of periods for depreciation

Period = Current period, i.e. period of the asset's life for which the calculated depreciation is required

Use: Calculates the depreciation of an asset for a specified period, using the using the Double-Declining Balance depreciation method. The final NBV is equal to the salvage value. This accelerated depreciation method depreciates the asset faster than @SLN and @SYD. Life can be any value greater than 2; see Car example below.

Formula: [Net Book value in period]*2/life of asset.

Note that this formula works until final depreciation brings NBV to salvage value.

Example

	A	B	C	D	E	F	G	H
99	Example:	Asset	Cost	Salvage	Life	Period	Dep'n	Cum.Dep/n
100								
101		Machine	20000	2400	4	1	10000.00	10000.00
102		Machine	20000	2400	4	2	5000.00	15000.00
103		Machine	20000	2400	4	3	2500.00	17500.00
104		Machine	20000	2400	4	4	100.00	17600.00
105								
106		Fittings	15000	0	10	5	1228.80	
107								
108		Car	18000	6000	2	1	12000.00	
109		Car	18000	6000	2	2	0.00	

Example showing formulae

	A	B	C	D	E	F	G	H
111	Example:	Asset	Cost	Salvage	Life	Period	Dep'n	Cum.Dep/n
112								
113		Machine	20000	2400	4	1	@DDB(C113,D113,E113,F113)	G113
114		Machine	20000	2400	4	2	@DDB(C114,D114,E114,F114)	G114+H113
115		Machine	20000	2400	4	3	@DDB(C115,D115,E115,F115)	G115+H114
116		Machine	20000	2400	4	4	@DDB(C116,D116,E116,F116)	G116+H115
117								
118		Fittings	15000	0	10	5	@DDB(C118,D118,E118,F118)	
119								
120		Car	18000	6000	2	1	@DDB(C120,D120,E120,F120)	
121		Car	18000	6000	2	2	@DDB(C121,D121,E121,F121)	

OBJECTIVE TESTS
Answers

Question Numbers:

SESSION:	1	2	3	4	5	6	7	8	9	10
1	C	B	D	C	D	D	A	B	A	A
2	B	A	A	B	C	D	B	B	D*	A
3	B	A	D	C	B	D	B	A	D	A
4	C	B	A	D	C	B	A	A	B	C
5	D	C	B	D	A	B	C	D	D	A
6	C	C	C	C	A	D	A	C	A	B
7	A	D	C	A	C	B	A	C	A	C
8	C	D	A	B	B	D	B	A	D	D
9	B	A	C	D	C	A	D	B	C	C
10	A	B	D	A	C	A	D	D	C	D

*C(VPP)

INDEX

References are to Sessions and Paragraph numbers:

For example: 8.3 represents Session 8, Paragraph 3; 6.1-9 represents Session 6, Paragraphs 1 to 9 inclusive Also: AppA.6 represents Appendix A, Paragraph 6.Preface.3 represents Preface, Paragraph 3

"Promoting Active Learning"

Spreadsheets for Business Students

An Active-Learning Approach

C West

ISBN: **1 870941 83 7** • Date: **1991** • Edition: **1st**
Extent: **176 pp** • Size: **245 x 190 mm**
Lecturers' Supplement ISBN: **1 873981 66 X**

Courses on which this book is known to be used
CBA; CMS; BA (Hons) Acc. & Fin.; BEd Bus. Studies; CLAIT II; Dip. Voc. Ed. Bus. & Fin.; HNC/D; ACCA Level 1; BA Business Studies; BTEC Nat.; HNC Bus. & Fin.; BEng; HND Computing; HND Manufacturing Management; IPM; DMS.

The aim of this book is to provide a 'user friendly' guide for students on the innumerable courses where acquaintance with the basics of spreadsheets is required.

It is very much a 'learning by doing' guide – requiring very little (if any) input by the lecturer and can be used on any machine/system with Lotus 1-2-3 version 2.0 (or above) or compatible spreadsheets such as VP-Planner and As-Easy-As.

All examples have a business emphasis and students progressively gain confidence in the basics of:

- constructing spreadsheet models
- saving and retrieving files
- graphics
- printing spreadsheets and graphs
- using a spreadsheet as a data base
- creating and using simple macros.

The lecturers' supplement is a copyright-free $5\frac{1}{4}$" (360K) PC-compatible disk, incorporating files in .WKS format for the models in the book, for checking students' activities.

Contents:

Models include:
VAT Calculations • Cash Flow Forecast • Integrated Cash Flow Forecast/ Profit & Loss Account/Balance Sheet • Accounting Ratios • Cost Behaviour • Cost Allocation and Apportionment • Cost-Volume-Profit Analysis.

Each session contains:
Objectives • Active Learning • Summary • Activities • Objective (Multi-choice) Test.

Review Comments:

'I like the worksheet approach enabling students to work at their own pace.' 'A wonderful time saver – congratulations.' 'Ideal for new modularised units – all activity based.' 'Tried it on 2 lecturers first – they found it easy, so able now to recommend it to students!' 'Good to use in open learning workshop.' 'Excellent in every way – a book like this, at its current price, has been wanted for years!' 'A very useful text – practical and easy to understand.' – ***Lecturers***

Free Lecturers' Supplement

dBase for Business Students

J. Muir

An Active-Learning Approach

"Promoting Active Learning"

ISBN: **1 873981 16 3** • Date: **June 1992** • Edition: **1st**
Extent: **200 pp (approx)** • Size: **245 x 190 mm**
Lecturers' Supplement ISBN: **1 873981 76 7**

This book is aimed at students on a wide variety of business courses who need to know how to use dBase IV (the industry-standard database management system for IBM PC and compatibles). The learning material in this book requires minimal, if any, input by lecturers and can be recommended for student self-instruction. It makes no assumptions about business or computing knowledge, but teaches dBase IV techniques and their business applications in simple terms.

All students can successfully use this book – from those needing only an introduction to those needing to go to advanced programming. It covers the **essentials** of dBase IV at **each** level. The text covers all three modes of dBase IV- menu-driven, command driven, and programming. dBase IV features are progressively introduced in the context of practical business activities.

Note: A copyright free $3\frac{1}{2}$" (750K) disk is provided free of charge to lecturers adopting the book as a course text. It includes all the programs, databases, etc used in the book.

Contents:

Introduction – Databases in Business • Using the Control Centre • Creating and Searching a Database • Views and Queries – Retrieving Selected Records • Modifying the Database Structure • Adding and Deleting Records • Indexing and Sorting • Producing Printed Reports • Designing Data Entry Screens • Checking User Output • The Applications Generator • Using the Dot Prompt to Create and Search a Database • Dot Prompt Commands • Creating and Running a Program • Program Debugging • Programming Using Screens, Queries and Printed Reports • Decisions and Conditions – IF and DO CASE Commands • Looping or Iteration – DO WHILE...ENDDO • Locating Duplicate Records • Using Multiple Databases – Updating and Joining • Passing Parameters Between Programs • Conclusion – Bringing It All Together.

Free Lecturers' Supplement

"Promoting Active Learning"

MS Works

An Active-Learning Approach

D Weale

ISBN: **1 873981 30 9** • Date: **June 1992** • Edition: **1st**
Extent: **140 pp (approx)** • Size: **245 x 190 mm**

Courses on which this book is expected to be used
The many business courses requiring a basic knowledge of spreadsheets, databases and word processing via MS Works.

The aim of the book is to provide a 'user friendly' guide for students being introduced to spreadsheets, databases and word processing via MS Works.

It is very much a 'learning by doing' guide – requiring very little (if any) input from the lecturer, enabling students to learn and practice the commands and techniques using examples to which they can relate, ie business ones. A series of sessions, each self-contained, takes students step by step to a level at which they can happily use the program manual to master finer details.

Contents:

Free
Lecturers' Supplement

"The Complete Course Text"

Oliver and Chapman's

Data Processing & Information Technology *Revised by CS French*

ISBN: **1 870941 39 X** • Date: **1990** • Edition: **8th**
Extent: **432 pp** • Size: **245 x 190 mm**
Lecturers' Supplement ISBN: **1 873981 44 9**

Courses on which this book is known to be used
ACCA; CIMA; AAT; ICSA; IComA; City and Guilds; A Level Computing; BTEC National Computer Studies; BTEC HNC/D Business Studies; BSc Computer Studies; BSc Information Technology; IAM; BPICS II; CIPFA; Graduate Conversion Course; HND Information and Control Systems; HNC BIT; Combined Degree – Computing; C & G 424; BTEC National IP; BA Business Studies.

On reading lists of ACCA, AAT, IDPM, BCS, IComA, CBSI, ICM, ICSA and LCCI

This book provides a simplified approach to the understanding of data processing and information technology. It is intended for those with little or no knowledge of the subject.

The contents have been reorganised and extensively revised to provide a modern perspective. The text contains significant new material on work stations, structure methods, databases and 4GLs.

Contents:

Review Comments:

'Good core text, excellent price.' 'Good value text, succinctly written.' – ***Lecturers***

'This new edition has some very useful changes from the previous one. The wider page format helps in presentation of the material (and reading the book). The order of the contents is more logical than the last edition and there are some useful additions in the areas of 4GLs, databases and workstations ... The book's strongest point is its coverage of computer technology and data processing. It has some very useful examples throughout the text and is as up-to-date as textbooks reasonably can be.'

"ACCA Students' Newsletter"

ELBS

Also available as ELBS edition in member countries at local currency equivalent price of £2.50

Free Lecturers' Supplement

"Promoting Active Learning"

Accounting and Finance for Business Students

An Active-Learning Approach

M Bendrey, R Hussey & C West

ISBN: **1 873981 05 8** • Date: **July 1992** • Edition: **2nd**
Extent: **450 pp (approx)** • Size: **275 x 215 mm**
Lecturers' Supplement ISBN: 1 873981 34 1

Courses on which this book is known to be used
BTEC National and HNC/D Business and Finance; BA Business Studies; CMS/DMS; IPM; ICM; HND Business Information Technology; A Level Business Studies; BSc Engineering; BSc Computing; BEd in Business Studies; BA in Modern Languages and other management development courses.

On reading lists of IAM and ICM

This book provides a comprehensive introduction to accounting and finance. It includes numerous examples, with solutions in the text, to assist the student in understanding each topic. Also, for directed private study, there are student activities (assignments, objective tests, etc).

The opportunity has been taken in the second edition to improve the layout and presentation of the book. There is a new chapter on Manufacturing Organisations, and every chapter has been thoroughly reviewed and updated where necessary. The index has been expanded and the number of tasks, questions and assignments increased.

Contents:

Sources & Uses of Finance • Personal Finance • Business Finance • **Financial Accounting** • Sole Traders • Concepts & Control • Limited Liability Companies • Other Organisations • **Management Accounting** • Using Costs for Planning and Control • Using Costs for Total Costing • Using Costs for Decision Making • Project Appraisal.

Review Comments:

'Best textbook at this level [HNC Business & Finance].' 'Price and coverage are excellent.' 'Easily referenced sections – good, clear layout' 'Perfect for the course! [HNC Business & Finance]' 'Concise and easy for students to follow.' 'Gives a good introduction at an excellent price.' 'Assignments are excellent for classroom activities.' – ***Lecturers***

Free
Lecturers' Supplement

"Promoting Active Learning"

Understanding Business and Finance

Edited by J Hussey

An Active-Learning Approach

ISBN: **1 870941 74 8** • Date: **1991** • Edition: **1st**
Extent: **352 pp** • Size: **275 x 215 mm**
Lecturers' Supplement ISBN: **1 873981 69 4**

Courses on which this book is known to be used
BTEC National and Higher National Business & Finance; Certificate in Business Administration; ISM Diploma; CMS; HNC Business Information Technology; BA Business Studies.

The aim of this book is to provide a course text covering the whole of the core subjects of BTEC HNC/D Business and Finance. It will also be of considerable value to business and finance students on other courses.

It satisfies the need for a completely different kind of book which takes into account all the following requirements:

- the variety of ways the BTEC core subjects are implemented;
- all the themes, knowledge and skills required by the core subjects;
- the 'learning by doing', 'problem solving' and 'learning by discussion' approach central to BTEC philosophy;
- the tasks and assignments (both topic-based and integrated) appropriate to the level of the BTEC Higher student.

To summarise, it forms a single book that can be recommended by all lecturers on the core subjects.

The book itself does not try to teach. Within each specialist area the equivalent of the lecturer's notes (including key facts and formulae) are listed, to provide a checklist for students and lecturers of the topics that need to be covered. These guidelines are interspersed, as appropriate, with problem-solving activities which students can tackle only when they have acquired the understanding and associated skills. How the requisite knowledge and skills are acquired will depend on whether they are better researched by the student or explained by the lecturer. Guidance is given in the lecturers' supplement.

Contents:

Accounting and Finance • Business Environment • Business Law • Business Policy • Employee Relations • Marketing • Operations Management • People and Organisations • Quantitative Methods and Information Technology • Integrated Assignments.

Review Comments:

'Excellent exercises and case studies.' 'Extensive coverage of BTEC Modules, ideal for students.' 'Provides a welcome focal delivery of the key components [HND Business and Finance].' 'Approach new and refreshing.' 'An excellent overview of the syllabus, excellent presentation, reasonably priced.' 'Good coverage of syllabus in the book [HND Business and Finance].' – ***Lecturers***

Free Lecturers' Supplement

Refresher in Basic Mathematics

RN Rowe

ISBN: **1 870941 61 6** • Date: **1990** • Edition: **2nd**
Extent: **96 pp** • Size: **215 x 135 mm**

Courses on which this book is known to be used
HNC/D Business and Finance; HNC/D Computing; BA Business Studies; BA Economics; BA Social Sciences; Diploma in Health Administration; Accountancy Foundation courses; Access Courses and Foundation Courses; MBA; DMS; BSc Management Studies.

On reading list of AAT

This book is aimed at those students who have difficulty with basic mathematics as well as those who wish to refresh their understanding of the subject (perhaps due to a prolonged absence from study). The text covers ten units, each of which consists of an introduction to the topic and a series of worked examples (graded by level of difficulty) followed by exercises.

The book is suitable for use on any course in further or higher education involving a quantitative component.

Contents:

Fractions • Decimals • Percentages • Elementary Algebra • Powers • Coordinates and Graphs • The Straight Line • Simple Linear Equations • Simultaneous Equations • Quadratic Equations • Achievement Test • Tutors' Section • Appendices: Calculators; Rounding.

Review Comments:

'Well liked by students ...' 'It is an excellent book, much appreciated by student.' 'I can't get it back from a student!' 'A much needed self help text which will enable gaps in basic mathematical skills to be addressed in a non-intimidating manner.' 'Excellent! They don't seem to teach maths in schools these days – or the students forget it all!' 'Very clear; hard to find books that cover this simple range of work.' **– Lecturers**

**Free
Lecturers' Supplement**

"The Complete Course Text"

Business Mathematics and Statistics

A Francis

ISBN: **1 870941 02 0** • Date: **1988** • Edition: **2nd**
Extent: **432 pp** • Size: **275 x 215 mm**
Lecturers' Supplement ISBN: **1 873981 38 4**

Courses on which this book is known to be used
Accountancy Foundation courses; BTEC Business and Finance; ACCA; CIMA; ICSA; CII; AAT; IIM; CIPFA; IPS; CIM; Integrated Degrees Programme.

On reading lists of CIMA, ABE and IPS

This book provides a thorough grounding in basic mathematical and statistical techniques to students of business and professional studies. There are many self-testing exercises and fully worked examination questions.

Contents:

Review Comments:

'...it is a model of logical organisation and clear presentation. ...Students with examinations on the horizon will regard this book as an invaluable aid for intensive revision and reinforcement.'

"The Mathematical Gazette"

'This is the kind of book which business and accountancy students at undergraduate level will love – it is very detailed and thorough on the applied business side, and not too theoretical in nature.'

"IMA Journal"

ELBS

Also available as ELBS edition in member countries at local currency equivalent price of £2.30

Free Lecturers' Supplement